Revisiting Music Theory

Revisiting Music Theory: Basic Principles, Second Edition, surveys the basics of music theory and explains the terms used in harmonic and formal analysis in a clear and concise manner. Students will find *Revisiting Music Theory* to be an essential resource for review or reference, while instructors of introductory theory courses will find in these pages a solid foundation for cultivating musical thinking. Musicians of all kinds—amateur and professional alike—will find great value in augmenting and informing their knowledge of the art of music theory.

The text covers the basic principles of music theory, including:

- Musical notation
- Key signatures and scales
- Intervals, chords, and progressions
- Melodic and harmonic analysis
- Counterpoint and voice leading techniques
- Musical forms and structures

This second edition has been revised and reorganized to promote learning. Each section now includes an all-new selection of exercises, allowing readers to practice key skills and improve understanding. For students, instructors, and practicing musicians, *Revisiting Music Theory* offers an indispensable guide to the foundations of musical analysis.

Alfred Blatter joined the faculty for Musical Studies at the Curtis Institute of Music in 1989 and is Professor Emeritus at Drexel University.

Revisiting Music Theory

Basic Principles

Second Edition

ALFRED BLATTER

Curtis Institute of Music

Routledge
Taylor & Francis Group
NEW YORK AND LONDON

Second edition published 2017
by Routledge
711 Third Avenue, New York, NY 10017

and by Routledge
2 Park Square, Milton Park, Abingdon, Oxon OX14 4RN

Routledge is an imprint of the Taylor & Francis Group, an informa business

© 2017 Alfred Blatter

The right of Alfred Blatter to be identified as the author of this work has been asserted by him in accordance with sections 77 and 78 of the Copyright, Designs and Patents Act 1988.

All rights reserved. No part of this book may be reprinted or reproduced or utilised in any form or by any electronic, mechanical, or other means, now known or hereafter invented, including photocopying and recording, or in any information storage or retrieval system, without permission in writing from the publishers.

Trademark notice: Product or corporate names may be trademarks or registered trademarks, and are used only for identification and explanation without intent to infringe.

First edition published 2007 by Routledge

Library of Congress Cataloging in Publication Data
Names: Blatter, Alfred, 1937– author.
Title: Revisiting music theory: basic principles / Alfred Blatter.
Description: Second edition. | New York; London: Routledge, 2016. |
Includes bibliographical references and index.
Identifiers: LCCN 2016030134 (print) | LCCN 2016032118 (ebook) |
ISBN 9781138915886 (hardback) | ISBN 9781138915893 (pbk.) | ISBN 9781315689975
Subjects: LCSH: Music theory.
Classification: LCC MT6 .B643 2016 (print) | LCC MT6 (ebook) | DDC 781—dc23
LC record available at https://lccn.loc.gov/2016030134

ISBN: 978-1-138-91588-6 (hbk)
ISBN: 978-1-138-91589-3 (pbk)
ISBN: 978-1-315-68997-5 (ebk)

Typeset in Caslon
by codeMantra

Dedicated—with enduring gratitude—to all who struggle to replace dogma with truth, who labor to elevate the dreary through art and who strive to heal by replacing evil with love… thus, informing our understanding of life.

Contents

Preface	ix
Acknowledgments	x
Notes on the Use of This Book	xi

part 1: Notation: The Symbols of Music — 1

1. The Components of Sound and Music — 1
2. The Notation of Pitch — 2
3. The Notation of Duration — 12
4. The Organization of Time — 17
5. Movement, Language, and Musical Rhythms — 34
6. The Notation of Loudness and Style — 38
7. The Notation of Tone Quality — 43
8. Conducting Music — 44

part 2: Melody: Note Following Note — 49

1. Intervals — 49
2. The Modes — 62
3. The Major Scale — 71
4. Key Signatures for Major Scales — 75
5. The Minor Scale — 80
6. Other Minor Scales — 84
7. Key Signatures for Minor Keys — 89
8. Scale Degrees — 95
9. The Melodic Structure — 104
10. Expanded Melodic Sources — 108

part 3: Harmony: Note(s) with Note(s) — 115

1. Intervals — 115
2. Triads — 125
3. The Inversion of Triads — 137
4. Triads within Keys — 145
5. Seventh Chords — 149
6. Harmonic Progressions — 159
7. Harmonic Rhythm — 166
8. Cadences — 170
9. Secondary Dominants — 174
10. More Chords on the Secondary Level — 178
11. Other Chords — 188

part 4: Melodies in Harmony — 205

1. Part Writing — 205
2. Creating the Harmonic Structure — 215
3. Non-Harmonic Tones — 233
4. Analyzing Later Styles — 251
5. Nineteenth-Century Analysis — 257

part 5: Textures, Structures, Techniques, and Forms — 267

1. The Textures of Music — 267
2. Fundamental Structures — 274
3. Melodic Manipulation — 286
4. Form — 301

part 6: Appendices — 343

Appendix I	Systems for Identifying Pitches	343
Appendix II	The Harmonic Series	345
Appendix III	Tuning and Temperament	348
Appendix IV	The Circle of Fifths	354
Appendix V	Transposition	356
Appendix VI	All Major Scales in Four Clefs	362
Appendix VII	All Minor Scales in Four Clefs	366
Appendix VIII	Inversions of All Triads on All Pitches in Two Clefs	378
Appendix IX	Inversions of All Common Seventh Chords on All Pitches in Two Clefs	384
Appendix X	Primary Chords in All Major and Minor Keys in Two Clefs	392
Appendix XI	Chord Symbols Used in Lead Sheet and Fake Book Notation in Two Clefs	395

Index — 399

Preface

The first edition of *Revisiting Music Theory* would never have existed without Richard Carlin insisting that I write it. In his vision, the book would be a practical handbook for all who wish to learn *about* music theory rather than for those needing to develop basic skills. The initial stages of creating the book led me to cull through materials I had prepared for students at Drexel University, where for years my theory classes were filled with bright and eager engineering, business, and design majors. In structuring my courses for these non-majors, I was guided by the words of my friend Neely Bruce, who said, "Music theory is learning to think about music." To support this goal, the book needed to be both instructional and to serve future reference needs.

Constance Ditzel, my editor at Routledge, saw the value for such a book in the lives of students with varied backgrounds in music theory who need to review—and perhaps enlarge—their theory knowledge for a practical reason: transferring into a new music program, returning to school after a hiatus, placement in graduate school, or simply relearning what they may once have known. Now, several years later, it is Constance who has insisted on the creation of this second edition. Working together, we have based our revision on suggestions that she and I have received from colleagues, readers, friends, and users of the book.

The audience for whom the book should have value remains current students, returning graduates, and those who, like many of my friends and colleagues, are music lovers with varied interests. It is hoped that the book can answer questions and provide insights to concertgoers and audiophiles, amateur or semi-professional performers, and interested listeners of all types and levels of knowledge. In fact, anyone who is fascinated by how and why music works as it does, by the related acoustical phenomena and by the interactions of melody, harmony, and form, may find the content to be not only informative but also thought-provoking.

Alfred Blatter
Media, PA 2016

Acknowledgments

The list of people to whom I owe a debt for their contributions to this book is overwhelming. It begins with my parents, includes all of the musical acquaintances of my lifetime and—especially—all of my music teachers, and ends with all the students from whom I am sure I have learned more than they ever learned from me.

In a moment of optimism, I had hoped to list everyone by name…but quickly realized that the danger of omitting important contributors, due to my limited powers to recall all of my wonderful mentors and friends (a byproduct of the good fortune of having had a long and happy life), prohibited that approach.

So I must start by saying to everyone listed in the acknowledgments of the first edition I want to add everyone I may have overlooked then and everyone I have met and benefited from since. Especially, I need to add the names of Genevieve Aoki and Peter Sheehy who have joined with my editor and very supportive friend, Constance Ditzel, to bring about this reincarnation of the book. I truly appreciate their patience, professionalism, and confidence!

And I have too often taken for granted the support and opportunities afforded me by the educational and musical institutions that gave me both significant experiences and constructive challenges: The Kirkwood Symphony; The University of Illinois, Urbana-Champaign; The U.S. Army Band; The Roanoke Symphony; Marshall University; The Mark Foutch Brass Band; The College Music Society; Drexel University; The National Association of Schools of Music; The Orchestra Society of Philadelphia; The Musical Fund Society; The Curtis Institute of Music; The Chester County Band; The Chesapeake Brass Band; The Society for American Music; and The Lower Merion Symphony.

Finally, I must thank my family for whom all of this was undertaken: my wife, Marilyn; my children, Kristine and Nicholas and his wife, Tricia; and my grandchildren, Ethan, Julienne, Alexander, Aidan, Alyssa, and Sarah.

Alfred Blatter
July 2016

Notes on the Use of This Book

Revisiting Music Theory: Basic Principles, now presented in this second edition, is intended to serve various roles for students, teachers, and lovers of music. For all, it can be a reference and resource in matters of musical notation, organization, and structure. For those enrolled in the advanced study of music theory, it should prove to be a condensed, easy-to-use catalogue of the significant facts and concepts fundamental to the understanding of music. For some instructors, it will serve to augment their lectures, workbooks, and texts. For those preparing for advanced placement or graduate admissions exams in music theory, it should serve as a concise guide for reviewing their knowledge base. And no less important, it is intended to be a source of reliable information for the music lover, amateur performer, or anyone who may wish to learn more about musical notation, form, melodic and harmonic structures, traditional practices, and the many, many seemingly mysterious signs, symbols, and performance directives found in music of the last 300-plus years.

Over the years, the materials offered here have been developed and shaped by the interests and needs of the student for whom music theory is an eagerly sought out elective. The needs of *this* student, bright and highly motivated but with little prior musical knowledge, have encouraged me to present concepts, both basic and sophisticated, in a clear, no-nonsense manner with particular attention to the idiosyncratic nature of music.

Organization

As in the first edition, the organization of the book begins with the fundamental concepts of musical notation and continues on to more complex common-practice structures. The book is divided into separate articles that deal with specific topics and practices. In this way, a student, teacher, or casual reader may pick and choose those presentations that are most relevant to topics at hand. Main articles are followed with review bullets that summarize the presentation.

Although when structuring a book, materials must be rendered in a fixed sequence, the user should never feel bound by the resulting ordering. In fact, I have often used several quite different orderings in courses I've taught over the years—always in an effort to adapt to the objectives of the particular course and the interests of the current students. Since the selection of materials to present and how the presentations are scheduled depend upon the experiences of the instructor and students, the role of the course within a curriculum (and even whether the course is offered within a semester or quarter system), the final determination of which articles to use and in what sequence must be left, happily, with the instructor.

New to This Edition

Sets of Related Exercises have been added following the bullet summaries that the student/reader may complete in order to gain further insights and understandings. In a class situation, these exercises may be assigned and graded by the instructor. Also changed in the second edition are aspects of the writing style that have been made to present a more conversational style. I have also reordered some materials to reflect more accurately my usual preferences when teaching these subjects.

Versatility

Whenever possible, varied terminologies for identical concepts found in different texts and traditions have been included. For the adult user, who may encounter unfamiliar terms on CD covers or in program notes, and students, who wish to use the book as a study aid in support of another textbook, this catholic approach should facilitate understanding. Of special utility to all of these users is the extensive index. For those for whom *Revisiting Music Theory* will serve primarily as a reference, this may be its most valuable feature.

Topics rarely found in traditional texts are included here. Modes are explained and alternative scales introduced. An in-depth discussion of fundamental compositional techniques is included as are sections on musical form. Traditional theory and introductory contrapuntal concepts are covered as are harmonic analysis and basic conducting practices. The appendices provide quick reference to such basics as scales, transposition, tuning, and chord structures, including fake book notation along with articles on the harmonic series, pitch identification systems, and more.

part 1

Notation
The Symbols of Music

1. The Components of Sound and Music

Music is the art of sound and as such possesses the same properties as sound. In musical terms, these are pitch, duration, and loudness.

Pitch is our perception of the *relative* highness or lowness of a sound.
Duration is the *relative* length of a sound.
Loudness is the *relative* strength of a sound.

All of these properties have a common dimension: time. Thus, music is characterized as a *temporal* art.

From a scientific perspective, pitch is directly related to *frequency*, which is measured in vibrations per second or *hertz (Hz)*. Likewise, duration or length is measured in *seconds* while loudness is measured in *watts* (i.e. *joules* per second).

Sound also has another property called **tone color, tone quality,** or **timbre,** which, for music, is very important. Although not a fundamental component of sound, it is in fact the result of complex interactions between various pitches (*harmonics*), durations, and loudnesses over *time*. Scientists describe the timbres of musical instruments as **complex waves** and understand them to be the sum of many different simple (sine) waves. They know, too, that the distributions of these simple waves and their behavior over time give rise to the many different instrumental and vocal colors and effects found in the music of the world.

Notating the Auditory Experience

In the evolution of notation for Western music, the symbols for pitch came first (about the tenth century). Later, notation was developed for durations (about the thirteenth century) and their relationships in time. Newer additions to our set of musical symbols were indicators for loudness and changes in loudness (seventeenth century) and for tone color (eighteenth century). Changes and modifications to these symbols continue to appear as the content and nature of music continue to evolve.

Review

- The fundamental components of sound and music are pitch, duration, and loudness.
- Another important quality of sound and music is timbre or tone quality.
- Earliest symbols were for the notation of pitch. The notation of durations is newer.
- Notations of loudness and tone color are the more recent additions to our system.

Related Exercises

§ For each sound event listed below, select one or two words (such as *high*, *low*, *loud*, or *soft*) that you associate with the sound.

Whistling	Bird songs	Truck rumbling by	Fire siren
Cold wind	Thunder	Door closing	Ringtone
Electric guitar	Kittens	Dish washer	Electric razor
Door bell	Cars crashing	Children playing	Traffic jam
Walking on dry leaves	People talking	Helicopter	At the shore
Fans at basketball game	Airplane taking off	Orchestra tuning	Auction
Making espresso	Weather broadcast	Band marching by	In a restaurant

§ What are some everyday words that you use to describe sounds and/or the changes in sound?

2. The Notation of Pitch

Early notated European music was at first associated with (Latin) words, and therefore the symbols for the pitches (notes) were placed on the page along with the text to be sung. The order of the symbols from left to right, like the language, indicated the order in which the sounds were to be produced. The positioning of the notes up or down the page indicated the highness or lowness of the sound to be sung.

The Pitches

Western music uses the first seven letters of the alphabet to name the different pitches. In our system, *A* is lower than *B*, and *B* is lower than *C*, etc. (In German-speaking societies, the pitch name H is also used.) The fact that all of our music can be represented by using only seven letter names is due to the historical evolution of our Western notation system and the nature of the human ear.

The Special Properties of the Octave

If you play a pitch near the middle of the piano's range and ask a group of people to sing what has been played, the women (and children) will sing the pitch that was sounded. But most men will sing a pitch that sounds lower because it has half as many vibrations per second as the sounded pitch. In spite of this obvious difference, almost all listeners will agree that both groups sang "the same pitch." For this reason, we are comfortable with using only one letter for both pitches. We accept two pitches as being (octave) equivalents *if one has twice as many vibrations as the other*.

Early Western music notation and terminology divided the space between these two similar pitches into seven steps. In order to identify each of these steps, one of the letter names—A through G—was assigned in ascending order to each pitch. When the musical sound that possessed twice as many vibrations as the initial pitch was reached, it proved to be the eighth note. Since it sounded like the first note, it was called by the same letter name as the first note. Because it was the eighth note, its distance from the first note was labeled an **octave** (from the Greek base *okta* or the Latin base *octo*, both meaning "eight").

Though our modern keyboard pitch system now includes twelve separate pitches within an octave and our musical vocabulary possesses even more pitch names, the name *octave* has not been discarded. Usually, this is not a problem. However, as in the study of acoustics or music from other cultures, it can at times become a source of confusion, or even an impediment to accurate communications.

> In an effort at clarity in his writings on tunings, Harry Partch (1901–1974) referred to the octave as "the two to one" (2/1).

EXAMPLE 1.01 The layout of a modern keyboard, with its characteristic grouping of three black keys alternating with a group of two black keys. (Lower pitches are to the left of higher pitches.) Note the repetition of the pitch names in each octave. The white keys all have letter names, and each letter name has a unique position in the pattern.

The earliest pitch notations dealt only with what we would identify as (typically) the white keys on the keyboard. These pitches are the so-called **naturals**. Pitches that we know as the black keys, or **sharps** or **flats**, were sometimes used in early music but were often not notated, implying that the performers knew when to inflect the pitch.

The Staff

Modern notation uses one or more horizontal lines, called a **staff**, for the placement of our pitch and duration symbols. The usual form of the staff is five parallel lines, although, historically, other numbers of lines, especially four, have been used. Modern percussion music often uses one or two lines.

EXAMPLE 1.02 The modern five-line staff.

Musicians understand the staff as being composed of lines and spaces. Staff lines are numbered from the bottom to the top. When you need to identify a particular line, you use its number. Likewise, spaces are identified as first (lowest) to fourth (highest). Pitch symbols (the notes, usually elliptical in shape) may be placed in a space or on a line (i.e. the line passes *through* the symbol).

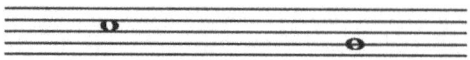

EXAMPLE 1.03 On the left, a pitch symbol (note) in a space. On the right, a note on a line.

The Clefs

A *clef* is usually placed at the beginning of the staff. The clef is a symbol that shows the reader which pitch will be assigned to which staff line. There are three clefs—the **G clef**, the **F clef**, and the **C clef**—each deriving its name from the pitch it locates.

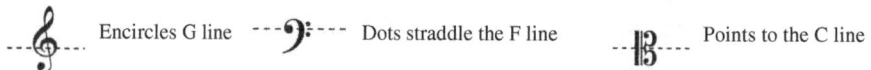

EXAMPLE 1.04 The three clef symbols found in Western music notation. From left to right: the G clef, the F clef, and the C clef.

In current practice, the commonly encountered clefs are the treble, bass, alto, and tenor, as shown below.

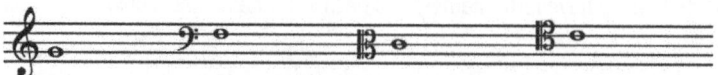

EXAMPLE 1.05 The four modern uses of the clefs and the pitch that each locates. From left to right: G above middle C in treble clef; F below middle C in bass clef; middle C in alto clef; and middle C in tenor clef.

When the G clef is placed on the staff so that the lower loop encircles the second line, it is called a **treble clef**. When the F clef is placed on the staff so that the two dots straddle the fourth line, it is called the **bass clef**. The C clef may be placed so that its central arrow points to the middle (third line), in which case it's called the **alto clef**, or to the fourth line, in which case it's called the **tenor clef**.

The most commonly encountered clefs are the treble and the bass. The alto clef is found in music written for the viola and sometimes in music written for the trombone. The tenor clef can be found in some music written for the violoncello, the bassoon, the trombone, and even the double bass.

Example 1.06 shows the pitches assigned to the lines and spaces of the treble, bass, alto, and tenor clefs.

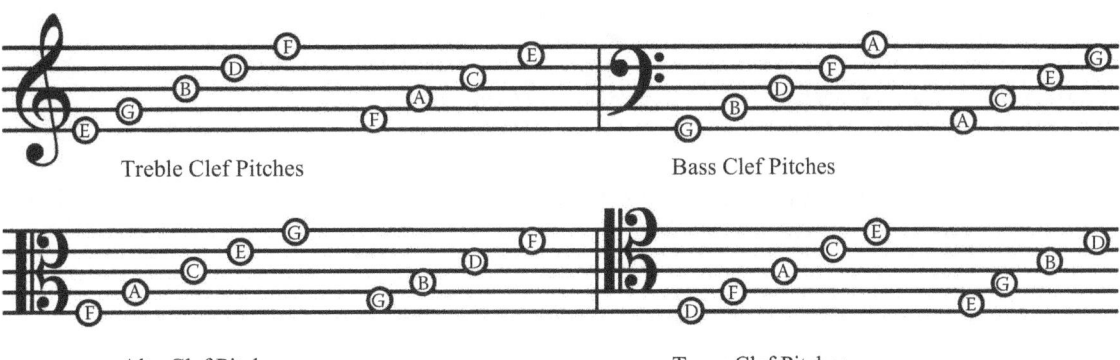

EXAMPLE 1.06   The pitch letter names represented by the lines and spaces found in each of the standard clefs. The practice is to assign successive letter names by alternating lines and spaces. Top left, the lines and the spaces in the treble clef. Top right, the lines and the spaces in the bass clef. Bottom left, the lines and the spaces in the alto clef. Bottom right, the lines and the spaces in the tenor clef.

Historically, clefs could be found in other positions on the staff. Each clef had a specific name and was selected to keep most of the notes in the staff.

EXAMPLE 1.07   On the left, an example passage in French violin clef. On the right, the same passage in treble clef.

The need for fluency in the reading of these ancient clefs is usually limited to scholars and performers who specialize in particular periods and styles of music.

> As recently as the early twentieth century (especially in vocal music), C clefs were placed on the first, second, and fifth lines producing the soprano, mezzo-soprano, and baritone clefs, respectively.

Ledger Lines

When a required pitch is too high or too low for the available staff lines, additional pitches can be written by using *ledger lines*. These short lines, drawn parallel to the staff lines and with vertical spacing identical to the staff, may be placed above or below the staff as required. Ledger lines are equivalent to extending the lines and spaces of the staff higher or lower as needed. Note the usage shown below.

EXAMPLE 1.08   Using ledger lines for pitches beyond the staff lines.

Ledger lines are placed between the staff and the notes with which they are associated but never beyond the notes.

EXAMPLE 1.09   On the left, unnecessary ledger lines added beyond highest or lowest notes. On the right, ledger lines used correctly.

Even Lower or Higher Pitches

On modern instruments, it is possible to play pitches much higher and lower than those available on our standard clefs. Even ledger lines may offer only limited assistance. An extended passage in an extreme portion of the musical range can become difficult to read. Therefore, it is not uncommon to find indications to perform a musical line an octave or two higher or lower than notated. These indications look like this:

> In some notation, particularly jazz/pops, *8vb* and *15mb* may replace *8va basso* and *15ma bassa*.

EXAMPLE 1.10 On the top, the use of *8va* and *8va basso*; on the bottom, the use of *15ma* and *15ma bassa*. When *8va* or *15ma* is no longer required, *loco* is often used to indicate a return to normal.

The Need for Greater Precision

One problem with the simple A-B-C-D-E-F-G system of identifying pitches was that it gave the performer no cue as to the distance between adjacent pitches. This presented little difficulty when these were assumed to be the only available pitches but led to notational complexity when it later became desirable to insert pitches between the original notes.

When you look at the keyboard, you see the result of this situation: Because the distance between B and C and E and F were small steps (what we now call **semitones** or **half steps**), no additional pitches could be inserted.

But because the distance between all the other adjacent pitches was larger (what we call a **whole tone** or **whole step**), additional pitches were inserted. This brought about the very familiar look of the modern keyboard.

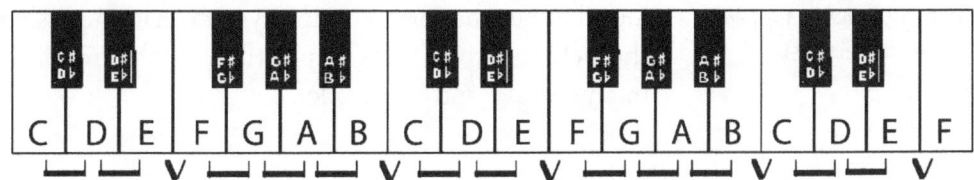

EXAMPLE 1.11 Keys marked ⌐⌐ are a whole tone apart. Those marked V are a semitone apart. Notice that everywhere the pitches are a whole tone apart, a black key is inserted. When the pitches are only a semitone apart, no black key can be inserted.

Sharps and Flats

To notate these added pitches (primarily the black keys), another set of symbols evolved, what we call *accidentals*. These symbols include the ***sharp***, ***flat***, and ***natural*** as well as the ***double sharp*** and ***double flat***. Here is how they function:

Sharp	♯	raises associated pitch by 1 semitone.
Flat	♭	lowers associated pitch by 1 semitone.
Double sharp	✕	raises the associated pitch by 2 semitones.
Double flat	♭♭	lowers the associated pitch by 2 semitones.
Natural	♮	removes effect of a sharp, a double sharp, a flat or a double flat.

> The symbol for the flat evolved from the letter *b*, the German name for B-flat. The sharp and natural symbols evolved from *h*, the German name for B-natural.

When these symbols are placed on the staff, they are positioned immediately before the note to be changed. Even though we say, "F-sharp," we always write sharp-F, because the performer needs to see the required change before sounding the note. (Discovering the accidental after the note has been played would obviously be too late.)

> It would be incorrect to state that a double sharp or a double flat altered the original pitch by a whole tone because two semitones may represent a distance slightly greater than a whole tone. (See Appendix III, p. 348.)

EXAMPLE 1.12 On the left, accidentals placed incorrectly (after their associated pitches). In this location, the accidentals are useless to the performer. On the right, accidentals placed correctly.

Additional Pitch Items

> Although microtones are found in music of other cultures and have been used by some Western composers, they remain beyond the scope of this text.

As music became more complex, additional pitches were added to the system. Example 1.13 shows *all* of the pitches found in our modern notation system. Although shown in the treble and bass clefs, any of these pitches may be found in any octave and in any clef.

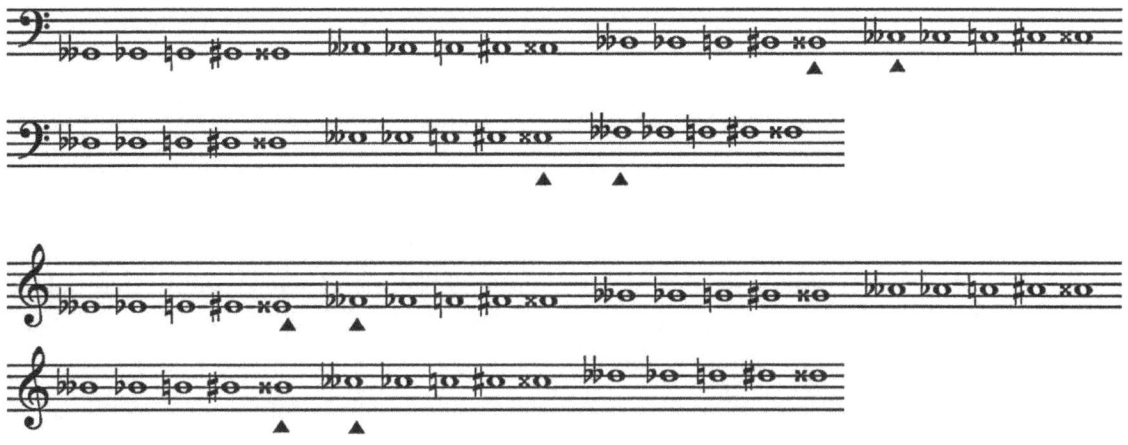

EXAMPLE 1.13 Pitches marked with a ▲ are rarely seen.

Enharmonics

Two pitches that are noted differently but played on a keyboard using the same key, such as G-sharp and A-flat, are said to be *enharmonic*. Enharmonic equivalents are generally avoided in music theory, although they may occasionally prove useful.

Review

- Pitch symbols are placed on a line or in a space on a staff that consists of one or more horizontal lines; the usual number is five.
- These symbols are read and performed from left to right.
- The letters used to name musical pitches are A, B, C, D, E, F, and G.
- The lines are numbered from the bottom upward.
- Clefs are placed at the beginning (left) of the staff to indicate pitch assignments.
- Each of the three clefs is named for the pitch letter it identifies: G, F, and C.
- Although clefs may be placed on the staff in various positions, modern usage finds only one normal position for the G and F clefs and only two normal positions for the C clef.
- Multiple clefs are needed to keep as many notes on the staff as possible.
- The G clef, with G on the second line of the staff, is called the treble clef.
- The F clef, with F on the fourth line of the staff, is called the bass clef.
- The C clef may be placed on the third or fourth line of the staff. When placed on the third line, it is called the alto clef; when placed on the fourth line, it is called the tenor clef.

- When pitches are too high or too low to be written on the staff, ledger lines are used to extend the range of the staff.
- The indications *8va, 8vb, 15ma,* and *15mb* are used for notating pitches too high or low for ledger lines.
- The distance between adjacent pitch names (letters) is either a whole step or whole tone (as between C and D, D and E, F and G, G and A, and A and B) or a half step or semitone (as between E and F and B and C).
- Accidentals are used to raise or lower the notated pitch and are always placed before (to the left of) the pitch to be affected.
- A sharp (♯) raises the pitch a semitone.
- A flat (♭) lowers the pitch a semitone.
- A double sharp (𝄪) raises the pitch two semitones.
- A double flat (♭♭) lowers the pitch two semitones.
- A natural (♮) returns the pitch to normal.
- Although a double sharp or double flat may be placed before any pitch, actual practice limits the likelihood of such figures.
- Especially in keyboard music and on fretted strings, two pitches that are spelled differently, such as A-sharp and B-flat, but played the same way are said to be enharmonic.

> In older editions, the combination of a natural and a sharp or a natural and a flat was used to return a double sharp or a double flat to the status of a single sharp or flat (respectively). Although a thorough and correct notation, it is rarely used in modern editions and manuscripts.

Related Exercises

§ On the staff—and in the clef given—place the note specified below the staff.

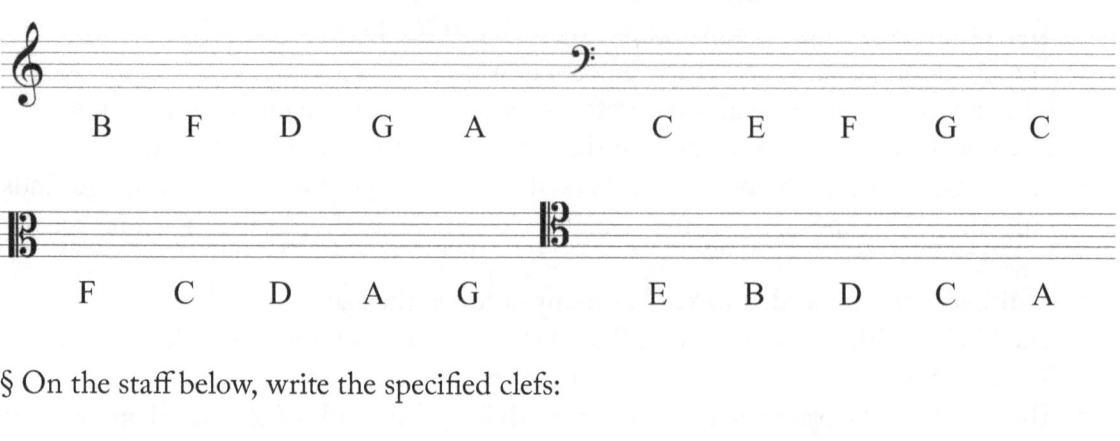

§ On the staff below, write the specified clefs:

Bass clef   C clef   F clef   Alto clef   Treble clef   Tenor clef   G clef

§ Name the pitches represented by these clef/staff locations:

§ Renotate these pitches onto the clefs/staves given below. Use ledger lines when necessary.

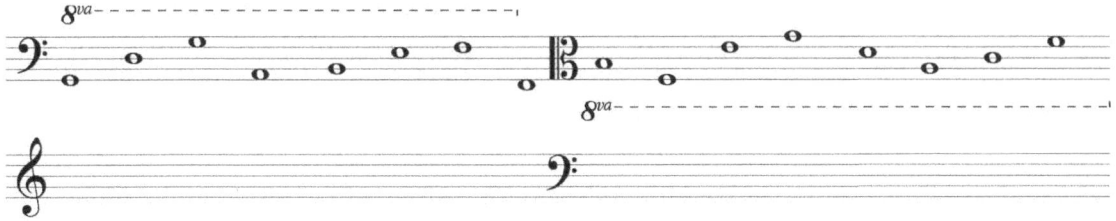

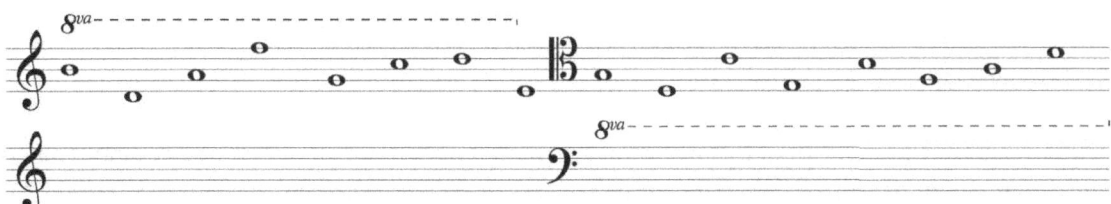

§ Mark the locations of all the semitones found on the given clefs/staves. One example is given.

§ Using sharps, create semitones below each given pitch. An example is done for you.

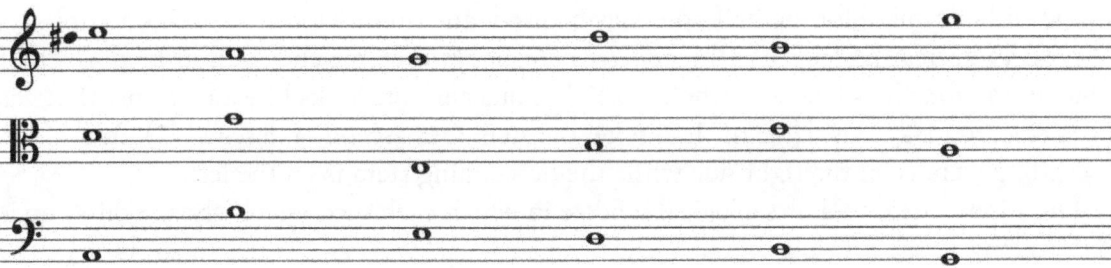

§ Using flats, create semitones above each given pitch. An example is done for you.

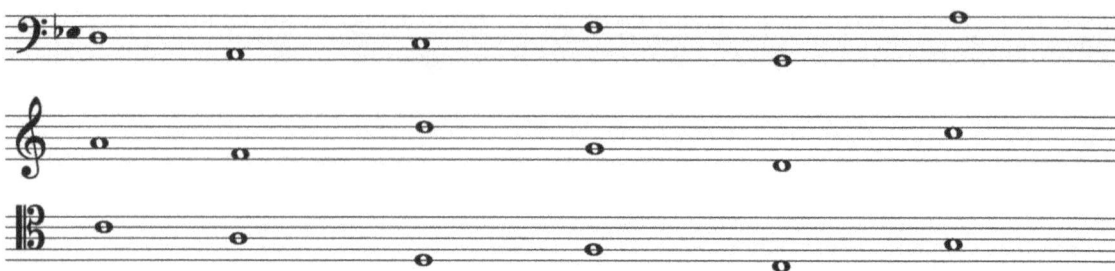

§ Next to each given pitch, write an enharmonic equivalent. An example is done for you.

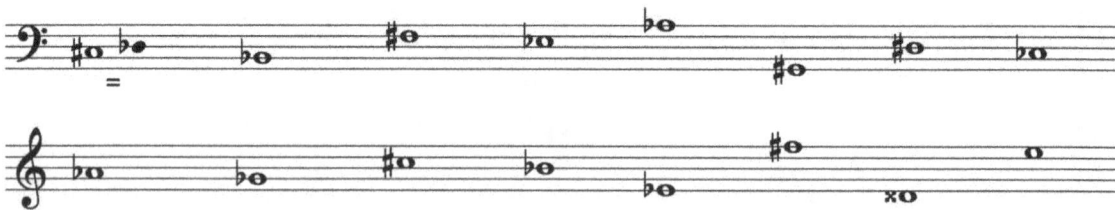

3. The Notation of Duration

The duration of a musical sound is communicated by the *appearance* of the symbol that is placed on the staff to indicate the pitch. But the duration characterized by that symbol is not an absolute value. All note lengths are *relative* to each other and are understood and performed in relation to one another.

The longest duration found in Western music is the ***double whole note*** or ***breve***. It looks like this: ⊚. The double whole note is fairly rare.

The longest duration routinely encountered is the ***whole note*** or ***semibreve***. It has an elliptical shape and looks like this: ○. The next longest note is the ***half note*** (minim) and, as the name implies, it is half as long as the whole note. The half note looks like a small whole note but with a vertical line, called a ***stem***, attached to it: ♩. The stem may ascend from the note head or may descend like this: ♩. Notice that when the stem ascends, it is attached to the *right* side of the note head, but when it descends it is attached to the *left*. In writing music, either symbol for the half note may be used, and no difference in sound occurs.

Next in decreasing length is the ***quarter note***, or ***crotchet***, which is half as long as a half note or one-fourth as long as a whole note. The quarter note looks like a half note that has been colored in (♩). Also, like the half note, the stem may ascend or descend (♩). Again, the ascending stem is on the right side while the descending stem is on the left.

Duration notation follows a logical scheme in which each successively shorter duration is half as long as the previous symbol. Thus, we have ***eighth notes*** (♪ or ♪) (quavers) half the length of quarter notes and *sixteenth notes* (♬ or 𝅘𝅥𝅯) (semi-quavers) half the value of eighth notes.

The eighth note looks like a quarter note with a tail. This "tail" is called a *flag* (♪) and is added to the stem. The sixteenth note is written with two flags. There are also *thirty-second notes* (demisemiquavers) with three flags, and *sixty-fourth notes* (hemidemisemiquavers) with four flags. The process may continue, although you will rarely see notes shorter in length than a *128th* note (five flags!). The flag (or flags) is always placed on the right side of the

> In Britain, the durations have different names. A double whole note is a breve, a whole note is a semibreve, a half note is a minim, a quarter note is a crotchet, an eighth note is a quaver, a sixteenth note is a semiquaver, a thirty-second note is a demisemiquaver, and a sixty-fourth note is a hemidemisemiquaver.

stem, regardless of the direction of the stem. However, flags attached to downward stems are "upside down" from those attached to upward stems.

Where two or more notes in succession are eighth notes or shorter, the flags may be replaced by *beams* without having any effect on the sound of the notes. Thus, ♪♪ and ♫ sound exactly the same and ♪♪♪♪ may replace ♬♬ with no audible change. Beams assist the performer to see how the notes are grouped or associated with one another.

Here is a table of most of the commonly found durations starting with a whole note. The total duration of the symbols on each line is the same, but every line consists of twice as many events as the line above.

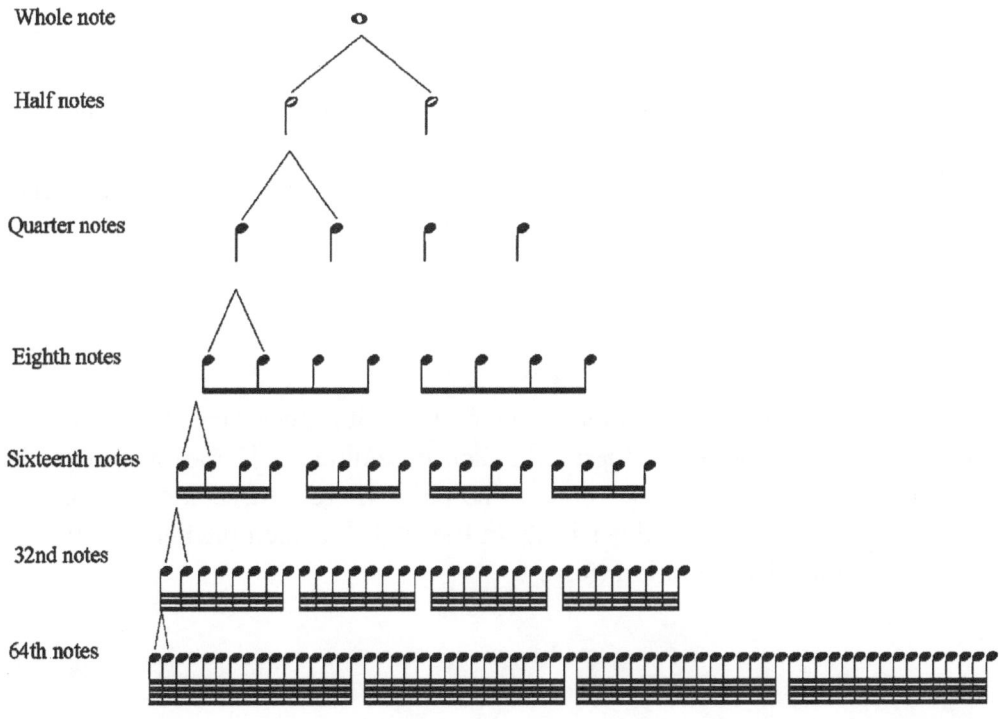

EXAMPLE 1.14   Chart showing the relationships between durations from whole note to sixty-fourth notes.

Ties and Dots

When longer durations are required, they may be notated by the use of a *tie*. A tie is a short curved line that connects the symbols to be combined and informs the performer that the pitch is to be sounded for a duration equal to the sum of all the connected durations.

EXAMPLE 1.15 Using ties. From left to right, two tied quarter notes equal a half note, a half note tied to two quarter notes equal a whole note, a half note tied to a quarter note in turn tied to two eighth notes equal a whole note, and two tied half notes equal a whole note.

In the special case where the duration of the note is to be increased by 50 percent of the value of the note, a ***dot*** after the note (or rest) may be used. Look at the following examples:

EXERCISE 1.16 From the left, the combination of a half note tied to a quarter note may be notated by the use of a dotted half note; the half note tied to a quarter note tied to an eighth note may be notated with a doubly dotted half note; a dotted whole note equals a whole note tied to a half note; and a doubly dotted quarter note is sounded for the same duration as a quarter note tied to an eighth note tied to a sixteenth note.

Notice that when a second dot follows the first, the duration of the whole event is increased by three-fourths of the initial symbol. Another way to think of this is that the first dot adds 50 percent of the initial symbol's duration to the initial symbol and that the second dot increases the total duration by 50 percent of the value of the first dot. Three or even four dots may be placed after a note or a rest. Each successive dot increases the total duration of the event by 50 percent of the value of the preceding symbol (dot). Single and double dots are the most common. Three or more dots are extremely rare.

Rests

In music, silence is often as important as sound and thus it is necessary to indicate to a performer when not to play and for how long this silence should last. To indicate these silences, **rests** are used. Because rests have duration but no pitch, there are a separate set of symbols. These symbols are usually centered vertically in the staff. For each pitched duration (note), there is an equivalent silent duration (rest).

Pitch Symbol	Name	Silence Symbol	Name
𝄺	double whole note (or breve)		double whole note rest
o	whole note		whole note rest
𝅗𝅥	half note		half note rest
𝅘𝅥	quarter note	𝄽	quarter note rest
𝅘𝅥𝅮	eighth note	𝄾	eighth note rest
𝅘𝅥𝅯	sixteenth note	𝄿	sixteenth note rest
𝅘𝅥𝅰	32nd note	𝅀	32nd note rest
𝅘𝅥𝅱	64th note	𝅁	64th note rest

EXAMPLE 1.17   Pitch and rest symbols from double whole note to sixty-fourth note.

When necessary, dots are applied to rests just as they are to notes. In contrast, ties are never used—or needed—with rests.

Grace Notes

We often find smaller notes, with or without slashes through them, associated with some pitches. These notes are called grace notes and are among the many, various decorative inflections composers add to pitches to make them expressive or more colorful.

EXAMPLE 1.18   On the left, a single grace note before the main pitch. On the right, a group of three grace notes to be played before the main pitch.

Exactly how these extra notes are to be performed is a matter of historic interpretation and style and is beyond this text. For now, you should recognize these notes as ornaments and understand that they are usually played very quickly. These notes may be played on the beat or immediately before the beat depending on the composer, period, and the tradition.

> In music from the late eighteenth century, small notes may be found that do not function as grace notes but which are a part of an older notation convention. Writings by Leopold Mozart (1719–1787; father of Wolfgang) and other scholars should be consulted with regard to the correct interpretation of these symbols. Also see non-harmonic tones on p. 233.

Review

- The duration of a musical sound is indicated by the appearance of the symbol (note).
- Notes do not convey an exact length but rather represent a relative length.
- Available notes range from the rare double whole note (breve) to the whole note (semibreve), half note (minim), quarter note (crotchet), eighth note (quaver), sixteenth note (semiquaver), thirty-second note (demisemiquaver), sixty-fourth note (hemidemisemiquaver), and even a 128th note. In this list, each note is half as long as the preceding note.
- These notes are graphically made up of an elliptical shaped note head and, as needed, shading, a stem, and flags or beams. The more components to the symbol, the shorter the duration.
- The direction of the stems makes no difference in the sound of the note.
- Beams may be substituted for flags with no affect to the sound.
- When a longer duration is required, ties may be used to connect two or more notes.
- Silences are indicated by rests. Each note has a rest that corresponds to it.
- In certain situations, dots are used to extend the length of a note or rest. No matter how many dots are used, each dot increases the duration of the initial note or rest by 50 percent of the length of the preceding symbol. It is rare to encounter more than two dots.
- Ties are never used with rests.
- Grace notes are smaller notes that are played quickly before their associated main note.

Related Exercises

§ Using the staves provided below, write the specified durations on a line or in a space as required:

1. Whole note on a line;
2. Whole note in a space;
3. Half note in a space;
4. Quarter note in a space;
5. Sixteenth note on a line;
6. Eighth note on a line;
7. Quarter note on a line;
8. Half note on a line;
9. Double whole note on a line;
10. Eighth note in a space.

§ For each duration noted above the staff, create the equivalent duration on the staff by using ties. The first one is done as an example.

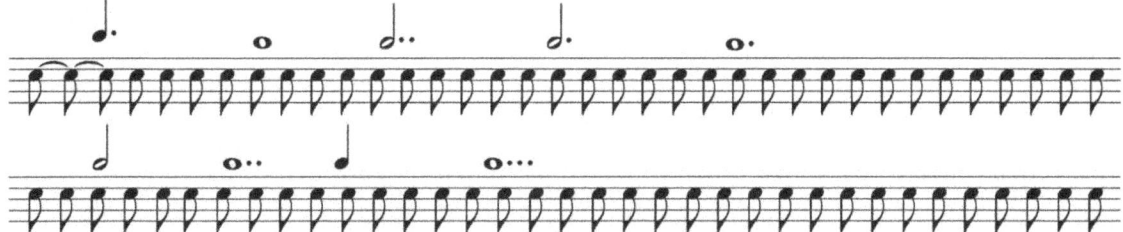

§ On the top staff (and on the third staff), various rests and notes are written. If a note is written, write the corresponding (same duration) rest on the staff below. If a rest is written, write the corresponding note on the staff below.

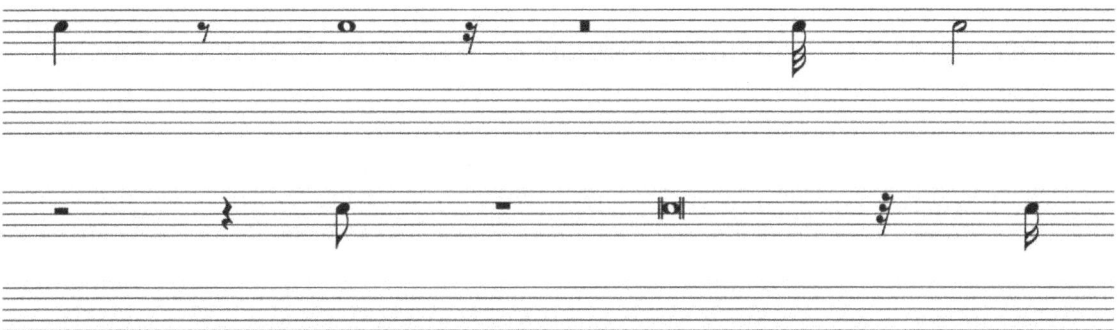

4. The Organization of Time

Western music is organized in time by an underlying *pulse* that is also called the *beat*. This beat may be of any speed desired by the composer, dictated by the conductor, and/or selected by the performer. The beat is always present, even though it may not be heard by the listener. It is, however, something of which the performer is always aware.

Tempo

The speed of the beat is called the ***tempo***, and the tempo may be indicated in the music by words (subject to interpretation), such as *Allegro* (fast) and *Largo* (slow), or by ***metronome*** marks, such as ♩ = 60. Frequently, the metronome indication is also combined with descriptive words.

As with much of the vocabulary of music, the source for many terms used to indicate tempo (as well as the word *tempo* itself) is the Italian language. When only words are used to define the tempo, the interpretation is left to the performer (or conductor) and may vary greatly from performer to performer.

With the above metronome indication for example, a speed of sixty quarter notes per minute, less ambiguity exists. The metronome will be set to click or flash sixty times every minute, and the performer will practice the music at that tempo.

Here are some of the commonly encountered terms (**tempo marks**) used to define the tempo of a piece of music. They are listed from slowest to fastest.

Grave –	extremely slow	*Moderato* –	moderate
Largo –	very slow	*Allegretto* –	not as fast as Allegro
Lento –	slow	*Allegro* –	fast
Larghetto –	not as slow as Largo	*Vivace* –	lively
Adagio –	comfortably slow	*Vivo* –	same as Vivace
Andante –	walking speed	*Presto* –	very fast
Andantino –	a little faster than Andante	*Prestissimo* –	as fast as possible

In addition, we have many terms that communicate a *sense* of tempo *and* a manner of performance. And other terms regularly associated with tempo marks clarify, modify, or otherwise refine the meaning. Among the more common of these, listed alphabetically, are

a –	by	*grazioso* –	gracefully
animato –	with life	*l'istesso* –	the same
assai –	very, enough	*ma* –	but, however
bravura –	boldly	*maestoso* –	dignified
brio –	spirit	*marcato* –	well marked, accented
con –	with	*molto* –	very much
dolce –	sweetly	*non troppo* –	not too much
dolore –	sadness	*pesante* –	heavily
e –	and	*più* –	more
espressivo –	expressively	*poco* –	little
fuoco –	fiery	*risoluto* –	with resolve
grandioso –	stately	*subito* –	immediately
		troppo –	too much

Changes in Tempo

During a performance, the composer may ask the performer to change to a new tempo, slow down the tempo, and/or speed up the tempo. Again, this is usually accomplished by the use of Italian words that tell the musician what to do. In music published after the first quarter of the nineteenth century, metronome marks may clarify the character and amount of change desired. As with tempos, most of the time any change is left to the performer to interpret.

Notation: The Symbols of Music

In addition to the above terms, here are some others that may be used with a tempo change.

a tempo –	return to previous tempo	*più mosso* –	faster
accelerando –	get faster	*rallentando* –	slowing down
affrettando –	becoming quicker	*ritard* –	gradually slowing
agitato –	faster, agitated	*ritenuto* –	a sudden slowing
allargando –	broaden and slow	*rubato* –	with rhythmic flexibility
l'istesso tempo –	retain the same tempo	*stringendo* –	get faster
meno mosso –	less motion, slower	*tempo primo* –	return to first tempo

Determining Actual Durations

Up to now, the question of the actual length of a note or rest has been left unanswered by saying that the "lengths are relative" because without a tempo a performer cannot determine how long any note or rest will last. Once the tempo is established at, for example, sixty quarter notes per minute, it then becomes obvious that a quarter note will last one second, a half note will last two seconds, and an eighth note will occupy one-half of a second.

Under the conditions specified above, the following series of durations (***rhythmic figures***) will last twelve seconds:

EXAMPLE 1.19 A rhythmic figure using half, quarter, and eighth notes at a tempo of sixty beats per minute (BPMs).

It can be difficult to keep your place when reading a series of durations like those in Example 1.19. For this reason, and to communicate to the performer the rhythmic structure of the music, musical notation usually includes vertical lines, called ***bar lines***, that separate the notes into smaller, easier-to-grasp groups. For example:

> BPMs or beats per minute can obviously be determined by using the metronome but only became a regular part of composers' vocabulary with the rise of computer-generated music for film and television.

EXAMPLE 1.20 The rhythmic figure from Example 1.19 but with bar lines added to clarify the rhythmic organization.

Each of these smaller rhythmic groupings is a ***measure*** or ***bar*** of music (i.e. between two bar lines). In the example above, all bars are equal in length, and at ♩ = 60, each bar equals, in actual time, four seconds (four quarter notes). In Western music, it is very common for most, or all, measures in a piece of music to be of the same length, but it is certainly not required.

In the notation of music, the composer usually indicates to the performer how the durations and beats are organized into measures by the use of a ***meter signature*** or ***time signature***. The time signature is expressed as two numbers, one over the other, and is placed at the beginning of the music. It is never shown again unless the composer decides to change it.

EXAMPLE 1.21   This example is identical to Example 1.20 but includes a time signature (⁴⁄₄) to clarify the rhythmic organization.

The upper number in the time signature indicates the number of beats per measure. The lower number shows the performer which of the various duration symbols the composer has selected to represent the beat. In Example 1.21, the lower four tells the performer that the quarter note has been selected to represent the beat. (As a matter of information, time signatures are never written as fractions.)

Example 1.21 could have been divided into measures differently. For instance, the composer could have chosen to use two quarter notes per bar (two-four time) rather than four per bar, in which case the passage would appear this way:

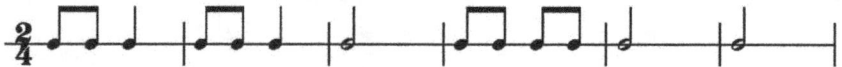

EXAMPLE 1.22   The passage from above with the beats grouped as two quarter notes per bar.

Or the same passage could be notated using the half note to indicate the pulse and with two half notes per bar.

EXAMPLE 1.23   The passage from above with the beats grouped as two half notes per measure.

In Example 1.24 below, the composer chose to represent the beat with an eighth note. Therefore, it *looks* different from Example 1.21. However, if performed at ♪ = 60, the sound will be identical.

EXAMPLE 1.24   Using a four-eight time signature and durations that are all half the length of those in Example 1.21 will produce the same perceived rhythm as Example 1.21 provided that the tempo is set at ♪ = 60.

Notation: The Symbols of Music

The most frequently encountered time signatures have two, three, four, and six as the upper numbers, but any number of pulses may be selected as the length of a measure. The lower number is selected from one, two, four, eight, sixteen, thirty-two, or sixty-four, representing whole note, half note, quarter note, eighth note, sixteenth note, thirty-second note, and sixty-fourth note, respectively. These are the available values from which the symbol for the beat *must* be selected.

> Some composers have used actual notes to indicate the lower number, such as ♪ for three-eight time or ♩ for two-four time.

The Structure of a Measure

Let's examine how a measure of music in four-four time may be structured. From the above discussion, we know that each four-four measure will be equal to four quarter notes in length, but it need not consist of (literally) four quarter notes. Any combination of durations (including rests) that add up to four quarter notes may be used.

Thus, these are some of the many possible configurations:

EXAMPLE 1.25 Twelve different rhythmic figures, each of which equals a complete measure in four-four time. Of course, many other possibilities exist.

As you can see, there are many ways to arrange notes and rests within a four-four measure. And there are as many different ways to arrange notes and rests within three-four bars, two-four bars, or any other time signature.

Duple and Triple Meters

Bars that consist of two, four, or eight beats are said to be in *duple meter*; those written with three pulses are examples of *triple meter*. Usually the first beat in a bar (the *downbeat* or *thesis*) is given the greatest stress or *accent*. In duple meter bars with four beats, the third beat may receive a secondary accent (not as great as accorded the first beat but slightly greater than either the second or fourth beat). The second and fourth beats are typically unaccented and are often called the *offbeats*. The last beat in a measure is called the *upbeat*, *arsis*, *anacrusis*, or *pickup*.

In a triple meter bar there is, of course, also a downbeat and an upbeat. However, the secondary accent, if it exists, may be *either* on the second beat *or* on the third beat. The location or existence of this secondary accent determines the characteristic rhythmic feel of the music.

Common Time and Cut Time (Alla Breve)

Two time signatures are unusual because they do not use numbers and look quite different from the others. These are **common time**, which is indicated as 𝐂 and **alla breve** time—usually called "cut time"—which is indicated by ₵. These symbols are remnants of an older system for notating time. The common time symbol is understood to be the equivalent to four-four time, while the alla breve symbol is equivalent to two-two time. They are both duple meters.

Other Time Signatures

The notation of musical meters is so strongly associated with beats per measure that are multiples of two—three being the primary exception—that our terminology has been affected. Most texts refer to six-eight (or six-four) meters as being compound duple meters. Similarly, nine-eight or nine-four measures are called compound triple meter. Musicians often encounter references made to meters such as five-four time or seven-eight time as irregular meters. These terms are widely employed so you need to be familiar with them. However, it is more important to understand how these various meters are constructed and also how they feel.

Compound Time

Time signatures that have upper numbers that are multiples of three (but not three itself) may display significantly different characteristics when performed at faster tempos than they do at slower tempos. When performed slowly enough, the feel of a six-beat measure is very clearly a pattern of six pulses. These measures may have internal accents on the first beat and on the fourth beat, or the accents may be found on the first beat, the third beat, and the fifth beat. The two accent patterns look like this:

EXAMPLE 1.26 The two typical accent patterns found in measures with six beats. On the left, two groups of three; on the right, three groups of two. Notice that the groupings are made clearer by the use of beams connecting the associated notes. This is a frequent use of beams.

At faster tempos, each measure of six will sound either like a measure of two stronger beats with each beat divided into three parts or, less commonly, like a three-beat measure. Though the first alternative is somewhat more common, composers sometimes alternate between the two. When it is heard as two groups of three pulses, the traditional description is **compound time**, or, more precisely, **compound duple time** (or **compound duple meter**). Obviously, when heard as three groups of two pulses, it sounds like simple triple meter.

In a similar manner, music with a time signature that has a nine as the upper number is often felt as a fairly fast three with each main beat divided into triplets. This, too, is a form of compound time. The other frequently encountered example of compound time is twelve-eight or twelve-four time, where at faster tempos you feel four strong beats and each of these beats is divided into triplets.

EXAMPLE 1.27 On the left, the typical accent pattern for nine-eight time. On the right, the accent pattern usually heard in twelve-eight time.

From the perspective of a listener, who cannot see the notation, the concept of compound time is not at all obvious. What may be perceived is a rapid triple meter with *measures* grouped by twos, threes, or fours.[1]

Irregular Meters

Time signatures with upper numbers of five, seven, ten, and eleven (or other numbers that are not powers of two or multiples of three) are sometimes called *irregular* (or *irrational*) meters. (They are neither.) But these pulse patterns are less common in Western music than they are in the music of some cultures. When encountered, we tend to hear and feel these patterns in certain specific ways.

Five Beats per Measure

Measures with five beats are almost always the combination of two pulses: one short and one longer. At slow tempos, all five beats are counted and/or felt. At faster tempos, an uneven two pulse is felt. This feeling has two versions:

EXAMPLE 1.28 The two usual five-beat patterns. On the left, a 2+3 grouping. On the right, a 3+2 grouping.

Seven Beats per Measure

The seven-beat pattern is an uneven three pattern. It may be 2+2+3, 2+3+2, or 3+2+2. Here are examples.

EXAMPLE 1.29 The three usual seven-beat patterns. On the left, a 2+2+3, in the middle is 2+3+2, and on the right the 3+2+2 grouping.

For purposes of clarity, composers will sometimes indicate the grouping of the notes within a measure by using two or more numbers for the time signature. In this manner, it is possible to clarify the desired internal accent pattern within a measure.

EXAMPLE 1.30 Using two and three numbers to clarify the accent pattern within a measure. On the left, a two-number indication for a five-eight measure. On the right, a three-number designation for a seven-eight measure.

This same sort of time signature can be used if the music groups the beats within a conventional meter in an unconventional manner, such as two groups of three eighth notes and one group of two eighth notes within a four-four meter. Or like these:

EXAMPLE 1.31 Using two and three numbers to modify the accent pattern within a measure. On the left, a two-number indication within four-four measure. On the right, a three-number designation for a nine-eight measure. Note the use of a dashed internal "bar line" on the example on the left to assist the performer in seeing the patterns. The use of a dashed bar line is optional, does not create an additional bar, and has no audible effect.

Incomplete Measures

Although a composition will usually consist of many measures, often all of the same length, it is not uncommon for the piece to begin with an incomplete measure. Commonly, it is the first measure that may have only one or two beats in it representing the last beat (or last two beats) of a measure. Collectively, these beats preceding the first complete measure are referred to as pickups. Familiar pieces that illustrate the difference between music with pickups and music without pickups are the "The Star-Spangled Banner," with two pickup notes ♪♫ on the syllable "Oh," and "My Country 'Tis of Thee," which has no pickup and begins with a complete measure. (The first complete measure of "The Star-Spangled Banner" begins with the word "say.")

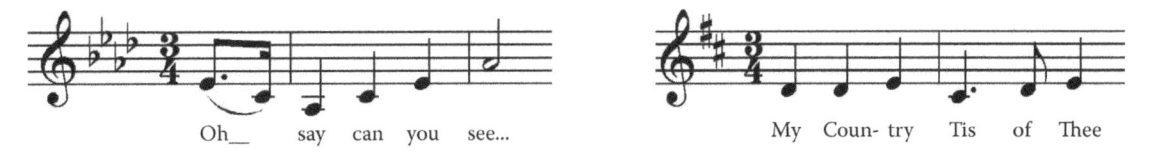

EXAMPLE 1.32 The beginning of "The Star Spangled Banner," on the left and "My Country 'Tis of Thee" on the right. "The Star-Spangled Banner" begins with a dotted eighth-sixteenth pickup. There is no pickup to "My Country 'Tis of Thee."

Usually a piece that begins with an incomplete measure also ends with an incomplete measure of sufficient length that, if combined with the pickups found at the beginning, would equal a complete measure. There are many exceptions, though.

> When numbering the measures in a piece that has a pickup measure, the pickup measure is not counted, and the numbering begins with the first complete measure.

Counting Time

When learning music and when performing music, musicians often need to count the time. Usually this is a matter of simply saying the beats of the measure at the tempo to be performed, thus, "one-two-three-four, one-two-three-four…," in each measure with four beats or "one-two-three, one-two-three…," in each measure with three beats.

Review

- Most Western music has an underlying pulse called a beat.
- The speed of the beat is called the tempo.
- Tempo may be described in words, by use of a metronome setting, or both.
- A series of musical durations, with or without associated pitches, is called a rhythmic figure.
- Beats are organized into specified groupings called measures or bars.
- Measures are separated by bar lines.
- The specified length of a bar and the notation used to designate the beat is communicated by a time signature.
- In a time signature, the upper number identifies the number of beats that define the length of the bar. The lower number identifies the durational symbol used to represent each beat and must, therefore, be a one, two, four, eight, sixteen, thirty-two, or sixty-four, meaning, respectively, whole note, half note, quarter note, eighth note, sixteenth note, etc.

- A measure may consist of any combination of durations, including pitches and rests, that are equal in length to the number of beats specified in the time signature.
- Time signatures with an upper number of two, four, or eight are said to be duple.
- Time signatures with an upper number of three are said to be triple.
- Time signatures with an upper number that is a multiple of three (but not three itself) are said to be compound time.
- Time signatures that are not multiples of two or three, such as five and seven, are sometimes called irregular.
- The first beat in a measure is called the downbeat or thesis and may be stressed.
- The last beat in a measure is called the pickup, upbeat, arsis, or anacrusis.
- Some measures, usually at the beginning of a piece, are incomplete. The notes in these measures are performed before the first downbeat and are called pickups or upbeats.

Related Exercises

§ Examine the rhythmic content of each measure given below (assume each measure is complete), and select a correct time signature for each measure based on the content.

§ In each measure given below, you are provided with a time signature. Place notes or rests of whatever duration you wish that will complete each measure.

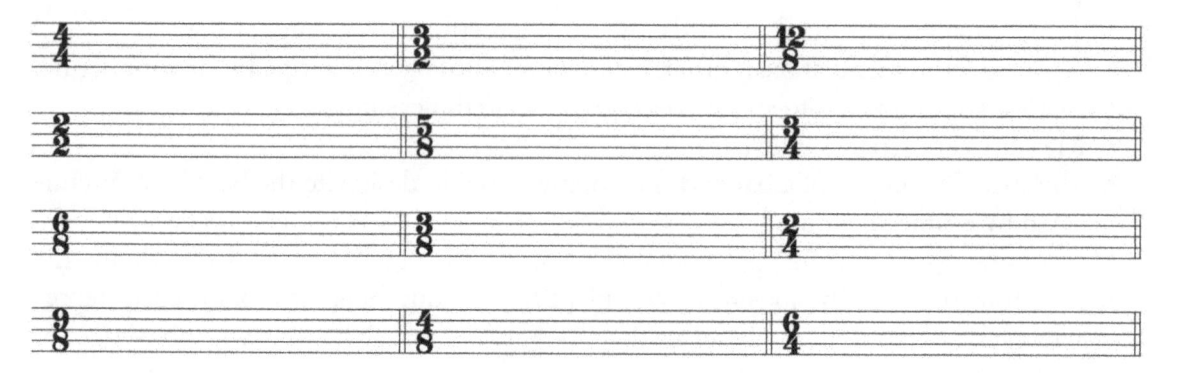

Notation: The Symbols of Music

§ Each measure below has a time signature and is filled with a number of notes. However, at the end of each measure, one note is missing. Supply the missing duration using the correct notation.

§ Study each staff below and determine an appropriate time signature for each. Place your time signature at the beginning of each staff. (Assume that each example begins on a downbeat.)

§ On each staff below is a rhythmic excerpt with a time signature. Assuming these examples begin on a downbeat, draw in the bar lines.

The Structure of the Beat

As described above, each measure of music is composed of one or more beats or pulses. The measure may be filled with various notes and rests in any desired combination that add up to the total number of pulses indicated by the upper number in the time signature. In the same way, each beat may be composed of any combination of notes and rests that add up to the duration specified in the time signature's lower number.

Among the most common beat durations encountered are half notes, quarter notes, and eighth notes although other durations are certainly used, too. Let's examine some typical ways to divide these standard beats.

EXAMPLE 1.33 Several ways in which beats may be structured in music: On the top, the half note is the equivalent of the beat. In the middle, the quarter note is the equivalent. On the bottom, the eighth note serves as the basis. Music between each pair of dotted bar lines equals a single beat of the designated duration.

The Triplet

As you examine the rhythmic figures in Example 1.33, note that all of these patterns involve durations with ratios with each other of 2:1, 4:1, 8:1 or multiples thereof. Often composers ask performers to divide the beat into combinations of durations that do not possess simple duple ratios. The most common of these alternative divisions is the ***triplet***.

A triplet is a grouping of three equal durations to be performed within one beat. Using the same representations for the beat as in Example 1.33, here is how the corresponding triplets would be notated:

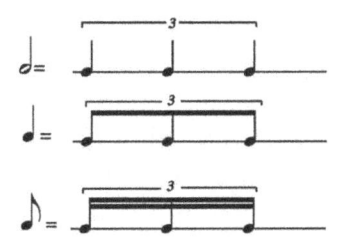

EXAMPLE 1.34   Triplets to be performed within a single beat. On the top, using a half note as the beat; in the middle, using a quarter note as the beat; and on the bottom, using an eighth note as the beat.

A triplet is understood as follows: The performer is to play or sing three equal durations within the same time span that two of the notated values would usually occupy. Thus, the top figure in Example 1.34 is interpreted as performing three shorter quarter notes within the time of two normal quarter notes. Since two quarter notes equal a half note, the performer also understands that this represents three equal durations within the time occupied by a half note.

The other two figures in Example 1.34 are translated similarly. For the middle figure: Perform three shorter eighth notes within the time of two normal eighth notes. For the bottom example: Perform three shorter sixteenth notes in the time of two normal sixteenth notes.

Musicians regularly identify the notes shown top to bottom in Example 1.34 as quarter-note triplets, eighth-note triplets, and sixteenth-note triplets. Simple math shows that each note of a triplet is two-thirds as long as its normal duration.

Other Divisions of the Beat

Unfortunately, virtually all other divisions of the beat are less easily notated and less easily understood. Even though the means of notating other divisions, such as five, six, or seven equal events per beat, follows a similar approach, the results can be ambiguous, slow to interpret (a big disadvantage when one is sight reading music), and even confusing to notate or understand. These indications of the division of the beat into groups of five, six, seven, or other numbers (other than multiples of two) are called ***quintuplets***, ***sextuplets***, ***septuplets***, etc. and, as a class, are sometimes called ***'tuplets*** (with or without the apostrophe).

> This term was first introduced with music notation software during the 1980s.

Here are some of the more commonly encountered 'tuplets.

EXAMPLE 1.35   All of these examples are based on a quarter note representing a beat. From left to right, five equal durations per beat, six equal durations per beat, and seven equal durations per beat.

The meaning of each of the rhythmic figures shown in Example 1.35 is as follows, from left to right: five equal durations (notated as sixteenth notes) within the time of four sixteenth notes; six equal durations (notated as sixteenth notes) within the time of four sixteenth notes; seven equal durations (notated as sixteenth notes) within the time of four sixteenth notes.

However, seven equal durations within the time of a quarter note are sometimes notated as in Example 1.36 below. In performance, both the last figure in Example 1.35 and the figure in Example 1.36 would sound the same. That is certainly not something that would be quickly grasped from the notation. Yet in written or printed music, either may be found.

EXAMPLE 1.36   Another way to indicate seven equal durations within the time of a quarter note.

Because the actual duration of each of the septuplet's notes is much closer to the length of normal thirty-second notes, many composers choose the notation in Example 1.36 instead of using sixteenth notes, as done in Example 1.35, which, though conventional, is somewhat further from the truth.

'Tuplets in Triple Meters

In meters such as three-four time or six-eight time, 'tuplets are used to instruct the performer to play two or four equal durations within the time normally occupied by three such symbols. Here are some examples.

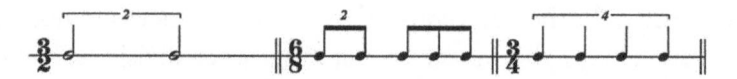

EXAMPLE 1.37   From left to right, two equal durations (called **duplets** and represented by half notes) within the time normally occupied by three half notes; two equal durations (represented by eighth notes) in the time normally occupied by three eighth notes; and four equal durations (called **quadruplets** and represented by quarter notes) in the time normally occupied by three quarter notes.

Notation: The Symbols of Music

As you may note by comparing Examples 1.35 and 1.37, the notation remains of a type with the original triplets, but the logic may seem less intuitive. At a glance, it may not be clear what forms the basis of the 'tuplets' relationship. Composers since the middle of the twentieth century have begun to add ratios to the notation to assist performers in interpreting the meaning of various 'tuplets. Here are some 'tuplets identified by ratios.

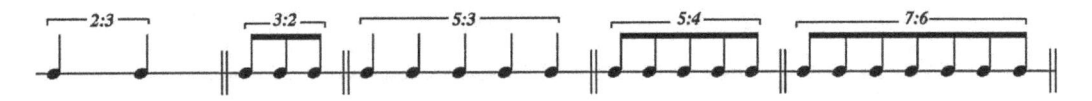

EXAMPLE 1.38 Various 'tuplets with the meaning of each clarified through the use of ratios rather than numbers alone. The ratios are based on the durations as notated.

Some composers have chosen an alternative to ratios. This notation tells the performer directly the duration within which the divisions of the 'tuplet are to be performed. Here are the same figures as given in Example 1.38, shown with this alternative notation.

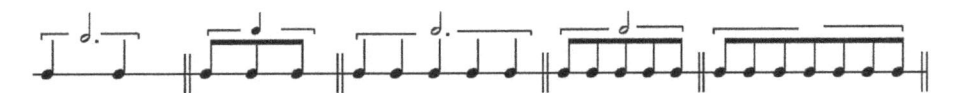

EXAMPLE 1.39 In this form of 'tuplet notation, the duration of the 'tuplet is given directly as a note value. The figures here are the same as those used in Example 1.38 above.

Just as measures and beats may be composed of any combination of durations that add up to the value of the measure or beat, 'tuplets may be constructed from various durations, including rests and notes, that total the duration of the 'tuplet. The first illustration involves triplets.

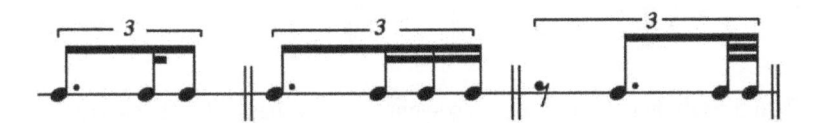

EXAMPLE 1.40 Various triplets, all of which are equal to a quarter note in length but each of which involves symbols of differing lengths. From left to right, a triplet composed of a dotted eighth note, sixteenth note, and eighth note; a triplet composed of a dotted eighth note and three sixteenth notes; and a triplet composed of an eighth note rest, a dotted eighth note, and two thirty-second notes.

As the palette of available 'tuplets expands, figures such as those given below are found. If a ratio notation or a durational equivalent is not provided, the performer often has to examine the measure and determine what part of it is to be occupied by the 'tuplet before being able to interpret the 'tuplet's value.

EXAMPLE 1.41 Four different measures of music, each including a 'tuplet on the top staff. The dotted bracket on the staff below each 'tuplet shows its durational equivalent.

Over the years, this cumbersome and arcane system wastes many hours of rehearsal time as musicians struggle to determine exactly what a composer may have meant by a particular 'tuplet notation.

Hemiola

When three equal durations occur during the time normally occupied by two events, as in triplets or as in the two passages illustrated below, it is referred to as hemiola. The use of hemiola is especially noteworthy in many of Russian composer Piotr Ilyich Tchaikovsky's (1840–1893) waltzes and in American composer and conductor Leonard Bernstein's (1918–1990) "America" from *West Side Story*.

> Some use the term *hemiola* for other rhythmic ratios, such as 4:3 or 5:4.

EXAMPLE 1.42 On the left, hemiola created in six-eight time; on the right, hemiola created with tied notes in three-four time.

Counting the Divisions of the Beat

When the tempo is slow and/or the rhythm is complex, it may become necessary to count both the pulse and the division of the beat. There are many ways to do this, but a basic way to count beats that are divided into two equal parts (duple) is to say: "One-*and*-two-*and*-three-*and*-four-*and*, one-*and*-two-*and*-three-*and*-four-*and*…." Or, in triple meter, "One-*and*-two-

and-three-*and*, one-*and*-two-*and*-three-*and*...." Because of this common practice, the second half of a beat may be referred to as the *"and"* of the beat. In rehearsals, musicians often say such things as, "I have an F on the *and* of three," which simply means that on the second half of the third beat, an F is written in the performer's music.

When a triple division *of the beat* needs to be counted, some musicians would use, "One-*and-ah*-two-*and-ah*, one-*and-ah*-two-*and-ah*...," to count a six-eight measure. Another option for counting the triple division of the beat is, "One-*la-lee*-two-*la-lee*, one-*la-lee*-two-*la-lee*...."

However the counting may be syllabized, the important skill is to keep the pulse steady and the division exact.

> Although throughout this discussion it has been assumed that notes with equal durations should be performed with equal lengths, that assumption is not always true. Historically, some musical styles have required unequal durations (although the extent of the inequalities is debated). In current performance practices, jazz or swing notation assumes unequal durations. In fact, in swing notation, one must specify "even eighths" when unequal durations are ***not*** wanted.

Review

- A beat may be composed of any combination of notes and rests that will total the exact length of the beat.
- As long as the divisions of the beat are duple (2:1, 4:1, 8:1, or some combination thereof), our standard notation will suffice.
- When a beat must be divided by a quantity such as three, five, six, or seven, 'tuplets are used.
- In the specific case when three even durations are performed in the time normally occupied by two equal notes, hemiola is created.
- In order to understand the exact rhythmic value of these figures, especially when they are complicated by the use of multiple note values, dotted notes, and rests, composers sometimes use ratios. As an alternative, they may show the total duration of a 'tuplet as a specific note value.
- When the interpretation of a 'tuplet is especially difficult to decipher, the performer will have to examine the composition of a measure to see what portion is occupied by the 'tuplet.
- Musicians count time in various ways usually by naming each beat and, when necessary, counting the subdivisions, duple, triple, or quadruple as required.

Related Exercises

§ In each of the measures shown below, a 'tuplet isn't marked. Place the proper 'tuplet indication over the notes (marked with a bracket) that need to be played as a 'tuplet.

§ The following measures do not have the correct number of beats in them. Find a way to correct the notation. How many different solutions can you find for each example? (You may write your solutions on the staves provided.)

5. Movement, Language, and Musical Rhythms

Historically, music and dance have enjoyed a symbiotic relationship since before the dawn of history. Many scholars believe that the most basic rhythmic patterns found in Western music come from the rhythms generated by natural and stylized movement of the human body. To this day, much music, including much concert music, originated as music for the dance.

Other sources for rhythmic structures are marches, religious processions, and other group activities that call for the coordination of the movement of groups of people. It is possible to list many of the rhythms that have become associated with these various activities and which composers have often used as an underlying pulse from which to generate music.

Among the more common dance figures are the following:

EXAMPLE 1.43 A few of the hundreds of dance patterns found in music of the last 400 years.

Certain dances have been important components of Western music since the Middle Ages. Some dance traditions, such as ballet, are art forms for which music is an important yet subordinate aspect. Other traditions, including folk dances, have found their way into various musical styles.

During the Baroque era (*c.* 1600–1750), keyboard suites were primarily composed of pieces based on then familiar dances. These included the allemande, courante, saraband, and gigue among others.

In the classical period (*c.* 1750–1810), the minuet was regularly used as at least one movement of most divertimentos and symphonies. Sets of dances of the period were composed by Mozart, Beethoven, and others.

For much of the nineteenth century, the waltz was the craze, and many ballroom and concert waltzes were written. Also during this time, dances derived from national traditions were introduced into piano and orchestral writings. Among these were Brahms's *Hungarian Dances* and Dvorak's *Slavic Dances*.

More recently, composers have written pieces intended only for concert performance but which have either been based on dances or which have used dance-like rhythms. Among these are Ravel's *Bolero*, Debussy's *Danses: sacrée et profane*, Kodály's *Dances from Galanta*, and Rachmaninoff's *Symphonic Dances*.

Since dance is movement of the human body, it is possible to conceive of all human motion as being dance-like and therefore (potentially) related to music. The fact that conductors regularly use body motions to transmit musical insights and nuances to groups of performers should not be surprising.

Poetic Meters

In a manner similar to the impact of movement on music, songs, and their underlying poetic structures, have long had an influence. One of the theories developed to explain the possible rhythmic performance of the earliest notated music (in which no rhythms were notated) was that the music was sung following the poetic rhythm.

Certainly some of the most ancient rhythmic figures found in music have a direct relationship to poetic meters. Here is a table of these meters showing the musical equivalent to the various poetic meters.

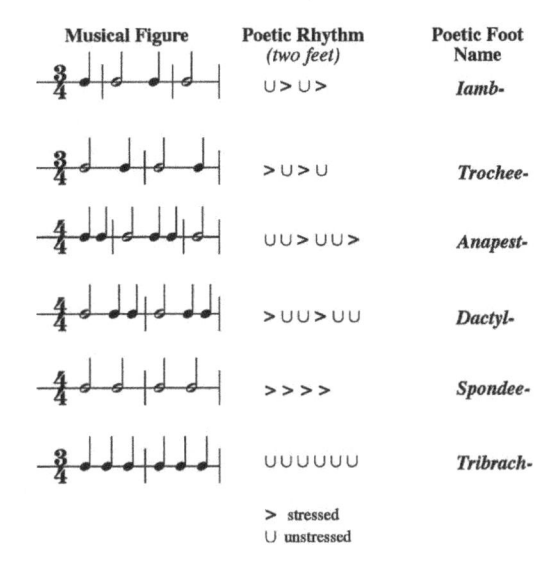

Musical Figure	Poetic Rhythm (two feet)	Poetic Foot Name
3/4	U > U >	*Iamb-*
3/4	> U > U	*Trochee-*
4/4	U U > U U >	*Anapest-*
4/4	> U U > U U	*Dactyl-*
4/4	> > > >	*Spondee-*
3/4	U U U U U U	*Tribrach-*

> stressed
U unstressed

EXAMPLE 1.44 The poetic meters.

Review

- Music and dance have long been associated.
- Various dances were components of Baroque suites.
- Classical symphonies and divertimentos used especially the minuet as a significant component.
- Dance remains important in the creation, understanding, and interpretation of music.
- Just as dance rhythms generated some of our fundamental musical rhythms, poetic meters influenced musical rhythms especially, but not exclusively, in vocal music.

Related Exercises

§ On the staves provided, notate the rhythm of the poetic lines.

1. The noble tree bowed to the wind that lofted through its bough.

2. Merrily the horses jumped, and merrily they gamboled.

3. I heard the cry—I felt the pain. I could not turn away.

4. Running through the rows of corn the children played hide and seek.

―――――――――――――――――――――――――

§ Select six dance rhythms from the examples given (on p. 37) and find at least one piece of music that is based on, or uses generously, each of your selected rhythms. Why did you select these rhythms?

6. The Notation of Loudness and Style

The notation used for loudness (and changes in loudness) and the notation used to indicate tone qualities are far less specific than the notations for pitch, duration, and time. These notational conventions are also relatively recent additions to the musician's vocabulary having appeared in the seventeenth and eighteenth centuries, respectively.

Loudness

While scientists and engineers use measurements of wattage and decibels to describe the energy produced by sound generators (musical instruments, speakers, etc.), musicians rely on their own senses of relative loudness to describe this aspect of sound. Musicians use the term *piano* (Italian for "soft") to describe or indicate quiet sounds and *forte* (pronounced for-´tay, the Italian word for "strong") to indicate or describe louder sounds.

In order to express louder, less loud, softer, or less soft sounds, other Italian-based terms may accompany these terms, such as *mezzo* (meaning "half"), *più* (meaning "more"), and *meno* (meaning "less") to provide finer distinctions. *Forte, mezzo,* and *piano* are usually abbreviated as *f*, *mf* and *p* (respectively) and may be combined as follows to indicate (from top to bottom) successively softer sounds:

fff	triple *forte*	as loud as possible
ff	fortissimo	very loud
f	forte	loud
mf	mezzo forte	half loud
mp	mezzo piano	half soft
p	piano	soft
pp	pianissimo	very soft
ppp	triple *piano*	as soft as possible

These abbreviations, called **dynamics**, are usually placed below the staff to communicate the composer's desired loudness to the performer. (In vocal music, they are often placed above the staff.)

In order to expand the range of dynamics available, starting in the nineteenth century, composers have used 4, 5, or even 6 *f*s or *p*s. It is also common to find the words *più* and *meno* added to *f* and *p* to produce *più f* (louder), *più p* (softer), *meno f* (not as loud), and *meno p* (not as soft).

As detailed as this information may seem, no standard exists for what constitutes a forte or a piano. Thus it is always a matter of interpretation modulated by the size and configuration of the performance space and the style and nature of the music being performed.

In performance, the musicians may become gradually louder or gradually softer. A *crescendo* (*cresc.*) indication tells the performers to become louder over time while a *decrescendo* (*decresc.*) or *diminuendo* (*dim.*) means to gradually become softer. This gradual dynamic change may be shown in the music by using the appropriate term or its abbreviation or by the use of two non-parallel lines. Thus, this ─────────── means crescendo and this ─────────── means decrescendo. These shapes are sometimes called "hairpins."

> The performance space, and especially its reverberation time or lack of reverberation time, is taken into account when determining effective tempos and articulations as well as dynamics.

Other terms that are used to indicate changes in dynamics include the following:

Term	Meaning	Term	Meaning	Term	Meaning
allargando	becoming slower and louder	*morendo*	dying away	*smorzando*	gradually dying away

Articulations and Accents

Somewhat akin to dynamics is articulation. Articulation refers to any modification of the attack and/or release of a sound (note.) These modifications are created by the performers' bows in string music or by their fingers on strings, piano, and percussion. The performers' breath and tongues create these effects on wind instruments, and the use of various sticks modify the articulation of percussion instruments.

Legato and Non-legato

Legato is a term indicating that notes are to be played smoothly connected with little or no break between them. The alternative is to play each note separately but without too much space. This is called ***non-legato***.

The slur (a line, shaped like an arc) indicates that the notes within the arc are to be performed in a legato manner. The slur may also indicate that the notes so connected are a part of the same musical gesture. Although the slur and the tie may look alike, the tie *always* connects two or more notes *of the same pitch*. The slur almost always connects two or more notes of different pitches.

> In orchestral string music, the notes so connected are usually to be played in a single bow stroke (i.e. without changing direction) but are not necessarily legato.

EXAMPLE 1.45   On the left, non-legato; in the middle, legato (slurred); and on the right, tied notes.

These articulations and modifications are frequently indicated by signs, symbols, and words placed above or below the notes to be affected. Different signs may have specific meanings for specific instruments so the following symbols and their executions should be understood only in the most general terms.

symbol	name	typical execution	symbol	name	typical execution
.	*staccato*	shortened, separated	*sfz*	*sforzando*	suddenly louder
—	*tenuto*	hold full value	*fp*	*fortepiano*	loud then suddenly soft
'	*staccatissimo*	extremely short	*fz*	*forzando*	strongly accented
>	accent	stress the start of the note	*rfz*	*rinforzando*	quickly becoming louder
∧	accent	a heavy accent	*sos.*	*sostenuto*	fully sustained

> In classical music, ∧ is a heavy accent. In popular and jazz notation, it is both heavy and (usually) very short.

Types of Accents

Audible stresses applied to selected notes within a musical phrase are called accents. Accents exist as four types: dynamic, agogic, metric, and tonic. A **dynamic accent**, usually indicated by symbols such as > or ∧ or with abbreviations such as *sfz* or *rfn*, indicates that the associated pitch is to be louder than the surrounding pitches. An **agogic accent** is created with an individual note that is *significantly longer* than the notes around it. A **metric accent** occurs on the downbeat of a measure. And a **tonic accent** occurs when a single pitch is significantly higher in pitch than the notes around it.

Other Useful Terms and Symbols

Da capo, dal segno, fine, and coda

Musicians encounter many terms on a daily basis that you may need to know in order to read and understand music. Among these are **da capo,** which is usually abbreviated DC or D.C. It instructs the performer to return to the very beginning of the piece (*da* = the, *capo* = head). Another instruction that casually looks similar but is distinctly different is **dal segno** (DS or D.S.), which instructs the performer to return to an earlier point in the music marked by a sign (*segno*). The typical sign is 𝄋.

Either *da capo* or *dal segno* may be accompanied by other instructions such as **a fine,** which means that the performer is to take the DC or the DS and then play until encountering the *fine* (pronounced fee-nay), which indicates the end of the piece. Or the instruction might be DC (or DS) **a coda,** which means that the performer is to take the DC or DS and play until encountering a ***coda sign*** (usually ⊕), at which point the performer must skip to another, later portion of the music (called the ***coda***), which is also marked by a ⊕. (The literal translation of coda is "tail," and it is a section of music used to bring the piece to a satisfactory conclusion.)

Repeats and Endings

Repeat signs are used to instruct the performer to play a section of music again immediately upon having played it the first time. These signs look like this :‖ and mean to go back to the repeat sign that looks like this ‖: and play the music in between again. (If the composer wishes for the performer to return to the beginning, the ‖: may be omitted.) It is common for the ending of the repeated section to be changed the second time through, and this introduces the need for first and second endings written this way:

EXAMPLE 1.46 Indication that the performer is to count six measures of rest, play the notes in the first ending, count another six measures of rest, and then play the notes in the second ending and stop.

Fermata, Cæsura, General Pause, and Commas

When reading or performing music, musicians encounter other symbols used to convey the composer's performance instructions. Among the more common is the ***fermata*** (⌒) placed over (or under) the note. A fermata indicates that the note associated with it should be held longer than its notated duration suggests. The rule of thumb is to increase the length by 50 percent, but many exceptions exist, and the performer usually holds the note for as long as it seems appropriate to do so.

When the composer wants the music to make a sudden stop or hesitation before continuing, a ***cæsura*** is used. It looks like this: //. A (usually) longer hesitation may be indicated by a ***general pause,*** which is notated as the letters **G.P.** (with or without the periods) within a measure that contains nothing else. A fermata may be added to the **G.P.** mark.

A short break in the musical line that does not alter the rhythm may be shown by a ***comma*** (ʼ) between two notes. For wind players, this usually indicates a point where a breath is to be taken so it may not always be clear as to its meaning. For many years, musicians have referred to the fermata as a "bird's eye", to the cæsura as "railroad tracks," and mistakenly called the general pause a "grand pause."

Review

- Notation to indicate relative loudness and softness first appeared in the seventeenth century.
- Most often Italian words and abbreviations are used to indicated the desired loudness.

- *Forte*, or its abbreviation (*f*), indicates loud while *piano*, or its abbreviation (*p*), indicates soft. Additional letters, such as *m* (*mezzo*) or words, such as *meno*, or replication of the *f* or *p* may be used to further define the degree of loudness or softness requested.
- Normal performance of a series of separate notes is called non-legato. When the notes are connected, the performance style is called legato.
- Articulations are modifications of the attack and/or release of a sound.
- Included among the common articulations are accents, staccato marks (·), tenuto marks, (-), and the indications *fz* and *fp*.
- Information is also provided to the performer to indicate how one is to proceed through the music and how the flow of the music is to be altered.
- Composers use repeat signs, endings, *da capo*, *dal segno*, coda signs, and *fine* to provide the performance map.
- Fermatas, cæsuras, commas, and G.P.s may also be employed to modify the flow of the music.

Related Exercises

§ Arrange the following dynamics in order from softest to loudest.

p   *mf*   *f*   *meno f*   *pp*   *mp*

§ Arrange the following dynamics in order from loudest to softest.

mf   *ff*   *pp*   *p*   *più p*   *fff*

§ Explain the "map" being specified for the performer to follow in the following example. In other words, starting with measure 1 (m.1), what measures are to be played and in what order? The whole piece will be how many measures in length?

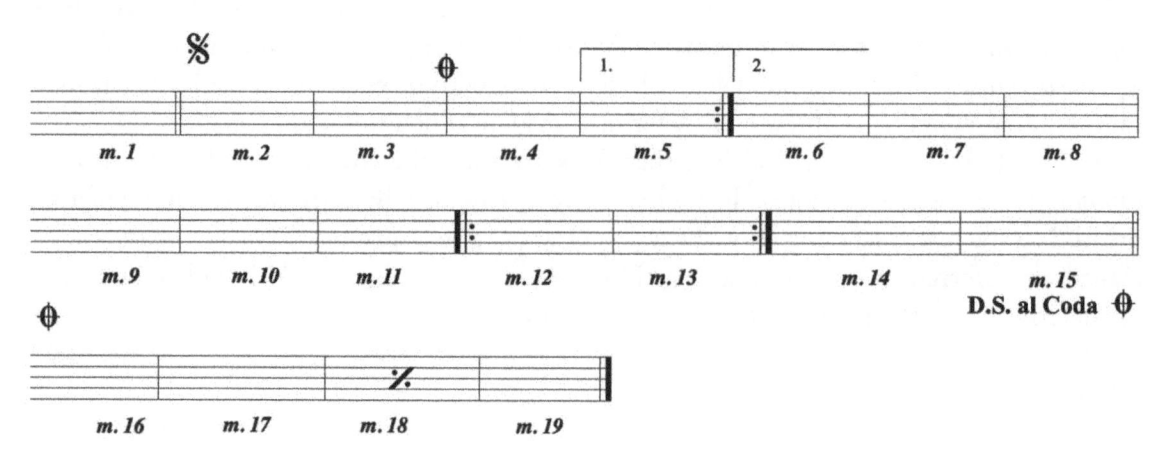

7. The Notation of Tone Quality

The usual manner in which tonal quality is specified is simply by stating the instrument to be used in the performance. More subtle tone color differences are usually not specified and are thus left to the performer to determine.

The vocabulary that is used for the altering of tone color depends on the instrument involved. For example, it is rare that a composer would ask for a flute to be played muted (it has been done), but certainly specifying that the instrument be played *without vibrato* would be a tone-quality change (since in the United States the normal flute tone includes vibrato).

Thus, strings are typically asked to play either *pizzicato* (plucked) or *arco* (bowed), and woodwinds and strings may be asked to play *harmonics*. The brass are at times asked to play bells up, and either the brass or the strings may be asked to play **with mute** or its opposite **without mute** (also called **open** in brass instruments), or the Italian equivalents **con sordino** (*sord.*) or **senza sordino**, respectively. Simply exchanging a musical line between two different players (or singers) of the same instrument (or voice quality) may result in a clear change in the color of the line.

> Vibrato is an undulation in pitch that occurs about five to seven times per second.

> Harmonics are produced when the performer overblows a woodwind or the string player lightly touches a string producing a higher, more transparent pitch. (See also Appendix II, p. 345.)

As sensitive as the human ear is to even slight variations in timbre, the notation of changes in timbre has rarely been explored beyond the most obvious possibilities. Individual composers from the twentieth century onward have experimented with mechanical and electronic alterations of the tone qualities of various instruments and voices as well as with the use of different vowels and consonants formed in the mouth and throat of singers and wind instrument players. String players have also been asked to bow and tap on various alternative parts of their instruments and/or to use different items, such as combs and drumsticks, in place of fingers and picks.

Performers make many changes in tone color as a normal part of performing on their instruments without any particular notation so indicating. These subtle but expressive changes are almost never specified, and there is certainly no commonly accepted set of terms or symbols that one finds for them. Standard notation for these effects simply does not exist.

Review

- Indications of tone quality are frequently limited to the specifying of particular instruments or specific voice qualities.
- The indication to use or remove mutes, add or remove vibrato, pluck or bow the strings, etc. provide changes in tone color.
- In the last one hundred years, composers have called for electronic and mechanical devices, altered vowels and consonants, and alternative bowing, tapping, and plucking locations to expand the range of tone colors.

Related Exercises

§ Here are some instructions used to inform performers of a particular tone quality or effect desired by the composer. What does each of these instructions mean? (Some may have more than one usage.) To what instruments (including the human voice) might these comments pertain?

ponticello	senza vibrato	con sordino
with plunger	brassy	pizzicato
sotto voce	flutter-tongued	una corda
cup mute	bells up	col legno

8. Conducting Music

To understand pulse (and style) in music, some basic concepts of conducting may prove helpful. For the non-performer, it allows a certain level of musical involvement not otherwise available. For the performer, it offers additional insights into the totality of the music beyond the demands of a single part.

The Role of the Conductor

When larger groups of musicians perform together, a conductor can often assist the players or singers to achieve rhythmic ensemble and dynamic balance. To this end, certain conducting patterns have emerged that convey quickly, and almost universally, the beat pattern of a composition. Other aspects of the conductor's gestures can communicate dynamic balance and even performance styles (such as staccato and legato) and indicate whether the music should be accented or placid. The tempo of the music is communicated through the speed of the beat while the dynamics are shown through the size of the motions.

The Beat

> However, the time signature may not always directly provide the actual pulse groupings. Sometimes triple meters require such a rapid tempo that the only practical way to communicate the pulse is one beat per measure. And very slow tempos may be indicated by dividing the beat into subdivisions, such as conducting a four-four meter in eight.

In order to communicate effectively with an ensemble, the conductor must learn to provide motion patterns that clearly indicate not only the tempo of the underlying pulse but also the grouping of these beats as is usually shown in the time signature. These gestures must become automatic and almost instinctive so that the conductor can concentrate on the other aspects of the performance and the overall musical effect being achieved. Over time, certain conventions have been established for the indication of the beat.

- The first pulse of each measure is a downward gesture called the ***downbeat***. Its arrival point is approximately at the conductor's waist.
- The last pulse of the measure is an upward gesture called the ***upbeat***. Its arrival point is approximately at the conductor's eye-level.

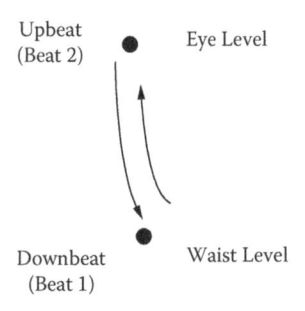

EXAMPLE 1.47 The locations of the downbeat and upbeat, as seen by the conductor. This is also the beat pattern usually used for two-four, two-two, or other duple time signatures. The two-beat pattern also forms the basis for conducting music that requires only one beat per measure.

When performing the pattern shown in Example 1.47, the conductor tends to "bounce" her/his hand or baton at the location of the downbeat and the location of the upbeat. These bounces help establish in the eyes of the performers the exact point at which each beat exists. (It sometimes helps if the conductor thinks of "pointing" the beats.)

Not all conductors use a baton. Some prefer to use only their hands while others will switch from hand to baton and back as they feel the music requires.

If the music requires a pulse of one beat per measure, the usual pattern is a strong (normal) downbeat with no rhythmic upbeat. The conductor will simply and smoothly lift his/her hand so that each successive downbeat can be made equally clear.

- The *next-to-last* pulse is indicated by a gesture to the conductor's right (performers' left). The vertical arrival point for this, and most other intermediary beats, is halfway between the upbeat and the downbeat, generally mid-chest.
- All other intermediate pulses are placed approximately mid-chest, too.

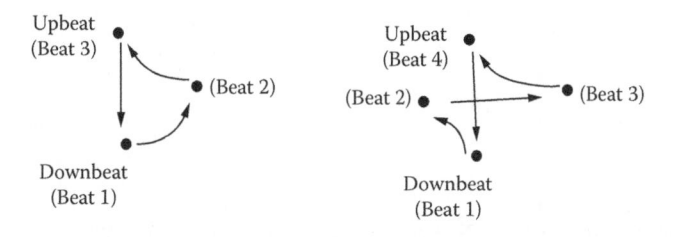

EXAMPLE 1.48 On the left, the three-beats-per-measure pattern. On the right, the four-beats-per-measure pattern. Note that the second beat is the next-to-last beat in triple time, so it goes to the conductor's right. In quadruple time, the second beat goes to the conductor's left, and the third beat (next-to-last) goes to the right.

Duple meters with triple subdivision, such as six-eight or six-four time, and triple meters with triple subdivisions, most often nine-eight time, look like the examples below.

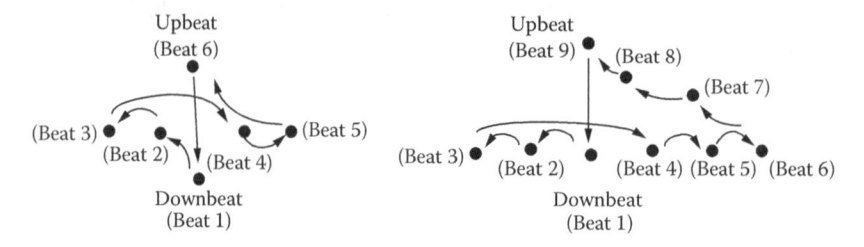

EXAMPLE 1.49 On the left, the pattern for two primary pulses, each divided into three subdivisions. On the right, the pattern for three primary pulses, each divided into three subdivisions.

Note that at slower tempos, the conductor may subdivide any of the given patterns (above or below) for clarity. In Example 1.50, the normal four-beat pattern is on the left while the subdivided pattern is on the right. In order to achieve the subdivision of a three-beat pattern, the conductor would similarly conduct a normal three-beat pattern but add an extra stroke at each of the three beat-points giving the effect of six pulses, two at each of the normal locations.

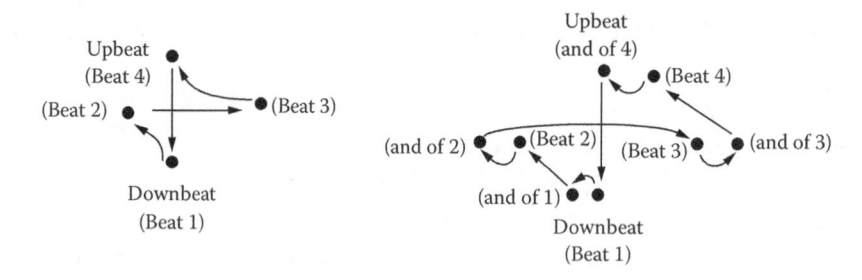

EXAMPLE 1.50 The divided four-beat pattern. On the left, the standard four-beat pattern as used in four-four, four-two, or four-eight time. On the right, the divided four-beat pattern used, for example, for a very slow, four-four pulse.

Time signatures with five or seven beats per measure are, typically, conducted as a duple pattern (five) or as a triple pattern (seven) with one beat that is longer than the other(s). Example 1.51 illustrates two of these beat patterns.

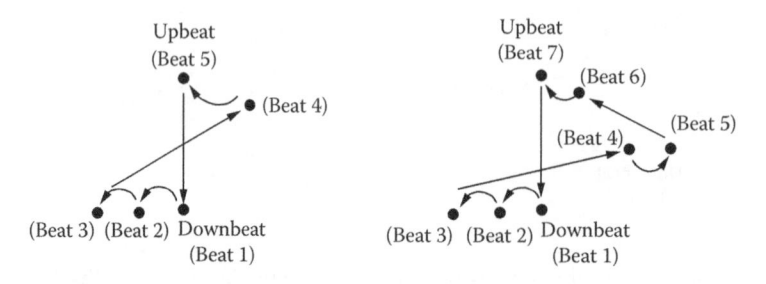

EXAMPLE 1.51 On the left, a five-beat pattern with a longer first "half" measure and a shorter second "half" measure. On the right, a seven-beat pattern with a longer first "third" and shorter second and third thirds of the measure.

If the five-beat pattern is short-long, then the cross-body movement would occur from beat 2 to beat 3, which would be located about when beat 4 is shown. Beat 4 would then be between where it is shown and the upbeat. In the seven-beat pattern, the longer (three-pulse) beat could occur where beat 4 is shown or where beat 6 is drawn.

The conductor connects all of the beat locations shown in the above examples by the continuous motion of his/her hand (or baton) in a manner that conveys *both* the music's flow *and* its loudness. Conductors must be clear and rhythmically accurate in their motions so as to enable the musicians to produce good ensemble.

In addition to the basic obligation of "beating time," the conductor also listens to the sounds that are being produced and makes indications to the performers as to what adjustments may be needed to obtain the desired effect. The conductor signals when the performers need to become louder and/or softer. Loud passages are indicated by large, bold gestures. Soft passages are indicated by smaller, more compact hand or baton movements.

To indicate that performers need to become louder, the conductor may either show a larger beat pattern or gesture with the free hand (the hand not holding the baton) in such a way as to indicate "louder." Typically this might be shown by raising the hand with the palm facing upward.

To signal the need to perform softer, the palm would be down or toward the musician(s) with a repeating downward "tapping" movement. Through eye contact, the conductor can tell the performers whether the gesture is directed toward all players, to just one section, or to a single person.

Legato, smoothly moving music requires smooth, very connected gestures while accented, rhythmic music would elicit shorter, jerkier movements. To indicate that the music should be performed staccato or marcato, the conductor will make the beat more rigid or pointed (a brief stopping at each beat point). To indicate the need for a smooth, connected sound, the beat pattern will become more flowing and less angular.

Professional conductors may not always seem to follow the above guidelines. As they become more experienced, conductors develop their own mannerisms that convey all the necessary information without looking just like every other conductor. However, less experienced conductors are well advised to begin by following the traditional patterns and gestures in order to communicate their desires as clearly as possible to the performers.

Review

- The primary responsibilities of the conductor are to set tempos, facilitate ensemble, communicate style, and adjust dynamic balances.
- Since speaking during a performance obviously would adversely affect the music, conductors communicate through gestures, eye contact, and body language.
- Although there are standard beat patterns, most successful conductors can communicate all the required information through their own, personal set of clearly understood gestures and mannerisms.

Related Exercises

§ To what time signature does each of the following beat patterns (as viewed from within the orchestra or band) correspond?

1.

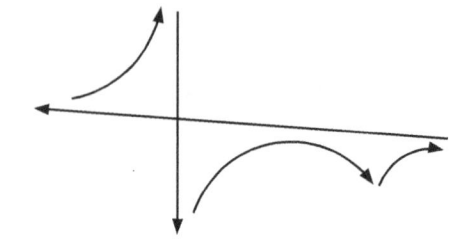

2.

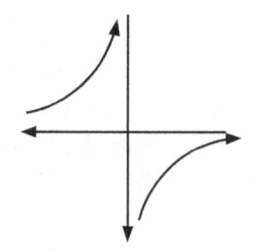

3.

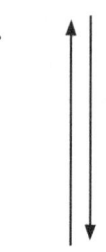

4.

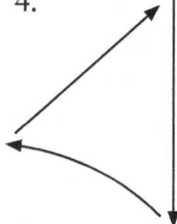

Note

1. Dr. John Buccheri of Northwestern University has for years pointed out that the term *compound time* is an artifact of the notation and not of the sound. Professor Buccheri has shown that the *listener* hears the grouping of accents on the primary and secondary levels. In most fast pieces in six-eight meter, these are groupings of threes collected together in a larger group of two.

part 2
Melody
Note Following Note

1. Intervals

Intervals in General

Music produced by the human voice or by a one-line instrument (like the trumpet or flute) is *melodic*—that is, note following note, one note at a time. *Melody* is also referred to as the *horizontal* component of music. In the study and practice of music, it is frequently necessary to express the distance between two pitches. This distance is expressed as an *interval*.

Although musicians understand that intervals express distances, the value of each interval is in reality obtained simply by counting the lines and spaces included from one pitch to the next. Thus, the following intervals are all called *seconds*.

EXAMPLE 2.01 Four examples of seconds. Each pair of notes involves a line and an adjacent space.

Note that in every case the second note is on a line (or in a space) immediately adjacent to the space (or line) of the first note. Seconds always look this way. Thus, at a glance, *you can identify a second by the way it appears.*

The following example shows what are called *thirds*. Two notes that are a third apart will be either both on adjacent lines or in adjacent spaces. Again, this makes rapid identification rather easy. As with seconds, thirds get their names from counting the pitches from one of the two pitches to the other pitch.

EXAMPLE 2.02 Four examples of thirds. Each pair consists of notes on adjacent lines or in adjacent spaces.

Two notes placed on the staff so that one is in a space while the other is on a line with a single skipped line and a single skipped space in between form a *fourth*.

EXAMPLE 2.03 Four examples of fourths. Each pair consists of a note on a line and a note in a space with one line and one space in between.

Fifths always involve either two notes on lines, with one skipped line and two skipped spaces in between, or two notes in spaces, with one skipped space and two skipped lines in between.

EXAMPLE 2.04 Four examples of fifths. Each pair consists of either two notes on lines with a line and two spaces in between or two notes in spaces with a space and two lines in between.

For many people, intervals greater than fifths are often more difficult to identify quickly. The *sixth*, being one pitch greater than a fifth, involves a pitch on a line and another pitch in a space with two lines *and* two spaces intervening. You may verify that these are indeed sixths by counting from one of the pitches to the other.

EXAMPLE 2.05 Four examples of sixths. Each pair consists of a note on a line and a note in a space with two lines and two spaces in between.

On the other hand, the *seventh*, like the third and the fifth, involves pitches either on two lines or in two spaces. When the pitches are placed on lines, there will be two skipped lines and three skipped spaces in between. And, when the pitches are placed in spaces, there will be two skipped spaces and three skipped lines in between.

EXAMPLE 2.06 Four examples of sevenths. Each pair consists of two notes on two lines with two lines and three spaces in between or two notes in two spaces with two spaces and three lines in between.

The *octave* should be easy to identify because both pitches possess the same letter name. However, in these examples, you cannot know the correct letter names so it may be easier to identify the interval graphically. Viewed this way, an octave involves a pitch on a line and a pitch in a space with both three lines *and* three spaces intervening.

EXAMPLE 2.07   Four examples of octaves. Each pair consists of a note on a line and a note in a space with three lines and three spaces in between.

Two pitches that are written on exactly the same line or in exactly the same space as each other are called *unisons* or *primes*.

EXAMPLE 2.08   Four examples of unisons or primes.

For intervals greater than an octave, sometimes called *compound intervals*, we may either continue to follow the counting pattern introduced above or identify the distance as an octave plus the appropriate smaller interval. This means that Example 2.09 may be identified either as a *ninth* or as an *octave plus a second*. An interval a step larger than a ninth would be a *tenth* or an *octave and a third*. Either description is correct. (Note that a ninth is equal to a second plus seven; a tenth equals a third plus seven; etc.)

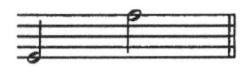

EXAMPLE 2.09   An interval a step greater than an octave may be called a ninth or an octave and a second.

Conjunct and Disjunct Motion

Melodies that move primarily from one pitch to another *adjacent* pitch—that, is moving by seconds and unisons—are said to have *conjunct* motion. Music that is easy to sing often consists primarily of these smaller intervals, as in this example:

EXAMPLE 2.10   An example of a conjunct melody.

Melodies that move mainly with intervals of a third and larger are said to display ***disjunct*** motion. Here is an example:

EXAMPLE 2.11   An example of a disjunct melody.

Although conjunct and disjunct motion may be found in a variety of music, disjunct motion is more characteristic of instrumental music. The expression "stepwise motion" is used for conjunct motion, and "movement by leaps (or skips)" is used for disjunct motion.

Review

- Two notes that follow each other are said to be melodic.
- The distance between any two notes is called an interval.
- Each sized interval has a unique appearance and sound.
- When determining an interval, one starts to count on the first note and counts each line and space in between until and including the second note.
- The interval between a note and another identical note of the same name is called a unison or a prime.
- Intervals greater than a unison include seconds, thirds, fourth, fifths, sixths, and sevenths.
- Intervals that are a step larger than sevenths are called octaves (not eighths).
- Intervals greater than an octave may be identified like other intervals (by counting from the first note to the second) or by beginning the count an octave (or two octaves) closer to the second note and expressing the interval as an octave (or two octaves) plus the smaller interval.
- Intervals greater than an octave are called compound intervals.
- Melodies that move stepwise exhibit conjunct motion.
- Melodies that move by thirds (or larger intervals) display disjunct motion.

Related Exercises

§ Identify each interval given on the staves below. Write the interval name on the line provided below each interval.

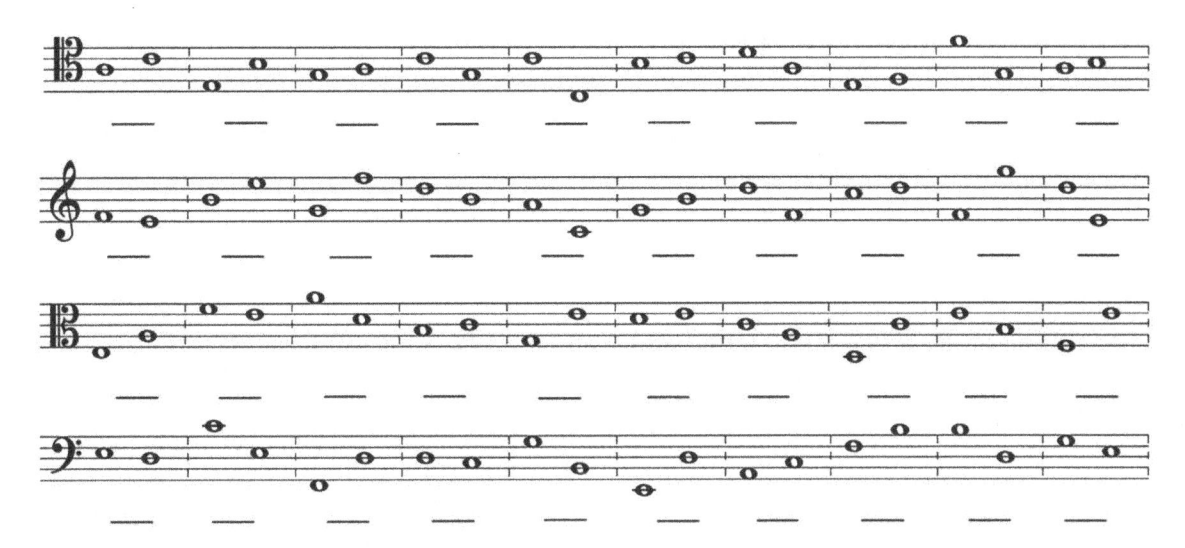

§ Under each note on the following staves is the name of an interval with an ascending or descending arrow. Write the specified melodic interval. (If the arrow is ascending, the second note should be above the given note; if the arrow is descending, the second note should be lower. In the case of unisons, there is no arrow.)

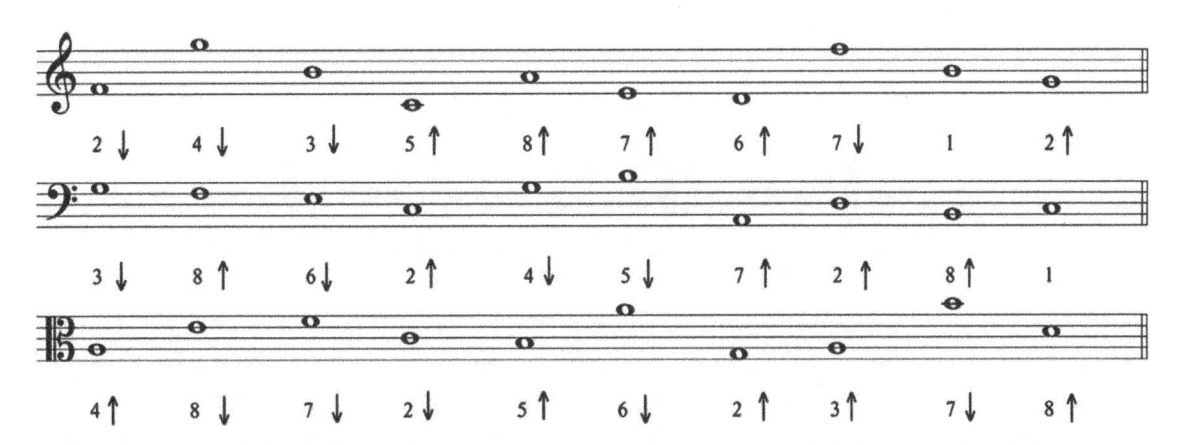

§ Study each of the following melodies, and then circle and mark the portions that feature conjunct motion and do the same for the portions that feature disjunct motion.

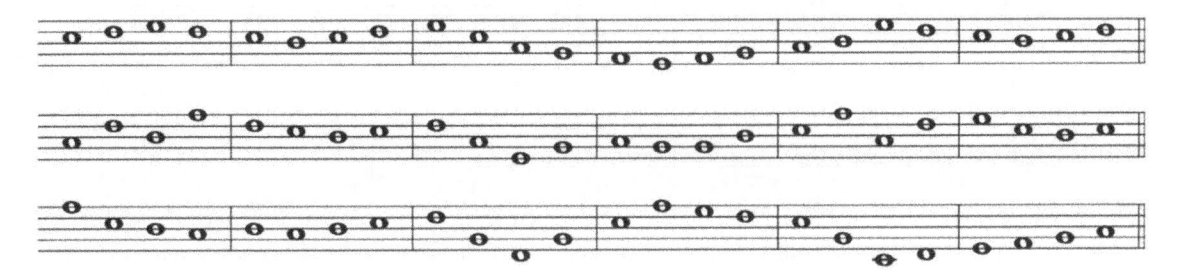

Naming Specific Intervals (Without Accidentals)

All of the above examples of intervals were presented on staves without clefs. This was possible because to name generic intervals, you do not need to know the specific pitches involved but only the distance between the pitches.

Seconds

In most situations, you deal with specific pitches and therefore you need to be more exact in naming the resulting intervals. Here are seven pitch combinations. It should be clear that all of these intervals are seconds:

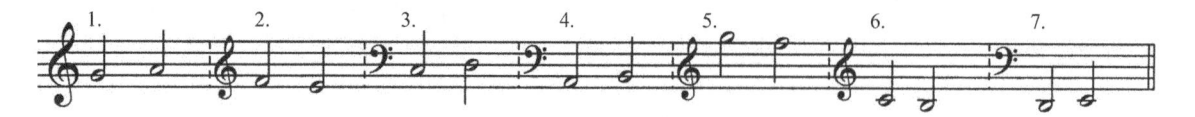

EXAMPLE 2.12   Seven examples of seconds as they appear in the treble and bass clefs.

To review how to "read" a keyboard, please refer to Examples 1.01 or 1.11 on pp. 3 and 7, respectively.

But an examination of these pitches on a keyboard reveals that they are not all the same size. Two of the combinations shown in Example 2.12, number 2 (F to E) and number 6 (C to B), are smaller than the other five. (Note that there are no black keys either between B and C or between E and F.)

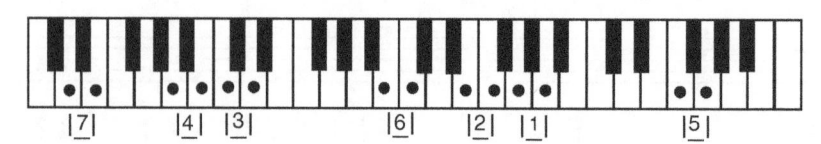

We call these smaller seconds *minor seconds*, while the larger seconds are called *major seconds*. These may be abbreviated as *m2* and *M2*, respectively. (Note that the minor second is equal to a semitone, or half step, and that the major second is a whole tone, or whole step.) Every possible second in our notation system is composed of one of these letter pairs: AB, BC, CD, DE, EF, FG, and/or GA.

In music theory, the term *minor* is used to indicate small, while the term *major* is used to indicate large.

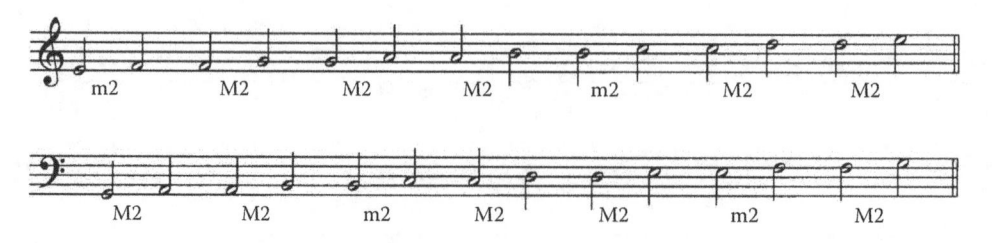

EXAMPLE 2.13   All possible seconds available in Western music, notated in the treble and bass clefs. These intervals may, of course, appear in any octave and in any clef.

Although these seconds may be written in any clef and anywhere on the staff, they exist in only the seven letter combinations shown above.

Thirds

Here are seven pitch combinations that we can classify as thirds:

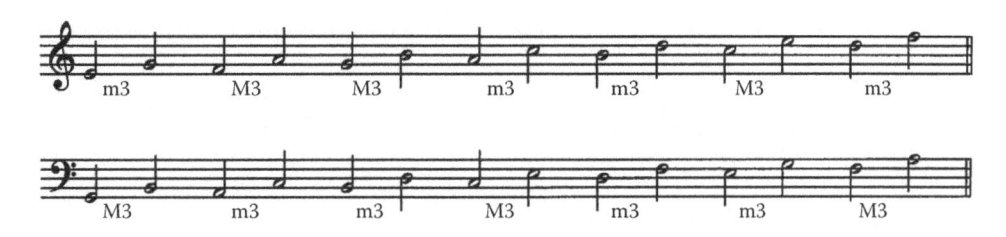

EXAMPLE 2.14 The seven pitch combinations that produce thirds shown in the treble and bass clefs.

Again, examination of these pitches on a keyboard reveals that they are not all the same size. Three combinations—C to E, F to A, and G to B—are larger than the other four. Following the same convention as was done for seconds, the smaller thirds are called *minor thirds*, while the larger thirds are called *major thirds*. These may be abbreviated as *m3* and *M3*, respectively. Again, there are only seven letter combinations that produce thirds: AC, BD, CE, DF, EG, FA, and GB.

A little thought should reveal that only seven discrete letter combinations can produce fourths, fifths, sixths, sevenths, and octaves.

Fourths

Notating those pitch pairings that produce fourths and examining the size of each, we discover that all fourths are the same size, except for the fourth produced between F and B. This latter fourth is larger than the other six by a semitone.

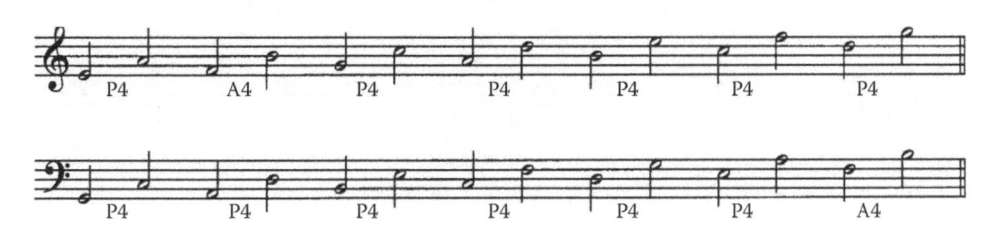

EXAMPLE 2.15 The seven examples of fourths as they appear in the treble and bass clefs.

The convention in music is to call the six "normal" fourths *perfect fourths* and to call the larger fourth an *augmented fourth*. The abbreviation for perfect fourth is *P4*, while the abbreviation for the augmented fourth is *A4*. Here are the letter combinations that produce fourths: AD, BE, CF, DG, EA, FB, and GC.

Fifths

Looking at the seven pitch combinations that produce fifths and examining the size of each, we discover that all fifths are the same size, except the fifth produced between B and F. This latter fifth is smaller than the other six by a semitone.

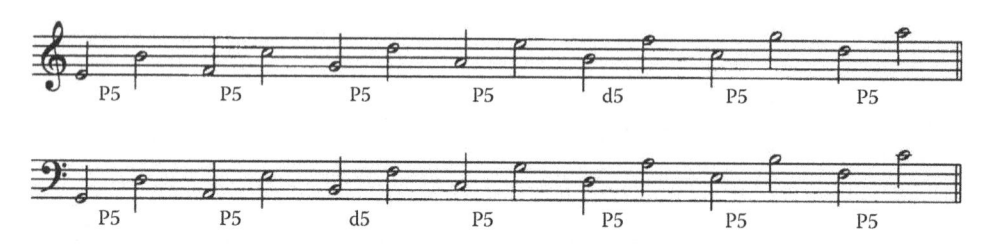

EXAMPLE 2.16 Seven examples of fifths as they appear in the treble and bass clefs.

> Augmented here means made larger by a semitone and may be applied to a perfect interval and to a major interval.

The convention is to call the six larger fifths ***perfect fifths*** and to call the smaller fifth a ***diminished fifth***. The abbreviation for perfect fifth is ***P5***, while the abbreviation for the diminished fifth is ***d5***. Here are the seven letter combinations that produce fifths: AE, BF, CG, DA, EB, FC, and GD.

> Diminished means made smaller by a semitone and may be applied to a perfect interval and to a minor interval.

Sixths

Examining the seven different sixths shows that four of them (C to A, D to B, F to D, and G to D) are larger and are called ***major sixths***, while the other three (E to C, A to F, and B to G) are each smaller by a semitone and are therefore called ***minor sixths***. The abbreviations are ***M6*** and ***m6***, respectively.

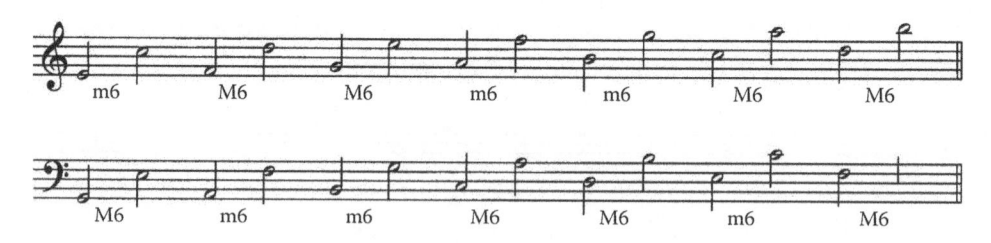

EXAMPLE 2.17 Seven examples of sixths as they appear in the treble and bass clefs.

The seven letter combinations that produce sixths are AF, BG, CA, DB, EC, FD, and GE.

Sevenths

The seven combinations that produce sevenths, when examined in detail, reveal that two of the sevenths are larger (C to B and F to E) and are thus called ***major sevenths*** (***M7***), and the remainder (D to C, E to D, G to F, A to G, and B to A) are smaller by a semitone and are called *minor sevenths* (*m7*). The seven letter pairings that produce sevenths are AG, BA, CB, DC, ED, FE, and GF.

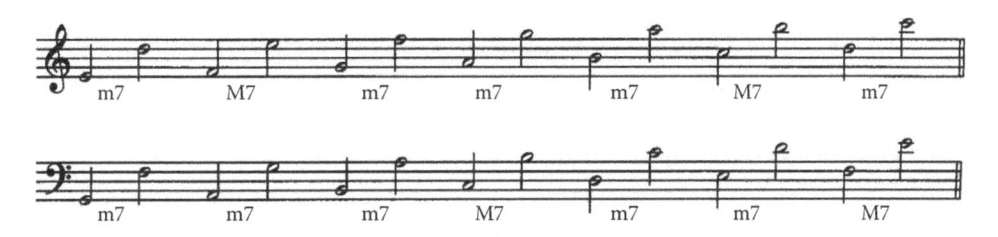

EXAMPLE 2.18   Seven examples of sevenths as they appear in the treble and bass clefs.

Unisons and Octaves

The seven unisons and seven octaves that we can notate, as we did the other intervals, are all the same size. In every case, the adjective used to describe them is, as in the case of fourths and fifths, *perfect*. Thus, these are all ***perfect unisons***.

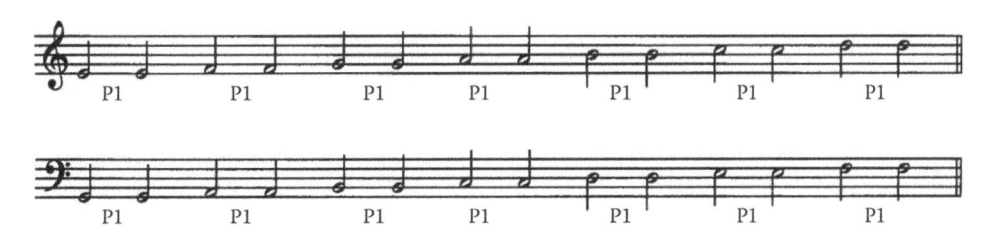

EXAMPLE 2.19   Seven examples of unisons as they appear in the treble and bass clefs.

These seven are all ***perfect octaves***.

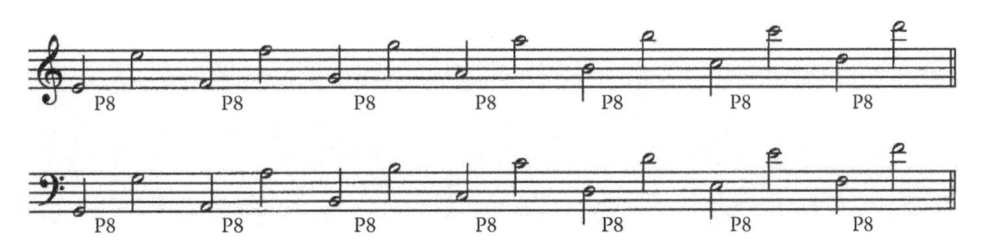

EXAMPLE 2.20   Seven examples of octaves as they appear in the treble and bass clefs.

As you can see, the corresponding abbreviations for unisons (or primes) and octaves are ***P1*** and ***P8***, respectively.

Review

- Seven unique pairs of pitches create each type of interval.
- For each interval class, seconds through sevenths, two sizes are generated. The two sizes differ by a semitone (half step).

- The larger seconds, thirds, sixths, and sevenths are called *major*.
- The smaller seconds, thirds, sixths, and sevenths are called *minor*.
- The smaller fourths are called *perfect*; the larger ones are *augmented*.
- The smaller fifth is called *diminished*; the larger fifths are called *perfect*.
- The modifier *minor* means small, while *major* means large.
- When describing intervals, *diminished* means to be decreased in size by a semitone, and *augmented* means to be increased in size by a semitone.
- All unisons and octaves are perfect.
- The abbreviations for the various modifiers are **M** (major), **m** (minor), **P** (perfect), **A** (augmented), and **d** (diminished).
- The term *prime* is sometimes used instead of unison.

Related Exercises

§ Identify the following intervals by interval class and size. Write your answers below the intervals provided on the staves.

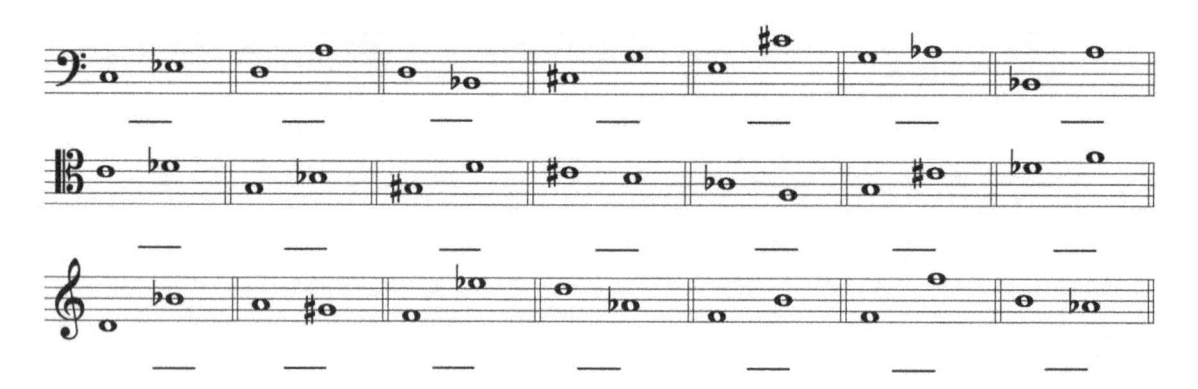

§ For each given pitch, write the specified interval above ↑ or below ↓ the given note.

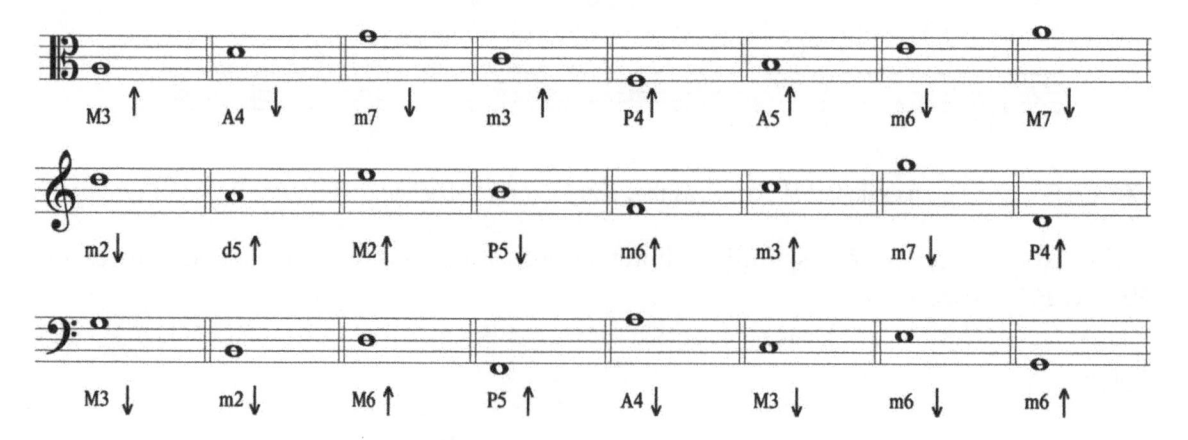

Naming Intervals with Accidentals

An Accidental on One of the Pitches

When intervals appear with accidentals attached to either pitch, the naming procedure becomes a two-step process. The first step is to name the basic interval by counting the pitches subsumed by the interval. The second step then accounts for the effect of the accidental. Here is an example:

EXAMPLE 2.21 An interval containing an accidental on the higher pitch.

By temporarily ignoring the accidental and its effect, you see that the base interval is C up to E, a distance that you know as a major third. However, the flat in front of the E lowers it, causing the *distance between the two pitches to be reduced* by a semitone. Thus, the size of the interval C up to E-flat is reduced from a major third to a minor third.

In Example 2.22, the basic interval is F up to B, which is an augmented fourth. But the written interval is F-*sharp* up to B. Since the sharp raises F by a semitone, thereby *decreasing* the distance between the two pitches involved, the resulting interval is a P4 (i.e. the interval a semitone smaller than an augmented fourth).

EXAMPLE 2.22 An interval containing an accidental on the lower pitch.

Accidentals on Both Pitches

If both pitches are modified by accidentals, the approach to the identification remains the same, but it now becomes a three-step process. The interval in Example 2.23 below is G-sharp up to B-flat. If, as a first step, you ignore both accidentals, you'll recognize the base interval as a major third.

Step two determines that the flat lowers the B by a semitone, reducing the interval from a major third to a minor third. Step three recognizes that the sharp raises the G by a semitone, further reducing the size of the interval. The illustrated interval is a semitone smaller than a minor interval and is, therefore, a diminished interval. The musical distance from G-sharp to B-flat is a diminished third.

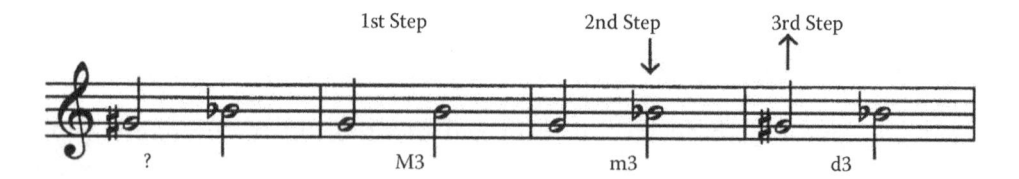

EXAMPLE 2.23 A diminished third and the step-by-step process by which this was determined.

The modifiers *diminished* and *augmented* may be applied to intervals other than unisons, fourths, fifths, and octaves in these situations:

- When a minor interval is reduced by a semitone, it becomes diminished.
- When a major interval is expanded by a semitone, it becomes augmented.

In Example 2.24, an accidental is associated with each pitch in the interval. The lower pitch is C-flat, and the upper pitch is F-sharp. To determine the correct name for this interval, first ignore the accidentals, and you'll find that C to F is a P4. Then, by raising the F to F-sharp, the interval becomes an A4. Finally, lowering the C by a semitone, the interval expands further from an A4 to a doubly augmented fourth (AA4).

EXAMPLE 2.24 A doubly augmented fourth and the step-by-step process by which this was determined.

If an augmented interval is expanded by a semitone, it is identified as doubly augmented. If a diminished interval is reduced by a semitone, it is identified as doubly diminished.

In those special situations when the same accidental is applied to both pitches, the resulting interval is the same size as the base, unmodified interval. Here are several examples.

EXAMPLE 2.25 In each example, the same accidental is applied to each pitch. If you know the size of the base interval, you will immediately know the size of the interval that has been modified.

Protocols for Naming Intervals

- Unisons, fourths, fifths, and octaves may be perfect, diminished, or augmented.
- Seconds, thirds, sixths, and sevenths may be major, minor, diminished, or augmented.

- Intervals a semitone larger than augmented are doubly augmented.
- Intervals a semitone smaller than diminished are doubly diminished.

Here are some miscellaneous examples:

EXAMPLE 2.26 Various sized intervals and the correct name for each. Be sure to understand how the correct answers were determined.

Review

- When either or both pitches of an interval have been altered by the use of a sharp, flat, or natural—whether this is due to a key signature or to the use of accidentals—you need to account for the effect of *each* of the accidentals.
- Raising the upper pitch and/or lowering the lower pitch creates a larger interval.
- Lowering the upper pitch and/or raising the lower pitch creates a smaller interval.
- *Never* use an enharmonic spelling when identifying an interval.

Enharmonic equivalents are G-sharp and A-flat, C-sharp and D-flat, C-flat and B-natural, etc. (See Part 1, p. 9.)

Related Exercises

§ Identify each interval by writing its name on the line below the interval.

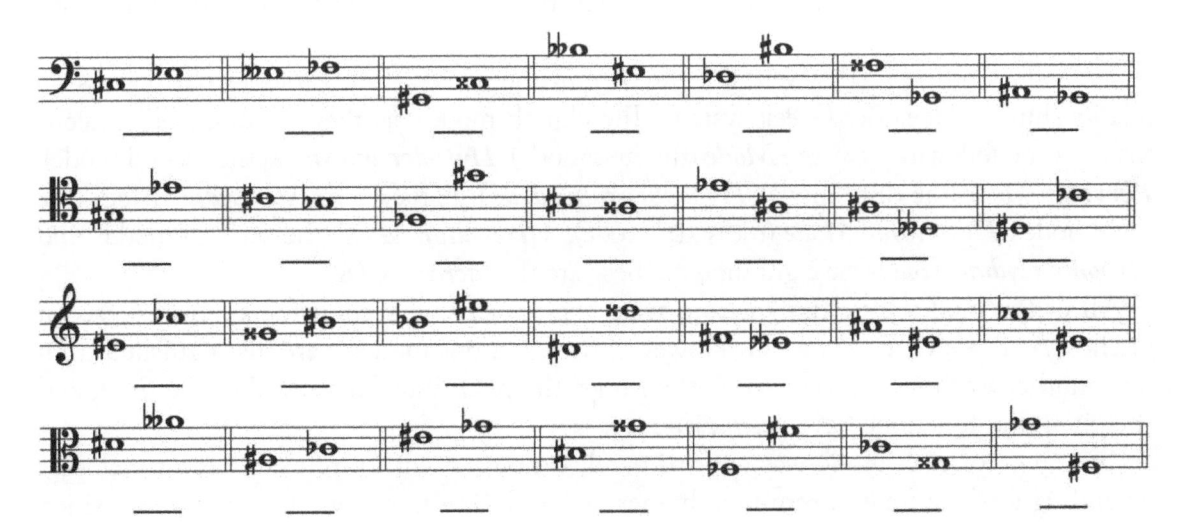

§ For each given pitch, write the specified interval above (↑) or below (↓) the given pitch. *Do not* alter the given pitch.

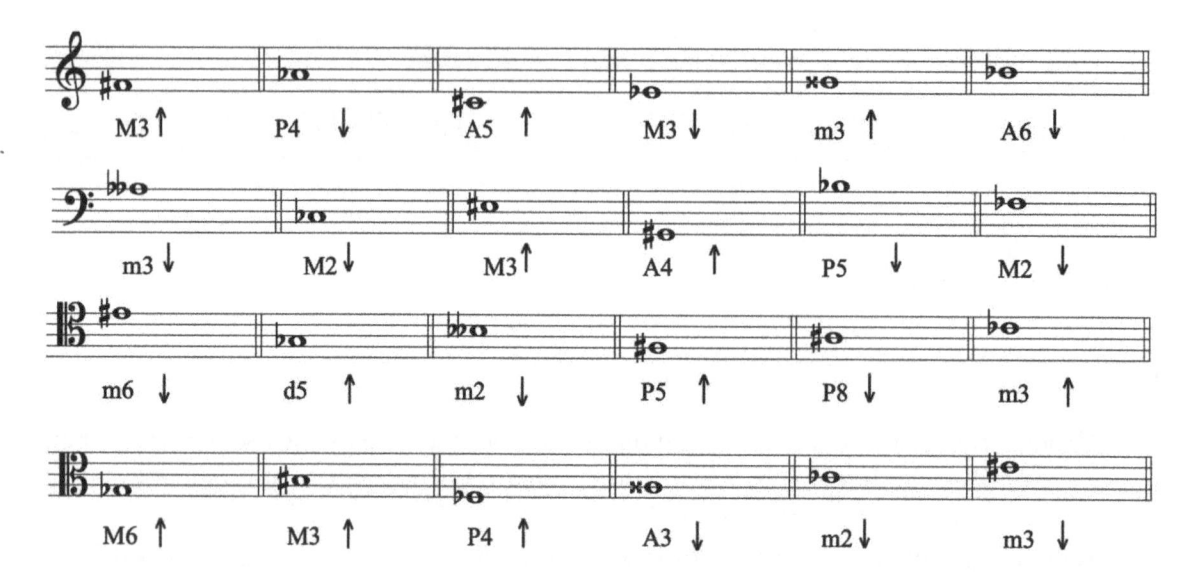

2. The Modes

Medieval Modes

Early Western music was based on *modes*. A mode is a collection of pitches with certain of these pitches possessing unique functions. The medieval modes were used to understand and to formulate the music used in the liturgy of the Roman Catholic Church during the Middle Ages (beginning about the ninth century and continuing through the thirteenth century).

The names of the modes were borrowed from the ancient Greek modes but possess no relationship to the earlier Greek system. The church modes, as they are often called, consisted of the following: **Dorian Mode** (the first mode), **Hypodorian Mode** (the second mode), **Phrygian Mode** (the third mode), **Hypophrygian Mode** (the fourth mode), **Lydian Mode** (the fifth mode), **Hypolydian Mode** (the sixth mode), **Mixolydian Mode** (the seventh mode), and **Hypomixolydian Mode** (the eight mode). These are the *sacred modes*.

All of the modes were drawn from what the reader will recognize as our basic set of pitches: A, B, C, D, E, F, and G. However, these various modes were distinguished from one another by three characteristics: the *range*, the pitch that functioned as the *final*, and the pitch that functioned as a *recitation tone*.

The range of each mode was approximately an octave with rare examples of melodies extending a whole tone or semitone higher or lower. The final was the pitch upon which modal melodies usually ended and on which they frequently began. The recitation tone, or *psalm tone*, was usually the most frequently sung tone within a modal melody.

The finals of the modes are as follows:

Root name *Dorian*, final is D
Root name *Phrygian*, final is E
Root name *Lydian*, final is F
Root name *Mixolydian*, final is G

Based partly upon range, modes were divided into two groups: ***authentic*** modes and ***plagal*** modes. Authentic modes have no prefix to their names, but plagal modes all have the prefix *hypo-*. Authentic modes consisted of (primarily) the pitches above the final. Plagal modes had the final near the middle of the singing range and used, about equally, notes below and above the final.

Hypo- means lower.

Note that the modal system uses no accidentals for notating the music because sharps and flats did not exist. However, because the esthetic of this type of music did not allow the melodic interval from F up to B (the A4) or from B up to F (the d5), it was necessary, when these intervals were encountered, to lower the B to "correct" the sound. Thus, the A4, F up to B, is changed to P4, and the

Other situations when it was believed that the B would be lowered include a melodic line that went from A to B and back to A or in some descending lines from C through B to A.

d5, B up to F, becomes a P5. Although these alterations of B were not notated, the variability of B made theorists of the day consider it an unstable pitch.

The recitation tone for each authentic mode can be determined by going up from the final a perfect fifth. However, when the P5 above the final is the unstable pitch B (as it is in Phrygian mode), the next closest stable pitch, C, is used instead.

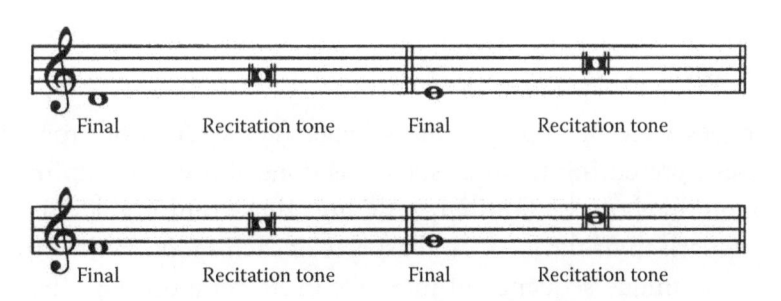

EXAMPLE 2.27 Finals and recitation tones for each of the four authentic medieval modes: upper left, Dorian; upper right, Phrygian; lower left, Lydian; and lower right, Mixolydian.

The recitation tone for the plagal modes is found by going down a third from the recitation tone used in the corresponding authentic mode. The same rule about the unstable B still applied, though. The recitation tone in Hypodorian is F, but in Hypophrygian it is

A (a third below Phrygian's recitation, C). In Hypolydian, the recitation tone is A, a third below Lydian's recitation tone of C. In Hypomixolydian, the recitation tone is C because descending a third from the Mixolydian recitation tone of D would cause B to be selected. Since that is not allowed, C (again) is substituted.

Here are all of the sacred modes showing each final, recitation tone, and approximate range.

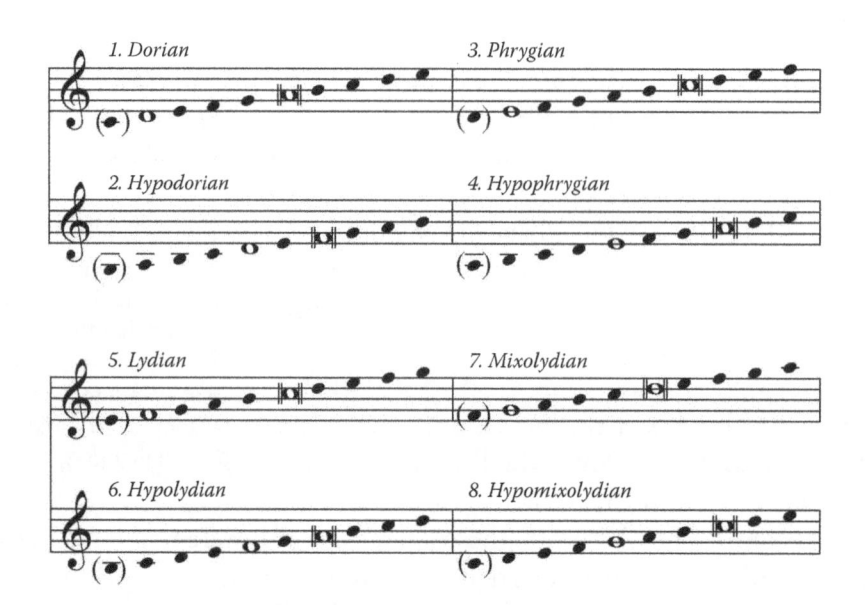

EXAMPLE 2.28 All of the medieval modes showing finals, recitation tones, and ranges. Finals are indicated by whole notes and recitation tone, by double whole notes. Pitches within parentheses are sometimes found in modal melodies.

The Structure of the Modes

Although the modes were not thought of as scales (i.e. a series of ordered ascending or descending pitches), presenting them as such—as done above—is helpful to modern students who are more likely to be familiar with, and thus comfortable with, scales. It also enables direct comparison of the structural aspects of each mode to the others.

Each mode has a unique sequence of intervals in its composition. The intervals of the Dorian mode, ascending from the final (D), are M2, m2, M2, M2, M2, m2, and M2. But the ascending Phrygian mode's composition is m2, M2, M2, M2, m2, M2, and M2.

In the chart below, each major second is marked with a ⊔, and each minor second is marked with a V. Note that no two modes share the same structure.

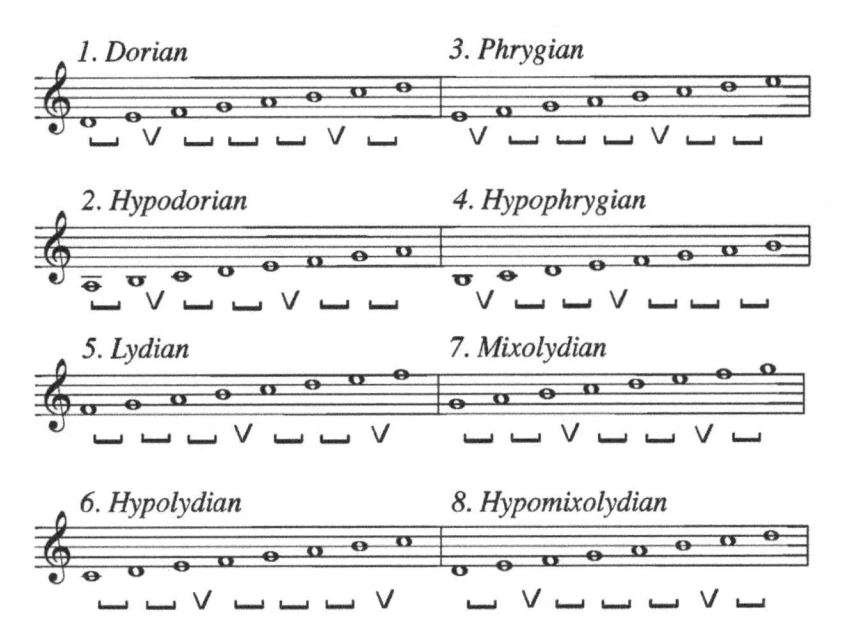

EXAMPLE 2.29 A comparison of the intervallic structures of the eight sacred medieval modes.

Other Modes

Using the same set of notes that were used in the modes discussed above, three other modes were constructed. One used A as the final, one used C as a final, and the third used B as its final.

The first two of these were considered inappropriate for use in Christian worship, thus they were called **secular modes**. (It may be inferred, therefore, that they did find use in music not intended for the church.) These two secular modes were named ***Æolian*** mode (final is A, recitation tone E) and ***Ionian*** mode (final C and recitation tone G).

The third of these avoided modes was ***Locrian***. From medieval times onward, it was considered only a theoretical mode since its final, B, was the unstable pitch, and there was no pitch a P5 above the final. (The likely recitation tone would have been F, but F was a d5 above the unstable final.)

> The interval of the A4 or d5 is also called the tritone because it is composed of three whole steps. (This interval is avoided by lowering B in performance.) This tritone was difficult to sing and, in early musical styles, awkward or impossible to use. Medieval musicians dubbed it "the devil in music" (*Diabolus in musica*) because, though it appeared to be an example of tonal perfection (containing three whole steps, and three being associated with the Trinity in Christian thought), it was useless or worse. Thus, like the devil, it appeared in the "likeness" of God only to tempt us. But, for the sake of the music, it had to be avoided.

Here are these secular/theoretical modes:

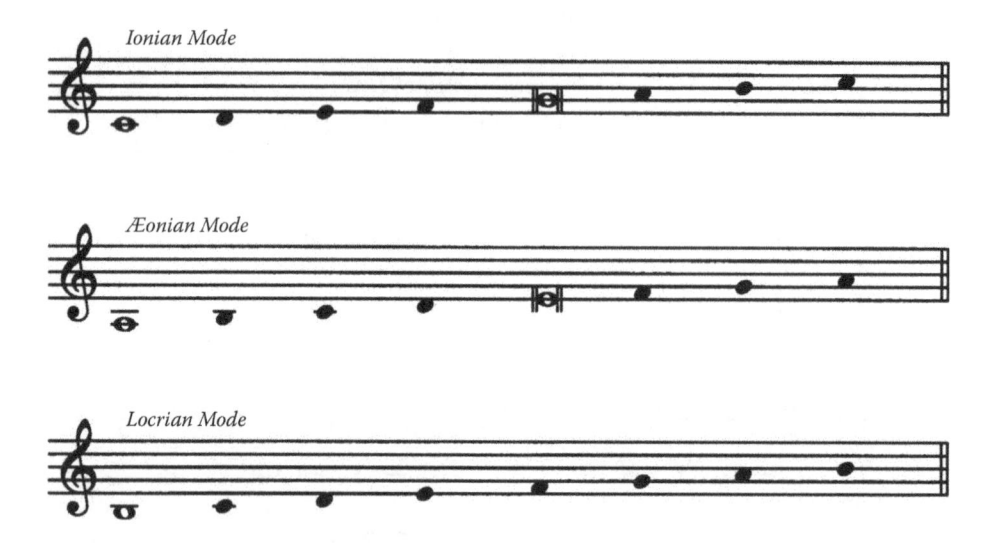

Ionian Mode

Æonian Mode

Locrian Mode

EXAMPLE 2.30   The two secular modes and the theoretical Locrian mode.

The Ionian mode is identical in intervallic structure to our major scale, and the Æolian mode is the same as natural minor. These facts lead many to believe they are the precursors of our major-minor system.

Review

- A mode is a set of pitches along with the functional relationships between these pitches.
- Medieval modes possessed Greek names but had no relation to ancient Greek practices.
- Each mode possessed its own unique final, recitation tone, and pitch range.
- The authentic modes were *Dorian*, *Phrygian*, *Lydian*, and *Mixolydian*.
- The plagal modes were *Hypodorian*, *Hypophrygian*, *Hypolydian*, and *Hypomixolydian*.
- The final for *Dorian* and *Hypodorian* was D. The final for *Phrygian* and *Hypophrygian* was E. The final for *Lydian* and *Hypolydian* was F. The final for *Mixolydian* and *Hypomixolydian* was G.
- The pitches used in melodies in the authentic modes were primarily above the final.

- The pitches used in the melodies in the plagal modes were distributed above and below the final.
- The recitation tone in an authentic mode was a P5 above the final unless the resulting pitch was B, in which case C was substituted.
- The recitation tone in a plagal mode was a third below the corresponding authentic mode's recitation tone unless the resulting pitch was a B, in which case C was substituted.
- The eight numbered modes discussed above were considered sacred modes because their use was appropriate for Christian worship.
- Although accidentals did not exist, B would regularly be lowered if it directly followed or immediately preceded F.
- The two secular modes are Æolian and Ionian.
- The final in Æolian mode was A, and the recitation tone was E.
- The final in Ionian mode was C, and the recitation tone was G.
- The theoretical mode was Locrian
- From medieval times, Locrian mode could not be used because the final (B) was considered unstable and was not, therefore, usable.
- When arranged in a scalar manner, each mode is seen as a unique sequence of major and minor seconds.

Related Exercises

§ Identify the possible modal roots of each of the following melodic fragments. What are the reasons for your choices?

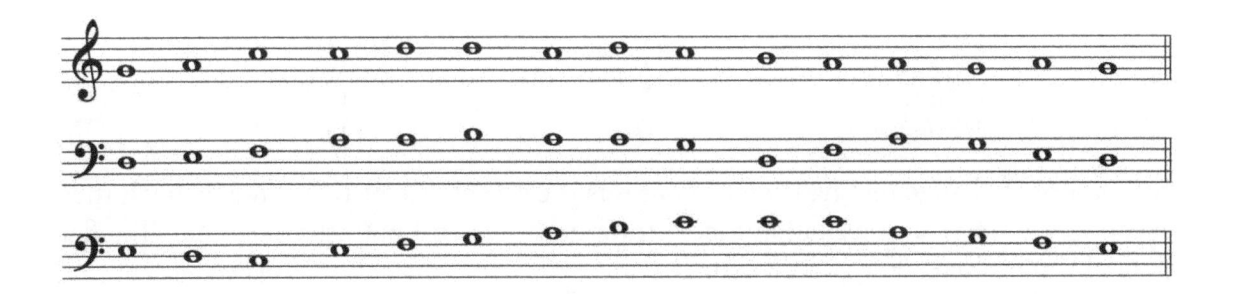

§ On each staff below, write an example of a modal excerpt in the given mode. Identify both the finals and the recitation tones in your example.

Lydian mode

Phrygian mode

Hypomixolydian mode

Hypodorian mode

The Renaissance Modes

The use of modes as the basis for Western (church) music lasted well into the Renaissance period (*c.* 1400–1600). However, the Renaissance modal practice had evolved from the medieval conventions.

No longer were modes separated into plagal and authentic forms. The recitation tone was no longer variable, and the range of pitches used was as large as needed. Thus, we have a simpler situation.

Mode Name	Final	Recitation Tone
Dorian	D	A
Phrygian	E	B
Lydian	F	C
Mixolydian	G	D

An important change that had come about was the acceptance of B as a usable pitch thus enabling it to serve as a recitation tone. However, it was still not used as a final. The flat symbol had evolved and was accepted. This allowed a new concept: ***transposed modes***.

Transposed Modes

In what were known as the transposed modes, the usable pitch set consisted of F, G, A, *B-flat*, C, D, and E. With these pitches, one can create an exact intervallic copy of Dorian mode, using G as the final and D as the recitation tone. Also, using A as the final and E as the recitation tone, one produced a form of Phrygian mode. A B-flat final with an F recitation tone possessed the same structure as Lydian mode, and using C for the final and G for the recitation tone yielded a structure identical to Mixolydian mode.

Below are the Renaissance modes with the normal form on the left and the transposed equivalent on the right. Note that there is no longer an authentic/plagal distinction.

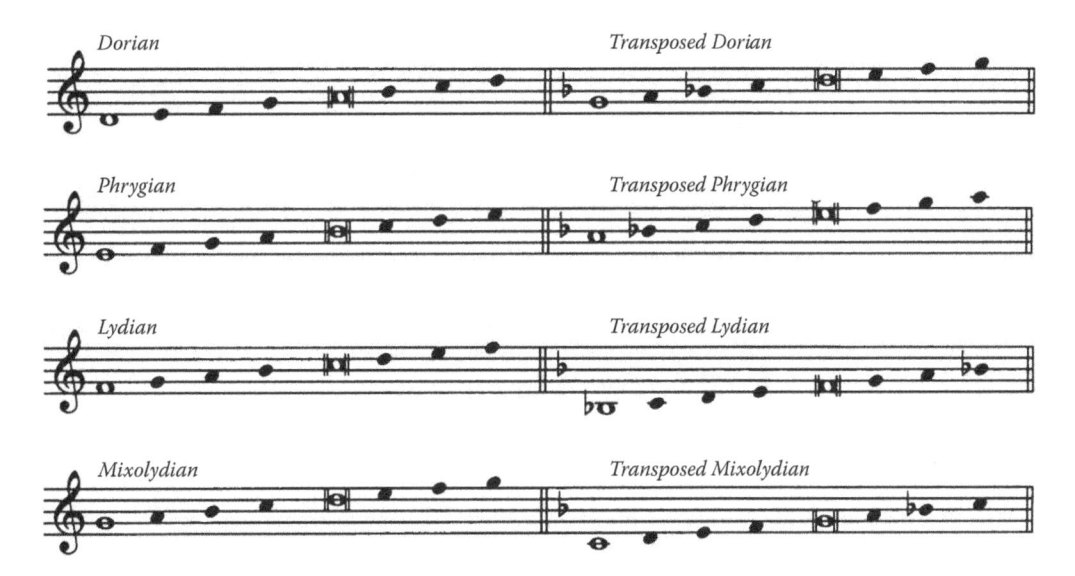

EXAMPLE 2.31 The four Renaissance sacred modes: original on the left and transposed on the right.

Although a symbol for flat now existed, it was usually applied only to B to indicate the lower pitched version of that note. (The flat sign, ♭, evolved from the lowercase *b* [see Part 1, p. 8].) But the concept of transposed modes meant that now the unstable interval (formerly F to B) would occur between B-flat and E, now prompting a need in certain passages to lower E to E-flat to avoid the tritone.

Review

- In the Renaissance, there were four sacred modes: Dorian, Phrygian, Lydian, and Mixolydian.
- These modes have, respectively, D, E, F, and G as finals.
- The recitation tone for Renaissance modes is always a P5 above the final.
- The range could be whatever was needed to accommodate the music.
- During the Renaissance, the use of the symbol ♭ became common.
- Because B and B-flat were no longer considered unstable, the modes could be transposed.
- Transposed modes used the same names and intervallic properties as the standard modes, but they were pitched a P4 higher (or a P5 lower) than the non-transposed forms.

Melody: Note Following Note

Related Exercises

§ Each example given below is an excerpt from a Renaissance form of a mode. Identify the recitation tone and final in each example and then recopy the excerpt on the blank staff below in its transposed form.

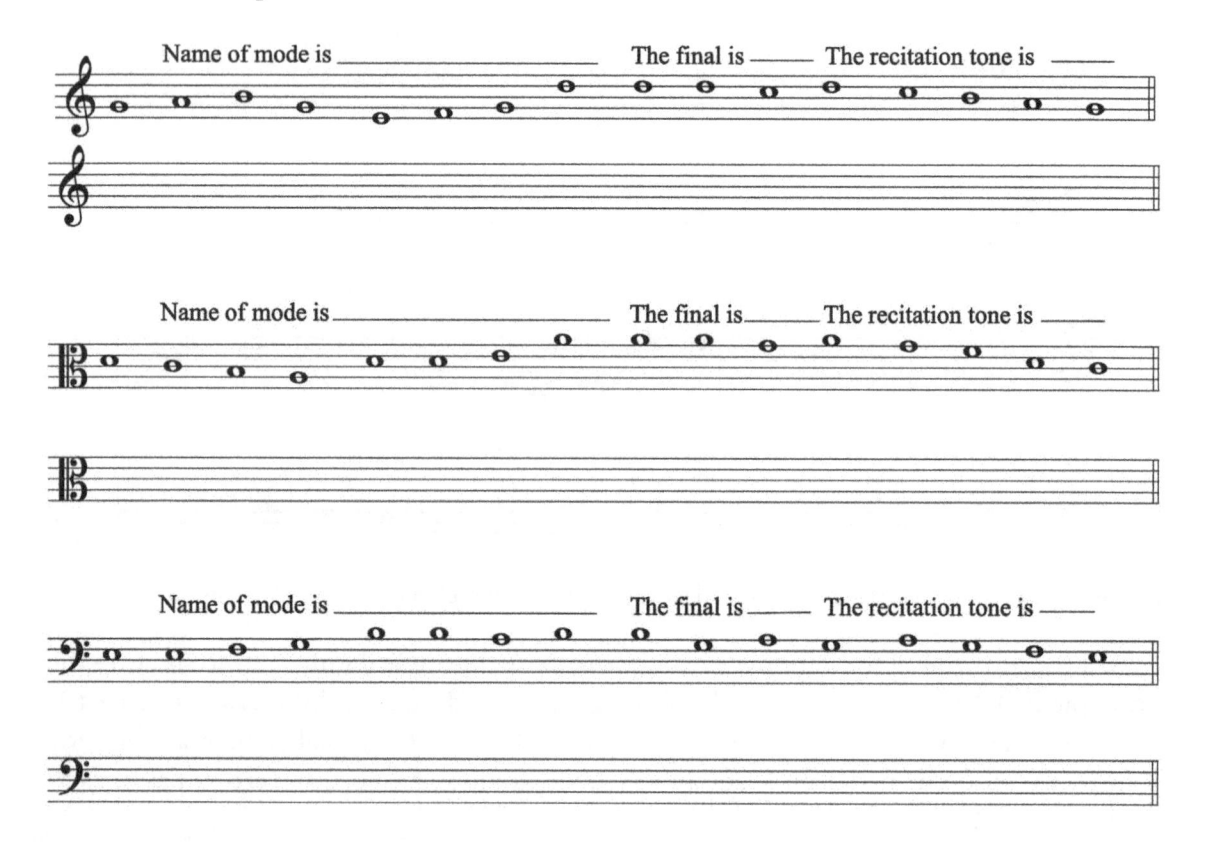

Name of mode is _____ The final is _____ The recitation tone is _____

Name of mode is _____ The final is _____ The recitation tone is _____

Name of mode is _____ The final is _____ The recitation tone is _____

The Modes Evolve into Major and Minor

Over the course of time, performers and composers gradually modified the modes by altering the location of some of the minor and major seconds. When the next-to-the-highest pitch in a mode was not a minor second below the upper final, as in Dorian, Phrygian, and Mixolydian, the practice was to raise this pitch to create a semitone that could progress smoothly to the final. When the note immediately above the lower final was not a whole tone above the final, as in Phrygian, it was sometimes altered to produce a major second. These changes took place gradually and changed the sound of the traditional modes into those heard in our modern major and minor scales.

   Modern usage—heard in folk, jazz, pop, rock, and other forms of music—shows a rediscovery of the modes, including the once unusable Locrian. In contemporary practice, dating from the late nineteenth century, any modal scale may be used with any pitch functioning as the final.

3. The Major Scale

The most familiar of the pitch structures that are the basis for music of the ***common practice era*** (roughly from 1600 to the present) are the ***major*** and ***minor modalities***. Because the pitches that characterize these modalities are often presented as ordered sets of ***ascending*** (or ***descending***) pitches, we usually call them ***major scales*** and ***minor scales***. These scales consist of a specific set of pitches, and each pitch within the scale serves a particular function.

The major scale is familiar to most of us by sound and by sight.

EXAMPLE 2.32 The C Major scale. Whole tones are marked with ⌐⌐ and semitones are marked with v.

The intervallic content of the (ascending) C Major scale shown is M2, M2, m2, M2, M2, M2, and m2. Expressed in terms of steps and half steps, it is whole step, whole step, half step, whole step, whole step, whole step, half step. It is a very familiar pitch sequence that we may also recognize by the ***solfege*** syllables *do, re, mi, fa, sol, la, ti, do*.

Tetrachords

Another model used to illustrate the construction of a major scale is that of a pair of ***tetrachords***—two sets of four notes each. Each of these tetrachords is composed of two whole tones and a semitone like this:

EXAMPLE 2.33 A basic tetrachord formed of two whole tones and a semitone.

By selecting an initial tetrachord starting on C and a second tetrachord linked to the first one by a whole tone (sometimes called a disjunct tetrachord), the C Major scale is formed. The use of tetrachords to construct major scales is especially helpful when used at the keyboard because the structure is both visually and tactilely evident.

These syllables were derived from those found in the text of the Latin hymn *Ut queant laxis,* in which each line of the text began on a successively higher pitch (starting with C). Guido of Arezzo (eleventh century) was attributed with first using this mnemonic to teach sight singing. The six successive Latin syllables that begin the six lines of the hymn are *ut, re, mi, fa, sol,* and *la*. *Ut* has been replaced by the more easily sung *do*, and *ti* was later provided for completeness. (In the Romance languages, *si* is used instead of *ti*. The French retain the syllable *ut*.)

According to some understandings of the ancient Greek system, the basic interval of music was the P4, and the various tunings came about by placing two other notes in between the fourth. The tetrachord used here is one possible (but certainly not the only) distribution satisfying this condition.

Tetrachords that share a common tone, such as C-D-E-F and F-G-A-B♭ are called ***conjunct*** tetrachords.

EXAMPLE 2.34 A C Major scale viewed as two disjunct tetrachords.

Because all major scales possess the same sequence of intervals, they all sound the same except for differences in highness or lowness. This fact means that all major scales share the same intervallic structure, and thus creating any major scale, beginning on any pitch, merely requires replicating the structure.

Using the ascending pattern M2, M2, m2, M2, M2, M2, and m2, you can create a major scale starting on any pitch. To build a major scale on G, the result would be as seen in Example 2.35.

EXAMPLE 2.35 The G Major scale. The arrow points to the F-sharp that had to be added to assure the correct interval sequence.

Note that by following the model, it was necessary to alter F to F-sharp. This provides both the last M2 and the final m2 required in an ascending major scale.

For musicians who use the "movable *do*" system of solfege, the syllables applied to each note of the major scale remain *do*, *re*, *mi*, *fa*, *sol*, *la*, *ti*, *do*, reflecting the fact that all major scales, regardless of starting pitch, possess the same sequence of intervals and, thus, the same sound. For musicians who prefer the "fixed *do*" system, the sequence of syllables for G Major is *sol*, *la*, *ti*, *do*, *re*, *mi*, *fi*, *sol*.

Following this pattern, you can create a major scale beginning on *any* pitch. Some guidelines for creating major scales are these:

> In solfege practice, whether using movable *do* or fixed *do*, raised pitches are *di* for raised *do*, *ri* for raised *re*, *fi* for raised *fa*, *si* for raised *sol*, and *li* for raised *la*. Lowered pitches thus become *ra* for lowered *re*, *me* for lowered *mi*, *se* for lowered *sol*, *le* for lowered *la*, and *te* for lowered *ti*.

Guidelines for Major Scales

Start on the letter (pitch) for which the scale is named and ascend to its octave.
Use all seven letter names.
Never skip a letter name.
Do not repeat any letter names (except the upper, ending pitch).

Never mix sharps and flats in the same scale.
The ascending intervallic pattern must always be M2, M2, m2, M2, M2, M2, m2.

Other Useful Principles

- Except for F Major, all major scales that contain flats have "flat" in their names.
- Except for C Major and F Major, all scales with a name devoid of sharps or flats are sharp scales.

Here is a major scale starting on A-flat.

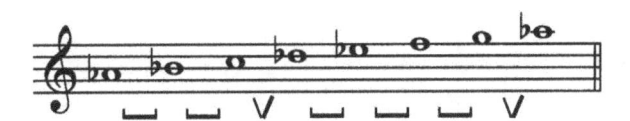

EXAMPLE 2.36   The A-flat Major scale.

Note that the intervallic pattern remains the same as that found in the C Major and G Major scales. But it is necessary to create this scale by using flats so the appearance of the scale differs from both that of the C Major scale and of the G Major scale. By following the guidelines given above—and being sure to create the M2, M2, m2, M2, M2, M2, m2 ascending sequence of pitches—it was possible to build an A-flat Major scale.

Review

In Western music, scales constructed so as to produce the following series of ascending intervals are called major: M2, M2, m2, M2, M2, M2, m2.

> Some people prefer to think of the pattern as whole step, whole step, half step, whole step, whole step, whole step, half step.

- The descending sequence of intervals in a major scale is always m2, M2, M2, M2, m2, M2, M2.
- The C Major scale has neither sharps nor flats. All other major scales will include either only sharps or only flats in their composition.
- Except for the starting pitch, which is repeated, each pitch name is used only once.
- No pitch names are skipped.
- The pitches found in every ascending major scale *may be* sung using the solfege syllables *do, re, mi, fa, sol, la, ti, do* regardless of the actual starting pitch. (This is known as movable *do*.)
- If a musician prefers a fixed *do* system, then the solfege syllable that corresponds to the starting pitch would be used for the first pitch and the other syllables would follow in order, being altered as required to account for raised or lowered pitches. (See sidebar on p. 72.)

Related Exercises

§ Here are a series of major scales written without the necessary accidentals. Remembering that the ascending sequence must be whole step, whole step, half step, whole step, whole step, whole step, and half step, add the missing sharps or flats as required.

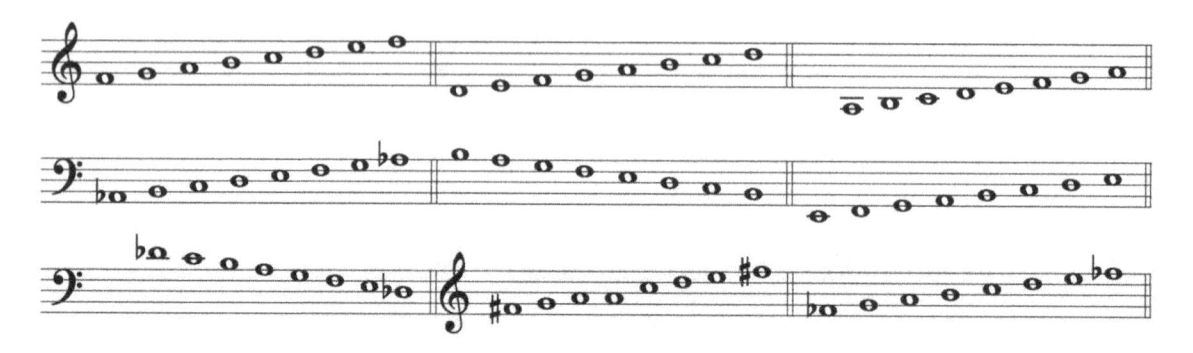

§ Study the major scales below. Decide, based on pitch content, the tonic in each example. Circle your answer.

§ On the staves below and in the clefs provided, write the specified major scales.

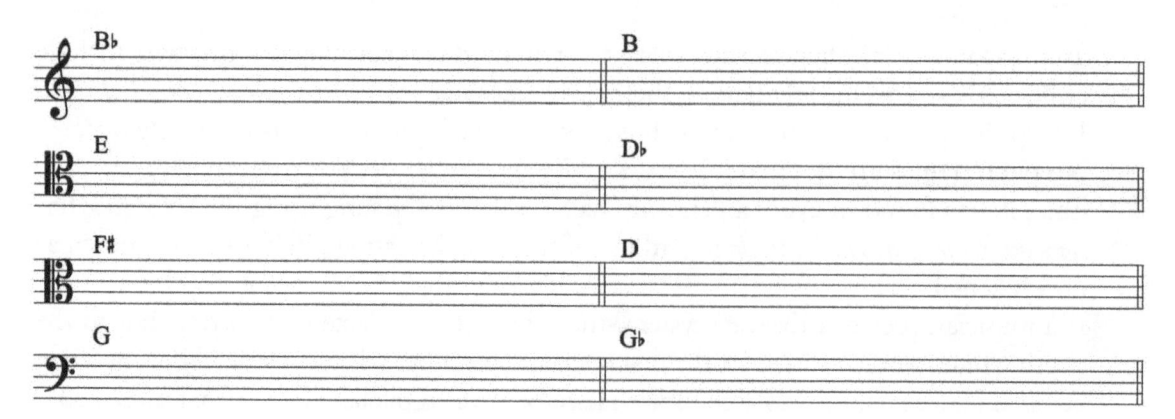

B♭   B

E   D♭

F♯   D

G   G♭

§ Using the fixed *do* system, write the scales that are being communicated through solfege below as pitches on the staff.

re-mi-fi-sol-la-ti-di-re

fa-sol-la-te-do-re-mi-fa

la-ti-di-re-mi-fi-si-la

me-fa-sol-le-te-do-re-me

§ In each of the examples below, you are provided with the seven unique pitches found in a major scale. Using moveable *do*, write the accepted solfege symbols for the given scale. (If preferred, you may do this exercise in fixed *do* instead.)

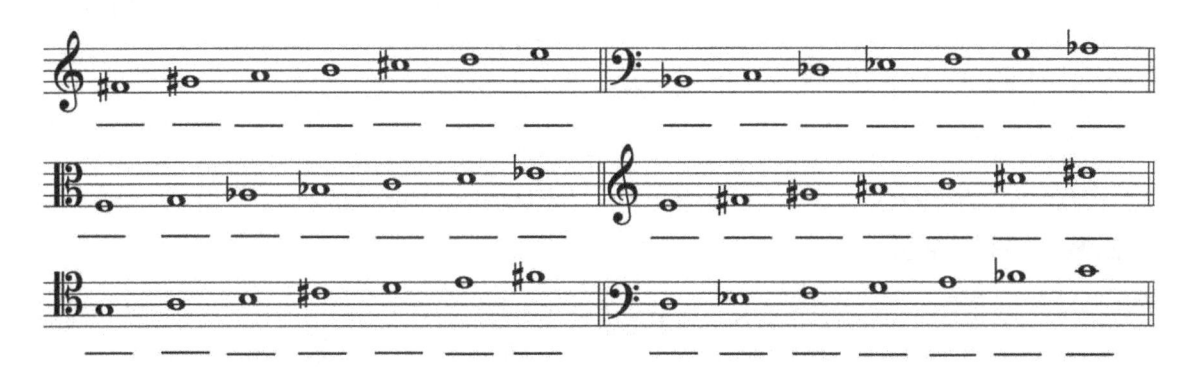

4. Key Signatures for Major Scales

Creating the major scales by following the procedures provided above can serve one very well. But if a significant amount of music must be notated, the task of placing the appropriate sharp or flat before each pitch that is to be modified can quickly become redundant. Hundreds of years ago, a shortcut was introduced called the ***key signature***.

Key signatures inform the performer that, unless specifically instructed otherwise, all encountered pitches of a certain letter name, such as—for instance—all Fs are to be sharped or all Bs and Es are to be flatted. This convention saves the composer/copyist the job of placing a sharp before all the Fs or flats before all the Bs and Es.

The appropriate key signature can be determined by observing the pitch content of the scale. Thus, the A-flat Major scale (Example 2.36) is seen to possess four altered pitches: the A-flat, the B-flat, the D-flat, and the E-flat. To inform the performer of this situation, one uses a key signature. It might look like this:

EXAMPLE 2.37 On the left, an unconventional way to indicate the accidentals used in A-flat Major. On the right, the conventional A-flat Major key signature.

If you have performed much music, the key signature shown on the left in Example 2.37 should seem strange. It is not that the key signature is necessarily incorrect. It does indeed provide information that the notes A, B, D, and E should all be flatted. However, it appears unusual because there are *conventions* for the construction of key signatures. The key signature on the right follows those conventions.

These conventions determine how the flats (or sharps) are to be placed, from left to right, on the staff. The pattern used is the order in which the flats or sharps are introduced into the major scales beginning with one flat (or sharp) on to two, three, four, five, six, and finally seven flats (or sharps). (A C Major scale requires no sharps or flats, which makes it the starting point.)

> The maximum number of sharps or flats to be found in a key signature is seven, namely, one for each of the seven pitch names.

Major Scales with Sharps

Constructing a scale with just one sharp could involve trying all the various possibilities. But it would finally be discovered that the major scale starting on G is the only major scale that satisfies the criterion. This scale has only one sharp, which is F-sharp. So F-sharp is the first sharp to appear in *any key* signature. (Note also that F-sharp is a minor second below G, the pitch that the G Major scale is built on.)

EXAMPLE 2.38 A G Major scale written using the conventional key signature.

Seeking a major scale with two sharps will eventually yield D Major as the solution. D Major has both an F-sharp and a C-sharp. The initial sharp (F-sharp) is retained, and a second sharp, C-sharp, is added. Thus, our two-sharp key signature shows, from left to right, an F-sharp and a C-sharp. (And again, the newest sharp, C-sharp, is located a minor second below the key tone, D.)

EXAMPLE 2.39 A D Major scale written using the conventional key signature, which consists of F-sharp and C-sharp.

A three-sharp key signature will consist of an F-sharp, a C-sharp, and a G-sharp. This key signature is generated by constructing an A Major scale. Thus, the key signature with three sharps indicates to the performer the key of A Major.

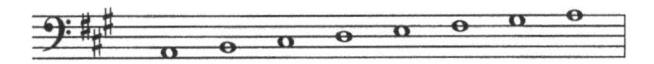

EXAMPLE 2.40 The A Major scale written using the conventional key signature, which consists of F-sharp, C-sharp, and G-sharp.

Here are the important guidelines for creating sharp key signatures:

The first sharp is always F-sharp.
The second sharp is always C-sharp, a perfect fifth (P5) above F-sharp.
The third sharp is always G-sharp, a P5 above C-sharp.
The fourth sharp will then be D-sharp, a P5 above G-sharp.
Continuing the pattern, the fifth sharp is A-sharp, the sixth sharp is E-sharp, and the seventh (or last) sharp is B-sharp. Each of these successive new sharps is a P5 above the preceding sharp.

Naming the key indicated by a sharp key signature is a matter of looking at the last (i.e. farthest to the right) sharp and knowing that it is a minor second below the pitch that gives the scale its name. Thus, with four sharps, the last sharp is D-sharp, a minor second below E, and the key represented must be E Major.

> This process works only for major keys that use sharps. Be sure to read the discussion of key signatures containing flats that follows.

Here are all of the sharp key signatures from one sharp to seven sharps, as they usually appear, in all four clefs.

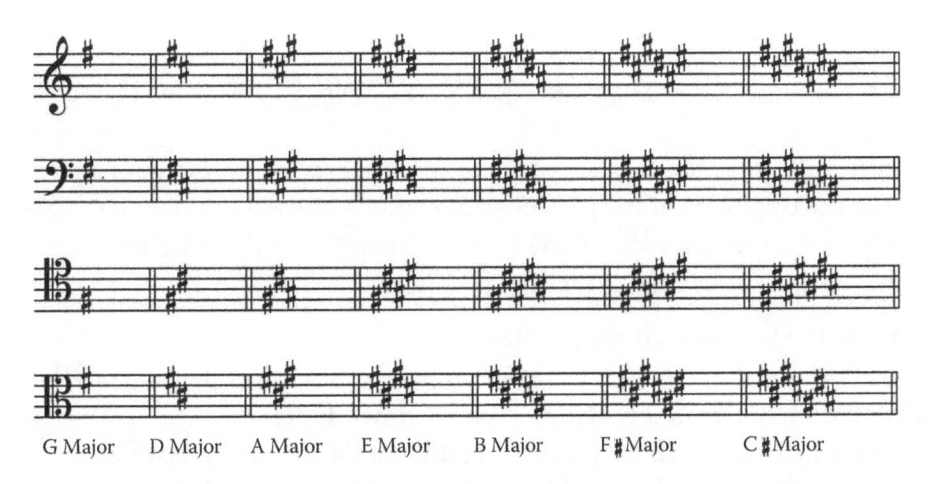

G Major   D Major   A Major   E Major   B Major   F♯ Major   C♯ Major

EXAMPLE 2.41 The seven key signatures that contain sharps written as they conventionally appear in all four clefs.

These should be memorized!

Major Scales with Flats

To create key signatures using flats, the approach is similar to working with sharps, but the details are different. Seeking a major scale that requires only one flat will eventually reveal F Major to be the only appropriate scale. It also turns out that the note that must be flatted is B. B-flat is a perfect fourth (P4) above F.

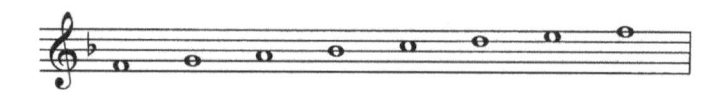

EXAMPLE 2.42 The F Major scale, the major key that contains only one flat, written with its conventional key signature.

Going on to create a scale using two flats results in a scale that has B-flat as its starting pitch and a new flat, E-flat. Note that E-flat is a P4 above B-flat. This is the pattern for the flats.

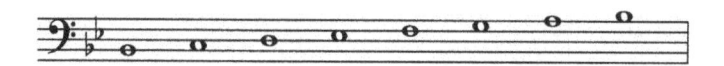

EXAMPLE 2.43 The B-flat Major scale, the major key that uses two flats, written with its conventional key signature.

The scale with three flats begins on E-flat, adds an A-flat, and still continues to use the original B-flat. You have probably anticipated that the latest addition, A-flat, is a P4 above E-flat.

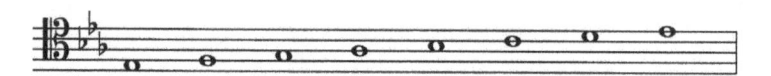

EXAMPLE 2.44 The E-flat Major scale as written using a key signature.

In much the same way that each successively more sharp scale started on a pitch that was a P5 above the starting pitch of the previous scale, each successively more flat scale starts on a pitch that is a P4 above (or a P5 below) the starting pitch of the prior scale.

The guidelines for flat key signatures are as follows:

The first pitch to be flatted is always B.
The second pitch to be flatted is always E, a perfect fourth (P4) above B-flat.
The third pitch to be flatted is always A, a P4 above E-flat.
The pattern continues with each new flat added a P4 above the last flat.
The remaining flats, in order, are D-flat, G-flat, C-flat, and F-flat.

Here are the seven flat key signatures in order, from left to right, from one flat to seven flats as they conventionally appear in all four clefs.

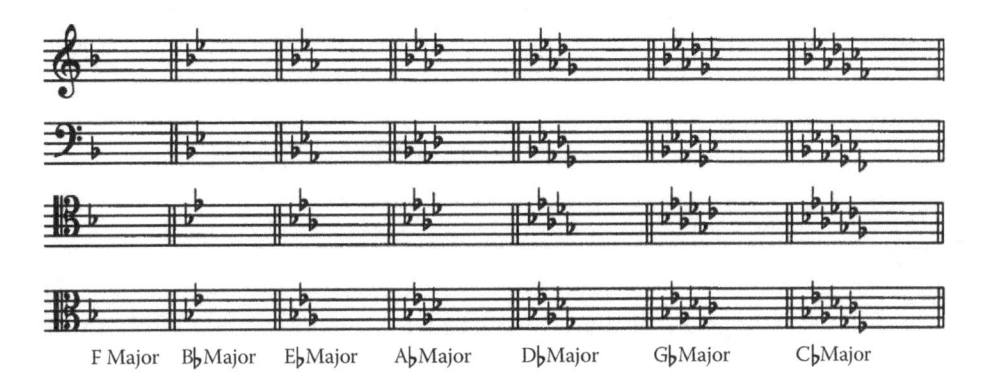

F Major   B♭Major   E♭Major   A♭Major   D♭Major   G♭Major   C♭Major

EXAMPLE 2.45 All seven conventional flat key signatures in all four clefs.

These, too, should be memorized!

The order in which the first four flats appear, B, E, A, and D, spells the word *bead*. The order in which all seven flats are added—B, E, A, D, G, C, and F—is exactly opposite to the order in which the sharps are added—F, C, G, D, A, E, and B

> Musicians have also observed that when pairing sharp and flat scales built on the same letter name (such as D Major and D-flat Major) the total number of sharps and flats is always seven. The D Major scale has two sharps, the D-flat Major scale has five flats (2+5=7). The A Major scale has three sharps, and the A-flat Major scale has four flats (3+4=7).

Review

- Sharps and flats are used to create the various major scales/keys used in Western music.
- In pieces of music written in these keys, key signatures set the "default" pitch pattern that forms the basis for each key. This avoids the necessity of placing a flat or sharp before every pitch in the music that requires such alterations.
- Key signatures may contain no sharps or flats or may consist of from one to seven sharps or from one to seven flats.
- Conventional key signatures do not mix sharps and flats.
- Key signatures are formed in a specific manner with the accidentals arranged, from left to right, in the order in which they are introduced.
- For sharp key signatures, the order of sharps from left to right is F, C, G, D, A, E, and B.
- For flat key signatures, the order of flats from left to right is B, E, A, D, G, C, and F.

> Beginning in the twentieth century, some composers who wrote with a complex pitch vocabulary used no key signatures but rather placed a sharp, flat, or natural before *every* pitch.

- When identifying the major key indicated by a key signature containing flats, the name of the key is always the name of the next-to-last flat.
- When identifying the major key indicated by a key signature containing sharps, the name of the key is always that of the pitch, which is a minor second above the last sharp.
- C Major has no sharps or flats in its key signature.
- F Major has only one flat (therefore, there is no "next-to-last" flat).

Related Exercises

§ On each staff provided, and in the clef specified, write the indicated major key signatures.

§ Below, you are given a key signature. Assuming it represents a major key, what is the name of the key? Write that pitch on the staff.

5. The Minor Scale

In addition to the major modality used in common-practice music, there is the ***minor modality***. Our minor modalities differ significantly from major in sound, which also means that they must differ from major in the manner in which they are constructed.

The primary distinguishing characteristic of a minor scale is the fact that the third pitch (ascending) is a minor third (m3) rather than a major third (M3) above the first pitch. Thus, the first five pitches in the ascending f minor scale are F, G, *A-flat*, B-flat, and C, which create the succession of intervals M2, m2, M2, and M2. See the example below.

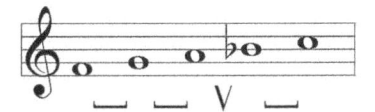

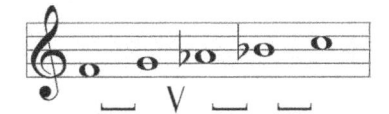

EXAMPLE 2.46 On the left, the first five pitches of an F Major scale. On the right, the first five pitches of an f minor scale. Note how the order of the intervals has changed.

The content of the rest of the scale is determined by the type of minor scale to be constructed. There are three types: ***melodic minor, harmonic minor***, and ***natural minor***. Each type possesses a unique pattern.

The Melodic Minor Scale

The c minor version of the melodic minor scale is structured like this:

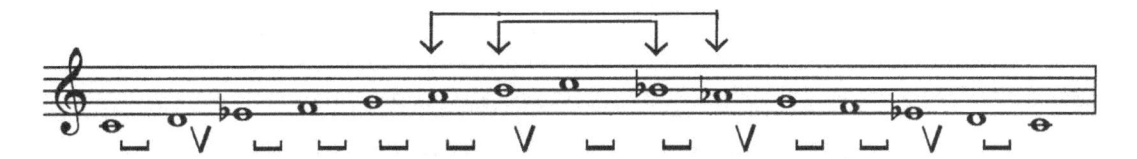

EXAMPLE 2.47 A melodic minor scale starting on C. Note that this scale has both an ascending form and a descending form. The differences are indicated by the bracketed arrows.

Although the ascending and descending forms of scales found in other cultures often differ, the melodic minor scale is the only common Western scale that does so.

The sequence of intervals found in an ascending melodic minor scale is M2, m2, M2, M2, M2, M2, m2. Except for the lowered third, it strongly resembles a major scale. The descending sequence is M2, M2, m2, M2, M2, m2, M2.

The generally accepted reason for the differences between the ascending and descending forms of the scale is that these particular pitch sequences are easy to sing. The melodic minor scale gets its name from the fact that it is frequently found as the central set of pitches used in melodic lines of music created in a minor modality. (This appears to be true both for common-practice music and much Western folk music.)

To create a melodic minor scale begining on a pitch other than C, simply follow the intervallic sequence given above. Thus, a d melodic minor scale would be as follows:

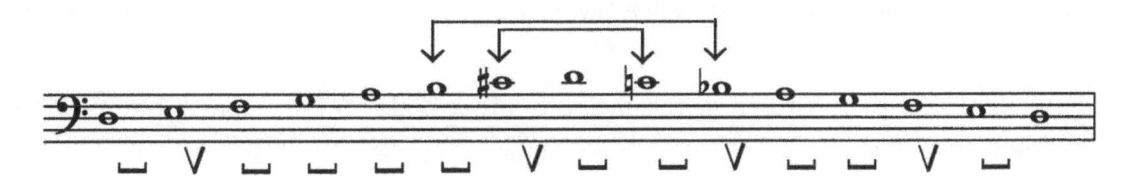

EXAMPLE 2.48 A melodic minor scale starting on D.

Note that this scale uses both flats (B-flat) and sharps (C-sharp). Unlike major scales, minor scales, in two instances (g minor and d minor), use both.

A melodic minor scale may also be created by beginning with a major scale. To create an f melodic minor scale, start with an F Major scale, ascending and descending, like this:

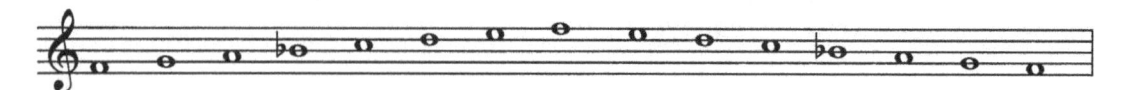

EXAMPLE 2.49   An F Major scale written both ascending and descending.

Next, lower the pitch of the note a third above the starting F—that is, change A to A-flat—both ascending and descending.

EXAMPLE 2.50   An F Major scale with the third pitch (A) lowered to A-flat.

Now, lower the pitch immediately below the upper F (E) to E-flat in the descending portion of the scale only.

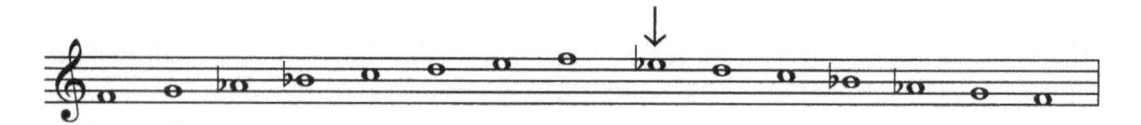

EXAMPLE 2.51   An altered F Major scale with the third pitch lowered and the pitch immediately below F in the descending scale (E) lowered to E-flat.

And, finally, lower the pitch a third below the upper F (D) to D-flat in the descending portion of the scale only.

EXAMPLE 2.52   An altered F Major scale with A lowered to A-flat, E lowered to E-flat, and the pitch a third below F in the descending scale (D) also lowered to D-flat.

Either approach to constructing the melodic minor scale will, of course, produce the same results.

Melody: Note Following Note

Review

- In Western music, scales with this sequence of intervals, ascending—M2, m2, M2, M2, M2, M2, m2—and this sequence descending—M2, M2, m2, M2, M2, m2, M2—are called melodic minor.
- Melodic minor scales represent the collection of pitches most commonly used in creating melodies in minor modalities.
- Unlike major scales, two minor scales (d minor and g minor) mix sharps and flats.
- Except for the starting pitch, which gives the scale its name and which is repeated at the top of the scale, each pitch name is used *only once* ascending and *once* descending.
- No pitch names are repeated or skipped in the ascending or descending forms.
- Musicians using movable *do* usually assign these syllables to a melodic minor scale: ascending, *do, re, **me**, fa, sol, la, ti, do*; descending, *do, **te**, **le**, sol, fa, **me**, re, do*.
- Musicians using fixed *do* assign the solfege syllables that correspond to the letter names regardless of any accidentals. (Any C is always a form of *do*, any D is always a form of *re*, etc.) Thus, for the f melodic minor example, the ascending syllables would be *fa, sol, le, te, do, re, mi, fa*, and descending would be *fa, me, ra, do, te, le, sol, fa*.

Related Exercises

§ One way to create a melodic minor scale is to alter a major scale by always lowering the third degree of the scale and, when descending, also to lower the seventh and sixth degrees. Using the example given below, and assuming that the first note is tonic, create a major scale on that pitch. Then, alter each thus created major scale into a melodic minor scale.

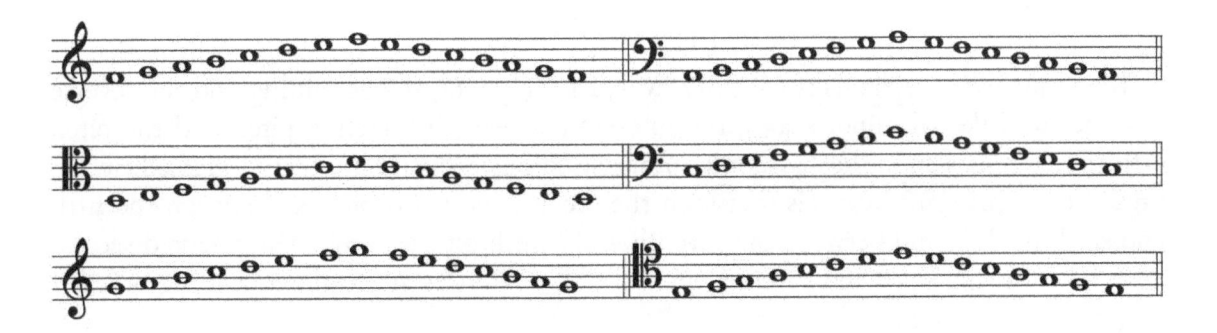

§ In each of the following examples, you are presented with a melodic minor scale. However, the example may not begin and/or may not end on the tonic. Examine each example, determine the tonic, and then show it by circling it.

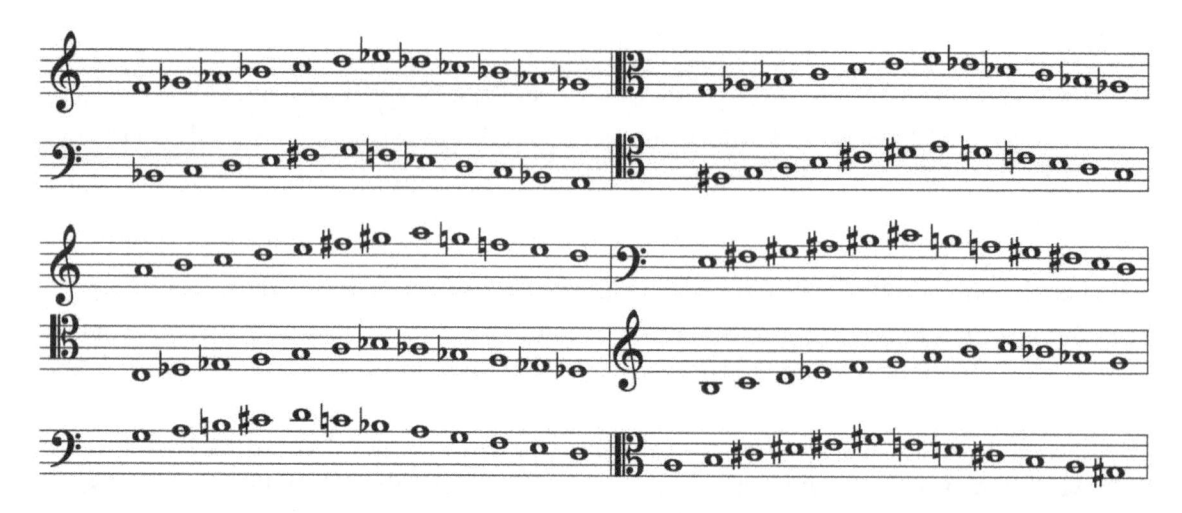

§ Practice singing major and the melodic minor scales using your preferred solfege syllables.

6. Other Minor Scales

The Harmonic Minor Scale

The c minor version of the harmonic minor scale is structured like this:

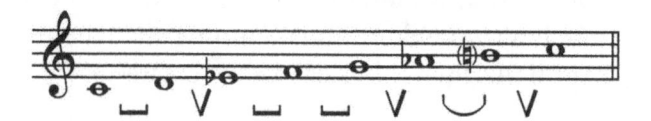

EXAMPLE 2.53   A c harmonic minor scale. Harmonic minor uses M2s, m2s, and an A2 (⌣).

The sequence of intervals is M2, m2, M2, M2, m2, *A2*, m2 ascending and the reverse descending. Like all minor scales, the interval between the starting pitch and the pitch a third above is a m3. The harmonic minor scale has a distinctive sound created by the presence of three m2 intervals (between the second and third pitches, between the fifth and sixth pitches, and between the seventh and eighth pitches) and an augmented second (A2) between the sixth and seventh pitches. (All references are to the ascending order of the scale.)

The harmonic minor scale is traditionally not used as a scale for melodies in Western music. The harmonic minor scale is much like a statistic in that it is the collection of those pitches most often used to harmonize a minor melody.

To construct a harmonic minor scale on a given pitch, it is necessary only to replicate the above interval pattern beginning with the given pitch. Thus, an e harmonic minor scale would be E, F-sharp, G, A, B, C, D-sharp, and E. This has the required sequence of intervals: M2, m2, M2, M2, m2, A2, m2.

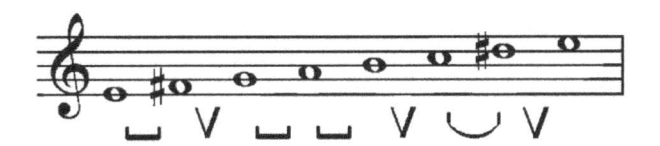

EXAMPLE 2.54 The e harmonic minor scale.

To create a harmonic minor scale starting from a major scale, you must lower both the third and the sixth pitches. Thus, starting with a B-flat Major scale, you get the following:

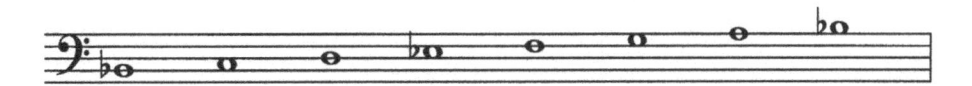

EXAMPLE 2.55 The B-flat Major scale.

As a first step, the third pitch, D, is lowered to D-flat. Then the sixth pitch, G, is lowered to G-flat. This produces a b-flat harmonic minor scale, which consists of B-flat, C, D-flat, E-flat, F, G-flat, A, and B-flat again, possessing the ascending interval sequence of M2, m2, M2, M2, m2, A2, and m2.

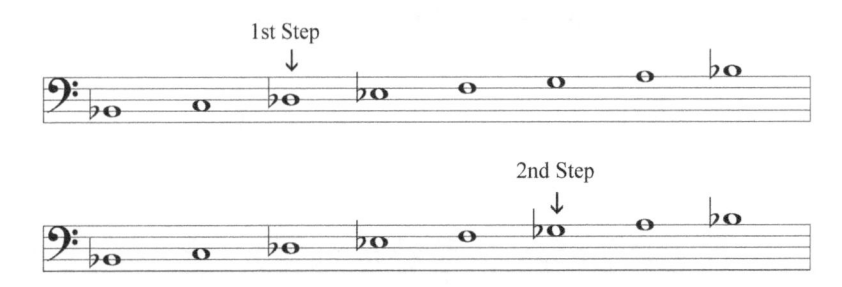

EXAMPLE 2.56 Transforming the B-flat Major scale into the b-flat harmonic minor scale. Step one (top staff), lower the third pitch to D-flat. Step two (lower staff), lower the sixth pitch to G-flat. This produces the harmonic minor scale with three minor seconds, three major seconds, and one augmented second.

Review

- The harmonic minor scale is composed of those pitches most often found in the chords that accompany Western music in the minor modality.
- The intervallic sequence found in the ascending harmonic minor scale is M2, m2, M2, M2, m2, A2, m2.
- The unique sound of the harmonic minor scale comes from the A2 interval between the sixth and seventh pitches above the starting pitch.
- One rarely finds the harmonic minor scale used in the melodic lines in common practice era music.
- The pitch content for the descending form of the harmonic minor scale is identical to the pitch content of the ascending form.

Related Exercises

§ Assuming that each of the following incomplete scales starts on the correct tonic, add the necessary accidentals to convert each example into a harmonic minor scale.

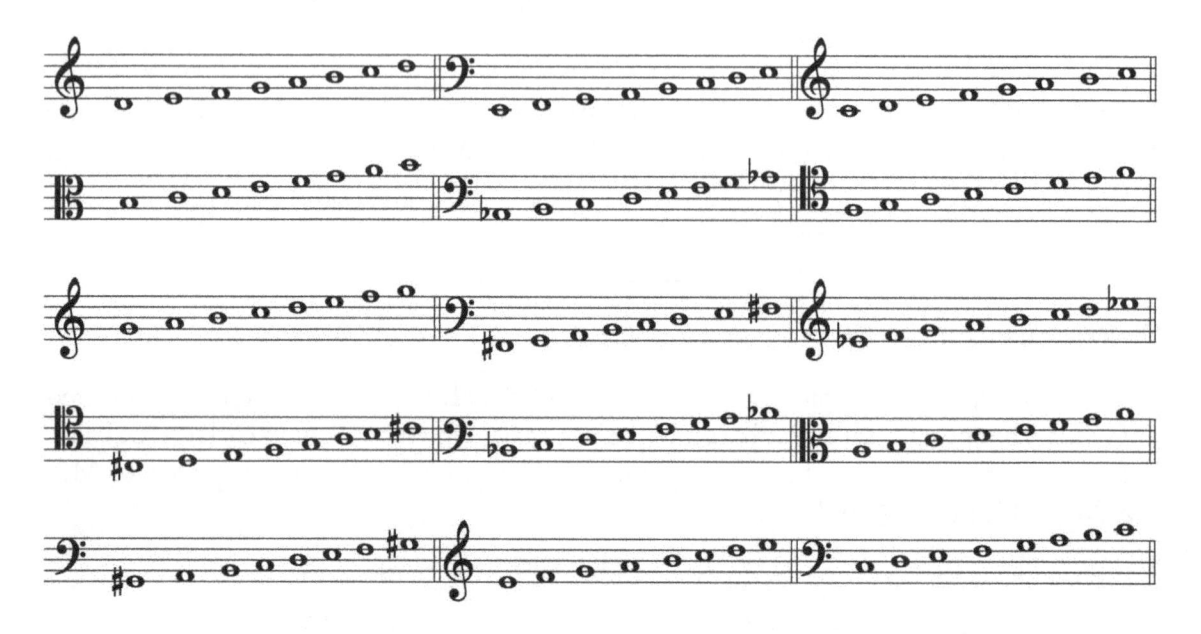

§ Using the given tonic, write the major, melodic minor, and harmonic minor scales on the staves provided.

§ Examine each of the following melodic fragments and determine whether the example is major, melodic minor, or harmonic minor. Circle the **tonic** in each example.

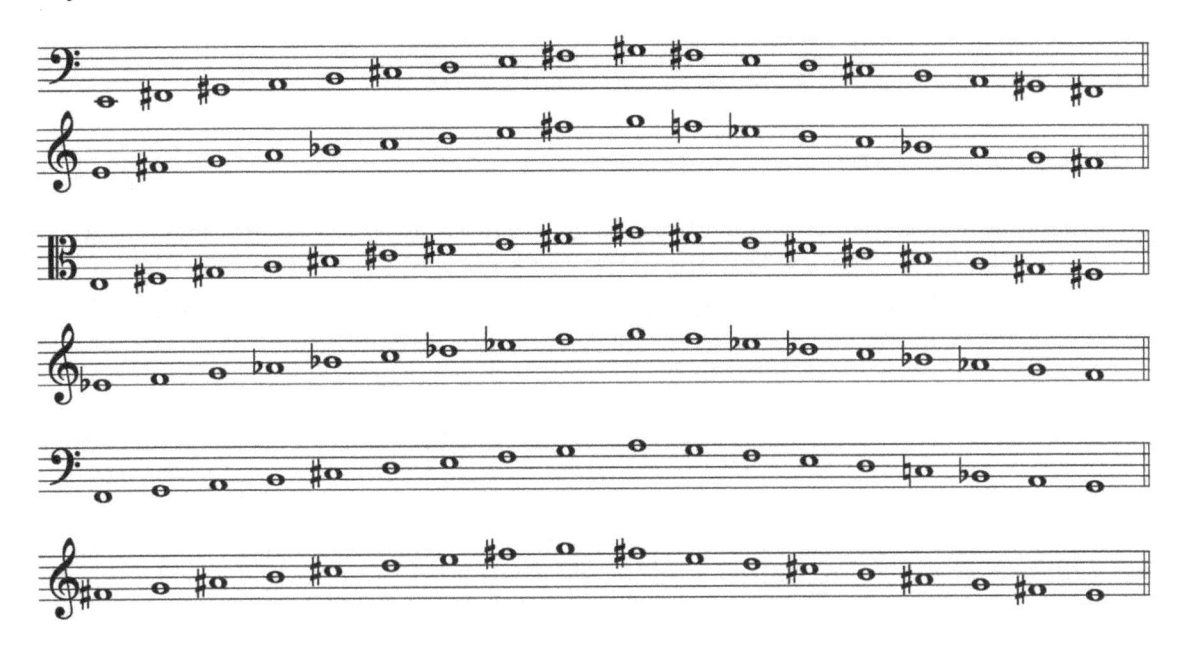

The Natural Minor Scale

The c minor version of the natural minor scale is structured like this:

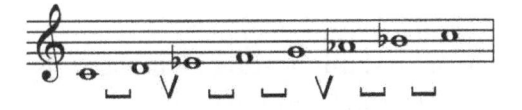

EXAMPLE 2.57 A natural minor scale starting on C.

This creates the ascending sequence of intervals M2, m2, M2, M2, m2, M2, M2.

A natural minor scale starting on G would be G, A, B-flat, C, D, E-flat, F, and G and is obtained simply by following the same interval pattern.

EXAMPLE 2.58 The natural minor scale starting on G.

To create a natural minor scale from a major scale, simply lower the third, sixth, and seventh pitches of the major scale.

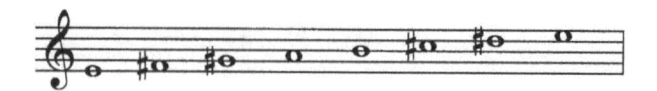

EXAMPLE 2.59   The E Major scale.

Thus, a natural minor scale built from an E Major scale (E, F-sharp, G-sharp, A, B, C-sharp, D-sharp, and E) would consist of E, F-sharp, *G-natural* (lowered from G-sharp), A, B, *C-natural* (lowered from C-sharp), *D-natural* (lowered from D-sharp), and E.

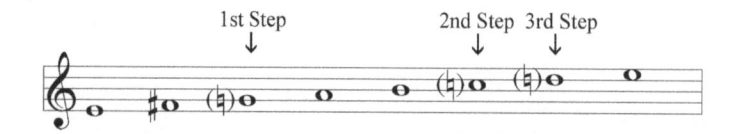

EXAMPLE 2.60   The natural minor scale starting on E. Notes preceded by naturals in parentheses are the pitches that had to be lowered to convert an E Major scale to an e minor scale.

Review

- The ascending intervallic sequence of the natural minor scale is M2, m2, M2, M2, m2, M2, and M2.
- Natural minor can also be created by lowering the third, sixth, and seventh pitches of the ascending major scale.
- The pitch content of the natural minor scale is the same ascending and descending.
- All minor scales use all seven pitch letter names.

Related Exercises

§ Using each of the given pitches as tonic, write out the natural minor scale.

7. Key Signatures for Minor Keys

As with major keys, key signatures are used to minimize the use of accidentals in minor keys. The same fifteen key signatures used for major keys are also employed for minor keys, but the relationship between the key signature and the name of the scale is different.

The practice is to use the set of pitches employed in the natural minor scale as the key signature for the minor key. Here is an example:

C Minor

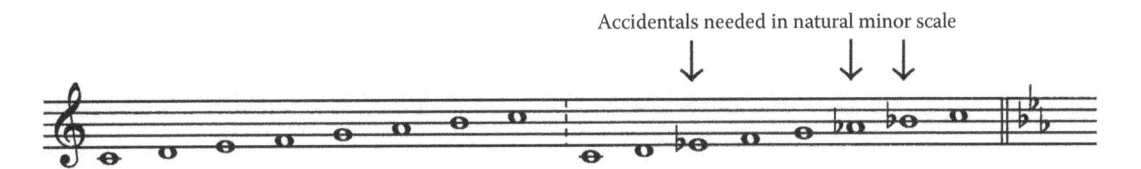

EXAMPLE 2.61   From left to right, the C Major scale; the c minor scale with accidentals; and the correct key signature (taken from the accidentals needed to convert major to natural minor).

This scale uses an E-flat, A-flat, and a B-flat. Therefore, the key signature would be three flats and is identical to the key signature used for E-flat Major.

This reveals an important point: To identify the name of a key based on the given key signature, it is first necessary to determine the modality of the music (i.e. is it a major or minor key?). Using notation, the modality can be determined only if pitches are provided. (By ear, the determination is usually easier.)

When a key signature is shown without music, remember that it could be indicating either a major key or a minor key. In the case above, the three flats indicate either c minor *or* E-flat Major. Without actual music, it's not possible to determine which modality is intended.

In the same manner, the key signature for e minor can be shown to be a single sharp (F-sharp) and is, therefore, identical to the key signature for G Major.

EXAMPLE 2.62   The G Major scale and the e melodic minor scale use the same key signature. (Because of the key signature, the accidentals in parentheses are not required but are shown here as reminders.)

In *all cases*, the minor key represented by a key signature is a minor third below the major key represented by the same key signature.

Here are all of the major and minor key signatures commonly used in Western music. The whole note identifies the pitch for which the major scale is named while the quarter note head represents the pitch that names the minor scale.

All Major and Minor Key Signatures that use sharps

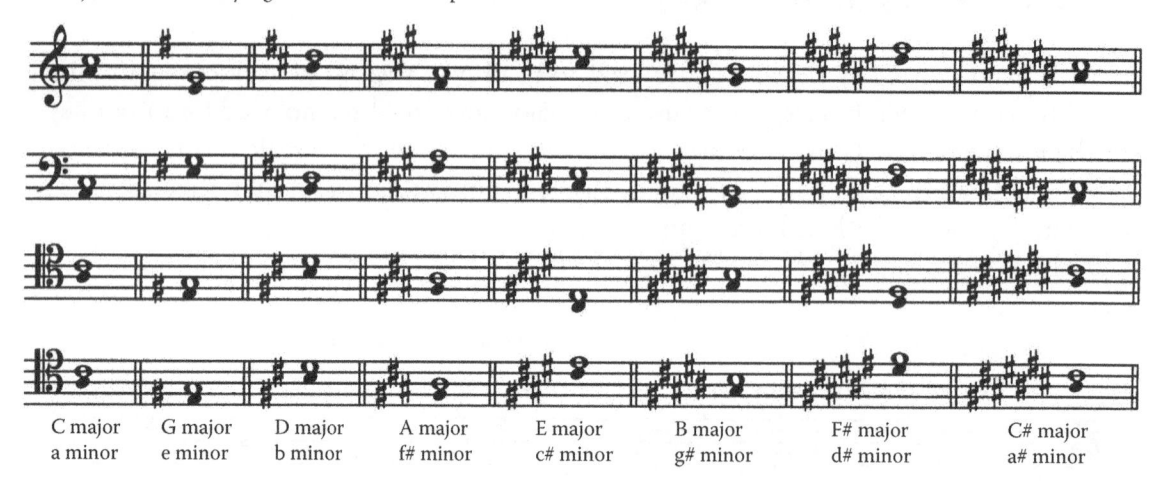

| C major | G major | D major | A major | E major | B major | F# major | C# major |
| a minor | e minor | b minor | f# minor | c# minor | g# minor | d# minor | a# minor |

All Major and Minor Key Signatures that use flats

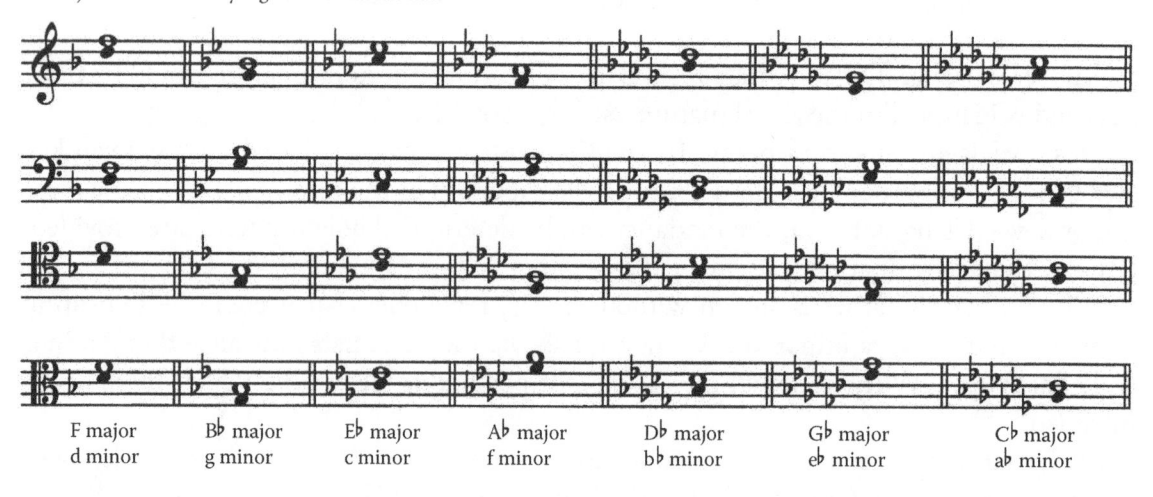

| F major | B♭ major | E♭ major | A♭ major | D♭ major | G♭ major | C♭ major |
| d minor | g minor | c minor | f minor | b♭ minor | e♭ minor | a♭ minor |

EXAMPLE 2.63 All of the key signatures in all four clefs showing the major tonality (represented by whole notes) and the minor tonality (represented by quarter note heads).

Having memorized all of the major key signatures, the reader is now encouraged to memorize all of the minor key signatures.

Review

- The key signature for any minor key is reflected in the pitch content of descending melodic minor or of the natural minor scale.
- The same fifteen key signatures found in major are also used in minor.

- To determine the name of the minor key indicated by a key signature, find the pitch that is a minor third below the major key associated with the same key signature.
- Another way to identify the name of the minor key indicated by a key signature composed of flats is to find the pitch a major third above the last flat.
- Another way to identify the name of the minor key indicated by a key signature composed of sharps is to find the pitch a major second below the last sharp.

Related Exercises

§ On the staves provided, write the specified key signatures.

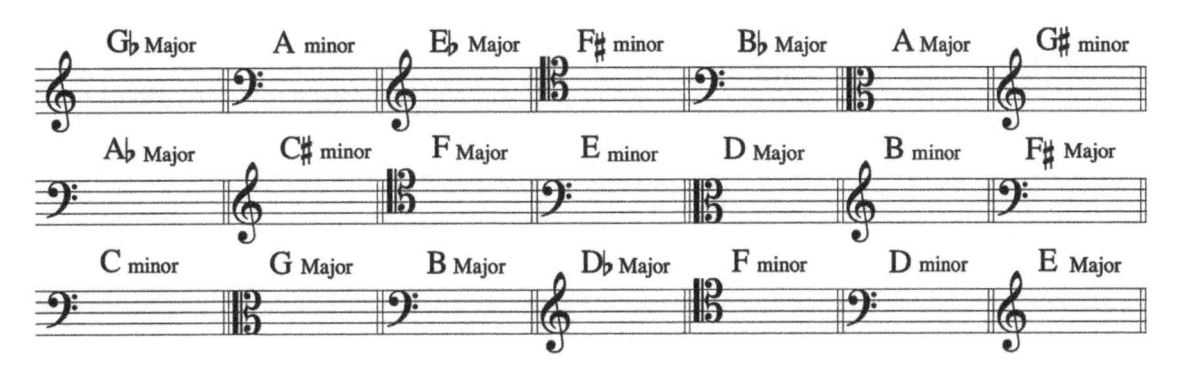

Using Key Signatures

You may have noticed that writing a major scale when you know the correct key signature is a fairly trivial task. Simply place the key signature on the staff and draw a series of ascending or descending pitches.

EXAMPLE 2.64 Drawing a G-flat Major scale. On the left, the correct key signature. On the right, the key signature with a series of ascending pitches starting on the G (flat) line producing a correct G-flat Major scale.

Drawing a natural minor scale is equally simple.

EXAMPLE 2.65 The correct key signature for d minor and the d natural minor scale.

Associating Major and Minor Keys

Major and minor scales that have the *same key signature* are said to be **relative** to one another. Thus, C Major is the relative major to a minor, and c minor is the relative minor to E-flat Major. And, of course, the reverse is true: a minor is the relative minor to C Major, and E-flat Major is the relative major to c minor.

However, you can also form a minor scale by altering a major scale (lowering the third pitch and, as needed, the sixth and seventh pitches). When you do this, you produce a minor scale with the ***same tonic*** as the original major scale. When a major and minor scale possess the same tonic, the two scales are said to be **parallel**. Thus, C Major is parallel to c minor, and f minor is parallel to F major.

EXAMPLE 2.66 Top, two scales relative to one another. On the left, A Major; on the right, f# minor. Bottom, two scales parallel to one another. On the left, E Major; on the right, e minor.

To determine the key signature of a minor key, when starting from its parallel major, you simply add three flats to (or take three sharps away from) the major key signature. In several situations, the alteration involves a combination of adding flats and removing sharps, as in forming d minor (one flat) from D Major (two sharps).

Using both relative majors and minors and parallel majors and minors, composers are able to move easily through various keys and modalities within a composition.

Review

- Major and minor keys are said to be relative to one another when both share the same key signature.
- Major and minor keys are said to be parallel to one another when both are named for the same pitch.
- A minor key will always have a key signature with the equivalent of three more flats than its parallel major.

Related Exercises

§ On the staves, key signatures are provided. Mark the major tonic with a o; the minor tonic with a •.

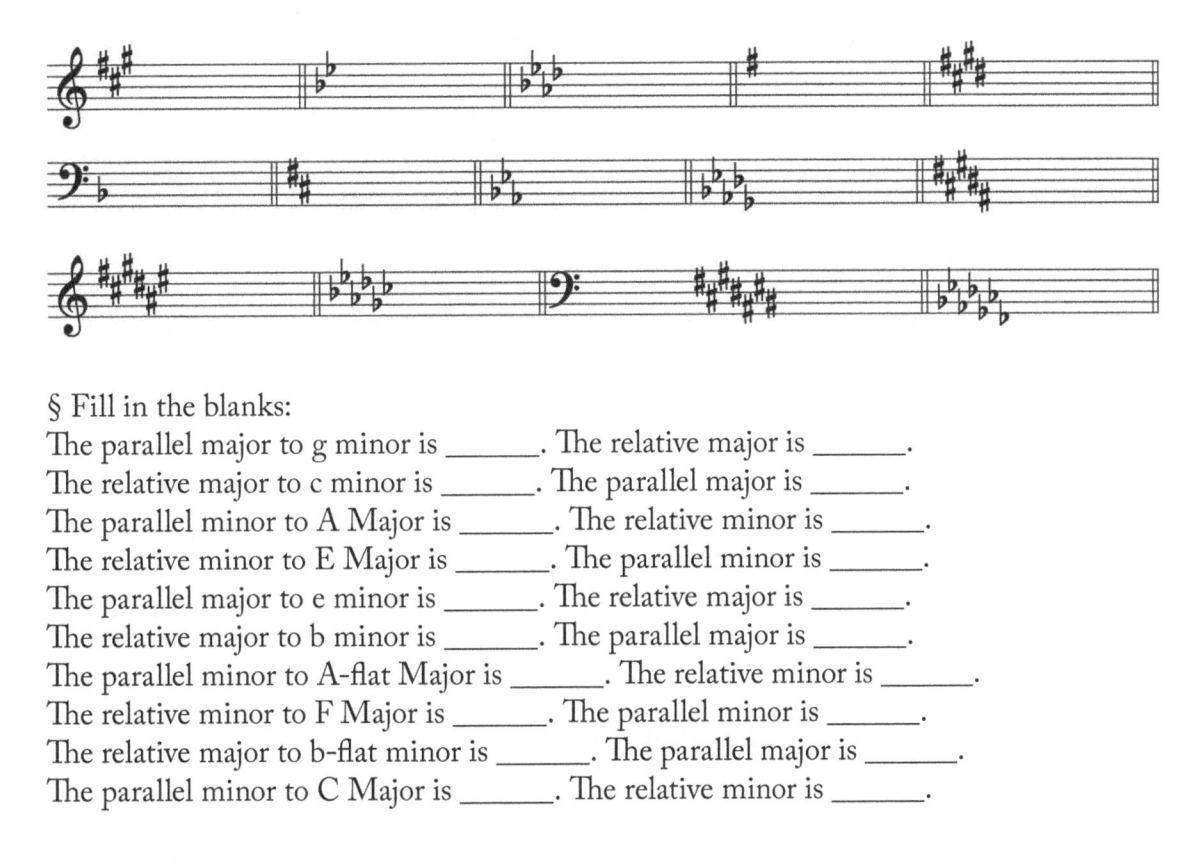

§ Fill in the blanks:
The parallel major to g minor is _____. The relative major is _____.
The relative major to c minor is _____. The parallel major is _____.
The parallel minor to A Major is _____. The relative minor is _____.
The relative minor to E Major is _____. The parallel minor is _____.
The parallel major to e minor is _____. The relative major is _____.
The relative major to b minor is _____. The parallel major is _____.
The parallel minor to A-flat Major is _____. The relative minor is _____.
The relative minor to F Major is _____. The parallel minor is _____.
The relative major to b-flat minor is _____. The parallel major is _____.
The parallel minor to C Major is _____. The relative minor is _____.

Using Accidentals

A major or a natural minor scale is easily constructed by selecting the correct key signature and writing in the pitches that belong to that scale. But constructing either a harmonic or melodic minor scale starting with a key signature also requires the use of accidentals. Here are examples.

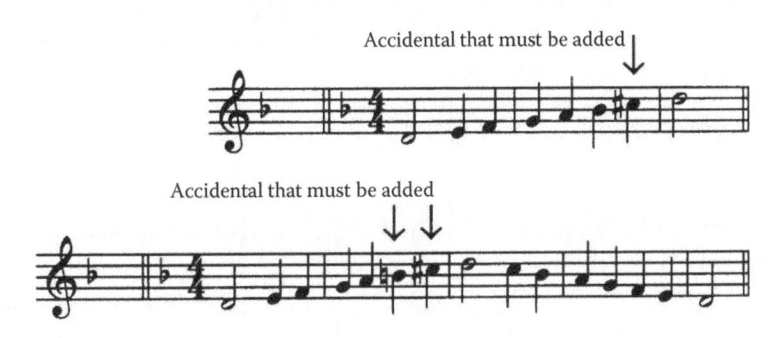

EXAMPLE 2.67 Top, the key signature for d minor used to draw the harmonic form of the scale. Bottom, the same key signature used to draw the melodic minor scale.

Notice the top illustration in Example 2.67. In the harmonic minor scale, an accidental had to be introduced in the second measure of the scale to indicate the C-sharp required to produce the harmonic form. In the lower example, the B-natural and C-sharp both had to be placed in the second measure to raise the sixth and seventh notes. Nothing needed to be done in the next measure to remove the accidentals due to the rules governing accidentals,

> Accidentals are added or removed as needed by placing sharps, flats, double sharps, double flats, or natural signs before any pitch, thereby temporarily negating the effect of the key signature. This alteration of the default pitch content applies *only* to the *specific pitch in the specific octave* where it is used, and any such changes last only until the next bar line, or until removed by the use of a different accidental.

At the bar line, all accidentals are canceled, and the default (the key signature) is reinstated. That is what happened at the end of the second measure in the melodic minor scale above.

An exception is found in the case of *tied notes,* where a pitch in the following bar is tied to an altered pitch in the preceding bar. In this situation, the tied pitch, too, is altered.

Courtesy accidentals may be used to clarify the notation and *should be used in any context in which the usage may be misunderstood.* Below are four passages that use accidentals. Each usage is correctly notated, but each of the upper examples carries the risk of being (easily) misread. The lower examples are improved through the use of courtesy accidentals (reminders) as shown.

EXAMPLE 2.68   Various use of accidentals. Top left, the bar line cancels the F-natural so the first pitch in measure 2 must be F-sharp. Top middle, the C-sharp ties across the bar line, but the second beat of measure 2 is a C-natural. Top right, the low B-flat has no effect on the upper B, which remains a B-natural. On the lower staff, the courtesy accidentals remind the performer of the correct pitch to be performed. At the far right, the B-natural clarifies that the writer did not "accidentally" omit a B-flat. (If the upper B were to be flatted, a flat would have had to be placed before it.)

Review

- Accidentals are in effect only during the bar in which they appear.
- Bar lines cancel all accidentals.
- Accidentals apply only to pitches in the octave in which they are introduced.
- An accidental attached to a pitch that is tied into the next measure alters both the original pitch and all pitches to which it is tied. When the tie ends, the accidental is canceled.

Melody: Note Following Note

Related Exercises

§ Using accidentals as needed, write the specified scales (ascending and descending) on the staves provided and within the designated key signatures. (Remember the rules for the use of accidentals.) The key signatures given may not be correct for the requested scale (or even close to correct). Start on the tonic, and use four quarter notes per measure and a half note for the final pitch in the descending scale.

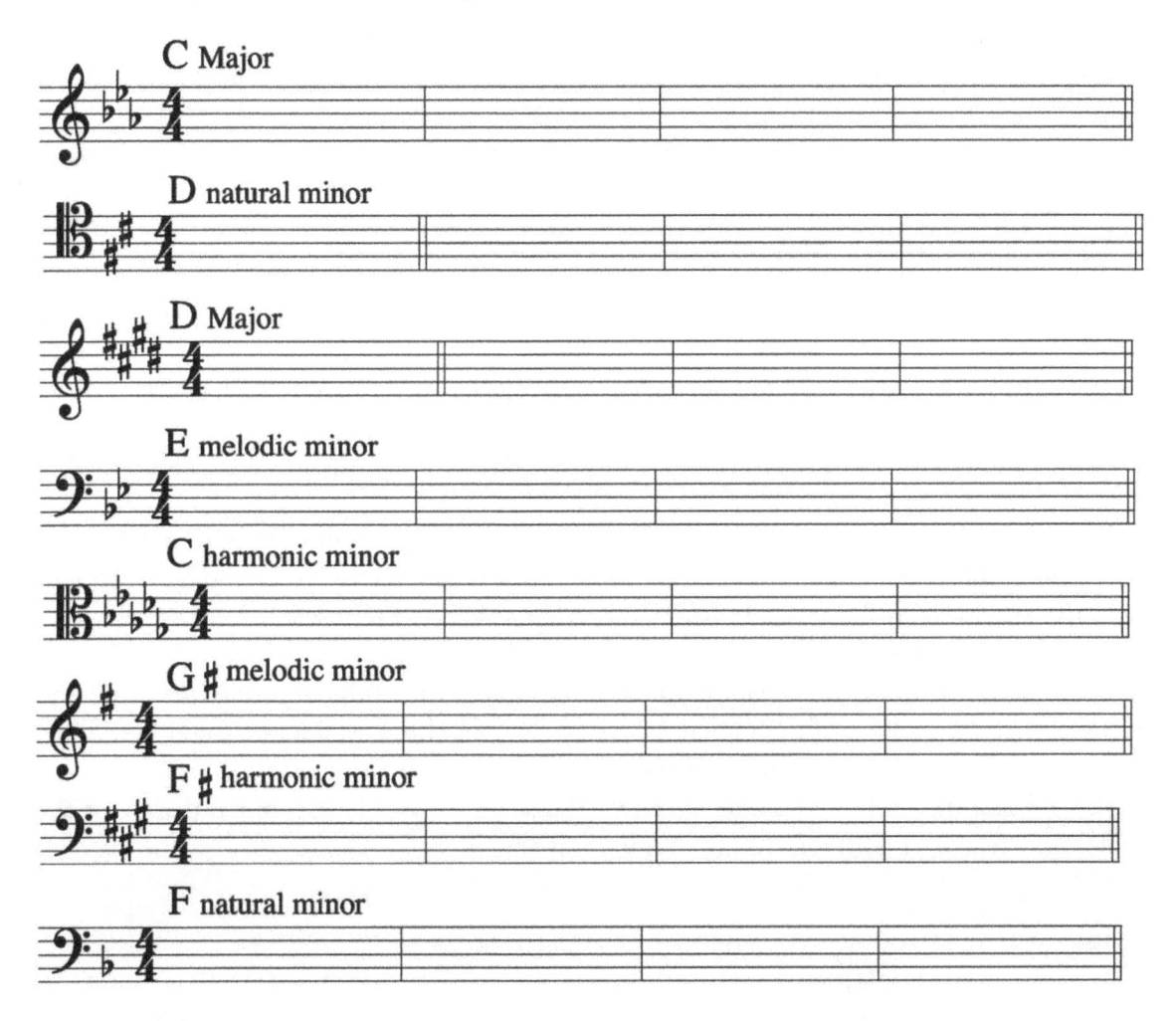

C Major

D natural minor

D Major

E melodic minor

C harmonic minor

G♯ melodic minor

F♯ harmonic minor

F natural minor

8. Scale Degrees

Identifying a pitch within a scale is cumbersome if you have to say "the fourth pitch of the ascending form of the *X* Major scale." You can avoid this wordiness and eliminate confusion by using the convention of ***scale degrees***.

Thus, within an ascending major or minor scale, the starting pitch (the pitch that gives the scale its name) is identified as the first degree of the scale.

- This may be written as 1st, 1° or $\hat{1}$ depending on the reader's (or theorist's) preference.
- By the same process, the second pitch of the ascending scale is called the second degree of the scale, or 2° or $\hat{2}$.

The process continues with the upper note of the scale being called either the eighth degree or the first degree, whichever (in context) proves to be more convenient.

By using the degree of the scale to identify a pitch, it becomes unnecessary to add the explanation "in the ascending form of the scale" or "in the descending form of the scale" to the description. Ascending is the specified direction from which scale degrees are defined.

EXAMPLE 2.69 The A Major scale with each pitch identified by scale degree using both of the usual notations.

Each scale degree has a name, too. Frequently, the name is more clearly understood—especially in oral communication—than the degree.

The first degree of the scale is called the ***tonic***. (This comes from the same root as ***tonal*** and ***tonality***.) It is the modern equivalent of the ancient modal final. The tonic is the pitch that gives its name to the scale. Thus, in an A Major or an a minor scale, A is the tonic and first degree of the scale.

A P5 *above* the tonic is the ***dominant***. The dominant is the fifth degree of the scale and is the modern equivalent of the modal recitation tone. In the A Major or the a minor scale, E is the dominant, the fifth degree of the scale.

A P5 *below* the tonic is the ***subdominant***. The subdominant is the fourth degree of the scale; in A Major or a minor, the subdominant is the pitch D.

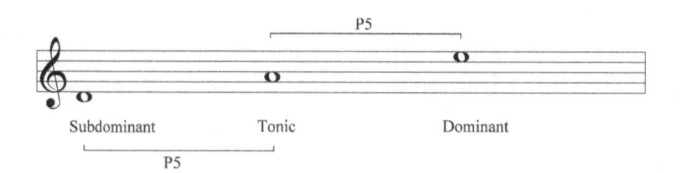

EXAMPLE 2.70 From left to right, the subdominant, tonic, and dominant pitches in A Major and a minor.

Halfway between the tonic and the dominant is the third degree of the scale. This scale degree is called the ***mediant***. In an A Major scale, this is the pitch C-sharp. In a minor, the mediant is C-natural. The selection of the mediant pitch determines the *modality* of a scale. The term *mediant* is from the Latin for "middle."

Halfway between the tonic and the subdominant (i.e. below the tonic) is the **submediant**. In an A Major scale, this would be the pitch F-sharp. In the a harmonic minor scale and in a natural minor and the descending form of the a melodic minor scale, it would be an F-natural. In an ascending a melodic minor scale, it would be F-sharp. Thus, the choice of the submediant pitch contributes to determining the *quality* of the minor scale created.

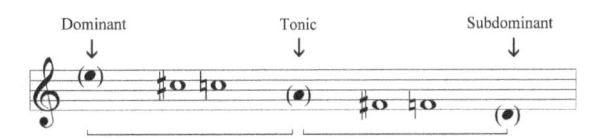

EXAMPLE 2.71 From the left to right, the mediant in A Major, the mediant in a minor, the submediant in A Major and a melodic minor (ascending), and, finally, the submediant in the natural minor, harmonic minor, and the descending form of a melodic minor scales.

The second degree of the scale is called the **supertonic**. In an A Major or an a minor scale, this would be the pitch B. (Note that the prefixes *super-* and *sub-* are from the Latin for "above" and "below," respectively.)

The remaining scale degree, the seventh, is called the **leading tone**. This comes from the effect it creates when you listen to ascending major, harmonic minor, or melodic minor scales. (Play an ascending major scale and stop on the seventh degree. It probably sounds incomplete, unfinished. It sounds as though this seventh degree pitch needs to *lead* back to the tonic. This strong tendency has given the seventh degree its practical and functional name.) In an A Major and an a minor (melodic ascending or harmonic) scale, the leading tone is G-sharp.

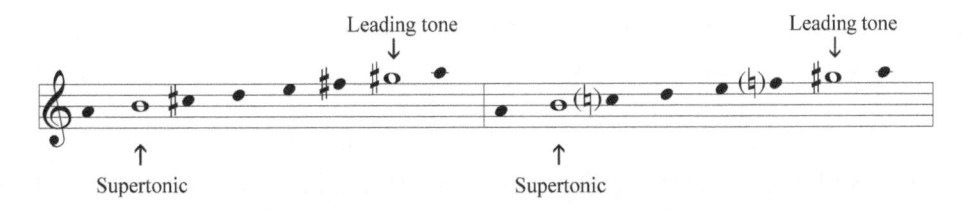

EXAMPLE 2.72 The supertonic and the leading tone in the A Major scale (on the left) and in the a melodic minor (ascending) scale (on the right). The leading tone is also the seventh degree of the harmonic minor scale.

In the natural minor and descending melodic minor scales, the seventh degree is not the leading tone but rather a lowered seventh degree or (less logically) a lowered leading tone. Although this pitch has no generally accepted name, some call it the **subtonic**.

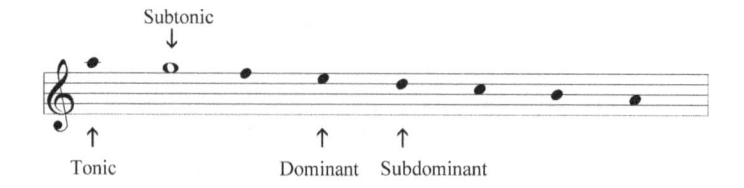

[Musical staff showing scale with labels: Subtonic (↓), Tonic (↑), Dominant (↑), Subdominant (↑)]

EXAMPLE 2.73 The subtonic (the seventh scale degree) in the natural minor and the descending melodic minor scales. Not all musicians use this term.

Although sometimes used to represent the degrees of the scale, Roman numerals are more commonly associated with chords as discussed in Part 3 of this book.

Many musicians use solfege syllables instead of (or in addition to) the names given above. Here is a chart showing these various equivalents. (Note: Roman numerals in parentheses represent the minor or lowered form of the scale degree; the brackets indicate that this symbolic representation is not universally used or understood.)

Symbol 1	Symbol 2	Name	Functional Name	Solfege/Major (Movable *do*)	Solfege/Minor (Movable *do*)	Function
1°	$\hat{1}$	first degree	tonic	do	do	I
2°	$\hat{2}$	second degree	supertonic	re	re	II
3°	$\hat{3}$	third degree	mediant	mi	me	III (♭III)
4°	$\hat{4}$	fourth degree	subdominant	fa	fa	IV
5°	$\hat{5}$	fifth degree	dominant	sol	sol	V
6°	$\hat{6}$	sixth degree	submediant	la	la (le)	VI (♭VI)
7°	$\hat{7}$	seventh degree	leading tone	ti	ti	VII
[♭7°]	$\hat{7}$	lowered or flatted seventh degree	(subtonic)	(te)	te	♭VII

EXAMPLE 2.74 Various means of identifying the degrees of the scale.

Review

- The protocol for the determination of scale degrees is based on the ascending scale.
- The first degree of the scale gives its name to the scale and key; it is called the tonic.
- The other degrees of the scale are numbered in sequence from the first degree.
- The second scale degree is called the supertonic.
- The third scale degree is called the mediant.
- The fourth scale degree is called the subdominant.
- The fifth scale degree is called the dominant.
- The sixth scale degree is called the submediant.

- The seventh scale degree is called the leading tone.
- The lowered seventh degree, found in descending melodic minor and natural minor, is sometimes referred to as the subtonic.

Related Exercises

§ Fill in the blanks so that the following statements are true.
In _____, F is the dominant.
In A Major, G-sharp is _____.
In g minor, _____ is the mediant.
In _____, E-flat is the subdominant.
In F Major, D is _____.
In D-flat Major, _____ is the supertonic.
In _____, B is the submediant.
In e minor, F-sharp is _____.
In C-sharp Major, _____ is the leading tone.
In _____, A is the leading tone.
In a minor, C is _____.
In G-flat Major, _____ is the subdominant.
In D Major, E is the _____ degree of the scale.
In B-flat Major, the second degree of the scale is _____.
In g minor, E is the _____ degree of the scale.
In c minor, the fourth degree of the scale is _____.
In E Major, C-sharp is the _____ degree of the scale.
In g-sharp minor, the seventh degree of the scale is _____.
In C-flat Major, A-flat is the _____ degree of the scale.
In f-sharp minor, the fifth degree of the scale is _____.

The Chromatic Scale

A scale or scale fragment that contains all successive semitones is called a chromatic scale. When written ascending and descending, it looks as shown below in Example 2.76.

> Chromatic refers to pitches not a part of the key. Thus, in G Major, F-sharp is not a chromatic pitch, but A-flat would be as would G-sharp and F-natural.

EXAMPLE 2.75 A chromatic scale from C to C.

When ascending, the chromatic scale is written with sharps; when descending, it is written with flats. When a chromatic passage is written within a key signature, the same conventions are used, but the key signature is given priority. In Example 2.76, the correct way of notating an ascending chromatic passage in a flat key is shown as is the correct way to notate a descending chromatic passage in a sharp key.

EXAMPLE 2.76 On the left, an ascending chromatic passage in E-flat Major. On the right, a descending chromatic passage in A Major. Each example shows the correct mix of accidentals both from the key signature (notated in parentheses because normally these would not be written in) and from the nature of the chromatic inflections (not in parentheses because these accidentals *must* be written in).

Tonal and Modal Scale Degrees

The tonic, subdominant, and dominant degrees of the scale are identical in both a major scale and in its parallel minor scale. In fact, if the music being performed did not use the mediant, submediant, or leading tone, it would not be possible for a listener to determine whether the piece was in a major or a minor modality. For this reason, the tonic, subdominant, and dominant pitches have often been identified as being ***tonal scale degrees***—those pitches that clearly establish in the listener's ear the tonic or tonal center of the music.

EXAMPLE 2.77 The D Major and d minor scales showing the tonal scale degrees represented with whole notes.

In contrast, the mediant, submediant, and leading tone are scale degrees that differ in the major modality from the minor modality and are, therefore, the pitches that enable the listener to identify the modality of the music. For this reason, these pitches have been identified as ***modal scale degrees***.

EXAMPLE 2.78 The D Major and d minor scales showing the modal scale degrees represented here with double whole notes.

The supertonic has some characteristics of both and for that reason may be heard as either a tonal scale degree or a modal scale degree.

Melodic Tendencies

As pointed out before, if you play an ascending major scale and stop on the leading tone, it is immediately clear that the scale seems incomplete. The need for closure is satisfied only by finishing the scale on the tonic.

Other scale degrees also imply motion to another pitch. Reverse the above experiment by playing a descending scale and stopping on the supertonic. Now the wish is to hear the descent to the tonic completed.

EXAMPLE 2.79   Shown in the key of G Major, the most obvious implied motion suggested by the leading tone, on the left, and the supertonic, on the right.

When performing a melody that is clearly in a key, stopping on the dominant causes the melodic journey to seem incomplete. However, leaping to the tonic (either up or down) or moving to either the upper or lower tonic (via some conjunct or disjunct path from the dominant) seems to satisfy most listeners.

EXAMPLE 2.80   Still in G Major, four possible paths to resolving the tension created by a melody that stops on the dominant. From left to right: upward leap to tonic; downward leap to tonic; upward conjunct motion to tonic; downward conjunct motion to tonic.

Other tendencies are both more subtle and less universally accepted. For example, in a major key, stopping the melodic line on the subdominant, after clearly establishing the tonality, often sets up a minor "discomfort" that can be eased (at least temporarily) by moving down to the mediant.

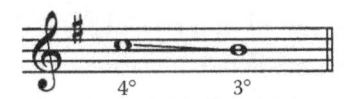

EXAMPLE 2.81   The subdominant (especially in major keys) tends to proceed downward to the mediant.

The tendency of the submediant in major and natural or descending melodic minor seems to be to go to the dominant. The tendency of the submediant in major and ascending *melodic* minor should be to continue to the tonic through the leading tone but is ambiguous enough even to seem directionless.

The mediant in major keys often offers a sense of stability second only to the tonic. In minor keys, the mediant seems, perhaps, a little less stable than its major equivalent. If it does have a tendency, it would be to descend to the tonic through the supertonic (or to be replaced with the major mediant).

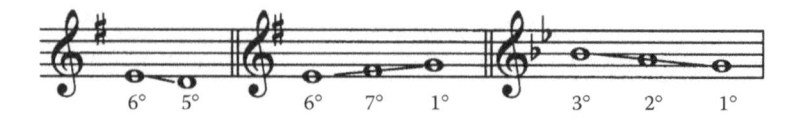

EXAMPLE 2.82 From left to right: submediant to dominant in major and descending melodic minor; submediant to leading tone to tonic in major (and ascending melodic minor); the minor mediant descending through supertonic to the tonic.

Active Tones

Many theorists describe the pitches of a major or minor scale—other than tonic, mediant, and dominant—as active tones. This terminology calls attention to the fact that, as melodies progress, a greater sense of stability is found when the tonic, mediant, and, to some extent, the dominant serve as points of repose.

In minor keys, the mediant may seem a little less stable to some ears than the mediant in major keys does. When a melody hesitates on an active tone, the listener is very aware of a need for additional motion on toward the tonic, dominant, or mediant.

Review

- Tonic, subdominant, and dominant, which are the same in parallel major and minor keys, may be considered tonal scale degrees because they establish tonality.
- The degrees of the scale that are altered between major and minor (mediant, submediant, and leading tone/subtonic) are modal because they contribute to the modality of the key.

> In minor keys, the supertonic is very slightly but perceptibly lower than in major keys. This property may partially account for the quasi-modal quality of the supertonic.

- The supertonic may be heard to function either as a tonal or a modal scale degree.
- The leading tone has a strong tendency to ascend to the tonic.
- The supertonic has a tendency to descend to the tonic.
- The dominant has a moderate tendency to leap up (or down) to tonic.
- The subdominant has a tendency, especially in major keys, to move down to the mediant.

- The mediant tends to move to the supertonic. But, especially in major keys, it also offers some stability.
- The submediant usually wants to descend to dominant. In ascending melodic minor, it often leads to the tonic through the leading tone.
- Active tones are all scale degrees *except* tonic, mediant, and dominant.

Related Exercises

§ Fill in the blanks.

The recitation tone in Hypophrygian mode is _____.

The leading tone gets it name from its tendency to return to _____.

The subdominant is a _____ degree of a scale.

The modal degrees of the scale are mediant, submediant, and _____.

The supertonic tends to go to _____.

The tonic, subdominant, and dominant are the same both in major and the _____ minor.

The _____ of the scale can function both as a tonal degree and a modal degree.

A minor scale and a major scale that have the same key signatures are said to be _____.

In what mode is B the recitation tone? _____

In Hypodorian mode, the final is _____, and the recitation tone is _____.

§ For each of the given key signatures below, identify the implied major key, **O**, and the implied minor key, **●**, and name the function of the given pitch in both the major key and the minor key. The first one is done as an example.

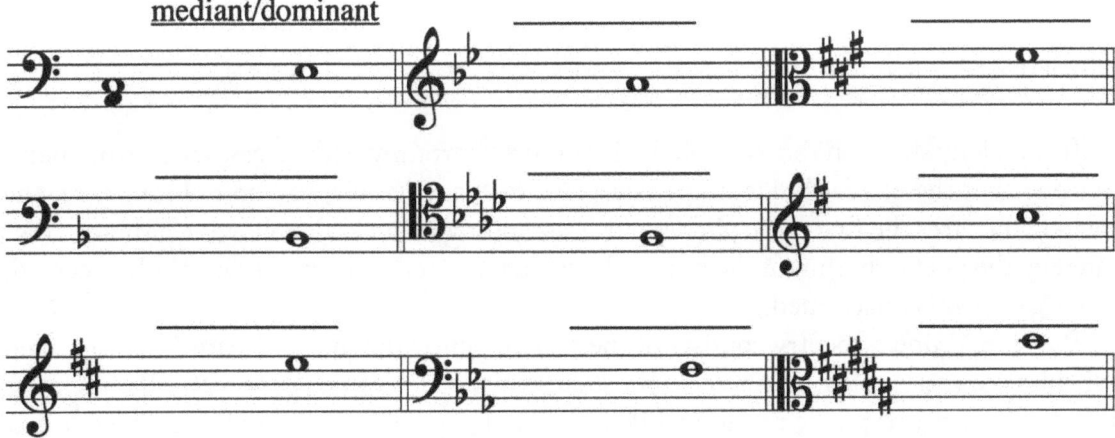

9. The Melodic Structure

One of the more compelling aspects of music is melody. In casual conversation, a melody is assumed to be more than merely a series of pitches, as may have been presented above, but is rather a combination of pitches and durations, dynamics, and articulation that give meaning to words or can suggest emotional, descriptive, or nostalgic images in sound.

An important characteristic of melody is the concept of **tonal goals**. A melody must be understood as not only a series of pitches but also as pitches *ordered* so as to *lead* the listener's ear to the various tonal centers. Dependent on the style and sophistication of the melody, the nature of the relationships among its tonal goals may be simple and apparent or obscure and complex.

All melodies possess structure: at the least, a beginning and an end. Between these critical points, one or more stops or temporary goals may lead, eventually, to the final goal. Even so, the discussion of the tendencies of scale degrees in the preceding section should not be seen as a prescription for writing melodies. Successful melodies need not follow the obvious paths.

To delve further into the nature of melodies, let us examine the very simple and familiar song "Row, Row, Row Your Boat."

EXAMPLE 2.83 "Row, Row, Row Your Boat," a familiar melody shown here in B-flat Major.

This melody starts on the tonic pitch. The tonic is certainly not a necessary starting point but one that the ear easily identifies as a place of tonal stability, a home. From here, the melody traverses the first three pitches of the ascending major scale following a rhythm dictated by the poetic rhythm of the lyric. (The words *row* and *boat* are all metrically accented. The word *your* is unaccented.)

The second line of poetry consists of the words "gently down the stream." The accented syllables are *gent-*, *down*, and *stream*. The unaccented syllables are *-ly* and *the*. The melody's rhythm reflects this poetic rhythm while the melody's pitch content continues more or less directly up the major scale.

Notice that the pitch D (*boat, gent-*, and *down*) is a sort of short pause along the melody's ascending path. The pitch F, which is the note on which the word *stream* falls also represents a pause but in this case longer. It is also halfway through the melody and represents the end of the first *phrase* of music. (A phrase is a musically coherent melodic line that concludes with a cadence.) This pitch, the dominant in the key of B-flat Major, is the first melodic goal of the piece.

> More details are found in Part 3, p. 170, and Part 4, p. 221.

The syllables *Mer-ri-ly, mer-ri-ly, mer-ri-ly, mer-ri-ly* are rhythmically strong-weak-weak, strong-weak-weak, etc., and each syllable is of equal duration. This characteristic (three pulses with equal lengths) translates into a triplet feeling with the first note in each group of three stressed. This portion of the melody begins on the upper tonic and leaps via the dominant and mediant to the lower tonic.

Although you might logically think that, because the melody has now returned to the tonic, there would be no need for additional material, we all know that this melody does not end here but rather with the words "life is but a dream." This last line has the accent pattern strong, weak, strong, weak, strong. And it provides a stepwise descent from the dominant to the tonic with the stable dominant, mediant, and tonic being stressed while the more active subdominant and supertonic are not. The portion of the melody from the upper tonic, on "merrily," to the final lower tonic, on "dream," is the song's second phrase.

The melody follows a pattern found in many melodies, even ones that are much more sophisticated and/or complex. This pattern is to begin with the sense of a stable tonal center (in this case, B-flat, the tonic), move away to another (perhaps) less stable pitch area (in this case F, the dominant), and then return to the initial tonality. As you listen, the melody seems to hesitate at certain places along this journey, most notably at the pitch area furthest from the tonic (i.e. the dominant in this case) and again at the end when the tonic returns.

These critical points of relative repose or hesitation are called **cadences** (from the Latin verb *cadare* meaning "to fall"). In "Row, Row, Row Your Boat," the first strong arrival and hesitation occurs on the word *stream*. Stopping at this point, the melody would seem incomplete or suspended. Because such a point of relative, but not final, repose is frequently found in the middle of simpler songs, this cadence (on *stream*) is called a **half cadence** or a **half close**. It might also be described as incomplete or unfinished.

> In the older modes, the cadence was almost always approached by a melodic line that descended (fell) stepwise to the final, hence the logical source for the term. In newer music, the approach need not be a descent and need not be stepwise.

The end of the melody, when the pitch sequence has completed its journey back to the tonic and the rhythm has again hesitated, makes our travels (in the tonal sense) seem to be completed. This last cadence, with its sense of return to final stability, is known as a **final cadence**, a **full cadence**, an **authentic cadence**, or as a **full close**.

As can be heard in this example, cadences function as the tonal goals toward which the various portions of a melody travel and (except for the final one) from which they eventually return. Thus, these cadence points form a tonal skeleton onto which the various details of the melody are attached.

Here is another melodic example:

EXAMPLE 2.84 "London Bridge Is Falling Down" in C Major.

In "London Bridge Is Falling Down," the melody begins on the dominant and does not reach the tonic until the last note in the song. Yet long before the tonic is reached, the listener can clearly hear that none of the preceding pitches sound final.

> Because this example is presented without harmony, we can only determine the cadential quality from the melodic pitch content.

The various parts of the melody do connect to significant tonal anchors as follows: "London Bridge is falling down" starts and ends on the dominant. The first *repetition* of "falling down" starts on the supertonic and ends on the subdominant. The second repetition of "falling down" is identical to the *initial statement* of "falling down" (i.e. beginning on the mediant and ending on the dominant). This arrival on the dominant also marks the first cadence. Because the cadential pitch is dominant, it is a half cadence.

The second half of the song begins just like the first half but ends with a new melodic pattern, not heard before, on the words "my fair lady." This last gesture begins on the supertonic and ends on the tonic producing a full cadence completing the melody.

More detailed information about cadences will be presented later when the effects of harmonic underpinnings and melodic complications are discussed. In the meantime, when listening to a melody, try to identify all the cadences and to mentally classify each as being either a half cadence or a complete cadence.

Review

- Melodies have beginning and ending tonal centers that may frequently, but certainly not necessarily, be the same.
- The ending pitch is almost always tonic.
- Between its beginning and end, a melody will usually have one or more tonal goals.
- Although any pitch may serve as a tonal goal, the most likely intermediate goal is the dominant.
- When a tonal goal is achieved, the forward motion of the line may be briefly interrupted.

Melody: Note Following Note   107

- Such a point of hesitation is called a cadence.
- The portion of a melody that ends with a cadence is called a phrase.
- When examining a melody by itself, one can observe that a cadence seems either incomplete (or unfinished) or complete (finished).
- An incomplete cadence is called a half cadence or a half close.
- A complete cadence is called an authentic cadence, a final cadence, a full cadence, or a full close.

Related Exercises

§ Study the following melody. What key is it in? Identify the four tonal goals within "America the Beautiful" and determine what sort of cadence each represents: authentic or half. (Suggestion: Play through the melody several times before answering.)

America the Beautiful — Samuel A. Ward

§ Here are five more melodies. For each, repeat the process you followed for "America the Beautiful": Identify the key, locate all the cadences, name the tonal goal, and, finally, name the type of cadence.

Abide with Me — William H. Monk

Sailing, Sailing — Godfrey Macks

Believe Me, If All Those Endearing Young Charms

Irish Air

My Bonnie

Traditional Song

Flow Gently, Sweet Afton

James E. Spilman

10. Expanded Melodic Sources

Western music, as it has been known for the past millennium or so, has been based on the modes and the major-minor system. Beginning in the nineteenth century, composers began looking for alternative pitch systems. Their searches led both to traditional music from around the world and to "invented" scales that offered alternative possibilities.

Scales Using Seven Pitches

Using exactly five whole tones and two semitones, a set of seven-note scales can be constructed, only a few of which are recognized as belonging to our modal and major-minor system.

> Note that this criterion *excludes* the harmonic minor scale.

Some of the scales below are used in the music of other cultures and traditions (to the extent that they are known, these are marked). Some other scales have particular names, which are also provided. The names for scales marked (P) were identified from the writings of Vincent Persichetti; those marked (S), from the writings of Dennis Sandole. Composers occasionally use scales, like those presented here, to create fresh sounds without moving too far away from the foundations of Western music.

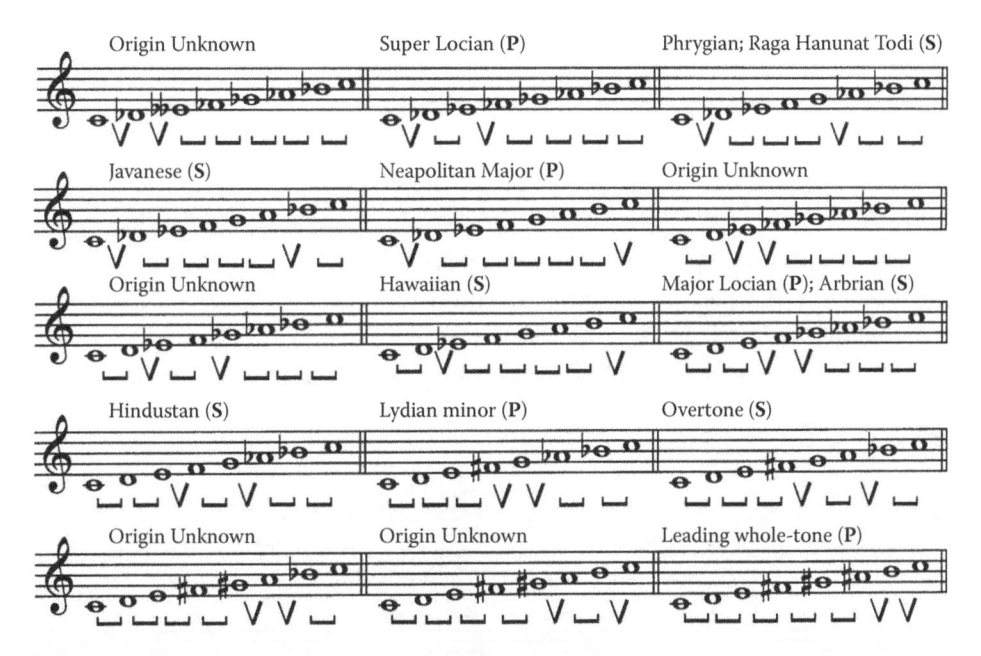

EXAMPLE 2.85 Seven-note scales that contain five whole tones and two semitones within one octave. As done earlier, semitones are indicated by V and whole tones by ⌐⌐.

The scales given above, all of which are notated as though the tonic were C, may be transposed to use any pitch as tonic. (The selection of C as tonic in Example 2.85 and in most of the following examples is intended to keep the presentation of the information consistent and clear.)

While Western musicians tend to take for granted the seven-note scale, other societies have long used scales containing varying numbers of pitches. These interesting scales are obviously constructed on different criteria. Among these are the nine following five-note (pentatonic) scales:

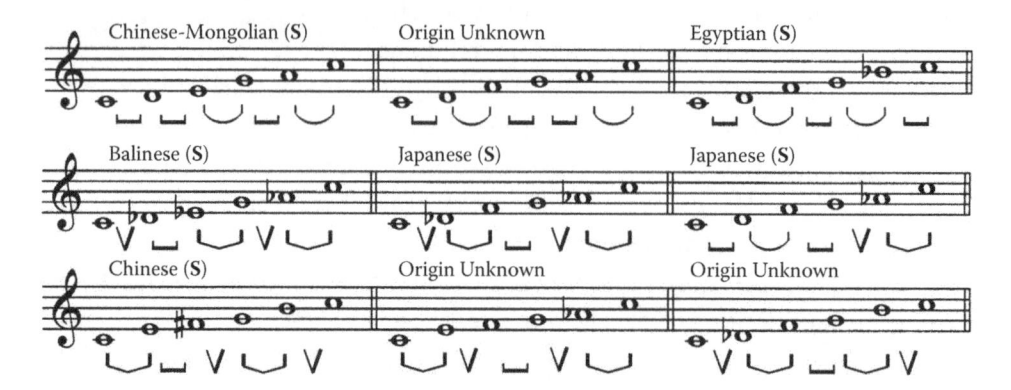

EXAMPLE 2.86 Nine different five-note (pentatonic) scales. Intervals marked ⌣ are three semitones (either a m3 or an A2) and those marked ⌐⌐ are two whole tones (M3).

Six-note scales have been used, too. For Western musicians, the more important of these are the whole tone scales used by Debussy and other impressionistic and post-impressionistic composers. Within our equal-tempered tuning system, the two possible whole tone scales are one including C and the other including C-sharp. Here are examples of four different six-note scales.

> The earliest known use of whole tone scales was by the Russian composer Mikhail Glinka (1804–1857), in his opera *Russlan and Ludmilla*.

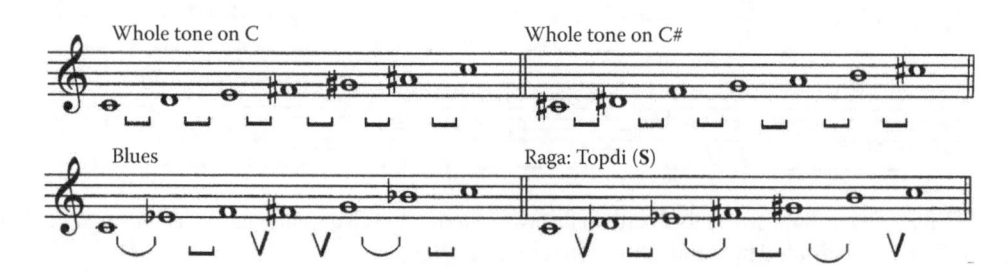

EXAMPLE 2.87 Four different six-note scales, including the two forms of the whole tone scale.

Below are nine different scales that use the familiar seven-notes per octave, but which are not limited to whole tones and semitones. Among these is a scale known as the Enigmatic scale (*scala enigmatica*) that was used by Italian opera composer Giuseppe Verdi (1813–1901) in his "Ave Maria" composed in 1889.

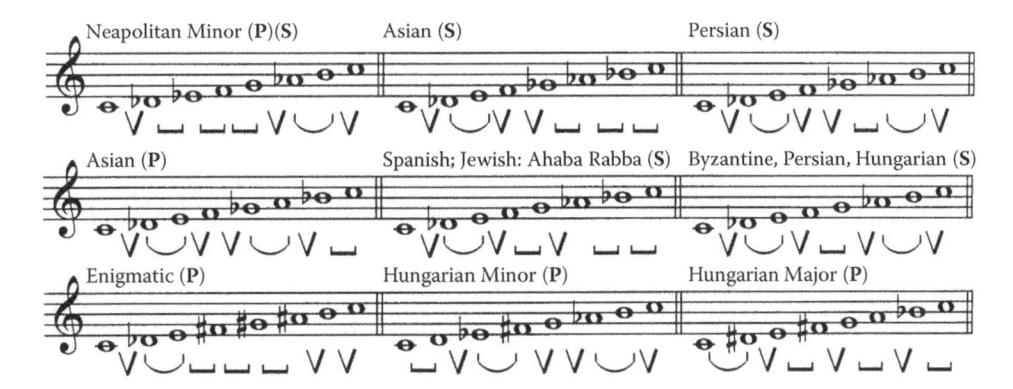

EXAMPLE 2.88 Seven-note scales that include intervals greater than a whole tone. (Harmonic minor also matches this criterion but is not shown.)

Scales that are composed of eight notes are found in other cultures and in jazz and blues compositions.

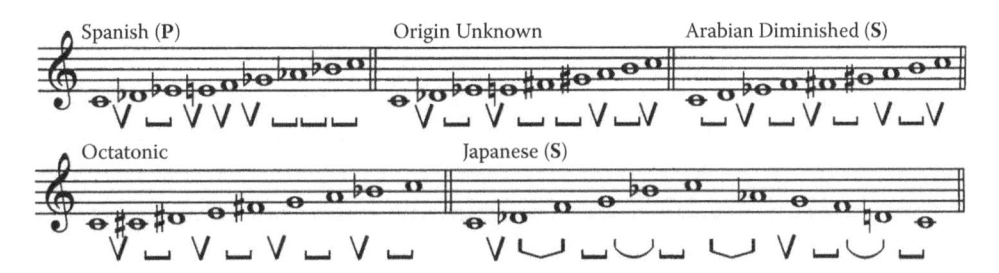

EXAMPLE 2.89 Examples of eight-note scales. The Octatonic scale is composed of alternating semitones and whole tones beginning with a semitone, while the Arabian Diminished is composed of alternating whole tones and semitones beginning with a whole tone. For this reason, these scales are considered a complementary pair. Note that the Japanese scale has both an ascending and descending form as does our melodic minor.

Many scales are also found in various music and societies that consist of more than eight pitches. Example 2.90 illustrates four of these. Three of these scales possess a range greater than an octave.

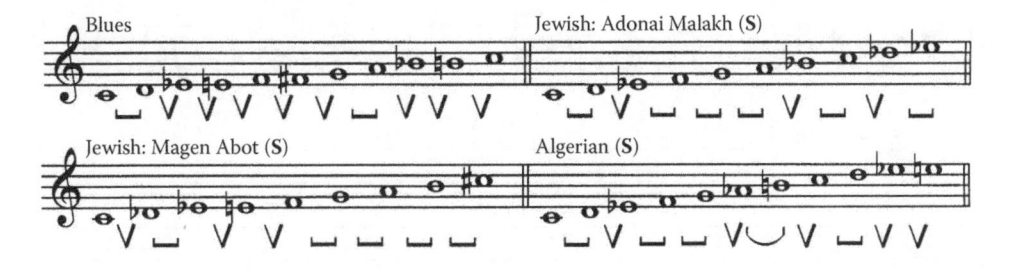

EXAMPLE 2.90 Scales with nine or more notes.

Review

- Other cultures, times, and various musical styles have created scales with five and more notes containing intervals of semitones, whole tones, three semitones, and two whole tones.
- Composers working in many styles, jazz musicians, and traditional folk ensembles regularly work with and within these scales.
- Some of the ethnic scales are also strongly associated with the dance and/or song rhythms of their cultures.

Related Exercises

§ Select a scale from among those presented in Examples 2.86 through 2.91. With your selected scale, create a melody that has at least three tonal goals (i.e. three phrases and three cadences). What scale did you choose? Why? Why did you select the tonal goals that you used? Can you describe each of your cadences as half (incomplete), authentic (complete), or neither?

§ This familiar Scottish melody was originally pentatonic. Rewrite it on the staves provided below the melody, restoring its pentatonic modality.

Auld Lang Syne

Traditional Scottish Song

§ This equally famous French Song, *Ah! vous dirai-je, maman*, is printed below. Select one of the scales provided in Examples 2.86 through 2.91 and rescore this melody in that alternative modality on the staves provided. What happens to the melody when it is thus altered?

Ah! vous dirai-je, maman

18th c. French melody

part 3

Harmony
Note(s) with Note(s)

1. Intervals

Harmony is the vertical component of music. When two or more pitches are sounded simultaneously, harmony is produced. The adjective *harmonic* applies to pitches "sounded at the same time" as opposed to *melodic*, which, as discussed in Part 2, is the adjective that means "note after note." We discussed intervals in Part 2, where the measuring of musical distances was considered in the context of melody. It is, of course, necessary to discuss and measure pitch distances in the harmonic context, too.

Due to acoustic phenomena, when two notes of different frequencies are sounded together, the sound waves of each tone interact with the others, producing reinforcements and cancellations that color the effect perceived by the listener. For this reason, harmony brings to music different effects than are found in purely melodic settings.

> Obviously, in imperfect listening situations, sounds can be distorted or otherwise blemished, which would adversely affect perception. In this discussion, we assume acceptable listening situations.

Lines or Voices

A melody is often identified as a musical *line*. Harmony is generated whenever two (or more) melodic lines are presented at the same time. Whether the lines are equally interesting or very unequal in their properties is unimportant to our fundamental understanding of harmony. That they sound simultaneously is sufficient.

Because producing two separate lines would usually require two human voices, musical lines are frequently called *voices*, even when produced by an instrument or instruments. The terms *lines* and *voices* are usually used interchangeably.

Here are two lines:

[Musical notation: two staves with upper voice in quarter notes (treble clef) and lower voice in half notes (bass clef), with intervals labeled below:]

P8 P5 m2 m3 M6 M2 P1 P4 M3 m7 m6 P8 d5 M7 P15

EXAMPLE 3.01 Although notated on two staves (to emphasize the fact that these are two, independent lines), one can certainly identify the interval created between each pair of simultaneous sounds (pitches). These are given below the music.

In Example 3.01, the upper voice consists of quarter notes, while the lower voice is composed of half notes. Below the lower line is an *analysis* of the harmonic intervals heard. As with other examples in this book, hearing the example played should prove instructive.

From the intervallic analysis given under Example 3.01, you see that the measurement of musical intervals does not change when done in a harmonic context. You will have observed, too, that during the sounding of each half note, two harmonic intervals are heard, one created by each quarter note.

Consonance and Dissonance

Tendencies of Harmonic Intervals

What should be immediately audible when listening to Example 3.01 is that some harmonic intervals sound smoother (or calmer or more pleasant) than others. Also, some intervals are much more rough or harsh than others. Seconds and sevenths, perfect fourths and all diminished (and augmented) intervals sound, to varying degrees, *unstable*, (i.e. *dissonant*). Intervals such as perfect unisons, perfect octaves, and perfect fifths sound *stable* and thus may be considered *consonant*. As we listen, we observe that some harmonic intervals may exhibit a tendency to *resolve* to other intervals.

Historically, the identification of which harmonic intervals sound consonant and which sound dissonant has evolved. In very early music, the perfect unison (P1), perfect fifth (P5), and perfect octave (P8) were the only accepted consonances. As time passed, the intervals of the major third (M3) and, less so, the minor third (m3), as well as the major and minor sixth (M6 and m6) were accepted—at least as *imperfect consonances*. Intervals such as the diminished fifth (d5) or augmented fourth (A4) as well as all seconds (M/m2) and sevenths (M/m7) were deemed dissonant. Even the perfect fourth (P4) was considered unstable and, therefore, a dissonance.

Perfect Consonances   Imperfect Consonances   Dissonances   Unstable (dissonant)

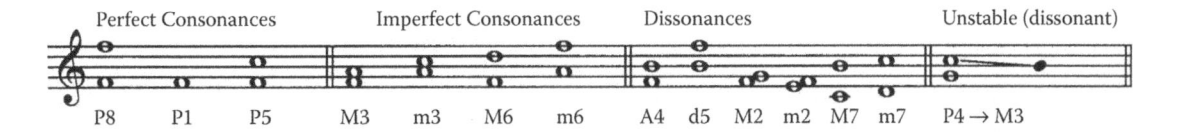

P8 P1 P5   M3 m3 M6 m6   A4 d5 M2 m2 M7 m7   P4 → M3

EXAMPLE 3.02 Historic attributions of consonance and dissonance to common intervals. From left to right: perfect consonances; imperfect consonances; dissonances; and the unstable (dissonant) P4 and its tendency to resolve to a M3.

In casual conversation, the word *consonant* is often used as a synonym for pleasant and *dissonant* as a synonym for disagreeable. For the purposes of music theory, *consonant* means stable while *dissonant* means unstable. It is important to understand this, perhaps more precise, usage.

Modern listeners have heard a lot of music in which a variety of intervals have been used in many different combinations. Most of us have learned to accept these diverse, often complex sounds. We may find it difficult—when hearing a perfect fourth, for example—to understand how it might ever have been construed as unstable. Thus, when attempting to understand older music and practices, contemporary listeners are frequently disadvantaged.

Review

- While the term *melodic* means pitches heard in succession, the term *harmonic* refers to pitches heard simultaneously.
- When two or more voices interact (by being performed simultaneously), harmonic intervals are formed between each voice and every other voice.
- A harmonic interval that sounds stable is said to be consonant, while an unstable harmonic interval is said to be dissonant.
- The determination of which intervals are consonant and which are dissonant will depend on the period and style of music under consideration.

Related Exercises

§ Rewrite the following melodic intervals as harmonic intervals (simply place the higher pitch above the lower pitch in the space to the right of the second note). The first interval is done as an example.

§ On the lines provided, label each of these harmonic intervals.

§ Write the specified harmonic intervals either above (↑) the given pitch or below (↓) the given pitch as indicated.

m3 ↑   P5 ↑   m7 ↓   P4 ↓   M7 ↑   m6 ↑

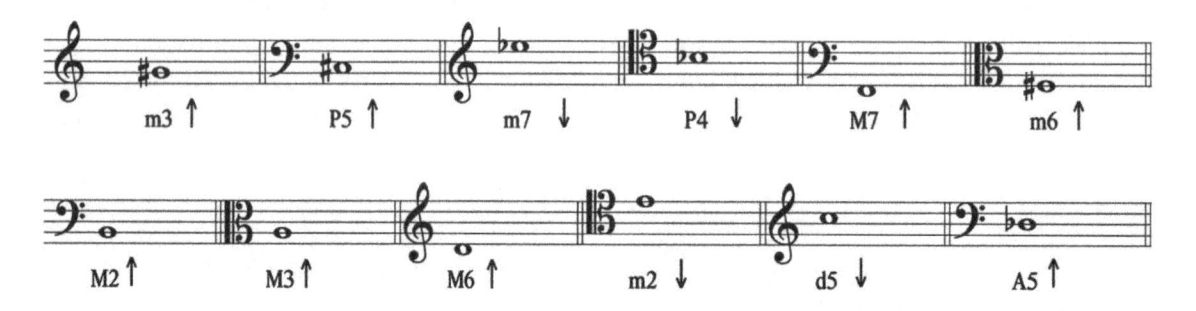

M2 ↑   M3 ↑   M6 ↑   m2 ↓   d5 ↓   A5 ↑

Intervals Found within Scales

Each pitch of a scale may be sounded with any other pitch of the scale, thus creating various intervals. Below are all of the intervals created by using the diatonic pitches of the major scale. Even though the example is in C Major, the results would be the same in any other major key.

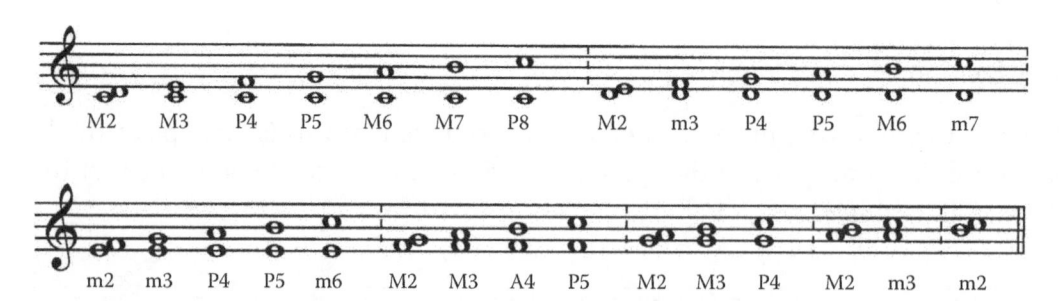

M2 M3 P4 P5 M6 M7 P8 M2 m3 P4 P5 M6 m7

m2 m3 P4 P5 m6 M2 M3 A4 P5 M2 M3 P4 M2 m3 m2

EXAMPLE 3.03 Intervals formed between each degree of the C Major scale and every other degree above the original.

The next example shows all the intervals created between various scale degrees using the pitch content of the harmonic minor scale to illustrate the outcomes of this process. This example is in c minor.

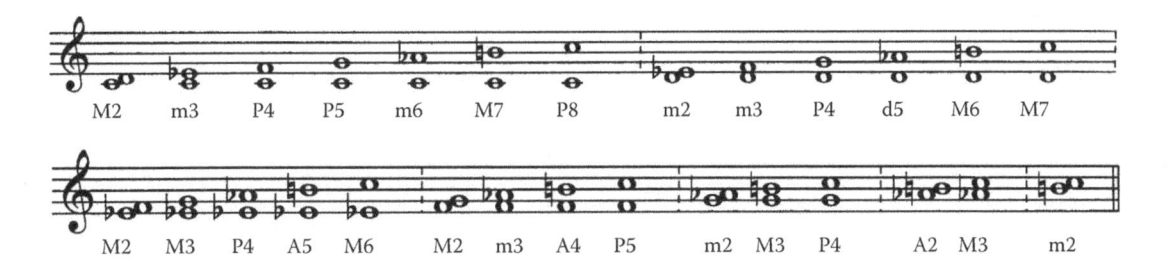

EXAMPLE 3.04 Intervals formed between each degree of the c harmonic minor scale and every other degree above the original.

Inverting Intervals

To determine the distance from the tonic *down* to the subdominant (from the information provided in Examples 3.03 and 3.04), you can use the principles of ***inversion***. All harmonic intervals may be ***inverted***. Inversion is accomplished by rewriting the interval with the original lower pitch ***transposed*** up an octave (or by transposing the original upper pitch down an octave).

If we take the interval formed by the pitch C and the F immediately above as our initial interval (a P4) and raise the lower note (or lower the upper note) an octave, we obtain the inversion of our original interval. This newly created interval still consists of F and C, but now the C is above the F and the interval between them has become a P5.

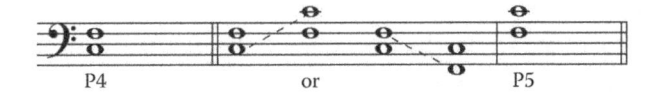

EXAMPLE 3.05 Inverting an interval. On the left, a P4 consisting of a C with the F above. In the middle, possible rewritings of the initial interval. On the right, the interval formed by an F with a C above, a P5.

The process may be repeated with any pair of pitches that form a P4, and the result will always be a P5. We say that *the inversion of a perfect fourth is a perfect fifth*. Thus, the distance from the tonic *down* to the subdominant is a P5.

Taking an interval, such as the m3 of D up to F, and inverting it, we obtain the interval of F up to D, which is a M6. In contrast, starting with the M3 of F up to A and inverting it, we end up with the interval A up to F, which forms a m6.

EXAMPLE 3.06 Inverting thirds. On the left, a m3 inverts to a M6. On the right, a M3 inverts to a m6.

An initial interval of D up to E, a M2, will, when inverted, yield a m7. And the interval from B up to C, which is a m2, will form a M7 when inverted.

EXAMPLE 3.07 On the left, inverting a M2 to form a m7. On the right, inverting a m2 to form a M7.

Two final examples: Starting with the A4 formed between F and B, we obtain, when inverted, a d5 from B to F. And when the P8 of G to G is inverted, a P1 is the result.

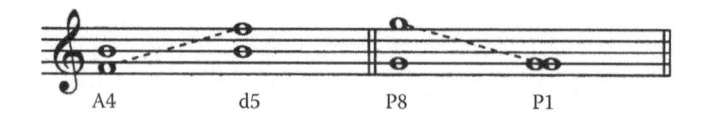

EXAMPLE 3.08 On the left, an A4 interval, B above F, and its inversion, F above B, forming a d5. On the right, the P8 G to G and its inversion, a perfect unison G to G.

From the illustrations above, we observe the following pattern:

>> **When inverted**:
   An octave becomes a unison, a seventh becomes a second, a sixth becomes a third, and a fifth becomes a fourth.
>> **When inverted**:
   A fourth inverts to a fifth, a third inverts to a sixth, a second inverts to a seventh, and a unison inverts to an octave.
>> **Perfect intervals** invert to perfect intervals.
>> **Major intervals** invert to minor intervals.
>> **Minor intervals** invert to major intervals.
>> **Diminished intervals** invert to augmented intervals.
>> **Augmented intervals** invert to diminished intervals.

Review

- Rewriting an interval such that the original upper pitch becomes the lower pitch produces the inversion of the original interval.
- Unisons invert to form octaves; octaves invert to form unisons.
- Seconds invert to form sevenths; sevenths invert to form seconds.
- Thirds invert to form sixths; sixths invert to form thirds.
- Fourths invert to form fifths; fifths invert to form fourths.
- Perfect intervals yield perfect intervals when inverted.

- Major intervals invert to minor intervals; minor intervals invert to major intervals.
- Augmented intervals invert to diminished intervals; diminished intervals invert to augmented intervals.

Related Exercises

§ For each interval given below, first identify its size by writing the correct name on the first line. Then invert the interval (either by drawing the lower note above the upper note or by drawing the upper note below the lower note). Name the resulting (inverted) interval on the second line. The first interval is done as an example.

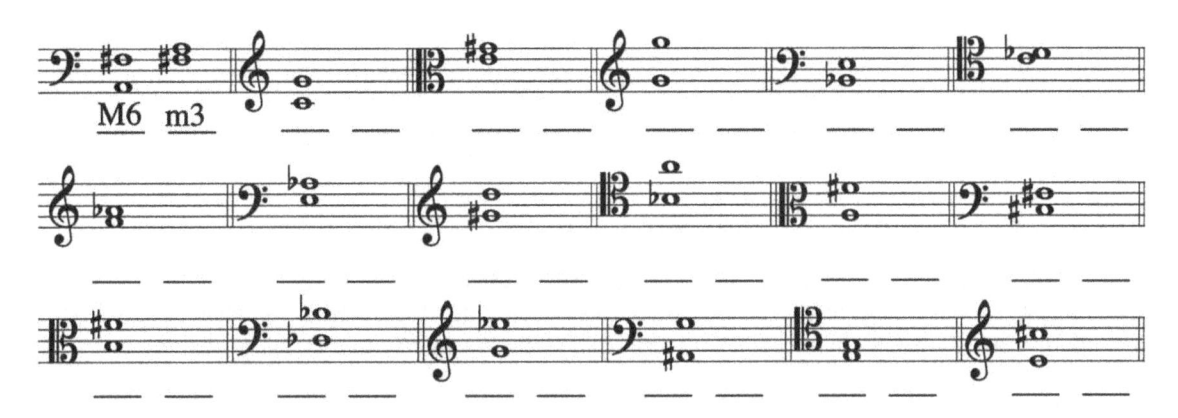

§ Correctly complete these statements:

A _____ inverts to become a fifth. A sixth inverts to become a _____. The inversion of a perfect interval is a _____ interval. A seventh inverts to become a _____. The inversion of a major interval is a _____ interval. A _____ inverts to become a unison. A doubly augmented interval inverts to become a _____ interval. A second inverts to become a _____. A minor interval inverts to become a _____ interval.

The Root of a Harmonic Interval

When an interval is played harmonically, one of the two pitches may be heard as the *root*, or the pitch upon which the sonority is based. In the case of perfect unisons, actually only one unique pitch is sounded, although in two voices, so that pitch *is* the root. But in all other cases, there are two distinct and separate pitches.

In a perfect octave, the lower pitch is the root with the upper pitch reinforcing the second partial of the lower sound. In a perfect fifth, many listeners perceive the upper pitch as a part of the harmonic series of the lower pitch, thus casting the lower pitch in the role of the root.

> Two pitches that are associated in some logical fashion are sometimes referred to as a dyad.

> For more information on the harmonic series, see Appendix II, p. 345.

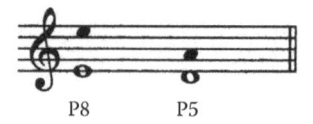

EXAMPLE 3.09 On the left, a P8 with the implied root indicated with a whole note. On the right, a P5 with the implied root indicated with a whole note.

The composer Paul Hindemith asserts that in a perfect fourth the upper note assumes the role of root. This is perhaps because the partials of the upper pitch include both the upper and the lower pitches while the partials of the lower pitch do not include the upper note.

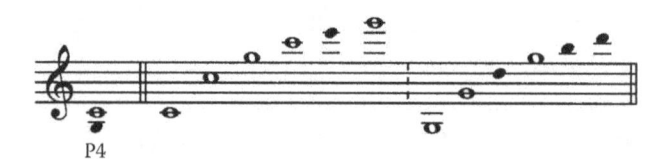

EXAMPLE 3.10 On the left, a G to C P4 with the implied root (C) indicated by a whole note. In the middle, the C harmonic series, which contains both Cs and Gs shown as whole notes. On the right, the harmonic series based on G showing that of the two pitches being considered only Gs (shown as whole notes) are to be found.

The determination of what constitutes the root of seconds, thirds, sixths, and sevenths is less clear. Many writers seem to agree that the root of the major third is the lower pitch but that the root of a minor third is the upper pitch. It is also suggested that the root of the major sixth is the upper of the two pitches while the root of the minor sixth is the lower pitch. Because of the unstable qualities associated with seconds, sevenths, augmented fourths, and diminished fifths, consensus as to which pitch may be the root is difficult to find.

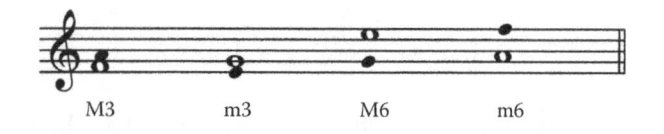

EXAMPLE 3.11 Several suggested implied roots. From the left, M3, m3, M6, and m6. The implied roots are shown as whole notes.

More Than Two Voices

When describing music with three (or more) voices, it is often useful to identify the musical distances between the various voices. In the example below, the intervals between the upper and the middle voices and between the middle

> Some theorists have cited the harmonic series as a basis for explaining both the evolution of consonance and dissonance in our music as well as an explanation of our perception of various sound phenomena. Although we can glean much from this approach, our fundamental understanding of sound and sound perception remains too limited for us to feel confident with such simple logic. However, the writings of David Cope and Howard Hanson are informative and thought-provoking reading for anyone with a greater interest in these topics.

and lower voices are identified on the upper, three-staff system. Compound intervals are reduced by an octave for clarity.

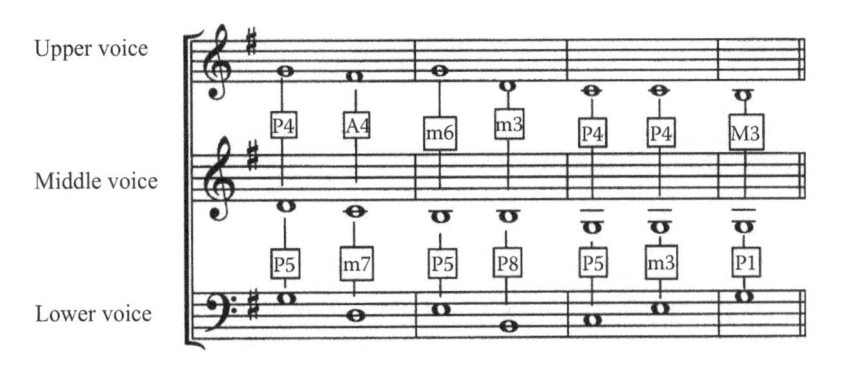

EXAMPLE 3.12 Three lines notated on three staves showing the harmonic intervals *between* the first and second lines and between the second and third lines.

The intervals between the upper voice and the lower voice are shown on the two-staff system below.

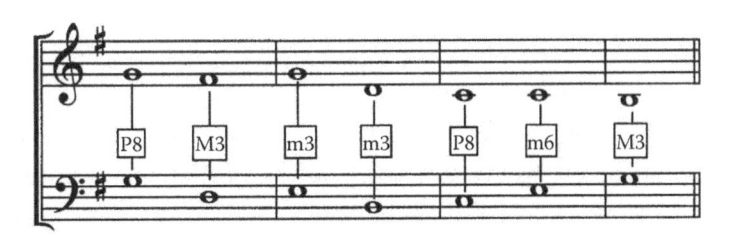

EXAMPLE 3.13 Here are the upper and lower voices from Example 3.12 isolated to show the harmonic intervals (compound intervals reduced to simpler forms) between them.

In the study of **counterpoint**, it is frequently necessary to examine *all* of the intervals found at any given moment between *all* of the voices (harmonic intervals) as well as the intervals between successive notes within the same voice (melodic intervals).

> When the interval between the lowest staff and the upper staff is greater than an octave, it is reduced by an octave. Thus, a M10 is identified as a M3. This is a common practice in many analytical situations.

Review

- When two pitches are sounded simultaneously so as to produce a harmonic interval, one of the two pitches may be heard to function as the root of the interval.
- It is generally agreed that the lower pitch sounds to be the root of perfect fifths and perfect octaves and that the upper pitch sounds to be the root of the perfect fourth.
- There is less general agreement as to the roots of other sized intervals.
- In music composed of more than two voices, one can identify harmonic intervals between each voice and every other simultaneously sounding voice.

Related Exercises

§ Assuming that the lower pitch is the root of a P5 and the upper pitch is, likewise, the root of a P4, circle the root in each of the following examples.

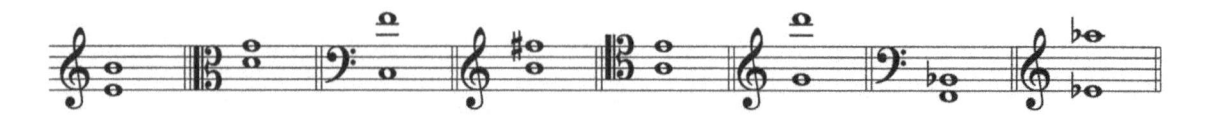

§ Here are a series of intervals formed by the simultaneously sounded pitches on the two staves. On the lines provided, write the name of each interval being produced. (Compound intervals may be reduced to simple intervals.)

§ Between the simultaneously sounding pitches given on these three-staff examples, there are three intervallic pairs: (1) between the top voice and the middle voice; (2) between the lowest voice and the top voice; and (3) between the lowest voice and the middle voice. Identify each of these intervals, and write your answer on the lines provided (numbered as given above). (Note: These are intended as interval identification exercises, not counterpoint examples.)

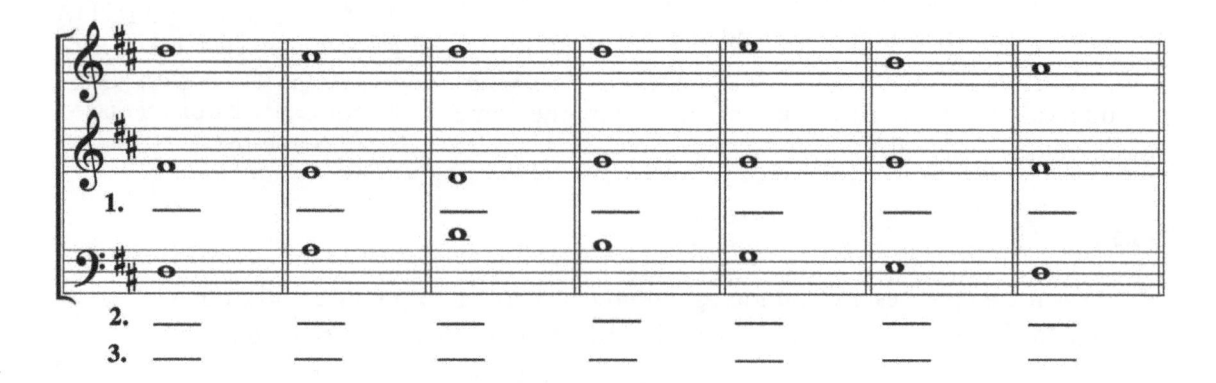

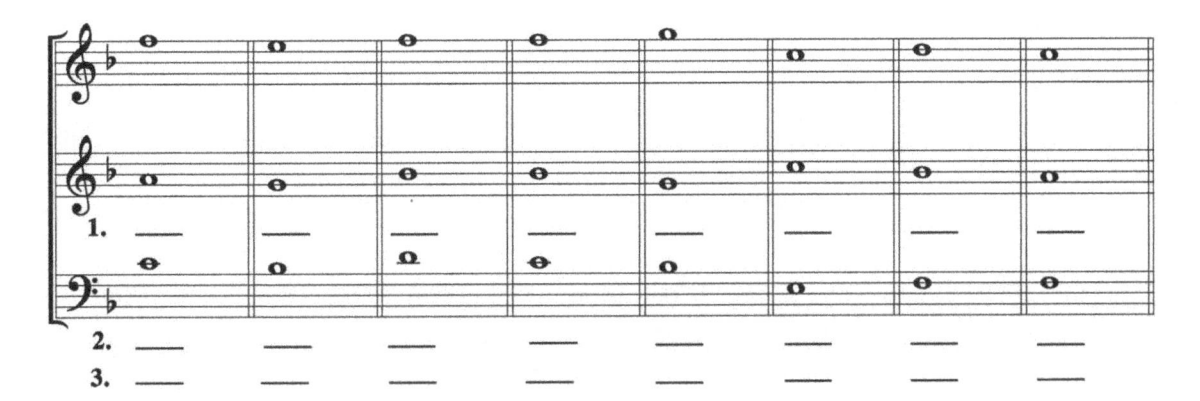

2. Triads

As Western music evolved, it became more and more common for music to be composed of three or four independent lines or voices. In the eighteenth century, a French composer/theorist Jean-Philippe Rameau (1683–1764) established a model for understanding harmonic structures that still influences our thinking (especially in academic settings) and much of the vocabulary used for harmonic analysis. Rameau suggested that the basis for harmony was the ***tertian triad***.

A ***triad*** is simply a chord composed of three different pitches. But the term ***tertian*** limits the triad to pitches related to each other by the interval of a third (either major or minor). Most of what is presented in the next few pages is rooted in Rameau's harmonic thinking.

Composers, especially in the twentieth century, have used other triads in their writings. Especially interesting have been quartal (or quintal) triads and triads built on seconds (or sevenths). Here are examples:

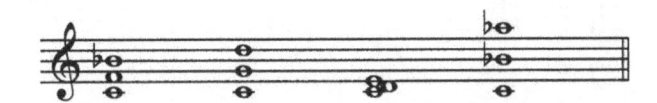

EXAMPLE 3.14 From left to right, examples of triads built on fourths, fifths, seconds, and sevenths

As interesting as the chords found in Example 3.14 may be, the use of the tertian triad, rather than any other possible triad, has been so widespread in Western music since before the eighteenth century that when musicians use the word *triad* it is always understood, unless stated to the contrary, to be a tertian triad. From now on in this text, the word *triad* will always mean a tertian triad.

The Basics of Triadic Harmony

Triads in Major Scales

Let us start with a major scale. In this case, we will use D Major, although any key would work. The pitches of the scale, in ascending order, are D, E, F-sharp, G, A, B, C-sharp, and D. And we know from earlier articles that these pitches are called the tonic, supertonic, mediant, subdominant, dominant, submediant, leading tone, and tonic, respectively. As Rameau observed, many of the chords commonly found in music are created by placing a second tone on the staff a third above (for each note of the scale) and another tone, again, a third above the second tone. All of the triads shown here are drawn from the pitch content of the D Major scale. Accidentals are shown only for clarity.

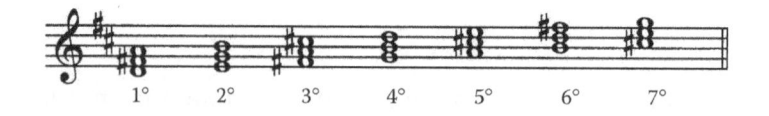

EXAMPLE 3.15 The D Major scale with a triad constructed on each scale degree.

Closer examination of the intervals used to construct the triads above reveals three different triad types. The triads built on the tonic, the subdominant, and the dominant all exhibit the same structure. They are called ***major triads***. Likewise, the triads built on the supertonic, mediant, and submediant also exhibit the same structure but one that is different from the first group. These are called ***minor triads***. Finally, the triad built on the leading tone is unlike either of the other two groups and is called a ***diminished triad***.

Here are the same triads, grouped by type.

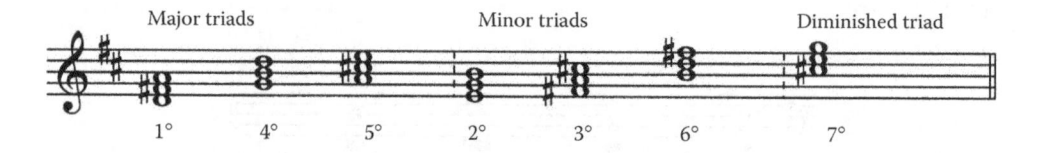

EXAMPLE 3.16 The three types of chords formed by stacking diatonic thirds on the pitches of a major scale. From left to right: major triads (constructed on the tonic, subdominant, and dominant); minor triads (constructed on the supertonic, mediant, and submediant); and a diminished triad (constructed on the leading tone).

The structure of these three different types of triads may be described in either of two ways:

- All of these triads are composed of the lowest pitch (called the ***root*** of the triad) plus the pitch a third above this root (called the ***third of the triad***) and another pitch a third above the second pitch (called the ***fifth of the triad***).

- Or, as encouraged by many theory teachers, these triads may be described as being composed of the root, a third above the root, and a fifth above the root.

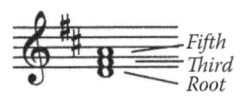

EXAMPLE 3.17 A D Major triad with the components labeled.

Examining the triads built on the supertonic, mediant, and submediant roots shows that they possess a second pitch a minor third above the root and a third pitch a perfect fifth above the root. All of these triads are called *minor triads*. Compare the sounds of these triads to the sounds of the major triads.

The remaining triad, the one constructed on the leading tone, is composed of the root, a minor third above, and a diminished fifth above. As with the major and minor triads, the components of this triad are identified as the root, the third, and the fifth. It is named the *diminished triad*.

Compared to the sound of the major or minor triads, you will notice that the diminished triad sounds much less stable.

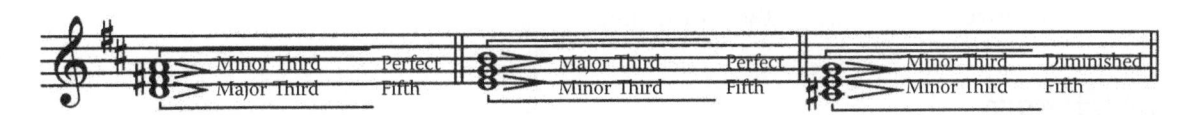

EXAMPLE 3.18 From left to right, the construction of the D Major triad, the construction of the e minor triad, and the construction of the c-sharp diminished triad. Each quality of triad can be seen to be a unique pairing of major and/or minor thirds.

Constructing triads on each pitch of every major scale would clearly show that all triads built on all the tonics, subdominants, and dominants are major triads; that those built on the supertonics, mediants, and submediants are all minor triads; and those built on the leading tones are all diminished triads.

Here are examples of these three types of triads built on different pitches:

EXAMPLE 3.19 Comparing the composition of the major, minor, and diminished triads, each set of three possessing the same root. On the left, root G; in the middle, root F-sharp; on the right, root B-flat.

Review

- The basic harmonic structure (chord) of Western common-practice music is the tertian triad.
- The tertian triad is constructed by stacking thirds above a root pitch.
- The root pitch gives its name to the triad either as a letter name or as a degree of the scale.
- The tertian triad is so common in Western music that it is usually simply called a triad; the fact that it is tertian is assumed.
- The parts of a triad are the root (the pitch upon which it is built), the third (the pitch a major or minor third above the root), and the fifth (the pitch that is a major or minor third above the third).
- The fifth will be perfect if the triad is built from the combination (in either order) of a minor third and a major third.
- If the triad is built from two minor thirds, the fifth will be diminished.
- Constructing triads on every degree of a major scale shows that only three types of triads are created: major triads, minor triads, and diminished triads.
- Triads constructed on the tonic, the subdominant, and the dominant consist of a major third and a perfect fifth above the root of the chord. These are major triads.
- Triads constructed on the supertonic, mediant, and submediant consist of a minor third and a perfect fifth above the root of the chord. These are minor triads.
- The triad constructed on the leading tone consists of a minor third and a diminished fifth above the root. This is a diminished triad.

Related Exercises

§ Identify the root of each triad in the examples below by circling it, and then identify the quality (major, minor, or diminished) by writing M, m, or d, respectively, on the line below the triad.

Harmony: Note(s) with Note(s)

§ Each example below has a key signature. Assuming a major key, write the triad(s) of the specified quality found in that key. Do not use accidentals! (You may write your triads in any convenient octave.)

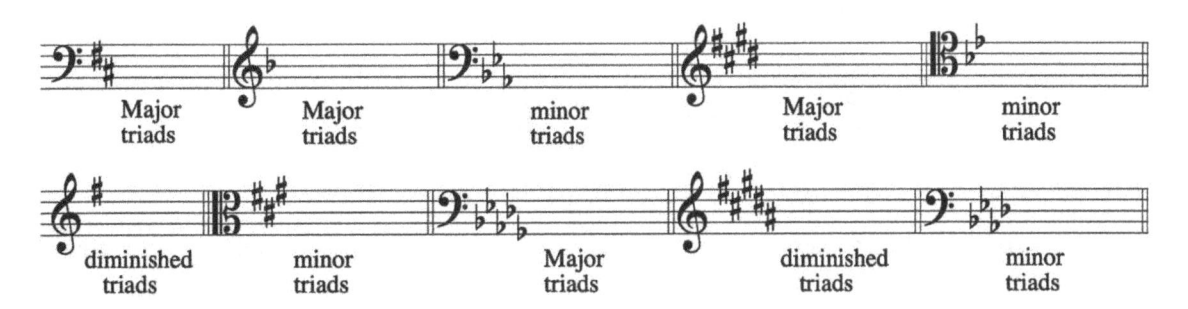

§ In each example below, you are given a triad. In what major key (or keys) does the notated triad naturally occur? Write the name of the key(s) on the line below each triad.

§ Draw the specified triads on the staff and in the clef provided. (Use any convenient octave.)

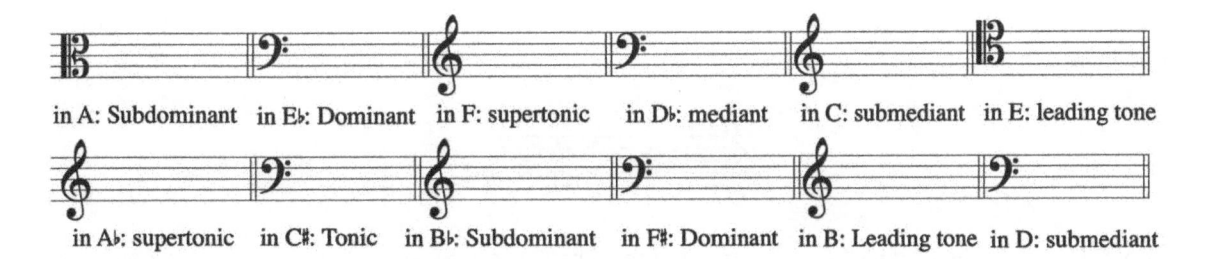

Triads in Minor Scales

If we repeat the process of constructing triads on each scale degree but use a minor scale, the results will be different. Before doing this, we need to decide which minor scale to use. We will start with harmonic minor because that is the scale derived from the pitches most likely to be used to harmonize music in minor modalities.

For now, we will use those pitches found in the d harmonic minor scale. The triad built on the tonic, D, would consist of D, F, and A; the triad formed on the supertonic, E, would contain E, G, and B-flat; the triad built on the mediant, F, would contain F, A, and C-sharp, and so on.

The example below shows the results from this approach.

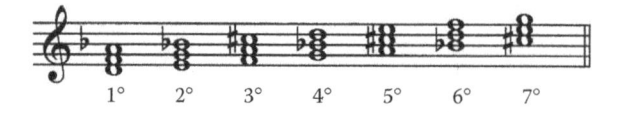

EXAMPLE 3.20 Triads built on each degree of the d (harmonic) minor scale and using only the pitches contained in the harmonic minor scale.

Examining this set of triads, we find that the tonic triad and the subdominant triad are both minor, the supertonic and the leading tone triads are diminished, and the dominant and submediant triads are major.

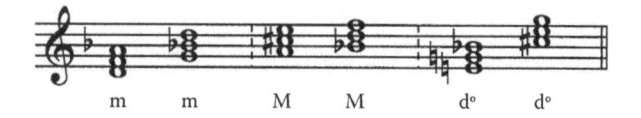

EXAMPLE 3.21 From the left, the tonic and subdominant triads, both minor. In the middle, the dominant and submediant triads, both major. On the right, the supertonic triad and the leading tone triads, both diminished.

But the mediant triad differs from the other triads found in this scale and in the earlier studied major scale. The mediant triad constructed from a harmonic minor scale has an interval between the root and the third of a major third, and the distance from the root to the fifth is an *augmented fifth*. This chord is known as an ***augmented triad***. Though an interesting sound variant, the augmented triad finds but limited usefulness in traditional harmonic practices.

EXAMPLE 3.22 The triad built on the mediant of the d harmonic minor scale. Notice the intervallic structure shown on the right.

As with major scales, building triads on every degree of every harmonic minor scale would show that the results are always the same: The tonic and subdominant triads are minor, the dominant and submediant triads are major, the supertonic and leading tone triads are diminished, and the mediant triad is augmented.

We have by the above processes created the four types of triads found in Western music. Each type of triad may be constructed using any pitch as the root.

Triads Formed from the Melodic Minor Scale

Although using the melodic minor scale as a basis for building triads will not provide any new *types* of triads, it does yield alternative associations of triads with scale degrees. Here is the d melodic minor scale.

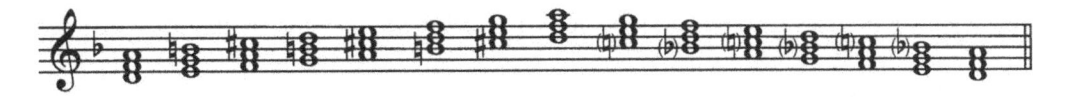

EXAMPLE 3.23 The d melodic minor scale ascending and descending with a triad built on each scale degree, producing, compared to harmonic minor, a new triadic distribution. Ascending: minor on the second, major on the fourth, and diminished on the sixth degrees. Descending: major on the flatted seventh, minor on the fifth, and also major on the third degrees.

Naming the Four Types of Triads

It is useful to be able to name specific triads. Triad names have two parts. The name of the pitch that serves as the **root** of the chord *and* the **quality** of the triad (namely, major, minor, diminished, or augmented). This information is notated as follows:

G   d   e°   F+

EXAMPLE 3.24 From left to right, a G Major triad, a d minor triad, an e diminished triad, and an F Augmented triad.

When abbreviating triads, **uppercase letters are used for major and augmented triads** (those triads with their third a *major* third above the root) and **lowercase letters are used for minor and diminished triads** (those triads with their thirds a *minor* third above the root). The augmented triad is indicated by the addition of a plus sign to differentiate it from the major triad, while the diminished triad is indicated by the degree symbol to distinguish it from the minor triad.

Triad names are used in several ways, depending on context. All approaches identify the root of the triad. Others add the quality to the description as shown above. Thus, the triad formed on the first note of the D Major scale may be identified as any of the following:

D Major triad, abbreviated D or DM
Tonic triad (in D Major), abbreviated I
The "one chord," abbreviated I or 1

Likewise, the triad built on the second degree of the D Major scale could be identified as

> In certain situations, the Arabic numerals would be understood as "Nashville Numbers." See also p. 147.

e minor chord (e, Emin, or Em)
Supertonic (ii or II)
The "two chord" (ii, II, or 2).

Other triads would be identified comparably.

Review

- As with major scales, triads may be constructed on each scale degree of a minor scale. This is usually (but not exclusively) done using harmonic minor.
- When built on the harmonic minor scale, the triads built on the tonic and subdominant degrees are minor.
- The triads built on the dominant and submediant scale degrees are major.
- The triads built on the supertonic and leading tone are diminished.
- The triad built on the mediant consists of a major third from the root to the third and an augmented fifth from the root to the fifth and is called an augmented triad.
- Constructing triads utilizing the pitch content of the melodic minor scale yields the following additions: major triads on the mediant, subdominant, and subtonic; minor triads on the supertonic and dominant; and a diminished triad on the raised submediant.
- The four triads found in Western, common-practice music are major, minor, diminished, and augmented.
- Triads are abbreviated by writing the pitch name of the chord's root in uppercase if the triad is major or augmented and in lowercase if the triad is minor or diminished. In addition, a plus sign (+) is added to identify an augmented triad while a degree symbol (°) is added to identify a diminished triad.
- The triad abbreviations B♭+, c♯°, f♯, and D are translated as B-flat Augmented, c-sharp diminished, f-sharp minor, and D Major triads, respectively.

Related Exercises

§ Circle the root of each triad in the examples below, and then identify the quality (major, minor, augmented, or diminished) by writing M, m, A, or d, respectively, on the line below the triad.

Harmony: Note(s) with Note(s)

§ Each example below has a key signature. Assuming harmonic minor, write the triad(s) of the specified quality generated by that scale. Use accidentals as required. (You may write your triads in any convenient octave.)

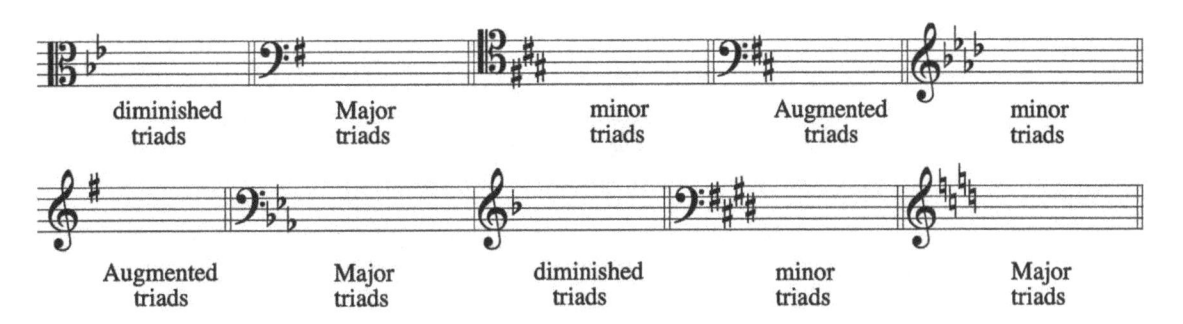

diminished triads — Major triads — minor triads — Augmented triads — minor triads

Augmented triads — Major triads — diminished triads — minor triads — Major triads

§ In each example, you are given a triad. In what minor key (or keys) does the given triad occur? Write the name of the key(s) on the line below each triad. (Any form of minor may be cited.)

§ Draw the specified triads on the staff and in the clef provided. Assume the harmonic form of minor. (Use any convenient octave.)

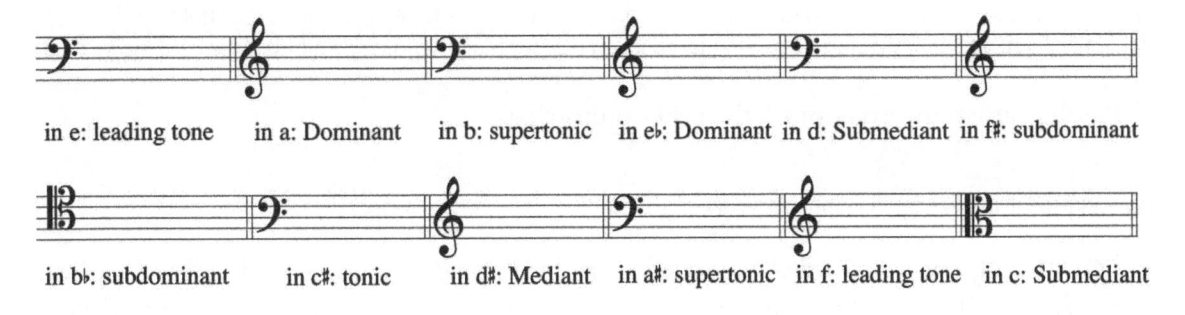

in e: leading tone   in a: Dominant   in b: supertonic   in e♭: Dominant   in d: Submediant   in f♯: subdominant

in b♭: subdominant   in c♯: tonic   in d♯: Mediant   in a♯: supertonic   in f: leading tone   in c: Submediant

Recognizing and Identifying Triads

Because triads, and the various rearrangements of them, play such a critical role in the harmonization of common-practice music and the study of Western music theory, you will find it valuable to learn to recognize triads quickly and to identify which of the three pitches is the root, which is the third, and which is the fifth. Fortunately, this is not an overwhelming task because only seven basic sets of pitches form triads:

A-C-E   B-D-F   C-E-G   D-F-A   E-G-B   F-A-C   G-B-D

These are shown below in both the treble and bass clefs.

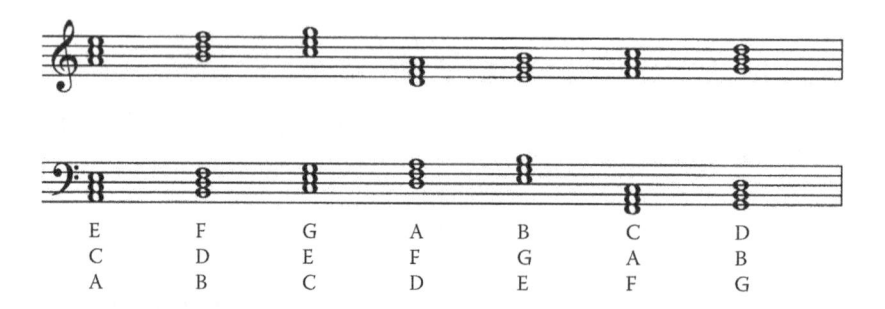

EXAMPLE 3.25   The seven fundamental sets of pitches that form the basis for all possible triads shown in both treble and bass clefs. In each of the given examples, the lowest pitch shown is the root, the middle pitch is the third, and the top pitch is the fifth.

A little experimentation will show that no other pitch combinations are available. All of these are compacted stacks of thirds and might be called ***prototriads.***

Thus, when some form of F (i.e. F, F-flat, F-sharp, F-double flat) is the root, the third will always be some form of A, and the fifth will always be some form of C. Here are all the possibilities for creating major triads (including a few examples that you are unlikely ever to see) using the FAC set of pitches:

EXAMPLE 3.26   The five *major* triads that possess a root that is some form of F. From left to right, an F-double flat Major triad, an F-flat Major triad, an F Major triad, an F-sharp Major triad, and an F-double sharp Major triad.

Parallel situations exist for *all* the other prototriads.

Rearranging Pitches to Form a Compacted Stack of Thirds

When reading music, the pitches notated may be located in various parts of the musical space. In order to correctly name the triad in use, it is necessary to rearrange the pitches—

mentally or otherwise—into a stack of thirds that will look like one of the prototriads shown above.

You can do this by writing on a staff any one of the pitches involved. Then write another of the pitches, as close to this first pitch as possible. Finally, as close to the first two as possible, write the third pitch. If this results in a stack of thirds, you simply identify the root (the bottom of the stack) and analyze the triad's quality.

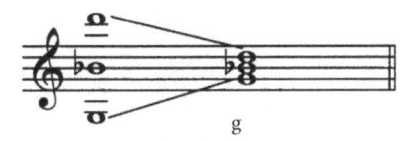

EXAMPLE 3.27 Rearranging the pitches within a chord to produce an easier-to-read stack of thirds.

If the initial rearrangement does not result in a stack of thirds, a second rearrangement is done.

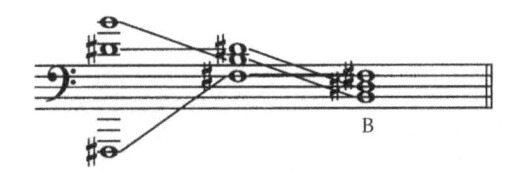

EXAMPLE 3.28 Obtaining a stack of thirds in two steps.

Review

- Only seven combinations of pitch letters can be found in triads. These are ACE, BDF, CEG, DFA, EGB, FAC, and GBD.
- As expressed above, the first letter is always the root, the middle letter is always the third, and the last letter is always the fifth.
- When the components of a triad are located on different staves and/or octaves of a piece, it may be necessary to rearrange them into a stack of thirds in order to name the quality of the triad and to identify the root.

Related Exercises

§ Below, the upper staff provides three pitches that form a triad. Circle the pitch that is the root of the given triad, and then, on the lower staff, copy the triad as a stack of thirds (with the root on the bottom). The first example is done for you.

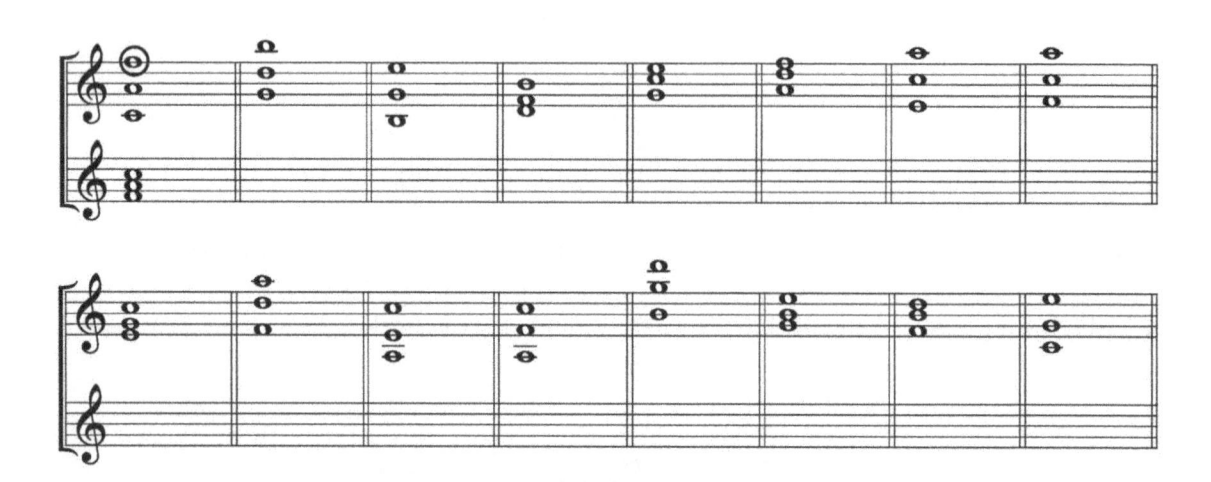

§ On the score below, each measure consists of a triad with the root on one staff, the third on another, and the fifth on the remaining staff. Label each pitch in each measure as R (for root), 3 (for third), or 5 (for fifth). Again, the first example is done for you.

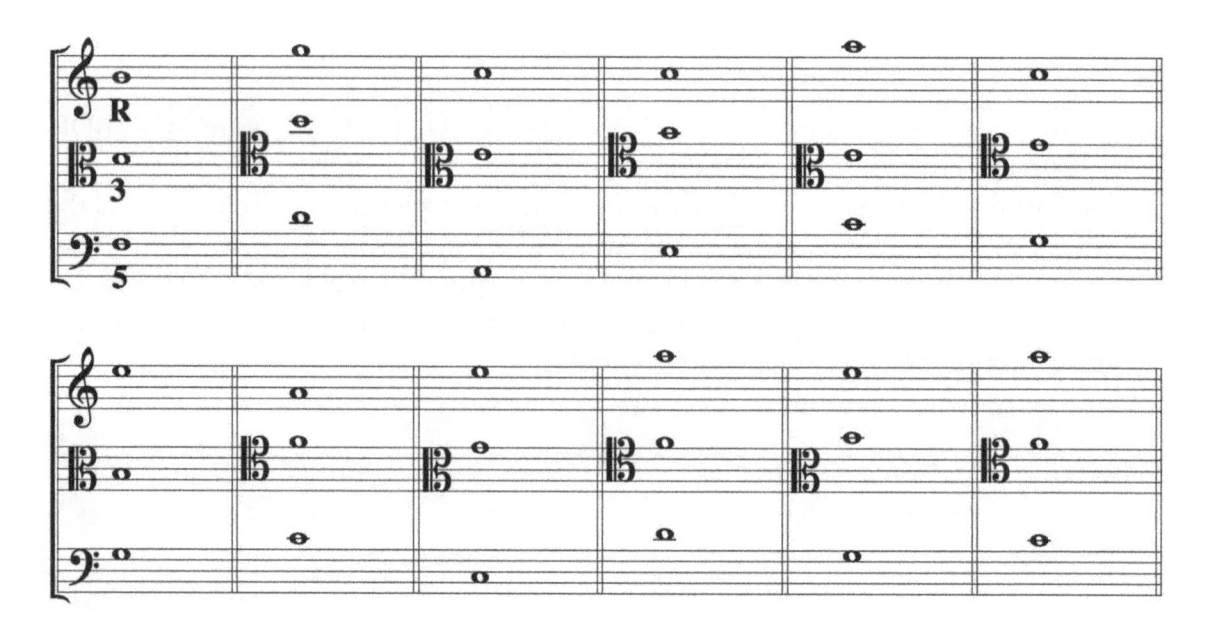

§ Circle the root of each triad represented on the staves below. On the line below each example, identify the quality of the triad as major (M), minor (m), augmented (A or +), or diminished (d or °).

3. The Inversion of Triads

The Process

Earlier in Part 3 (p. 119), the concept of the inversion of intervals was introduced. A similar operation can be performed on triads. Take this B-flat Major triad, for example:

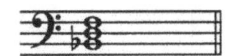

EXAMPLE 3.29 A B-flat triad written with the root, B-flat, in the lowest position.

Obviously, by the rules presented above, we can tell that the root is B-flat, the third is D, and the fifth is F. *It makes no difference where in musical space the components of this triad appear; the function of each pitch is the same.* Thus, these are all B-flat Major triads:

EXAMPLE 3.30   Various ways of distributing the pitches of a B-flat Major triad. Regardless of how each chord above may look or how the pitches are distributed, each of these chords is a B-flat Major triad.

But perhaps less intuitively so are the examples below. These examples are all *inversions* of the original triad.

EXAMPLE 3.31   Various inversions of the B-flat Major triad.

To name a triad completely, you must identify not only the root (in Examples 3.29 through 3.31, B-flat) and the quality of the triad (in all of these examples, major) but also the *inversion*. The three triads on the left in Example 3.31 are said to be in ***first inversion***, and the three examples on the right are identified as ***second inversion*** triads.

The quick way to identify the inversion of any triad is to determine which of the three pitches is in the ***bass*** (i.e. which pitch is the lowest pitch). If the root is in the bass, the triad is said to be in root position. If the third of the triad is in the bass, then the triad is in first inversion. If the fifth is the lowest pitch, then the triad is said to be in second inversion. *The vertical arrangement of the pitches* above *the bass does not affect the determination of the inversion.*

A point of great confusion for some is the difference in meaning of the terms *root* and *bass*. The root is the pitch upon which a triad or chord is built and from which the triad or chord gets its name. The bass is the lowest voice present in the music and, hence, whatever pitch is found in this voice. The root and the bass may, in some cases, be the same, but often they are not.

Harmony: Note(s) with Note(s)

Review

- Triads may be inverted—written with a pitch, other than the root, in the lowest (bass) voice.
- When a triad is written with the root as the lowest pitch, it is in root position.
- When a triad is written with its third in the lowest voice, it is in first inversion.
- When a triad is written with its fifth in the bass, it is in second inversion.
- The name of a triad and its quality are unaffected by any vertical rearrangement of the pitches.
- The determination of the inversion of a triad is based solely on which of the three components of the triad—the root, the third, or the fifth—is placed in the bass voice.

Related Exercises

§ In each of the following triads (presented on a staff without a clef), circle the root, and, on the line below, identify the *lowest* pitch as being the root, the third, or the fifth of the triad. The first one is done as an example.

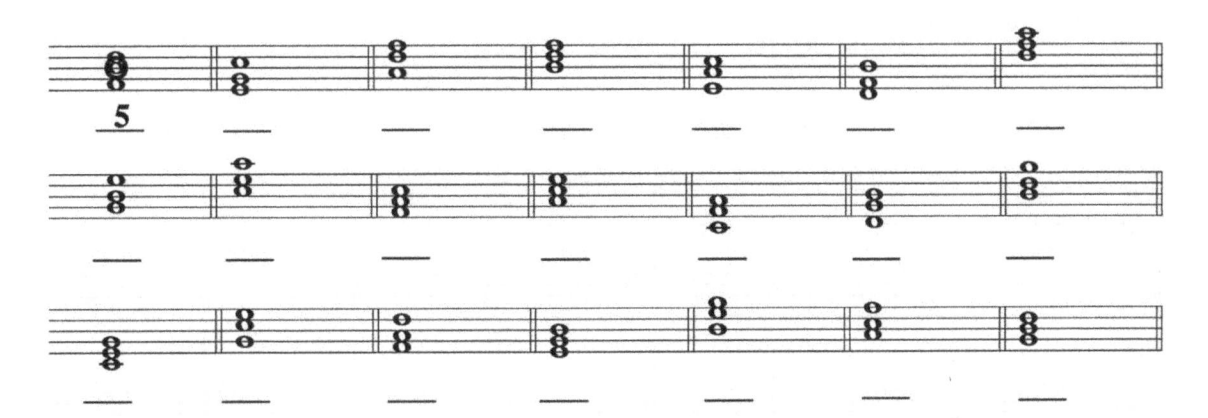

§ In the following exercise, the pitches are notated on three staves (rather than one) and clefs are provided. As before, circle the root and identify the *lowest* pitch as being the root, the third, or the fifth.

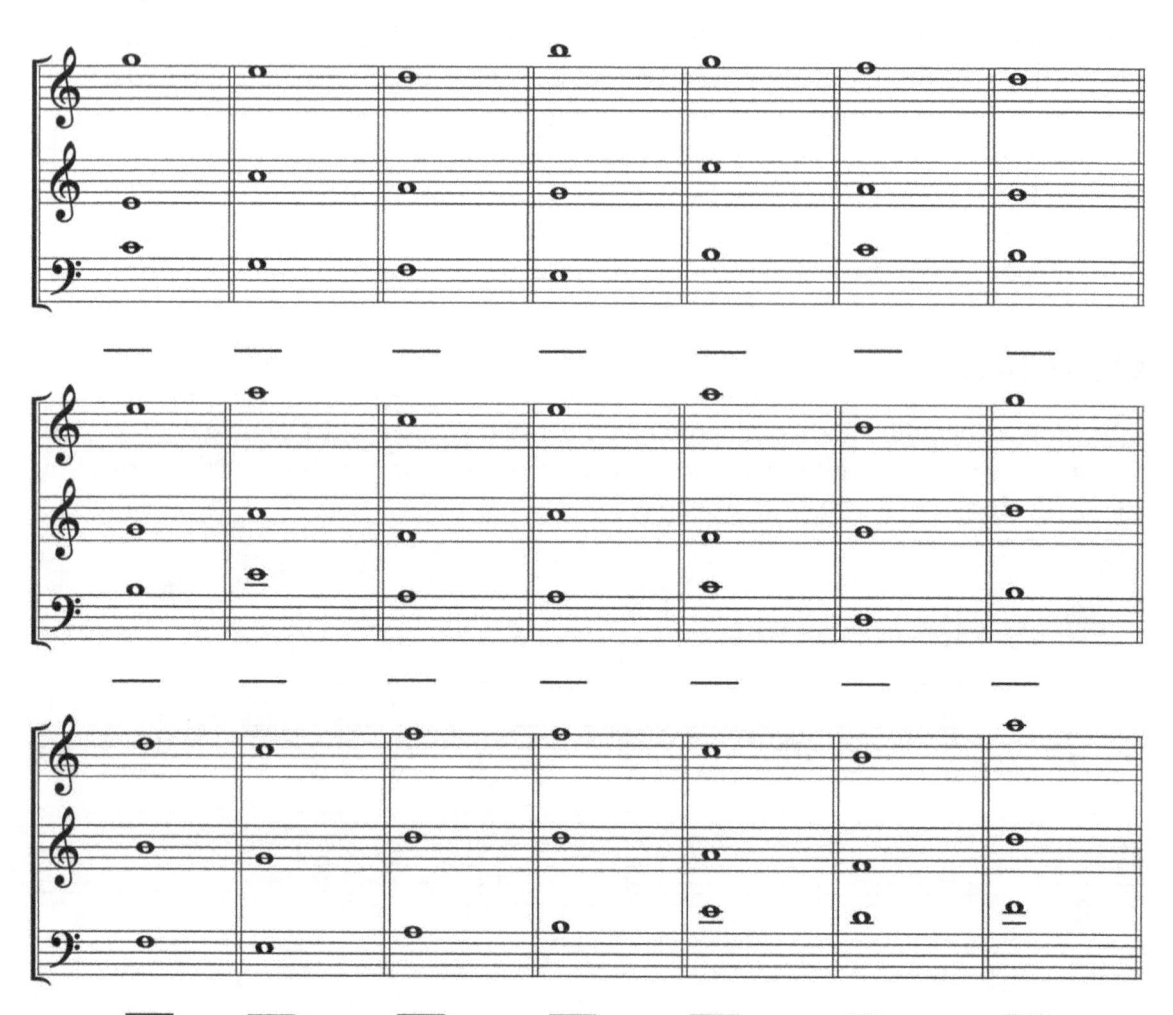

Harmony: Note(s) with Note(s)   141

§ Name the following triads according to the root and the quality of the triad. Show this information on the (upper) line below the chord. On the lower line, using R, 3, or 5, indicate the role of the bass note within the given triad. The first two are done for you as examples.

A♭ M   c♯ m   __   __   __   __   __   __

5   3   __   __   __   __   __   __

__   __   __   __   __   __   __   __

__   __   __   __   __   __   __   __

__   __   __   __   __   __   __   __

__   __   __   __   __   __   __   __

Abbreviating Inversions

Notating a root position triad as stacked thirds results in a configuration that is quite familiar. If you have to notate a first or second inversion triad in a compacted manner, the result is not a stack of thirds but rather a combination of a third and a fourth. See these examples:

5   6   6
3   3   4
1   1   1

EXAMPLE 3.32 Compacted triads. From left to right, a root position triad, a first inversion triad, and a second inversion triad. The numbers shown under each triad are identifying the intervals found between the bass note and each pitch (and every pitch) upward from the bass, including the bass itself. Obviously, the bass is in unison with itself regardless of the configuration while the upper pitches may be a third, a fourth, a fifth, or a sixth above the bass.

Example 3.32 does not use a clef to demonstrate that you can recognize stacked triads and their inversions by appearance without knowing the specific pitch content. In certain situations, this becomes a convenient method to identify quickly the inversion encountered.

Just as triads can be identified by using upper- and lowercase letters and, when necessary, adding a + or a °, we also have conventions to indicate both inversions. These involve small Arabic numbers, called *inversion symbols*, and are placed to the right of the chord symbol.

$$B\flat \qquad B\flat^6 \qquad B\flat^6_4$$

EXAMPLE 3.33 Abbreviations for the B-flat Major triad. From left to right, root position, first inversion, and second inversion.

All of the symbols shown in Example 3.33 tell us that we have a B-flat Major triad. On the left, we are told that it is in root position, in the middle is the symbol for a first inversion B-flat Major triad, and on the right is the symbol for a second inversion B-flat Major triad.

These symbols are derived from *figured bass* notation that was used hundreds of years ago to tell keyboard players what chords to use to create their improvised accompaniments. Because the purpose of this notation was to communicate performance information, brevity and clarity were especially desirable. Unnecessary or redundant information was avoided. (Compare the detailed information in Example 3.32 to the more efficient presentation provided by the lower staff in Example 3.34.)

> This explanation of figured bass notation is deliberately simplistic and quite incomplete. Readers who wish to know more should seek out a good reference on figured bass practices.

In the figured bass convention, the performer was given a bass note and under it perhaps a symbol.

EXAMPLE 3.34 On the lower staff, an example of figured bass notation. On the upper staff is a possible realization (interpretation) of the symbols.

If no symbol was present, the performer played the diatonic pitches a third and a fifth above the bass. (These pitches could be played in any octave desired.)

However, if the number 6 was given, the performer played both the pitch a third above the bass note and the pitch a sixth above the bass. Again, the determination of the octave was left to the performer. The figured bass symbol of a 6 over a 4 instructed the performer to play the pitch a sixth above the bass and the pitch a fourth above the bass as desired.

> The bass note was usually played by a bass instrument, such as the violoncello, while the full chords were the responsibility of the keyboardist.

Experimenting with this notation will show that the results are a root position triad, a first inversion triad, and second inversion triad, respectively.

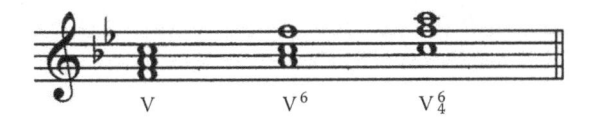

EXAMPLE 3.35 From left to right (in B-flat Major), a root position dominant triad, a first inversion dominant triad, and a second inversion dominant triad with the conventional inversion symbols below each. Remember that the convention for root position is the lack of any inversion symbol.

Review

- Inversion symbols are derived from the numbers that were originally used in figured bass notation.
- Inversion symbols are Arabic numbers applied as superscripts to the triad's identity.
- To minimize writing, inversion symbols use as few numbers as possible.
- If no inversion symbol is provided, the result is a root position triad (i.e. a stack of thirds). For both figured bass and chord inversions, this is the default.
- If only a superscript 6 is shown, the triad identified is in first inversion. The 6 indicates that the default fifth above the bass has been replaced by a sixth.
- In the case of second inversion triad, the 6 and the 4 are both needed because the fifth has been replaced by a sixth and the default third has been replaced by a fourth.

Related Exercises

§ Here are a series of triads notated on three staves. Circle the root of each triad. On the line provided below each triad, write the quality of the triad (M, m, +, or °). Next to this symbol, indicate the inversion: Add nothing for root position, a 6 for first inversion, and a 6 over a 4 for second inversion. The first one is completed for you.

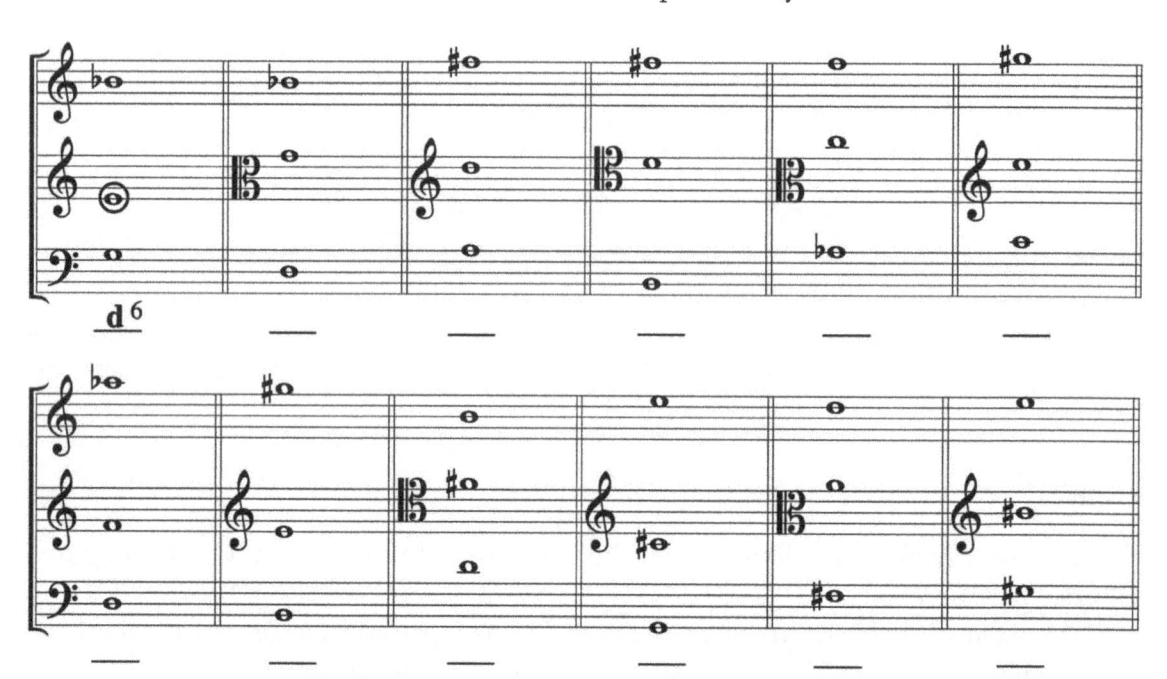

§ For each of these triads, identify the root, quality, and inversion. Name the root by writing its pitch name on the line provided, and identify the triad's quality by using upper- or lowercase letters—with or without + and ° as needed. Indicate the inversion by adding nothing, 6, or 6 over 4.

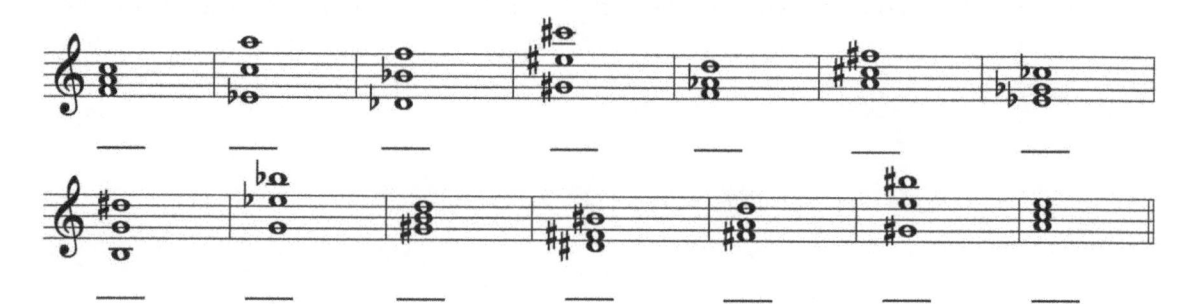

4. Triads within Keys

Harmonic Analysis

Although any consistent method for naming triads and their inversions is useful, identifying the function of triads *within the context of a major or minor tonality* provides the basis for **harmonic analysis**. In harmonic (or **functional**) analysis, triads are identified by a Roman numeral and, if inverted, by added Arabic numbers.

When the text first introduced triads, they were constructed on each degree of the major and minor scales, and the structure of each triad, as associated with each scale degree, was identified. Thus, the triad constructed on the tonic is identified with the Roman numeral one (I), the triad constructed on the supertonic is identified by the Roman numeral two (ii), and so on. (Some texts use uppercase Roman numerals to identify all triads while others—this book included—use a combination of upper and lower cases.)

Following this convention, the triads found in the E-flat Major scale would be constructed and named as shown below in Example 3.36. Note that as a first step in our harmonic analysis, the tonality of the example (E-flat Major) is given below the clef sign. (Some like to identify the triads built on the tonic, subdominant, and dominant pitches as primary triads, while triads on other scale degrees are considered secondary.)

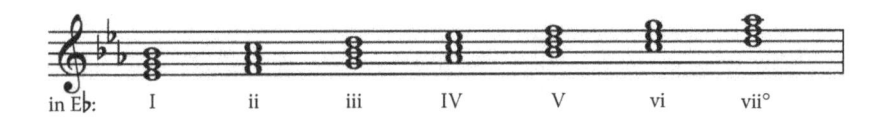

EXAMPLE 3.36   The triads formed from the E-flat Major scale and the Roman numerals associated with each. The tonality is given by "in E♭:" written below the clef.

Below are the triads created in a minor scale (in this example, a minor) complete with the Roman numeral correctly associated with each triad. In both Examples 3.36 and 3.37, note the use of upper- and lowercase numerals (and when required, a degree symbol or a plus sign). The tonality upon which the analysis is based is always given at the beginning.

> In some texts and some jazz conventions, the minus sign (–) may be used instead of the degree sign (°). Because the minus sign is sometimes used to designate minor, the practice can lead to misunderstandings.

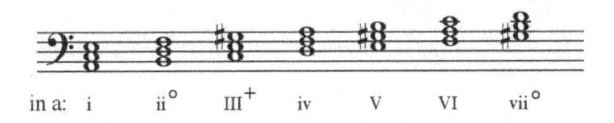

EXAMPLE 3.37   Roman numerals associated with the a harmonic minor scale. The tonality of the analysis again appears below the clef sign.

When using Roman numerals to identify triads within a given key, inversions are identified with Arabic numerals. Here are all of the triads in D Major with each triad shown and identified in root position, first inversion, and second inversion.

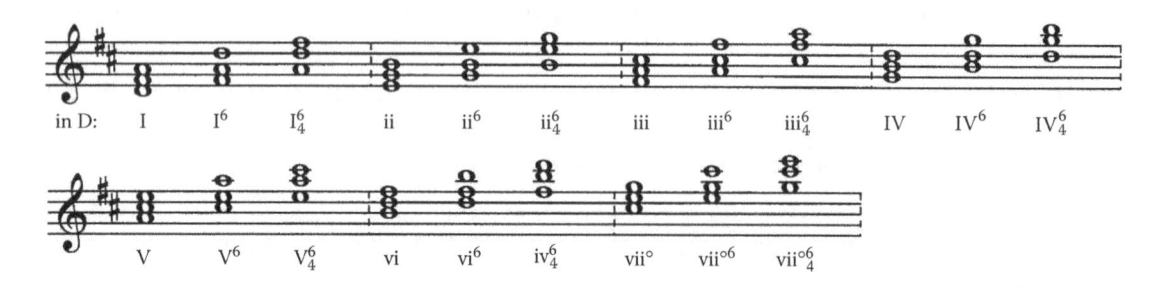

EXAMPLE 3.38 Roman numerals and inversion symbols associated with the D Major scale.

The Roman numerals communicate immediately the quality of the triad (major, minor, diminished, or augmented) and the inversion of the triad. Obviously, because the selection of the correct Roman numerals depends on knowing the tonic and modality, for complete clarity, the key (major or minor) also must be provided. By providing all of this information, a ***harmonic analysis*** or a ***functional analysis*** is produced.

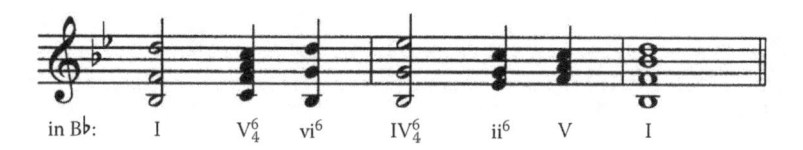

EXAMPLE 3.39 A series of chords with a functional (harmonic) analysis.

From this system of notating triads comes terminology frequently encountered in musical conversations and discussions. Commonly used terms include "a one chord" (written as I), "a four chord" (written as IV), and "a five chord" (written as V). Although many theorists prefer that instead of saying "a one chord" students would say "a tonic chord" and instead of calling it "a five chord" they would identify it as "a dominant chord" etc., it is probably not possible to change habits that date back through many generations of musicians!

> For example, if one hears, "Two six four six four" is the meaning ii-vi-IV($_4^6$), ii(^{6})-IV($_4^6$), or ii-vi-IV-vi-IV?

Yet when orally communicating the information contained in a harmonic analysis, you can avoid much of the aural confusion by using the following terms:

Symbol as Shown	As Spoken
I (or i)	tonic
ii (or ii°)	supertonic
iii (or III+)	mediant
IV (or iv)	subdominant
V	dominant
vi (or VI)	submediant
vii°	leading tone
6	first inversion
6/4	second inversion

Nashville Numbers

A practical variant on this system is found in what are known as ***Nashville Numbers***, in which performance information is communicated by referring to each triad as its scale degree, and this information is written and otherwise communicated as Arabic numbers. (Nashville Numbers do not attempt to communicate inversions.) The use of Nashville Numbers is predicated upon the performers possessing knowledge as to what chord quality is found on each scale degree. See also "Fake Book and Lead Sheet Notation" (p. 395).

Doubling

The reader has probably noted in printed music that chords sometimes contain duplicated pitches. A G Major triad may be written with two Gs, a D, and a B. These extra notes, because they duplicate notes already in the chord, do not change the identity of the chord. However, the duplication of a pitch within a triad constitutes what is called ***doubling***.

Review

- Harmonic analysis takes place within a tonality.
- A tonality is identified by using uppercase letters for major keys and lowercase letters for minor keys.
- Harmonic analysis includes the identification of triads by expressing the root of the triad as a degree of the scale using Roman numerals.
- In this process, the quality of the triad (major, minor, diminished, or augmented) may be communicated through the use of upper- and lowercase Roman numerals and, as needed, degree symbols (°) or plus signs (+).

- Uppercase Roman numerals are used for major and augmented triads with the plus sign added to differentiate the latter.
- Lowercase Roman numerals are used for minor and diminished triads with the degree sign used to differentiate the latter.
- Inversions are shown by the use of the inversion symbols: 6 and ($^6_4$).

Related Exercises

§ You are given a series of chords forming a harmonic progression within a major key. For each chord, circle the root, and, on the line below, place a Roman numeral indicating the degree of the scale that is the root of the chord. Show the triad's quality by using upper- and lowercase Roman numerals and by adding + or ° when required.

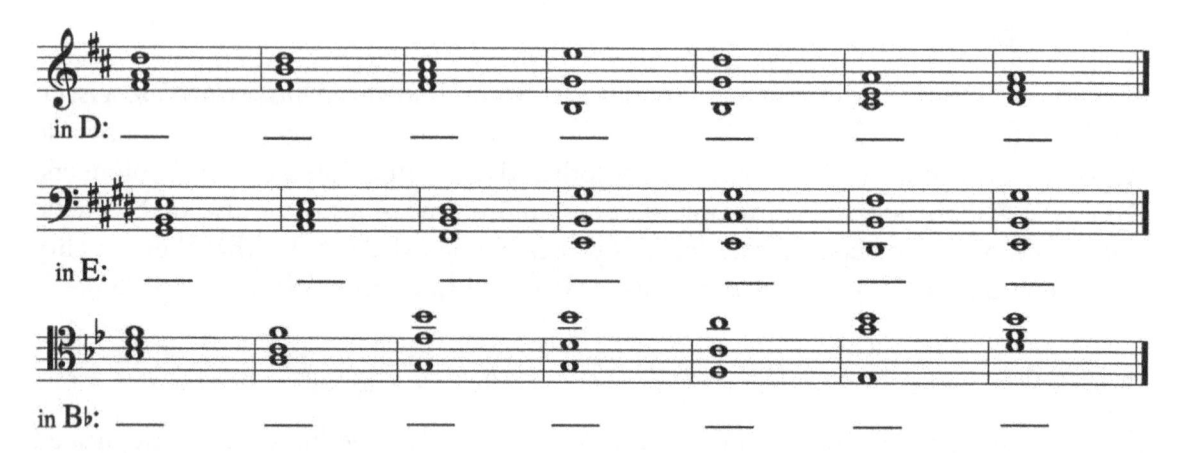

§ In the following harmonic progressions, identify the root, quality, and inversion of each chord by placing on the line provided the appropriate Roman numeral—in the proper case and with whatever modifier is required—and then adding the correct Arabic numerals (when required) to show the inversion.

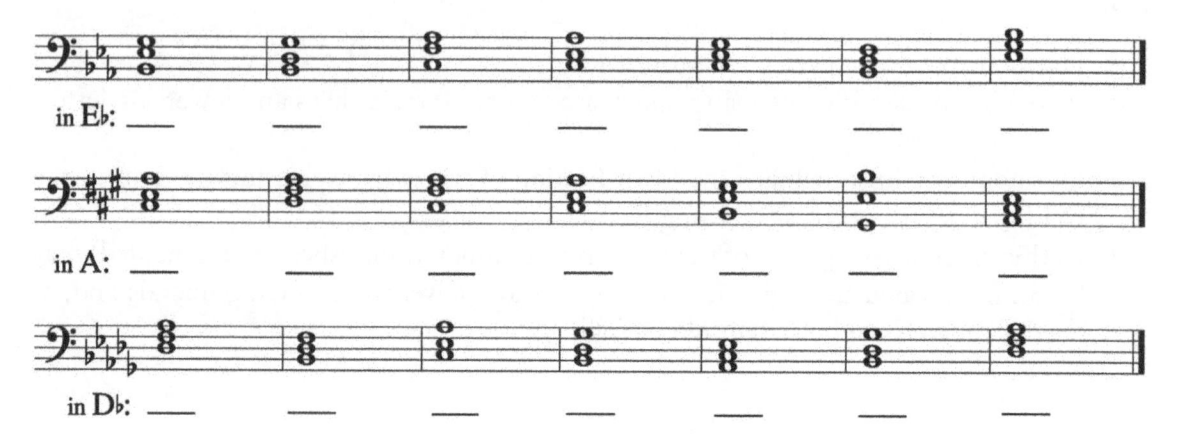

§ The following harmonic progressions are drawn from both minor and major keys. Otherwise, the instructions are the same as the exercises above.

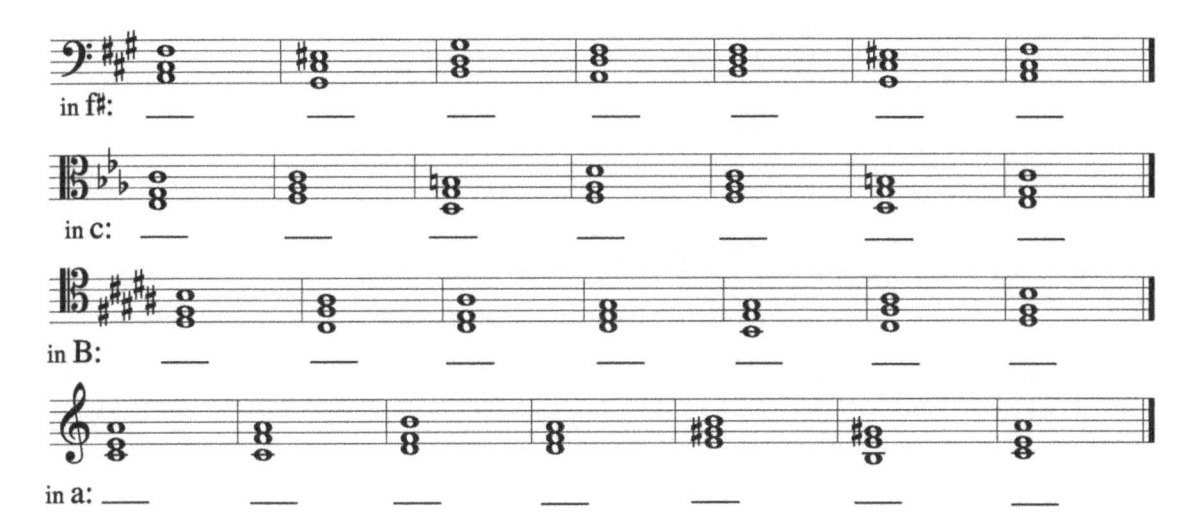

in f♯: ___ ___ ___ ___ ___ ___ ___

in c: ___ ___ ___ ___ ___ ___ ___

in B: ___ ___ ___ ___ ___ ___ ___

in a: ___ ___ ___ ___ ___ ___ ___

Triad Tendencies

As was seen with individual degrees of the scale, triads built on certain scale degrees seem to possess tendencies to generate harmonic motion (action) to other scale degrees. The most fundamental of these tendencies is that of the dominant, which pushes the harmonic motion toward the tonic. Similarly, the triad built on the leading tone strongly implies the arrival of the tonic, too.

The mediant and submediant triads do not possess especially strong tendencies and may be followed by almost any other triad without either a sense of surprise or inevitability. But the supertonic triad frequently precedes the dominant, although with less urgency than the dominant implies tonic.

The subdominant triad can go very comfortably to the tonic, and in much folk music it does exactly that. But the subdominant, like the other degrees of the scale, also represents an alternative tonal goal toward which the harmonic component of the music may progress.

5. Seventh Chords

As has been seen, our system of constructing chords includes stacking up a combination of major and/or minor thirds, yielding our familiar major, minor, diminished, and augmented triads. Years ago, composers extended this concept to produce four-note stacks. Because the distance from the root to the fourth pitch in such a four-note stack forms the interval of a seventh, these four-note chords are referred to as ***seventh chords***.

Below is the anatomy of the seventh chord.

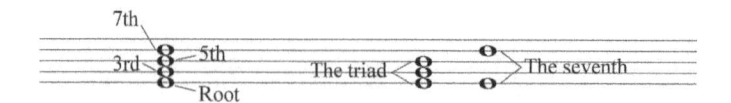

EXAMPLE 3.40 The composition of the seventh chord. On the left, a seventh chord with each pitch labeled. On the right, the basic triad with the (added) seventh, which, together, form the seventh chord.

Types of Sevenths

> The whole matter of tuning systems and their impact on music theory is often ignored in basic theory study. Yet many of our notational principles, such as the correct spelling of chords and intervals, are predicated on an assumption of certain tunings. More information on tunings can be found in Appendix III, p. 348.

The four likely sevenths to be found in our system include the major seventh, the minor seventh, the augmented seventh, and the diminished seventh. Of these, the augmented seventh is observed to yield no new sound because, in the equal-tempered system of tuning keyboards, the sound of the augmented seventh cannot be aurally distinguished from the perfect octave. In a discussion such as this one, the augmented seventh is usually omitted.

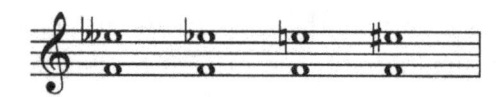

EXAMPLE 3.41 From left to right, the diminished seventh, the minor seventh, the major seventh, and the augmented seventh.

Systematically creating a set of seventh chords based on the four basic triad types and the three viable versions of the interval of the seventh gives the following twelve chords:

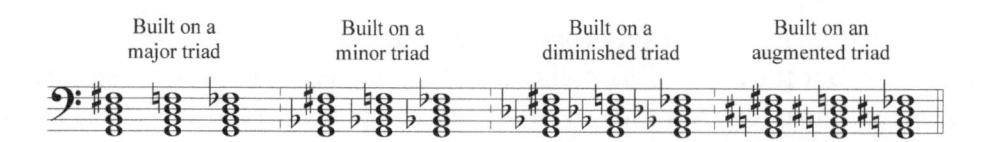

EXAMPLE 3.42 From left to right: first group, sevenths built on a major triad; second group, sevenths built on a minor triad; third group, sevenths built on a diminished triad; last group, sevenths built on an augmented triad. Within each group, left to right: major seventh, minor seventh, and diminished seventh.

To name these four-note chords in an unambiguous way, seventh chords are frequently identified by abbreviations of their *two* properties: the quality of the triad upon which they are based and the quality of the added seventh. In Example 3.42 above, the abbreviations of the sevenths, from left to right, would normally be given as M-M7, M-m7, M-d7; m-M7, m-m7, m-d7; d-M7, d-m7, d-d7; and A-M7, A-m7, and A-d7.

Composers have found these twelve types of seventh chords useful in various situations and styles of music. But the seventh chords usually encountered in common-practice music are only these four: M-m7, m-m7, d-m7, and d-d7. Here they are constructed with F as the root.

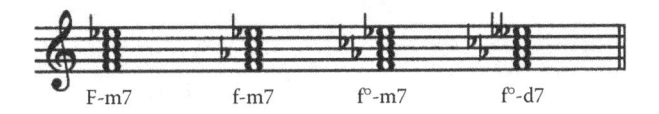

F-m7   f-m7   f°-m7   f°-d7

EXAMPLE 3.43 The four most commonly used seventh chords notated with F as the root. From left to right, F Major-minor seventh, f minor-minor seventh, f diminished-minor seventh, and f diminished-diminished (fully diminished) seventh.

Review

- Seventh chords are four-note chords produced by stacking three thirds.
- The term *seventh chord* is derived from the fact that the top note in the four-note stack is a seventh above the root.
- Seventh chords can be seen as a combination of a triad plus a seventh.
- The usual sevenths used are the major, minor, and diminished.
- You state the quality of seventh chords by stating the quality of the triad and the size of the seventh: M-M7, M-m7, d-d7, m-M7, m-m7, m-d7, d-M7, d-m7, or d-d7.
- Although twelve distinctive seventh chords may be formed, in common-practice music, the use of seventh chords is usually restricted to M-m7, m-m7, d-m7, and d-d7.

Related Exercises

§ In each example below, identify the root of the seventh chord by circling it, and then identify the quality of the basic triad (major, minor, or diminished) by writing M, m, or d, respectively, on the lower line and the quality of the seventh (M, m, or d) on the upper line below the example.

§ Each example below has a key signature. Assuming a major key, write the specified seventh chords. The root of the chord is given.

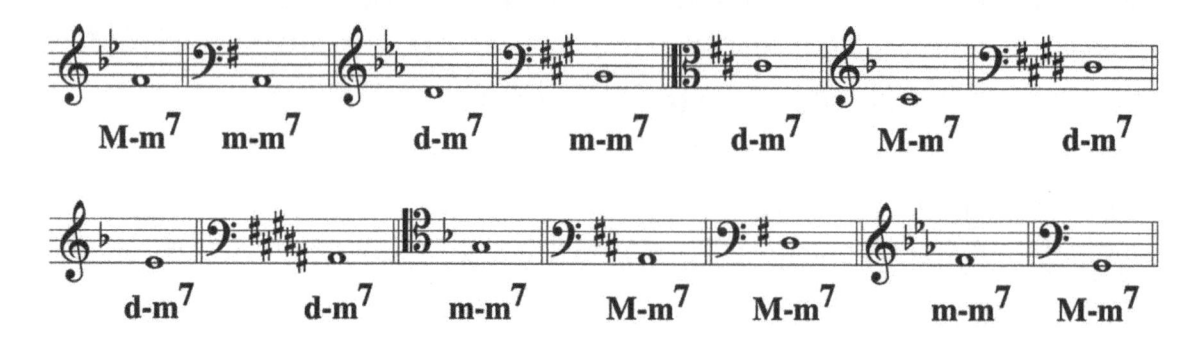

M-m⁷   m-m⁷   d-m⁷   m-m⁷   d-m⁷   M-m⁷   d-m⁷

d-m⁷   d-m⁷   m-m⁷   M-m⁷   M-m⁷   m-m⁷   M-m⁷

§ Each example below has a key signature. Assuming a minor key (harmonic), write the specified seventh chords. Some chords will require you to use an accidental. The root is given.

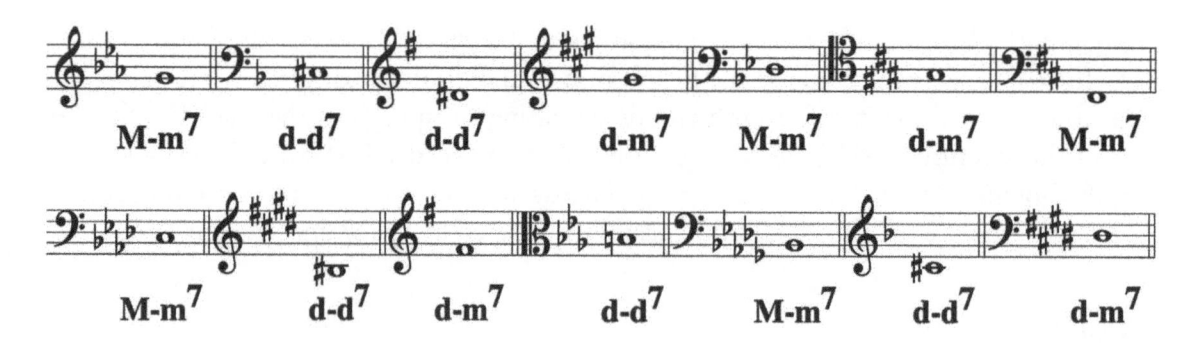

M-m⁷   d-d⁷   d-d⁷   d-m⁷   M-m⁷   d-m⁷   M-m⁷

M-m⁷   d-d⁷   d-m⁷   d-d⁷   M-m⁷   d-d⁷   d-m⁷

Seventh Chords Found within Keys

As was done with triads, seventh chords can be constructed on each pitch of the major and harmonic minor scales. However, in common-practice usage, the only seventh chords regularly encountered are those constructed on the supertonic, dominant, and leading tone scale degrees. Here are these most useful chords as constructed in a major key.

ii⁷   V⁷   vii°⁷

EXAMPLE 3.44   Seventh chords constructed in E Major; from left to right, m-m⁷ (on F-sharp), M-m⁷ (on B), and d-m⁷ (on D-sharp).

These are the standard seventh constructions found in minor keys.

EXAMPLE 3.45 Seventh chords constructed in f harmonic minor; from left to right, d-m^7 (on G), M-m^7 (on C), and d-d^7 (on E-natural).

Note that the three seventh chords formed in a major tonality are the m-m7 built on the supertonic, the M-m7 built on the dominant, and the d-m7 built on the leading tone. In minor tonalities, the three seventh chords are the d-m7 built on the supertonic, the M-m7 built on the dominant, and the d-d7 built on the leading tone.

If we add to the list those sevenths that can be constructed in melodic minor, the following are found: M-m7 chords on the mediant, the subtonic (lowered seventh), and the subdominant; m-m7 chords on the supertonic and the dominant; and a d-m7 chord on the raised submediant.

Roman numerals are used to identify seventh chords within keys. As with triads, the Roman numeral is based on the degree of the scale of the root while the case is determined by the quality of the triad within the seventh chord.

In major keys, the symbol for the supertonic seventh chord is ii^7. This symbol indicates that the root of the chord is the second degree of the scale, the quality of the triad is minor, and a minor seventh has been added. By a similar logic, the dominant seventh is written as V^7, indicating a major triad built on the dominant also with a minor seventh.

In minor keys (harmonic minor is assumed here), the dominant seventh is also V^7, indicating as above a major triad built on the dominant with an added minor seventh. The leading tone seventh is vii^{o7}, indicating a diminished triad built on the leading tone with an added diminished seventh.

In major keys, the leading tone seventh is written as vii^{ø7}. The same convention is used for the supertonic in minor: ii^{ø7}. This notation indicates a diminished triad built on a particular degree of the scale and an added minor seventh.

Carefully examining the symbols used for the four *typical* seventh chords, it will be noted that there are four unique symbols. The symbol ii^7 is understood to mean a minor triad with an added minor seventh built on the supertonic. This particular seventh chord is overwhelmingly likely to be found on the supertonic, hence its common nickname **two-seven chord**.

The seventh chord built on the dominant, in both major and harmonic minor, is a major-minor seventh, and its Roman numeral symbol is V^7. The nickname for this seventh chord is the **dominant seventh**. In minor keys, the

> If a musician uses the term *diminished seventh*, he is usually referring to the fully diminished seventh chord. But he could also mean (specifically) a diminished triad on the leading tone.

leading tone seventh is typically a diminished-diminished seventh represented as vii°7 and called a ***fully diminished seventh*** because *both* the basic triad *and* the added seventh are diminished.

Finally, the seventh chord built on the leading tone in major, a diminished-minor seventh chord, is represented as vii^{ø7}, and its common name is ***half-diminished seventh*** because, although the triad is diminished, the seventh, being minor, is not. Thus, the chord is said to be half-diminished.

> These two symbols, with the same meanings, are sometimes found in the chord changes used in pops and jazz writing.

Note the use of ° for diminished and ø for half-diminished. While the ° may be used with both triads and seventh chords, the ø is associated only with seventh chords.

Review

- In common-practice music, the four types of sevenths are primarily found on the second, fifth, and seventh scale degrees.
- In major keys, these are ii^7 (m-m7), V^7 (M-m7), and vii^{ø7} (d-m7) chords.
- In minor keys, these are ii^{ø7} (d-m7), V^7 (M-m7), and vii$^{°7}$ (d-d7) chords.
- In casual conversation, the term *dominant seventh* is often used to describe any M-m7 quality chord.
- In casual conversation, the term *two-seven (chord)* is often used to describe any m-m7 quality chord.
- In casual conversation, the term *half-diminished seventh* is often used to describe any d-m7 quality chord.
- In casual conversation, the term *fully diminished seventh* is often used to describe any d-d7 quality chord.

Related Exercises

§ On the staves provided, write the specified seventh chords. Some may be identified by their structures (e.g. major-minor seventh) and some by their use within the key (dominant seventh, half-diminished seventh, etc.). The root of the chord is provided.

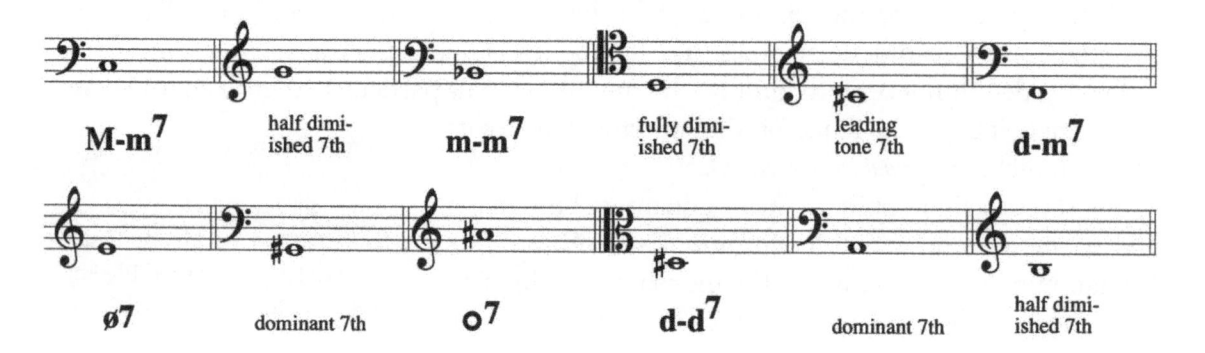

M-m^7 | half diminished 7th | m-m^7 | fully diminished 7th | leading tone 7th | d-m^7

ø7 | dominant 7th | °7 | d-d^7 | dominant 7th | half diminished 7th

§ As in the prior exercise, you are asked to write specific seventh chords but instead of being provided with the root, you are told only the key (major or minor). You will need to determine and notate the key signature and write the chord on the staff.

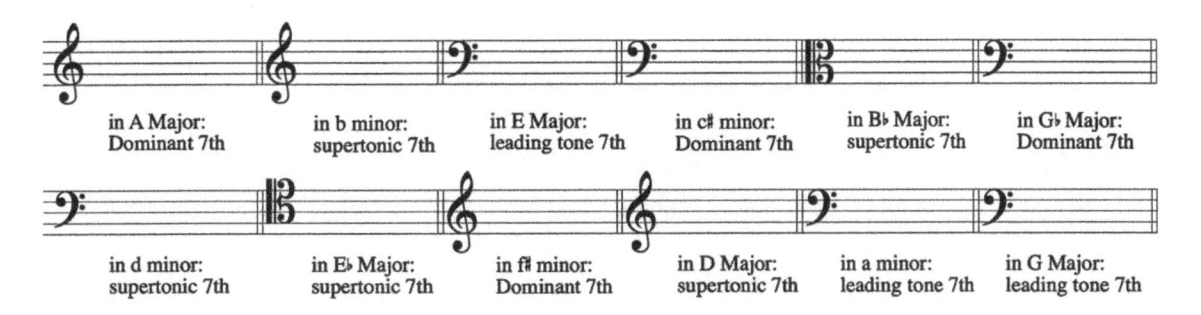

| in A Major: | in b minor: | in E Major: | in c# minor: | in B♭ Major: | in G♭ Major: |
| Dominant 7th | supertonic 7th | leading tone 7th | Dominant 7th | supertonic 7th | Dominant 7th |

| in d minor: | in E♭ Major: | in f# minor: | in D Major: | in a minor: | in G Major: |
| supertonic 7th | supertonic 7th | Dominant 7th | supertonic 7th | leading tone 7th | leading tone 7th |

Inverting Seventh Chords

Just as triads may be inverted, seventh chords, too, are invertible. Because four pitches are involved, seventh chords can be found in root position plus *three* inversions. The symbol for a root position seventh (a seventh chord with its root as the bass note) is what we have been using: ^{7}.

First inversion (with the third in the bass) is shown by $^6_5$.

Second inversion sevenths (with the fifth in the bass) are shown as $^4_3$.

The ***third inversion***, with the seventh in the bass, is represented by ^{2} or by $^4_2$.

> Some texts indicate the third inversion seventh by placing the 4 over the 2 but enclosing the 4 in parentheses.

Here is the dominant seventh chord in A Major shown in root position and in all three inversions:

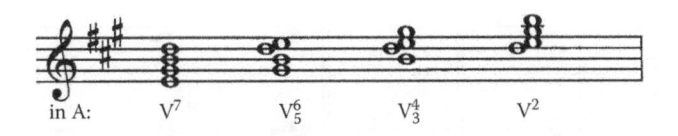

in A: V^7 V^6_5 V^4_3 V^2

EXAMPLE 3.46 From left to right, the dominant seventh in A Major shown in root position, first inversion, second inversion, and third inversion.

As an aid to remembering the inversion symbols for sevenths, simply count backward from seven, so the inversion symbols for seventh chords are *seven, six-five, four-three, two*—an order that represents root position, first inversion, second inversion, and third inversion.

As with triads, inversions of seventh chords in stacked thirds can be recognized by the configuration of the notes regardless of the specific pitches involved. Note these examples.

EXAMPLE 3.47 Various inversions of seventh chords. From left to right, third inversion, first inversion, root position, second inversion, first inversion, third inversion, and second inversion.

Review

- As with triads, seventh chords may be inverted.
- Because sevenths contain four pitches, they have three inversions in addition to the root position.
- When written with the root in the bass, the seventh chord is in root position, and the abbreviation is ^{7}.
- When written with the third in the bass, the seventh chord is in first inversion, and the abbreviation is $^6_5$.
- When written with the fifth in the bass, the seventh chord is in second inversion, and the abbreviation is $^4_3$.
- When written with the seventh in the bass, the seventh chord is in third inversion, and the abbreviation is ^{2}, $^4_2$ or $^{(4)}_2$.
- As with triads, the quality (M-m7, m-m7, d-m7, or d-d7) of the seventh chord is not affected by the selected inversion.

Related Exercises

§ In each of the following examples, you are given a seventh chord. Circle the root, and, on the line below, identify *the lowest pitch* as being the root, the third, the fifth, or the seventh. The first one is done for you.

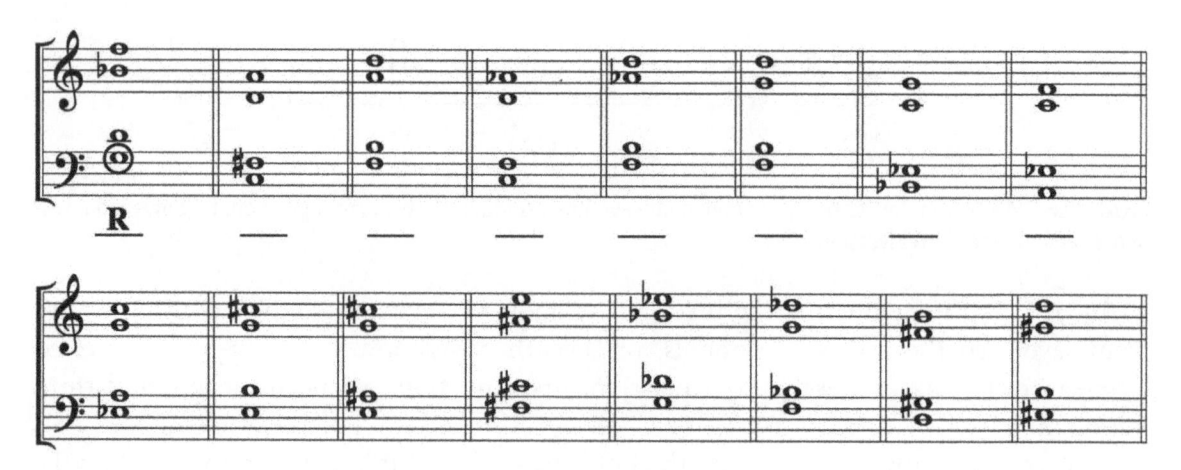

R

§ On the staff below, write the specified seventh chords in the spaces provided. The pitches may be distributed in any legible manner, but the lowest pitch needs to be as specified below the space for the answer.

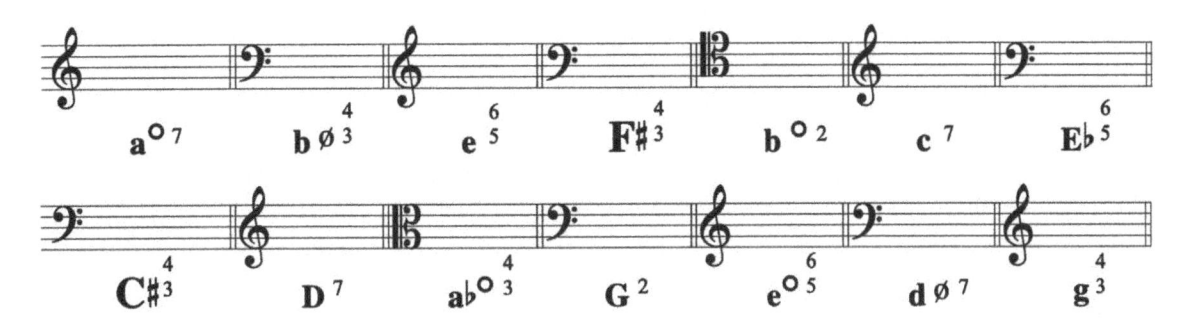

a°7   bø$^4_3$ e$^6_5$ F#$^4_3$ b°^{2} c^7 E♭$^6_5$

C#$^4_3$ D^7 a♭°$^4_3$ G^2 e°$^6_5$ dø^7 g$^4_3$

Using Seventh Chords

Seventh chords by virtue of their more dissonant (unstable) nature create a strong harmonic drive toward a resolution. The strongest and most familiar of these is the dominant seventh chord, which almost compels the arrival of the implied tonic chord. This familiar progression, found at the end of thousands of pieces and sections of pieces, looks like this:

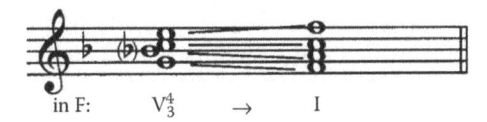

in F: V$^4_3$ → I

EXAMPLE 3.48 The dominant seventh chord in F Major progressing to the tonic. Note that each pitch of the dominant seventh in this example travels fairly directly to the appropriate pitch in the tonic triad. Compare these motions with pitch tendencies discussed on p. 101.

The leading tone sevenths, either the half-diminished version generated by the major tonality or the fully diminished seventh generated in minor, also have strong tendencies to resolve to the tonic. These can be seen in the following examples:

in G: viiø$^4_3$ → I   vii°$^4_3$ → I

EXAMPLE 3.49 On the left, the leading tone seventh in G Major resolving to tonic. On the right, the leading tone seventh in c minor resolving to the tonic.

The supertonic sevenths in both the major and minor keys seem to lead to the dominant (or dominant seventh) chord for its resolution. This harmonic push is not as strong as the push to the tonic created by the dominant seventh or by the two leading tone sevenths, but it is nonetheless compelling.

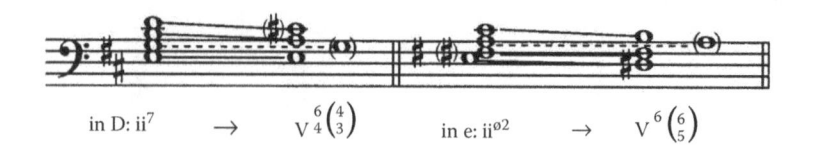

in D: ii^7 → V$^6_4$ ($^6_3$)   in e: ii^{ø2} → V^6 ($^6_5$)

EXAMPLE 3.50 On the left, the supertonic seventh in D Major resolving to the dominant or dominant seventh. On the right, the supertonic seventh in e minor resolving to the dominant or dominant seventh.

Because of their inherent instabilities, composers have found these seventh chords to be valuable for creating harmonic motion. And by avoiding—or working contrary to—their implications, these seventh chords may serve as mechanisms for prolonging and transforming musical passages.

Review

- Seventh chords are unstable and have strong tendencies to resolve in certain ways.
- The dominant seventh tends to resolve to the tonic.
- The leading tone sevenths tend also to resolve to the tonic.
- The supertonic sevenths tend to progress to the dominant.

Related Exercises

§ In each example, you are given a seventh chord and the correct key signature. After each given chord, write the root of the most likely following chord. The first one is done for you.

6. Harmonic Progressions

Traditional Chord Orderings

In most music, we are aware that the chords being used to accompany the melody change from time to time. Traditional music frequently (but certainly not always) begins with the tonic pitch or triad. If the piece is major in modality, the tonic triad will be a major triad. If the piece is minor in modality, the initial tonic chord will likely be a minor triad.

In common-practice music, the last chord heard in the piece is most likely going to be tonic. But in minor tonalities, the last chord may be altered from a minor triad to a major triad. This change of the final tonic triad in minor keys into a major triad probably dates back to about 1500, at a time when a minor third was still considered to be too dissonant to serve as the final sonority of a piece. The practice continued until around the end of the Baroque period (*c.* 1750). This altering of the last tonic is still done in some situations either because people enjoy the sound of this change in modality or because it evokes an older music. The name applied to this altering of the minor triad by raising the third of the chord is the **Picardy third** or *tierce de Picardie*.

Between the first and last chord of a piece, many other chords may be inserted to support and color the melody, to illuminate any words, and to evoke emotions appropriate to the music. The chords chosen and the order of the chords vary greatly from piece to piece, composer to composer, and style to style. However the chords may be arranged, the order in which the chords appear, from the beginning to the end, is called the ***harmonic progression***. The nature of its harmonic progression is an important characteristic of every piece.

Although the composer may choose any chord at any moment and in any order in a piece of music, certain patterns are more frequently encountered than others. Here is one that the reader may readily recognize:

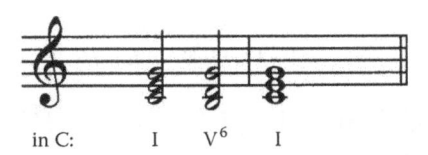

in C: I   V⁶   I

EXAMPLE 3.51   A very basic harmonic progression I – V – I as might be found in C Major.

This simple pattern does what harmonic accompaniments usually do: It takes the music from the "home" sonority (tonic) to a foreign sonority (the dominant) and back, thereby completing an auditory journey. Other simple harmonic patterns may also be found, such as the following:

> In all harmonic progressions illustrated here, the dominant triad, leading tone triad, and supertonic triad may be altered to be the dominant seventh, leading tone seventh, and supertonic seventh, respectively, at the discretion of the writer. By the same token, various inversions may be used.

EXAMPLE 3.52 Shown in B-flat Major, the harmonic progression I – IV – I.

The harmonic journey is often more extensive than those given above. These progressions are common:

$$\text{I} \quad \text{IV} \quad \text{V} \quad \text{I} \qquad \text{or}$$
$$\text{I} \quad \text{IV} \quad \text{ii} \quad \text{V} \quad \text{I}$$

The first progression—tonic, subdominant, dominant, and tonic— might look like this:

> All of the examples shown with this discussion present merely an ordering of triads or sevenths that *might* be used. In actual composition, concerns with voice-leading, pitch doubling, vocal and instrumental ranges, style, inversions, and coloring would also need to be addressed.

EXAMPLE 3.53 Shown in F Major, the harmonic progression I – IV – V – I.

And the second progression of tonic, subdominant, supertonic, dominant-seventh, and tonic would use these chords in the key of G Major:

EXAMPLE 3.54 Shown in G Major, the harmonic progression I – IV – ii – V – I.

A progression that may sound familiar is   I   vi   IV   V   I.
  Consisting of tonic, submediant, subdominant, dominant, and tonic, it is the basis of several songs that are easy to play and sing, including the ubiquitous "Heart and Soul." In E-flat Major, it would produce this sequence:

EXAMPLE 3.55 In E-flat Major, a common chord progression composed of these chords: I – vi – IV – V – I.

A common chord pattern that is found in the blues (and in much popular music) is as follows:

I   IV   I   V   IV   I

It is perhaps the most familiar of the twelve-bar blues progressions. In D Major, it would be

in D: I ——————————————— IV$^6_4$ ——— I ——— V$^6_4$ IV$^6_4$ I ———

EXAMPLE 3.56   A twelve-bar blues progression consisting of I – IV – I – V – IV – I in D Major.

Notice that in the blues progression the chords are specified and so is the *duration* of each chord. Knowing which chords to play and when to play them allows the creation of music that structurally and harmonically resembles the blues.

Major and Minor Progressions

The harmonic progressions shown in Examples 3.51 through 3.56 may be understood to work in either major or minor keys. In a minor key, the triads and sevenths associated with minor modalities would be used so that I – V – I would become i – V – i (or I) and I – vi – IV – ii – V – I would become i – VI – iv – ii° – V – i.

The Circle of Fifths

In larger and extended harmonic progressions, chords are often ordered in such a way that the root of one chord is the dominant to (the root of) the following chord, which is, in turn, the dominant to the next chord and (perhaps) so on. Such progressions are said to be following the ***circle of fifths***. Because tonics can always be preceded by their dominant, this sort of progression has been successful in many contexts and styles. (For a discussion of the circle of fifths, see Appendix IV on p. 354.)

Review

- The harmonic structure of much common-practice music consists of a series of chords the majority of which are related to the key of the music.
- These harmonic patterns may be expressed as a series of Roman numerals representing the roots and the qualities of the chords involved.
- Commonly, the harmonic pattern begins and ends with the tonic chord (either I or i).

- The final tonic is most likely (but not always) preceded by the dominant (V or V⁷) chord.
- Other frequently encountered chords are the subdominant (IV or iv), the submediant (vi or VI), and the supertonic (ii or ii°).
- Especially in extended progressions, it is not unusual to find a series of chords whose roots follow a portion of the circle of fifths.

Related Exercises

§ In the following examples, you are provided with a series of chords. Circle the root of each chord.

§ In the following examples, you are provided with a series of chords within a specified key. Circle the root of each chord. Then, on the line below each chord, write the Roman numeral that identifies the degree of the scale that is the root of that chord. (For chords with a major quality, you should use uppercase Roman numerals; for chords with a minor or diminished quality, use lowercase Roman numerals.)

A

in A♭: — — — — — — —

B

in A: — — — — — — —

C

in D: — — — — — — —

D

in E♭: — — — — — — —

Smoother Harmonic Progressions

It is often desirable to create a harmonic progression that seems to move subtly from chord to chord. In other situations, the composer may wish to create a harmonic progression that is more jagged or striking in its changes. Although tastes and times may dictate what constitutes a smooth harmonic motion versus a more angular one, some general guidelines can help achieve the desired effects.

A chord series in which only one pitch is changed from chord to chord creates a smooth progression. In the passage below, there is only one pitch change per chord. The horizontal lines show the pitches that do not change; the arrows identify the pitches that change.

in D: I   vi⁶   IV⁶₄   ii   vii°⁶   V⁶₄   iii   I⁶

EXAMPLE 3.57 A series of chords each of which differs from the preceding chord by a single pitch (i.e. each triad possesses two tones in common with both the preceding and following triad).

Changing a single chord tone through chromatic inflection is another means to obtain a smooth progression.

EXAMPLE 3.58 Movement from one triad to another by the use of semitones, chromatic or diatonic.

Other changes that can be made, while minimizing harmonic movement, are to change the inversion of the chord or the distribution of the upper pitches.

in F: V —————————————— V⁶₄ ——————————————

EXAMPLE 3.59 These eight chords are all from the same triad. From the left, a dominant triad in root position with four different distributions of the upper pitches. On the right, the same triad in second inversion with, again, four different distributions of the upper pitches.

When two or more chord tones change between two successive chords, the sense of harmonic change is increased. The example below shows several chords in a very normal progression but with each chord composed of pitches that are not a part of the preceding chord.

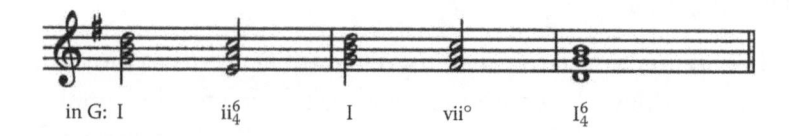

in G: I   ii⁶₄   I   vii°   I⁶₄

EXAMPLE 3.60 In this example, there are no common tones between successive triads.

In practice, the effort to create placid or athletic harmonic motion can be enhanced or negated by concomitant changes in tone quality, pitch range, dynamics, and/or rhythm.

Harmony: Note(s) with Note(s)

Review

- The more common tones between two successive chords, the smoother the harmonic motion.
- The lack of common tones between two successive chords creates a greater sense of harmonic change.
- Either effect can be minimized or increased by other factors, such as changing octaves, tone quality, dynamics, and rhythmic activities.

Related Exercises

§ Study each progression below and locate all the common tones between adjacent chords. Look for common tones within a voice and common tones between voices. Circle the pitch in a chord and draw a line from it to the same pitch in the next chord. The first example is done for you.

§ You are given a triad. On the staff next to it are two empty measures. In the first measure (1), write a chord that shares one (and no more than one) common tone with the given triad; in the second measure (2), write a chord with two (and no more than two) common tones.

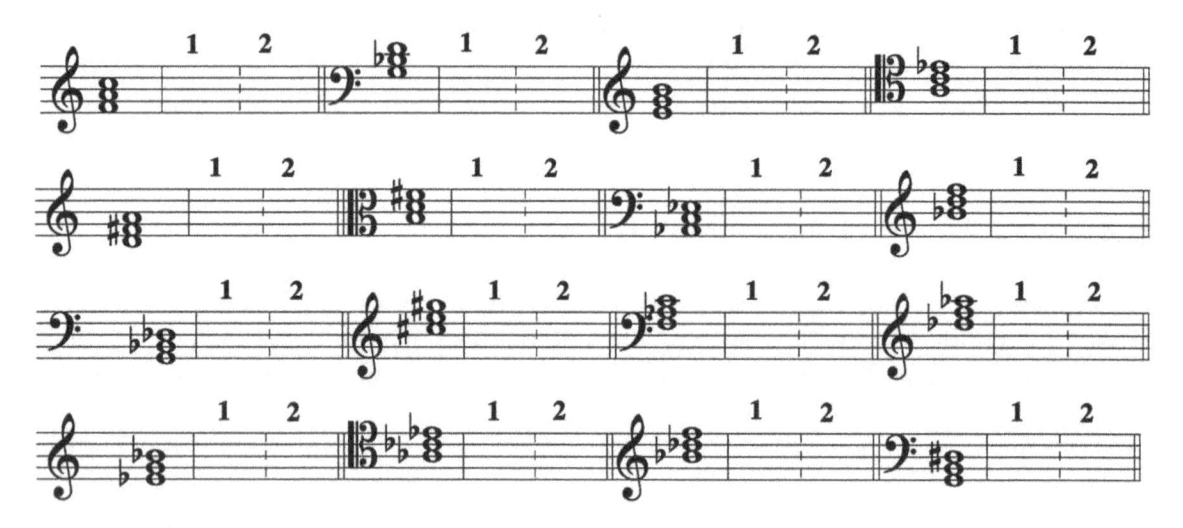

7. Harmonic Rhythm

The example of the twelve-bar blues progression given above (Example 3.56) can be used to introduce the concept of ***harmonic rhythm***. Harmonic rhythm is the rhythm generated by the changes in harmony (the harmonic underlayment) found in a piece of music.

As was noted before, in the twelve-bar blues progression, the first tonic harmony lasts for four bars. The following subdominant harmony is two bars long, and the return to tonic is also two bars long. The dominant harmony follows but lasts only one bar, as does the following subdominant. The concluding return to tonic is two bars long.

EXAMPLE 3.61   A twelve-bar blues progression showing the harmonic rhythm associated with this music.

In the blues, this repeating pattern establishes a harmonic framework upon which improvisation may take place. Within this repeating sonic foundation, the listener can easily tell where within the piece the performer is at each moment.

This phenomenon is of course not found only in the blues. Below is a folk melody with a simple harmonic accompaniment. Notice that the chords change in the rhythmic pattern shown in the bass clef. The melody in the treble possesses its own rhythm.

EXAMPLE 3.62 Given in the bass clef, the harmonic rhythm associated with "On Top of Old Smokey."

Example 3.63 has the following harmonic rhythm: two bars of tonic, four bars of subdominant, four bars of tonic, four bars of dominant, and then a return to tonic for about two bars. The melody has quite a different rhythmic pattern. In fact, if we compare the two, they look like this:

EXAMPLE 3.63 The melodic rhythm associated with "On Top of Old Smokey."

EXAMPLE 3.64 The harmonic rhythm associated with "On Top of Old Smokey."

And this pattern is repeated for each verse.

In Examples 3.61 through 3.64, the harmonic rhythm is quite slow with each chord lasting for one or more bars. However, in some music, the harmonic rhythm can change beat by beat, as in this chorale harmonization by J.S. Bach.

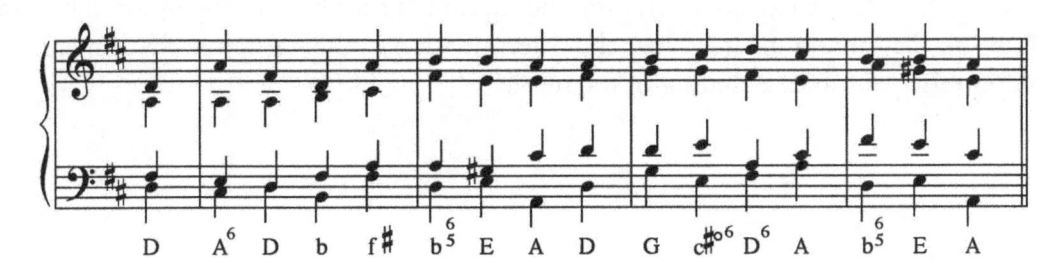

EXAMPLE 3.65 The harmonic rhythm associated with *"Wie schön leuchtet der Morgenstern."* Note that in this excerpt the melody and the harmony change on every beat.

Sometimes the harmony moves faster (more frequently) than the melodic rhythm. Here is an example.

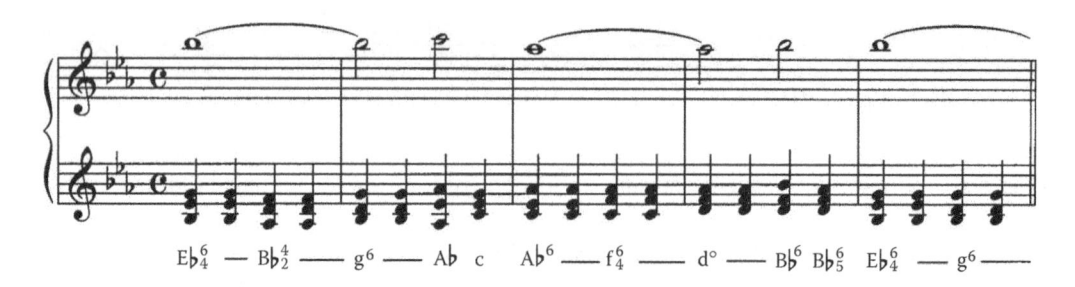

$E\flat^6_4$ — $B\flat^4_2$ — g^6 — $A\flat$ c $A\flat^6$ — f^6_4 — $d°$ — $B\flat^6$ $B\flat^6_5$ $E\flat^6_4$ — g^6 —

EXAMPLE 3.66 While the melody is stated in durations of whole notes tied to half notes and half notes, the harmony changes every half note and, in two places, every quarter note.

The defining characteristics of any piece of music include, among other elements, its underlying harmonic progression and associated rhythm (harmonic rhythm) as well as the melodic rhythmic and pitch structures.

Review

- Although melody and harmony may move together, they need not do so.
- The rhythmic pattern generated by the durations of the prevailing harmonies is called the harmonic rhythm.
- When attempting to understand the structure of a piece of music, the characteristics of the harmonic rhythm are significant factors.

Related Exercises

§ Several musical examples are presented below. On the single line staff provided below each example, write the harmonic rhythm (the rhythm of the chord changes) for that example. How do the three compare? Does the determination of the harmonic rhythm enhance or compromise your understanding of the music?

The Mill on the Brook
A — W. Tschirch

Aria from Rinaldo
B — G.F. Handel

Scherzo from Opus 24
C — L. van Beethoven

8. Cadences

In Part 2, melodic pitch goals and points of hesitation or repose were discussed. These points of hesitation are cadences. A primary use of chords is to support melodic lines and to intensify these cadences. Harmonized cadences, by the nature of their increased complexity, may be both more varied and also less ambiguous than purely melodic cadences.

> In pieces where the key frequently changes, this may not be the initial or the final tonic. It will rather be the pitch that is currently functioning as tonic.

Broadly speaking, there are two categories of cadences: those that sound final and those that do not. Those that sound final invariably conclude with the arrival of a tonic chord. Those that do not sound final conclude on a chord other than tonic.

Cadences That Sound Final

Authentic Cadences

Probably the most familiar cadence is the ***authentic cadence***. At its most fundamental, an authentic cadence consists of a dominant triad (or seventh) followed by a tonic triad. Other standard configurations include a supertonic or tonic six-four (or both) immediately before the dominant harmony. Here are some typical illustrations.

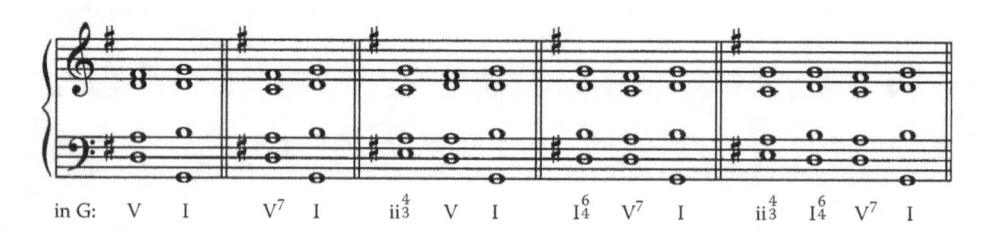

EXAMPLE 3.67 Various authentic cadence formulas in G Major. From left to right, dominant to tonic, dominant seventh to tonic, supertonic seventh to dominant to tonic, tonic six-four to dominant seventh to tonic, and supertonic seventh to tonic six-four to dominant seventh to tonic.

Leading tone triads or sevenths often replace the dominant chord in authentic cadences.

The Tonic Six-Four

This particular triad displays an unusual quality. Even though it is composed of the three pitches that belong to the tonic triad, when used in the second inversion (six-four), this chord sounds, and thus behaves, like a dominant chord. In early common-practice music, this will usually be the only appearance of the tonic chord in second inversion, as a precursor to the dominant. By listening to the last two cadences in Example 3.67, the reader should hear the dominant (unstable) quality of the tonic six-four chord.

An explanation for this unstable character is based on the fact that the bass is the dominant in the tonality and that both the root of the triad and the third can be heard as having tendencies to need resolution. The third seems to want to move stepwise downward to the supertonic (en route to an eventual arrival at the tonic).

The root of the tonic six-four seems surprisingly active, too, wanting as it does to move to the leading tone. This can be explained by the instability of the harmonic interval of the perfect fourth, which frequently wants to resolve to a major third.

Types of Authentic Cadences

Theorists have identified various standard configurations found in authentic cadence patterns. The two almost universally recognized types are identified as a ***perfect authentic cadence*** and an ***imperfect authentic cadence***.

A perfect authentic cadence will have the tonic pitch as both the highest and lowest tone in the final chord. An imperfect authentic cadence will not. The usual reason that an authentic cadence would be heard as imperfect will be due to the third or the fifth of the triad being presented in the highest voice. A less common—in fact, unlikely—variant is having the third or the fifth in the bass.

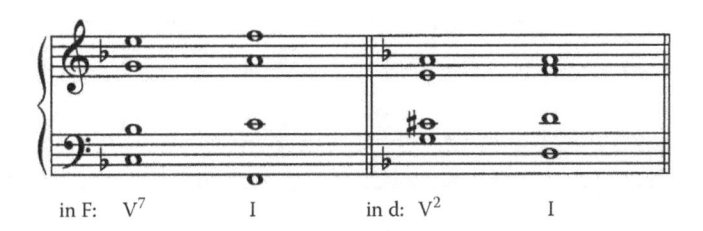

in F: V^7 I   in d: V^2 I

EXAMPLE 3.68   On the left, a perfect authentic cadence in F Major. On the right, an imperfect authentic cadence in d minor.

Plagal Cadences

The other final sounding cadence is the ***plagal cadence***, which consists of a subdominant chord followed by the tonic chord. There seems to be no logical reason for the name of this cadence. Because Protestant hymns have often concluded with an authentic cadence followed by an "Amen" sung to a subdominant-tonic harmonic pattern, music students have for years identified the plagal cadence as the "amen cadence."

However, the Greek root *plagio* is a prefix that is added to words to imply divergent or oblique. It may indicate that plagal modes and the plagal cadence were merely identified as "different" compared to authentic modes and cadences.

Here are several examples:

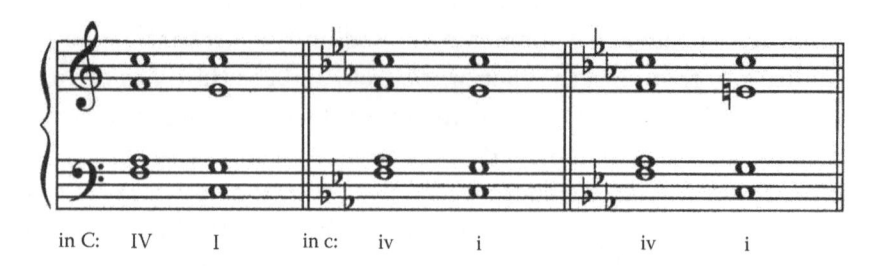

[musical notation: in C: IV I | in c: iv i | iv i]

EXAMPLE 3.69 Plagal cadences. From left to right, subdominant to tonic in C Major, subdominant to tonic in c minor, and subdominant to tonic in c minor but resolving on the C Major triad.

Cadences That *Do Not* Sound Final

Half Cadences

The ***half cadence*** is a hesitation on a pitch other than the tonic. Harmonically, the half cadence is usually a cadence on a chord that functions as a dominant. The half cadence pattern is typically a dominant (or dominant seventh) chord *preceded* by a supertonic, subdominant, or tonic six-four. Here are these three types.

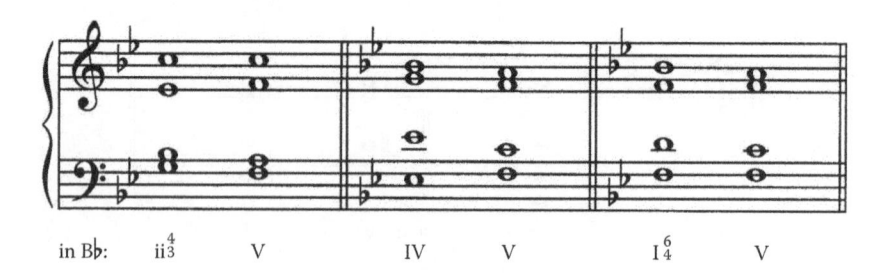

[musical notation: in B♭: ii$^4_3$ V | IV V | I$^6_4$ V]

EXAMPLE 3.70 Half cadences in B-flat Major. From left to right, supertonic (seventh) to dominant, subdominant to dominant, and tonic six-four to dominant.

Other chords may precede the dominant because the only requirement for a cadence to be a half cadence is that the cadence occurs with the dominant harmony.

Deceptive Cadences

The final generally identified type of cadence is the ***deceptive cadence*** (or sometimes called the interrupted cadence). A deceptive cadence is aptly named. To the listener, it sounds as though it is going to be an authentic cadence, but, instead of arriving on the tonic, the final chord in the pattern is *a chord other than tonic* (and other than dominant). The most typical chord found at the point of hesitation is the submediant, but other possibilities must be admitted. Here are three examples.

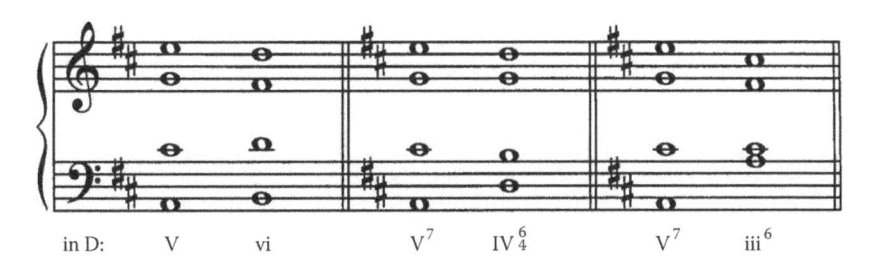

in D: V   vi V^7 IV^6_4 V^7 iii^6

EXAMPLE 3.71 Examples of deceptive cadences. On the left, ending on the submediant. In the middle, ending on the subdominant. On the right, ending on the mediant. All examples are in D Major. Because deceptive cadences commonly end on chords that contain the tonic pitch, the third example would be uncommon.

As with the discussion of authentic cadences, each of the other cadence types may be further identified as perfect or imperfect based on similar criteria: If the root of the final chord in the progression is found both in the bass and in the highest voice, it is a perfect cadence. Otherwise, the cadence is imperfect. (Usually this distinction between a perfect and an imperfect cadence is of little concern, especially as applied to cadences other than a final, authentic cadence.)

Review

- Harmony is used to support and intensify cadence points.
- Two types of cadences sound final because they end on the tonic chord. These are the authentic cadence and the plagal (or amen) cadence.
- The authentic cadence is, at the minimum, a dominant (or dominant seventh) chord followed by a tonic chord.
- The plagal cadence is a subdominant chord followed by the tonic chord.
- Likewise, two cadences usually do not sound final. These are the half cadence and the deceptive cadence.
- The half cadence concludes with a dominant chord preceded by such chords as the subdominant, supertonic, or tonic six-four.
- The deceptive cadence sounds as though it will become an authentic cadence, but instead of the dominant or dominant seventh chord resolving to the tonic, the chord of resolution is different. Frequently, this will be the submediant chord.
- Cadences may be said to be perfect if the root of the final cadential chord appears both in the bass and in the highest voice. Otherwise, the cadence is said to be imperfect.

Related Exercises

§ In the musical excerpts given below, you are provided with several cadences. Circle the root of each chord. On the line below each chord, write the correct Roman numeral for that chord within the specified key. Finally, on the longer line below the cadence, write the name of the cadence (authentic, half, plagal, or deceptive).

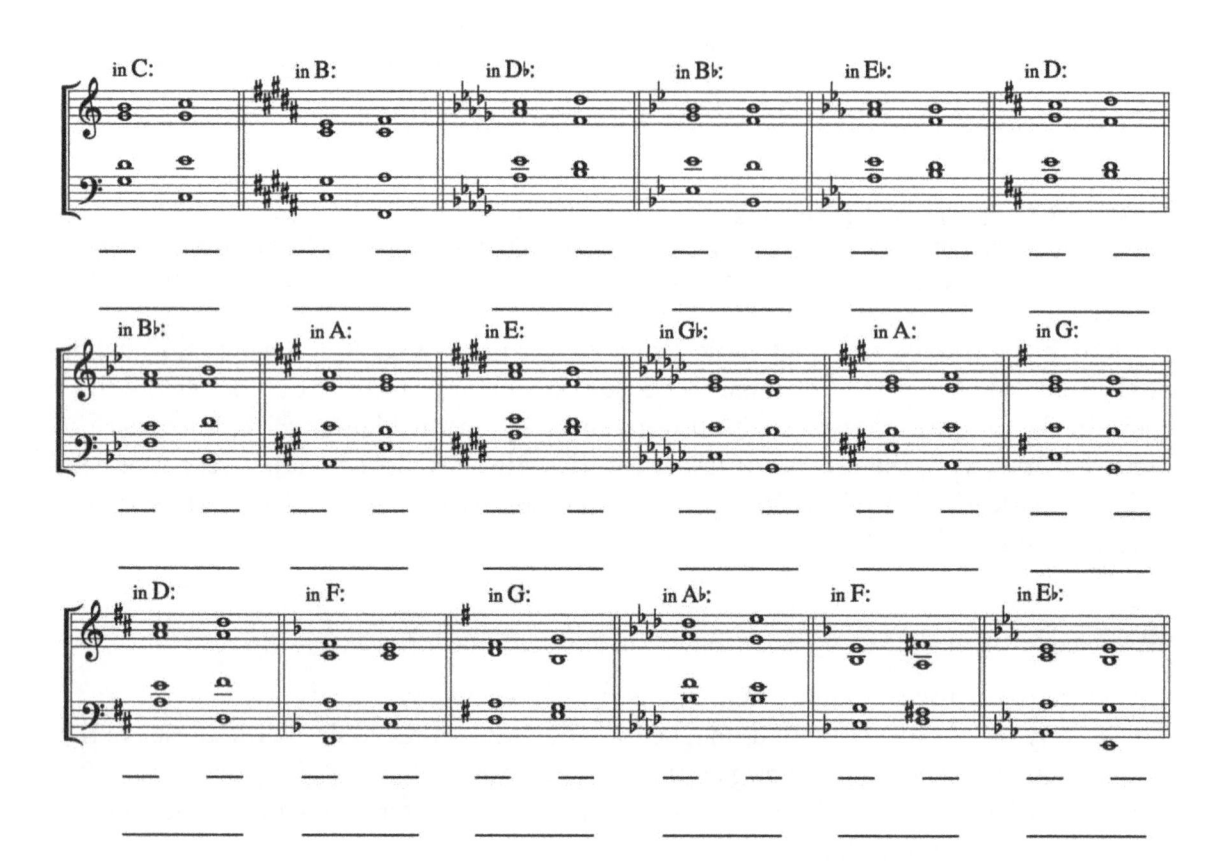

9. Secondary Dominants

Expanded Uses for Seventh Chords

A dominant seventh chord always implies that its tonic will soon follow. This ability to cause the arrival of the implied tonic to seem inevitable can be applied in many situations. Because for every pitch there is another pitch that functions as its dominant, every chord, no matter what pitch is its root, has a dominant. So if we know the dominant, we can construct a major triad or a major-minor seventh on that dominant pitch.

Harmony: Note(s) with Note(s)

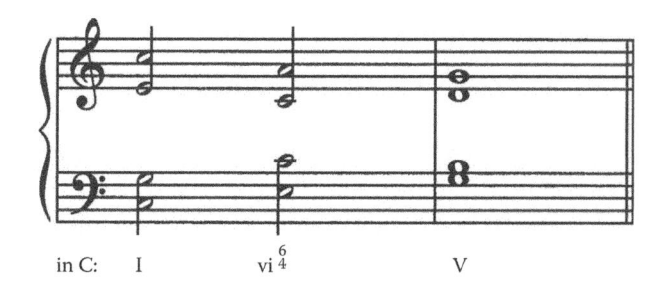

in C: I   vi $\frac{6}{4}$ V

EXAMPLE 3.72   A passage in C Major beginning on the tonic and progressing to the submediant and the dominant.

In Example 3.72, the second chord is an a minor chord, and the third chord is G Major. In the key of C, they are the submediant and the dominant chords, respectively.

The dominant of the a minor chord is E. The dominant of the G Major chord is D. Therefore, the progression *to* each chord can be made more insistent by preceding each with a triad (or seventh) built on its dominant.

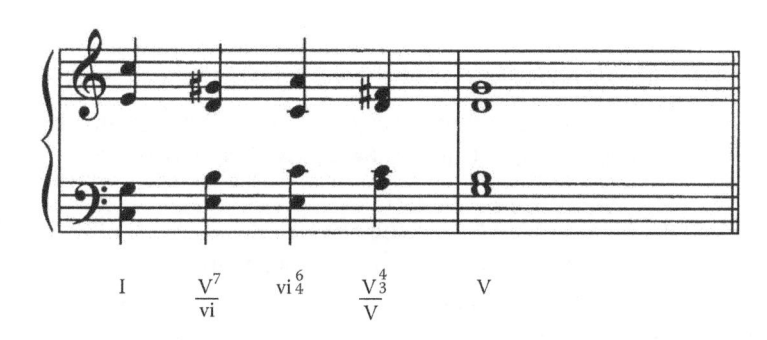

I $\frac{V^7}{vi}$ vi $\frac{6}{4}$ $\frac{V^4_3}{V}$ V

EXAMPLE 3.73   The same progression shown in Example 3.72, but now the submediant and dominant chords are each preceded by their respective dominant sevenths. These dominant sevenths, which lead to pitches other than the tonic of the key, are called secondary dominants.

We see in the revised example that now the submediant (vi) is preceded by a $\frac{V^7}{vi}$, and the dominant (V) is preceded by a $\frac{V^7}{V}$. These two chords, the $\frac{V^7}{vi}$ and the $\frac{V^7}{V}$, are ***secondary dominants*** and are quite useful to composers. Secondary dominants are sometimes called ***applied dominants***.

A secondary dominant may precede any chord (except of course the tonic) in any key. In analyzing these chords, the notation is $\frac{V^x}{y}$, where x is the inversion symbol for

Although in the example shown here, the analysis shows the dominant seventh of the submediant to be in second inversion, we usually describe these chords as the dominant seventh of the submediant, the dominant seventh of the dominant, etc., realizing that they may appear in any inversion.

the triad or seventh chord and *y* is the root of the destination chord. The "—" is read as "of." Thus, a description of $\frac{V^2}{ii}$ would be "the dominant seventh, in third inversion, of the supertonic."

When analyzing music, any accidental may *suggest* the presence of a secondary dominant. However, an accidental may be encountered without a secondary dominant being present for other reasons. A piece in a minor key is clearly one such situation. On the other hand, the lack of an accidental does not preclude the presence of a secondary dominant.

As indicated above, the secondary dominant chord *need not* contain the seventh. **The secondary dominant may appear as a triad or as a seventh**, depending on the composer's wishes or needs. Compare these two progressions.

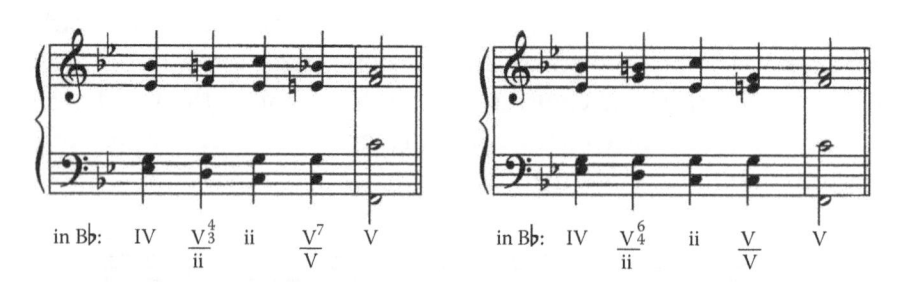

EXAMPLE 3.74 On the left, a passage using secondary dominant sevenths. On the right, the same passage using secondary dominants (without sevenths). Compare the sounds of the two excerpts.

The existence of secondary dominants suggests that other secondary relationships may prove useful, too. These will be discussed in the next section.

Finding an extended passage on a secondary level (i.e. using a pitch other than tonic as the tonal center) suggests that some form of ***tonicization*** has occurred. That is, a new, temporary tonal center is in operation at that point in the music.

Review

- Any chord may be preceded by a triad or seventh that is its dominant.
- Unless the chord thus preceded is the tonic, such dominants are called secondary or applied dominants.
- When analyzed, secondary dominants are indicated as V chords (with any necessary inversion symbols) above a horizontal line (—) followed by the analysis of the destination chord (expressed as a Roman numeral), namely $\frac{V^6}{ii}$ or $\frac{V^7}{vi}$ etc.
- An extended, but temporary, passage in which a pitch other than the tonic becomes the tonal center is an example of temporary tonicization.

Harmony: Note(s) with Note(s)

Related Exercises

§ In each example, you are provided with a key and a chord within that key. Analyze the given chord and circle its root. Then write on the staff (to the right of the given chord) the pitch that is the dominant of the circled pitch. The first example is done for you.

§ Each example consists of a pair of chords. The first is the secondary dominant of the following chord. Analyze the two chords within the tonality provided, and write your answers on the lines provided below the chords.

in B♭: ___ ___   in D: ___ ___   in E♭: ___ ___   in G: ___ ___   in A: ___ ___

in C: ___ ___   in A♭: ___ ___   in F: ___ ___   in E: ___ ___   in D: ___ ___

10. More Chords on the Secondary Level

Leading Tone Sevenths

In addition to secondary dominants, leading tone triads or sevenths can also be used to lead to pitches other than the tonic. For example, in the passage shown in Example 3.75, the second chord is a diminished-minor seventh chord, with a root of C-sharp, which is the *leading tone* to D, the dominant of the key. Note the analysis below the music.

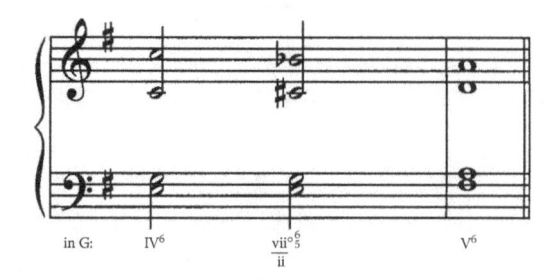

in G: IV^6 $\frac{\text{vii}°^6_5}{\text{ii}}$ V^6

EXAMPLE 3.75   In the above passage, the dominant is preceded by a fully diminished seventh chord, the root of which is the leading tone to the dominant.

Diminished triads, half-diminished seventh chords, and fully diminished seventh chords can be found functioning as secondary seventh (leading tone) chords. The general term for these leading tone triads or sevenths is **secondary sevenths** (sevenths, as in seventh degree or leading tone of the scale).

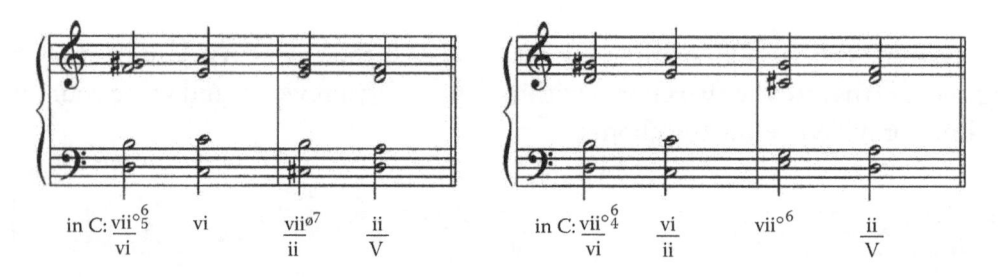

in C: $\frac{\text{vii}°^6_5}{\text{vi}}$ vi $\frac{\text{vii}^{ø7}}{\text{ii}}$ $\frac{\text{ii}}{\text{V}}$ in C: $\frac{\text{vii}°^6_4}{\text{vi}}$ vi $\frac{\text{vii}°^6}{\text{ii}}$ $\frac{\text{ii}}{\text{V}}$

EXAMPLE 3.76   On the left, a passage with two types of secondary sevenths. The first is a fully diminished seventh, and the second is a half-diminished seventh. On the right, the same passage, but now the the secondary sevenths are triads.

In a harmonic analysis, these chords are identified in a manner similar to the secondary dominants as $\frac{\text{vii}°^x}{y}$ or $\frac{\text{vii}^{øx}}{y}$, where x is the correct inversion symbol while the y is the root of the chord of resolution, expressed as a Roman numeral. Any of these three types of secondary sevenths may be found in any key or modality preceding any pitch within the tonality except for tonic.

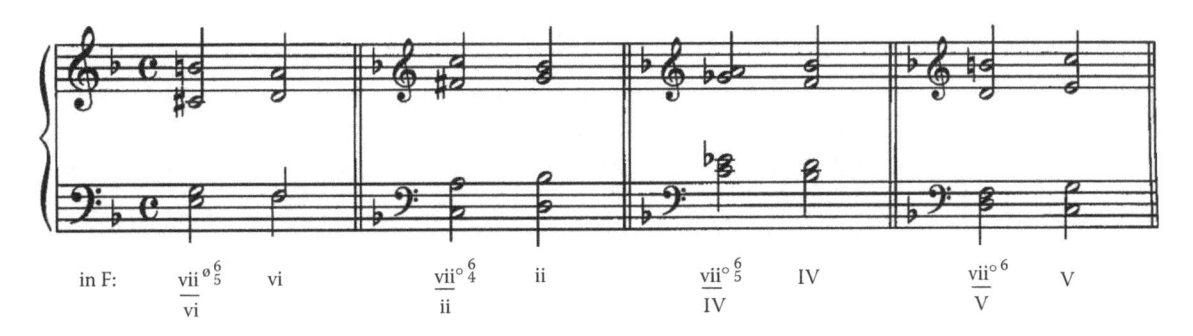

EXAMPLE 3.77 Four examples of secondary leading tone chords in the key of F Major.

Secondary Supertonic Chords

Another example of a secondary relationship is the secondary supertonic, often called the secondary two chord or **secondary second**. This chord may be either a minor or diminished triad or a minor-minor seventh or a diminished-minor seventh. Unlike secondary dominants or secondary sevenths, the secondary two chord does not lead to the temporary tonic but rather to the *dominant* of a tonicized pitch. Just as a frequent use of the supertonic is to lead to the dominant, the function of a secondary supertonic is usually to progress on to a secondary dominant.

EXAMPLE 3.78 An example of a secondary second chord (third chord from left). Note the analysis provided. Secondary seconds typically lead to secondary dominants.

Secondary second chords may be created from a major or from a minor modality. In the former case, the triad will be minor, and, if the chord is a seventh, it will be a minor-minor seventh. If the secondary second is created from the minor modality, the triad will be diminished, and the seventh chord variation will be a half-diminished seventh.

In providing the functional analysis, the notation will be $\frac{ii^x}{y}$, $\frac{ii^{ox}}{y}$ or $\frac{ii^{\o x}}{y}$, where x will be the correct inversion symbol and y will be the Roman numeral for the root of the temporary **tonic**. When a chord is analyzed as a secondary second, though it is implicit that the chord toward which the secondary second points is a dominant, *the analysis is related to the temporary tonic*.

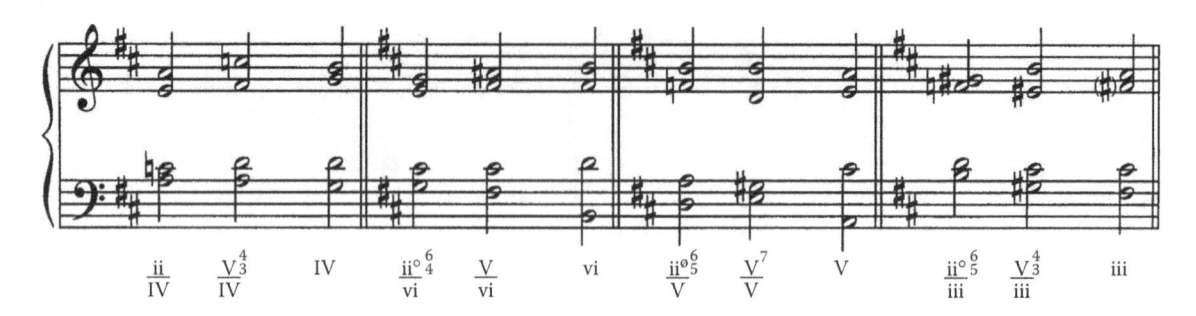

EXAMPLE 3.79 Secondary seconds in context in D Major.

Review

- Any chord (other than tonic) may be preceded by a triad or seventh constructed on the leading tone to the root of the aforementioned chord.
- Chords of this type are called secondary second, secondary seventh, or secondary leading tone chords.
- If a leading tone chord is a triad, it will be a diminished triad.
- If a leading tone chord is a seventh, the chord may be either half-diminished or fully diminished.
- Secondary leading tone chords are analyzed relative to the tonic toward which they point.
- Major triads (other than the dominant) may be preceded by a triad or seventh, the root of which is a perfect fourth below (or a perfect fifth above) the root of the aforementioned major triad.
- This type of chord is known as a secondary supertonic or a secondary two chord.
- A secondary supertonic, if a triad, may be minor or diminished; if a seventh, it may be a minor-minor seventh or a half-diminished seventh.
- Secondary seconds are analyzed relative to the tonic to which their destination chord is the dominant.

Harmony: Note(s) with Note(s)

Related Exercises

§ In each example, you are provided with a key and a chord within that key. Analyze the given chord and circle its root. Then write on the staff (to the right of the given chord) the pitch that is the leading tone to the circled pitch. The first example is done for you.

§ Each example consists of a pair of chords. The first is the secondary leading tone (secondary seventh) chord of the following chord. Analyze the two chords within the tonality provided and write your answers on the lines provided below the chords.

in A: ___ ___   in B♭: ___ ___   in G: ___ ___   in E♭: ___ ___   in D: ___ ___

in F: ___ ___   in A♭: ___ ___   in G: ___ ___   in E: ___ ___   in D♭: ___ ___

Avoidance of Resolutions

Even though secondary dominants, sevenths, and supertonics imply the eventual resolution of these unstable chords, the operational word is *eventual*. Just as within the primary tonality, chords are not always followed by their obvious chord of resolution, neither are secondary chords immediately resolved. In fact, in more complex and interesting pieces, the achievement of an implied harmonic goal may be delayed by several intervening chords. Thus, in analyzing a passage, you should be aware that a secondary chord's goal may need to be sought.

Modulation

Modulation refers to the act of changing the tonic within a composition. Before a composer can modulate, an initial tonic must be established. To accomplish this, the minimal requirements are usually the existence of a clear cadence in the tonic key. Different authors will suggest differing minimums. The amount of music required—in terms of numbers of phrases or measures needed to establish a key—will certainly be influenced by the total length of the piece being considered.

The problem for the analyst is often determining the difference between a temporary tonicization, an **intermediate** (or *false*) **modulation**, and a true modulation. Of these three terms, the usual distinction comes from the length of the sojourn into the new key and the manner by which the new key is approached and established. (Sources do not universally agree on this matter.)

Temporary tonicization refers to a very brief shift into a new key. Typically, this shift will last for less than a complete phrase. (The duration of the altered tonic passage relative to the total length of the piece being examined should inform the determination as to whether it is a modulation or merely a temporary tonicization. Therefore, the longer the composition, the longer a new tonal area may last while still considered a temporary tonicization.) After this brief passage in the new (temporary) tonality, the original tonic will return or another, new tonic will be explored or fully established.

An intermediate modulation (the better term because nothing is actually "false" about it) is somewhat longer than a temporary tonicization. It will last for a phrase or more but usually returns to the original tonality fairly soon. The new key may not have a really strong cadential passage. However, a "true" modulation requires, in the minds of most theorists, both the existence of a ***pivot chord*** and a complete (authentic) cadence in the new key.

A pivot chord is a chord that functions in both the key of origin and the key to which the modulation moves. Here is an example of a modulation including a pivot chord.

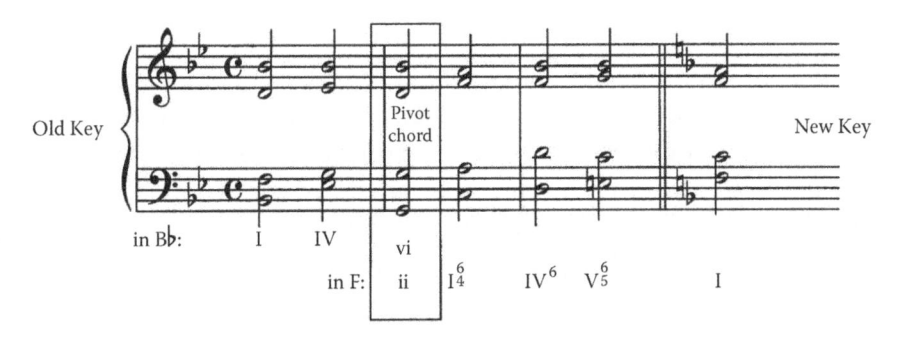

EXAMPLE 3.80 An example of a modulation as defined by most texts. Note that the submediant triad in the key of B-flat Major serves as the supertonic in the key of F and, in this passage, is the pivot chord.

Some texts also assert that to be a modulation, the change of key must also involve stepwise bass motion from the new dominant to the new tonic. (Note the bass line ascending from C to F in Example 3.80 above.) Although this stepwise may indeed happen, it is not universally required as a condition for determining the presence of a modulation.

> Some scholars prefer a stepwise descent to the new tonic.

Stylistically, composers may use many, varied and disguised changes of key to create a unique harmonic landscape for their compositions. Others, usually earlier historically, may create very clearly spelled out modulations and, most frequently, only between tonic and dominant, tonic and subdominant, or (in minor) tonic and the relative major. By the twenty-first century, all types of modulation may be used.

Standard literature, dramatic music, and various types of popular music may use examples of sudden or unprepared modulations as well as a great variety of pivot tones. In improvisation, the use of fully diminished seventh chords as pivot chords works well because, by the very nature of these symmetrically constructed chords, any of the pitches contained within the chord can be heard as leading to a tonic or dominant triad or to any other desired chord of resolution.

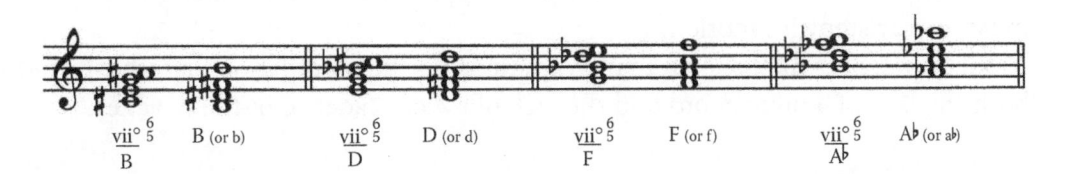

EXAMPLE 3.81 Examples of modulations via fully diminished seventh chords. Each initial chord is enharmonically the same. Each second chord represents a resolution of a leading tone seventh. From left to right, a-sharp fully diminished seventh to B Major; c-sharp fully diminished seventh to D Major; e fully diminished seventh to F Major; and g fully diminished seventh to A-flat Major. Note that the chord of resolution could (among many other options) be the new tonic, the new dominant, or the new subdominant.

Other frequently used modulation formulas include the addition of a minor seventh to a major triad, such as the subdominant or tonic in a major key or to the submediant in a minor key, to produce a dominant seventh chord in a new key. Also a chromatically altered minor triad, producing a diminished triad, can be used as a leading tone triad in a new key.

Composers and arrangers can chromatically alter any chord to function as desired in order to facilitate the modulation to another tonal center. Obscure progressions into a new key, using many secondary relationships, also provide harmonic variety and surprises.

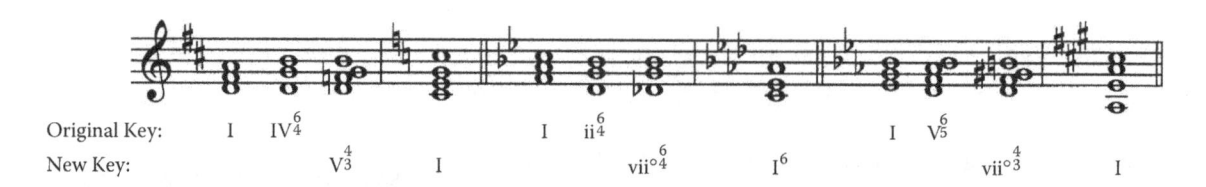

Original Key:	I	IV$^6_4$		I	ii$^6_4$		I	V$^6_5$	
New Key:		V$^4_3$	I		vii°$^6_4$	I^6		vii°$^4_3$	I

EXAMPLE 3.82 Other modulation formulas. From the left, adding a minor seventh to the subdominant to modulate to a tonic a whole tone lower; altering the supertonic to a diminished triad to modulate up a minor third; and altering the dominant seventh chord to a fully diminished seventh chord to modulate up an augmented fourth.

Review

- Moving from one tonality to another may be identified as temporary tonicization, intermediate modulation, or modulation depending, in part, on how long the new tonal center remains.
- For most authors, modulation requires a pivot chord (a chord that functions in both the original key and the new tonality).
- Modulation does not require a return to the original key, although it does not preclude it, either.
- Typically, a modulation will include a cadence in the new key.
- Some theorists believe that as the new key is approached in a modulation, the bass line must display stepwise motion.
- Modern practices have shown many variations on the modulation patterns, including both the lack of a pivot chord and the lack of a clear cadence in the new key.

Related Exercises

§ Each of the following excerpts modulates. Examine each example and identify the tonality (key) at the beginning of the example and at the end. Then circle those pitches that contribute to this change (modulation). You should pay particular attention to accidentals. If possible, discuss and/or explain how these pitches (chords) bring about the new tonal center.

Melody
Robert Schumann

The key here is: _____   The key here is: _____

Minuet
J.S. Bach

The key here is: _____   The key here is: _____

E-flat Major Piano Sonata
Joseph Haydn

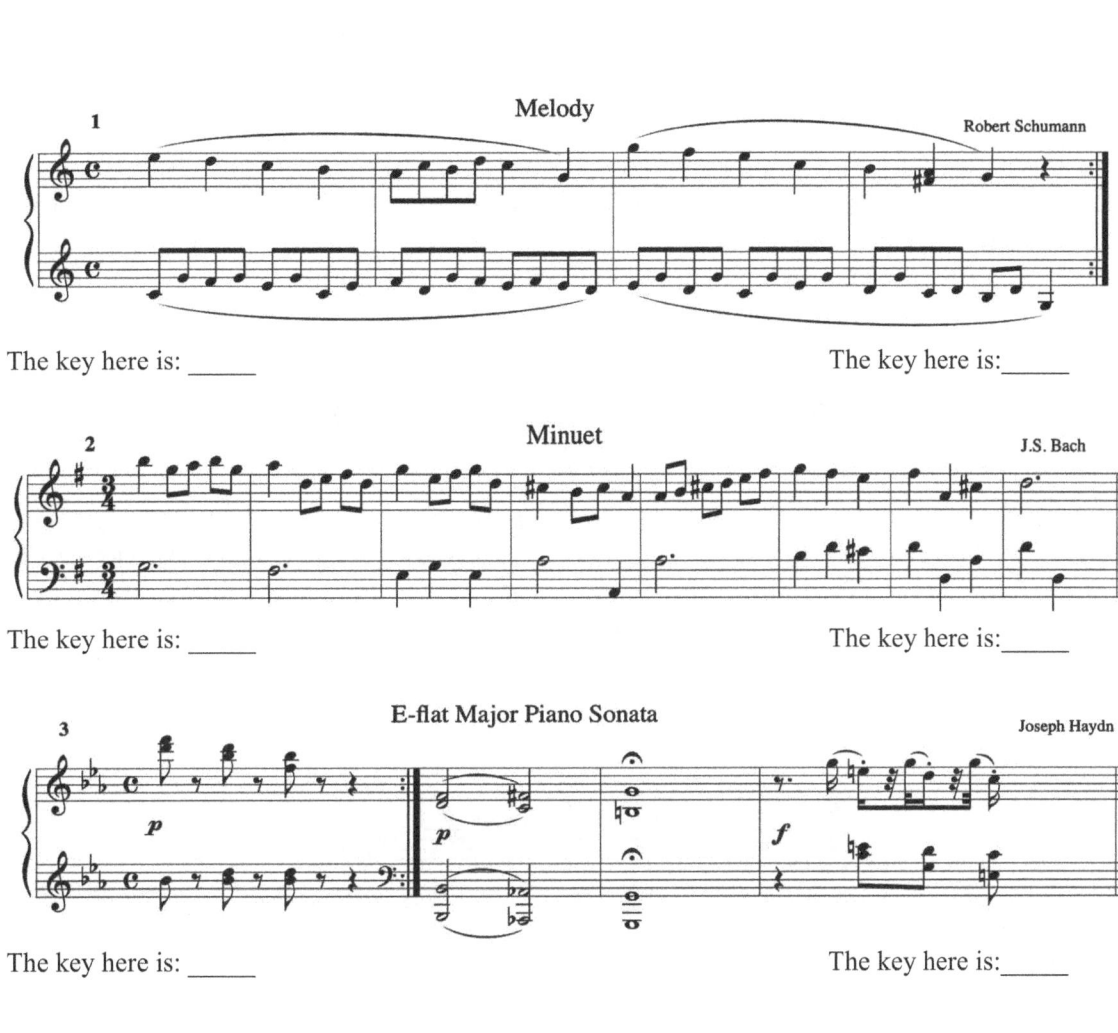

The key here is: _____   The key here is: _____

Herzliebster Jesu
J.S. Bach harmonization

The key here is: _____

The key here is: _____

Chord Alteration, Borrowing, and Substitution

Composers regularly replace expected chords with other chords to achieve fresh harmonic effects. An *altered chord* occurs when one of the standard, functional chords is given another quality by the modification of one or more components of the chord. An example would be changing the dominant triad into a minor chord by lowering the third.

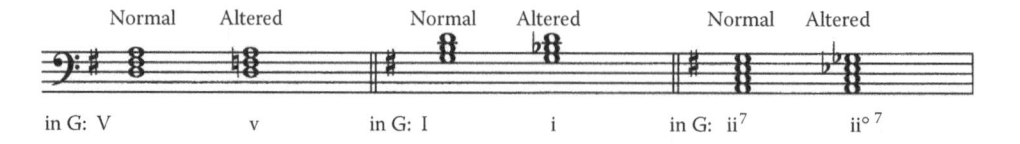

EXAMPLE 3.83 Examples of altered chords. On the left, a dominant triad with an altered dominant triad; in the middle, a tonic triad with an altered tonic triad; on the right, a supertonic seventh with an altered supertonic seventh.

A *borrowed chord* occurs when a chord, usually found in the minor modality, is used in place of the equivalent major modality chord or vice versa. A common example is using a fully diminished seventh chord on the leading tone in major or using a major triad as the subdominant in minor.

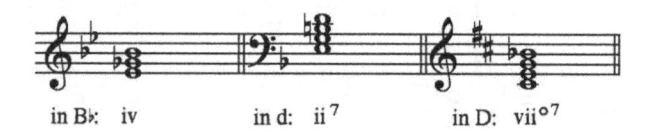

EXAMPLE 3.84 Examples of borrowed chords. On the left, a borrowed subdominant (from minor); in the middle, a borrowed supertonic seventh (from major); on the right, a borrowed leading tone seventh from minor.

A *chord substitution* occurs when a chord is replaced by another that is made to function like the original. Usually substituted chords possess two pitches in common with the triad that they are replacing. Here is a chart of some standard triad substitutions.

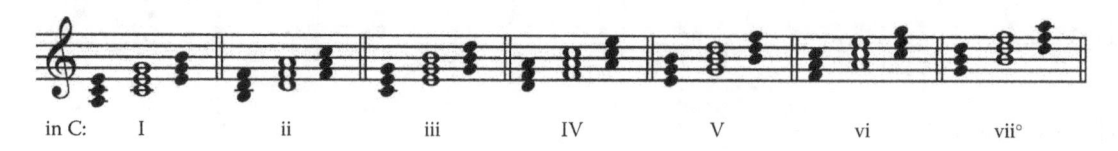

EXAMPLE 3.85 Examples of possible chord substitutions in C Major. The chords constructed from notes with shaded-in heads are the substitute chords while the triads in the middle (notated with whole notes) are original chords.

Harmony: Note(s) with Note(s)

Review

- To expand the harmonic vocabulary available, composers may use chord alteration, chord borrowing, and chord substitution.
- Altered chords are those that have been changed in quality by the use of accidentals or added pitches, creating chords not found on that scale degree in major or minor keys.
- Chord borrowing is using, in minor, a chord construction usually found only in major or using, in major, a chord construction usually found only in minor.
- Chord substitution involves replacing one chord with another, different chord. The substituted chord usually shares at least two common tones with the original chord.

Related Exercises

§ In each example, you are provided with a chord and given the key within which it is to be considered. Is the given chord an alteration or a borrowing? Show your choice by circling A for Altered or B for Borrowed.

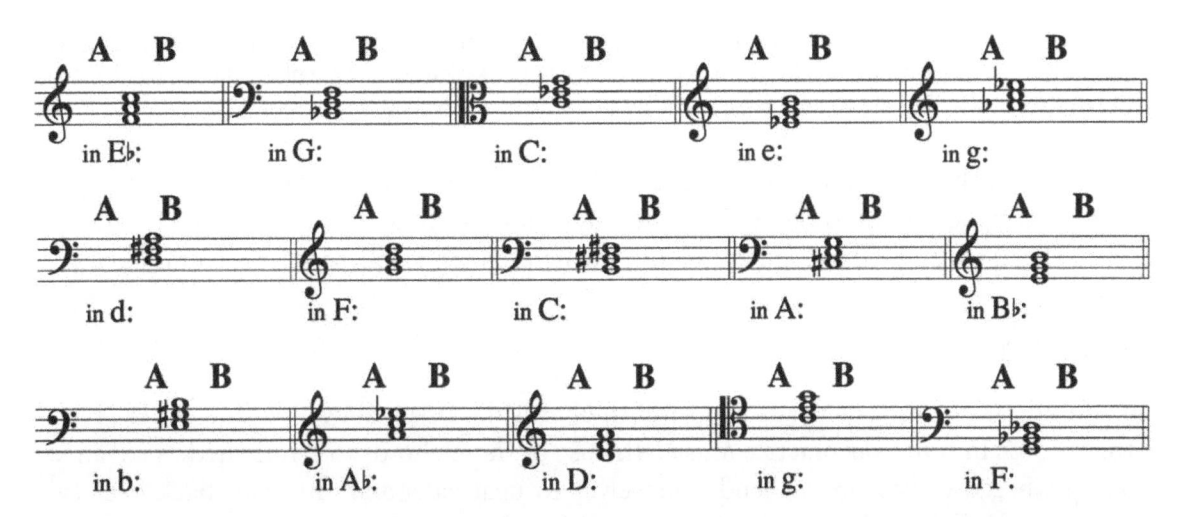

§ You are given a chord in a particular key. Suggest a substitute chord by writing your choice to the right of the given chord. How many possible answers are there?

11. Other Chords

Traditional Constructions

The Augmented Triad

The augmented triad is not used as often as are the other three types. A common role for the augmented triad is as an altered tonic chord in major keys. In such a role, it will be positioned between the tonic and the subdominant or between the tonic and the leading tone seventh (on the way to the dominant seventh chord). Here are those two uses:

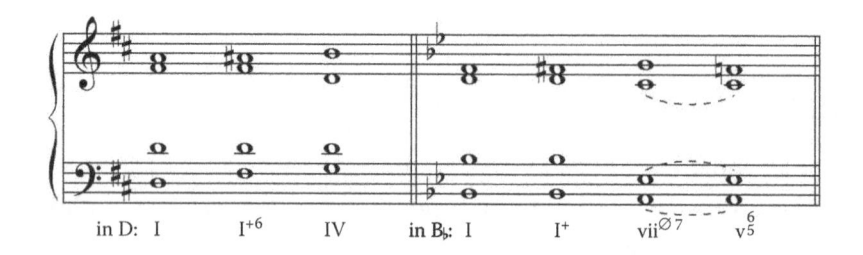

EXAMPLE 3.86 Typical uses of the augmented triad. On the left, a progression from the tonic to the augmented triad (with a tonic root) to the subdominant. On the right, a progression from the tonic to the augmented triad (with a tonic root) to the leading tone seventh and on to the dominant seventh (if desired).

Obviously, the progression from tonic to the subdominant is exactly parallel to the progression from dominant to the tonic. Thus, any dominant triad may be followed by an augmented triad (with the dominant as its root), which in turn is followed by the implied tonic.

Neapolitan Sixths

In addition to the various triads and seventh chords discussed above, we encounter several other chords in common-practice music. The use of these chords (often treated as advanced concepts because they do not lend themselves to neat categorization) dates back over two centuries. The first of these to consider is the ***Neapolitan sixth***.

The Neapolitan sixth is a chord built on the lowered (flatted) supertonic of the key. It is a major triad, so in the key of F Major or minor the components of the Neapolitan sixth would be a root of G-flat (the flatted supertonic in F), B-flat (the subdominant) as the third, and D-flat (the submediant) as the fifth. Note that in F Major, the submediant is D, not D-flat. This hints that the Neapolitan sixth may have evolved in the minor modality. But the chord is equally likely to be found in either major or minor.

The Neapolitan sixth traditionally resolves, either directly or eventually, to the dominant or dominant seventh chord of the key within which it is placed. The analysis symbol usually employed to identify a Neapolitan sixth is N^6.

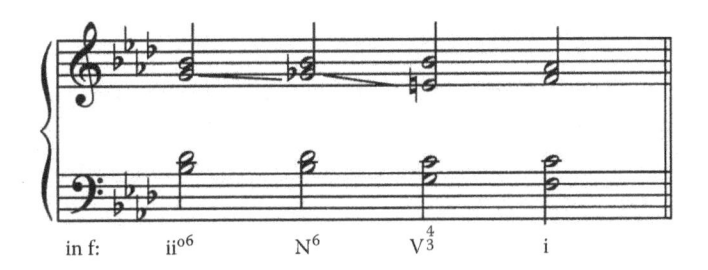

EXAMPLE 3.87 A typical appearance of the Neapolitan sixth following the supertonic and preceding the dominant. The progression of the root of the Neapolitan (in this case, G-flat) to the leading tone (E-natural) is frequently heard in this construction.

The lowered supertonic is itself sometimes referred to as the ***Neapolitan***. Whether this name comes from the chord built on it or whether the chord gets its name from this pitch is unclear. Also, no explanation appears in either context for the colorful name "Neapolitan," but it most assuredly has nothing to do with Naples.

Historically, it was almost always found in first inversion. However, this has not been true for more than two hundred years. Composers routinely use the chord in root position and second inversion, too. Sill, the name persists.

> Although some sources have observed that the Neapolitan sixth was used by composers associated with the Neapolitan school of the eighteenth century, the chord dates from the seventeenth century and has been used ever since by composers of many schools and nationalities, some that significantly predate the Neapolitan school.

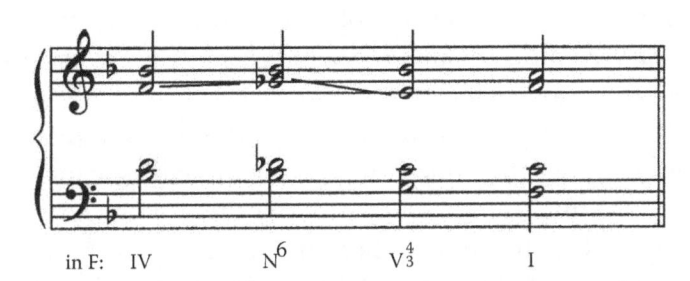

EXAMPLE 3.88 Here is a progression in F Major showing the Neapolitan sixth following the subdominant and preceding the dominant. Again, the Neapolitan to leading tone progression is commonly heard.

The lowered supertonic also has another name: the ***Phrygian second***. The reader may recall that the Phrygian mode has a minor second between the final and the note immediately above it. (In all other modes, except for the

> Some musicians strongly prefer the term Phrygian second (♭II) to Neapolitan sixth.

theoretical Locrian, this corresponding interval is a major second.) In modal practice, the minor second descent from F to E at the end of Phrygian melodies serves the same purpose as the upward minor second resolution (from leading tone to tonic) in common-practice majors and minors.

Dominant Ninth Chords

The structure of the seventh chord in root position is that of a stack of four pitches, each a third above the one below it. As early as the eighteenth century, in a desire to obtain an even more intense dominant, composers occasionally stacked five pitches in this same manner. Doing so created **ninth chords**. As seventh chords may be seen to be a triad with an added seventh, ninths may be seen as seventh chords with an added ninth.

A ninth is merely a displacement of an octave plus a second, sometimes called a compound interval. Because seconds are usually either major or minor, those are the two options generally associated with the traditional ninth chords. In traditional practice, ninths are only constructed on the dominant. Here are the two most traditional ninths:

EXAMPLE 3.89 On the left, the construction of a dominant ninth chord in G Major. On the right, the construction of a dominant ninth chord in g minor.

On the left in Example 3.89 is the ninth built on the dominant of a major key (G). Observe that it consists of a major triad plus a minor seventh and a major ninth. It is called a ***major ninth***. On the right in the same example is the dominant ninth constructed on the dominant of a minor key (g). It consists of a major triad, a minor seventh, and a *minor* ninth. It is called a ***minor ninth***. In spite of the origins of the two types of ninths, either may be used in major or minor keys.

Listening to both ninths illustrates that either ninth creates a great deal more tension than a seventh chord and that the minor ninth is the more dissonant of the two. Historically, composers used the ninth chord *only* in root position with the ninth as far removed from the root as possible. For this reason, there are in general use no inversion symbols for ninth chords. The analysis symbol is usually V^9 regardless of how the pitches are distributed vertically. Wherever a seventh chord might be used, whether on a primary or secondary level, a ninth chord may be substituted.

Since the nineteenth century, ninth chords have been built on other scale degrees. In addition, just as we constructed triads and sevenths in both major and minor modalities, the same may be done for the ninth chord. In certain styles of music, the added ninths serve as "coloration" for chords built on other scale degrees, including the tonic. In these situations, the ninth chord does not *function* in the traditional "extended dominant" sense but is used rather to introduce a certain stylistic complexity into the harmonic language. When a coloration ninth is added, the seventh may or may not be used.

I⁹   ii⁹   vi⁹

EXAMPLE 3.90   Ninth added to chords to create harmonic color. All examples are in G Major. Left to right: tonic with added ninth, supertonic with added ninth, and submediant with added ninth. These are only a few, limited examples of the possible use of "added ninths." (Note that the supertonic ninth *might be* functional if it creates a dissonance that is resolved by a dominant, dominant seventh, or dominant ninth chord. A submediant ninth and a tonic ninth are usually not heard as functional but rather as colored or enriched chords.)

When ninths are added to a triad, whether for coloration or to create greater tension, the seventh or even the fifth of the chord may be omitted. This is done either because there are not enough voices to cover all of the pitches or in an effort to create a particular sonic effect. Thus, in Example 3.90, the *sevenths are in parentheses*, indicating that their use, especially in these color chords, is optional. Also note the distribution of the pitches. In current usage, the ninth need not be an octave (or more) removed from the root.

Review

- The augmented triad may be used to serve as a bridge between a tonic chord and a following subdominant or leading chord. It may also serve as a bridge between a dominant triad and a following tonic.
- An alternative dominant preparation chord is called the Neapolitan sixth chord.
- The Neapolitan sixth is a major triad with a root that is the lowered second degree of the scale known either as the Phrygian second or as the Neapolitan (second).
- The resolution of the Neapolitan sixth is usually to the dominant or dominant seventh.
- Historically, the Neapolitan sixth has been found in first inversion (hence its name), but in actual practice it appears in any inversion.
- The dominant ninth is a five-note stack of thirds with, historically, the dominant as its root.
- The dominant ninth may have a major or a minor ninth in its composition.
- Initially, the dominant ninth appeared only in root position; this is no longer the case.
- Since the twentieth century, other scale degrees have been enriched with added ninths in an effect to color the harmony.

Related Exercises

§ Here are a series of authentic cadences. Analyze each chord in each cadence and write your analysis on the line provided. Circle any Neapolitan (Phrygian) second chords.

§ In the following examples, the dominant ninth chord may consist of a dominant seventh chord with a major ninth or a dominant seventh chord with a minor ninth. Identify each type by writing m9 or M9 on the line provided.

Augmented Sixth Chords

In an effort to smooth out the common progression from iv⁶ to V in minor keys, a chromatic inflection was sometimes introduced to the root of the subdominant chord. Over time, this change became so harmonically attractive that composers often chose to use this altered chord (the iv$^{\#6}$) rather than the original iv⁶. The raised root thus created forms the interval of an augmented sixth with the bass. This evolution is shown in Example 3.91.

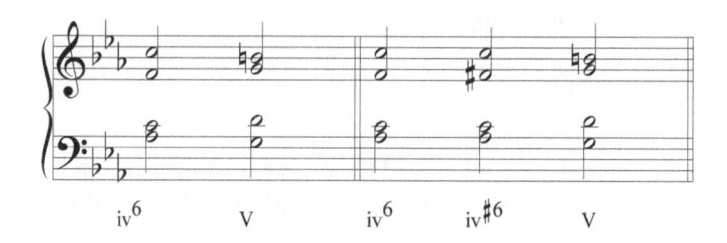

EXAMPLE 3.91   On the left (in c minor), the progression iv⁶ to V. On the right, the smoother progression iv⁶ to an augmented sixth chord to V.

The augmented sixth chord was not only used in minor but eventually it also became common in major. It could serve both as a chord between IV⁶ and V and as a substitute for IV⁶.

Composers would sometimes add additional pitches to this altered subdominant chord, eventually producing the three normally encountered versions: the ***Italian sixth***, the ***French sixth***, and the ***German sixth***.

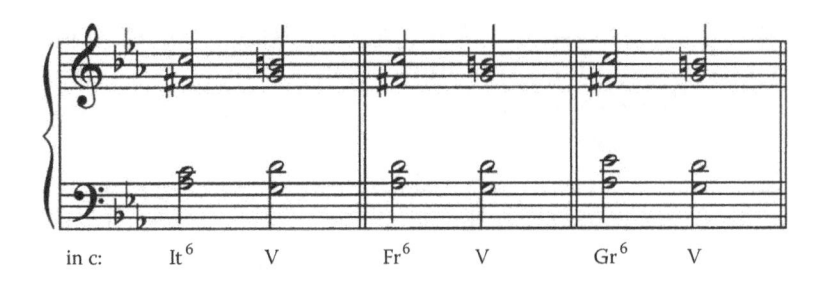

EXAMPLE 3.92 From the left to the right (in c minor), the Italian sixth, the French sixth, and the German sixth each proceeding to the dominant (V).

As with the Neapolitan sixth chord, the adjectives *Italian*, *French*, and *German* attached to these chords have no logical justification. The respective chords are not associated with or specifically used by composers of these nationalities. (The terminology seems to be a peculiarly American phenomenon because in most European languages these names are not used.)

The characteristics that enable identifications of an augmented sixth chord are

1. The resolution of the augmented sixth interval, which expands to form an octave, and
2. The octave thus formed is the root of the following chord of resolution and the dominant of the key in which the chord functions.

Here are the three augmented sixth chords as they would appear in C Major. The pitch composition is identical to that found in minor (see Example 3.92), but the use of accidentals is required due to the C Major key signature.

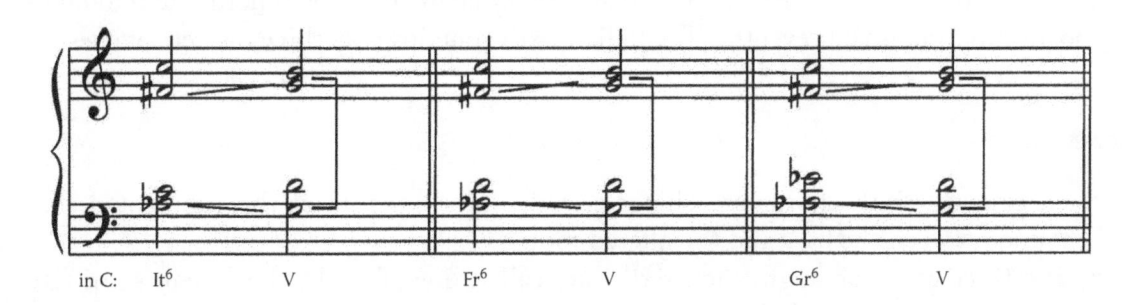

EXAMPLE 3.93 From left to right, in C Major, the Italian, French, and German sixth chords each progressing to the dominant. Note the expansion of the augmented sixth (A-flat to F-sharp) to the dominant octave (G) in each instance.

The fact that the German sixth chord is enharmonically the same as a dominant seventh chord has enabled composers to use it as another formulaic modulation chord. Treating the German sixth in an initial key as a dominant in a new key, the tonal center may be shifted up a minor second. Or, using it as a secondary dominant, the destination key may be as varied as down a major third or up a diminished fifth from the original key.

In addition to the three versions of the augmented sixth chord shown above, another related chord called the ***augmented six/doubly augmented four chord*** is also encountered. Although apparently an enharmonic variation of the German sixth, this chord does not resolve to the dominant but resolves instead to the major tonic *in second inversion*. This fact gives the augmented six/doubly augmented four its unique structure.

The outward resolution of the augmented sixth to the dominant octave is a characteristic of this chord, too. The difference is that the dominant is no longer the root of the following chord but is, rather, the bass (fifth) of the tonic six-four chord.

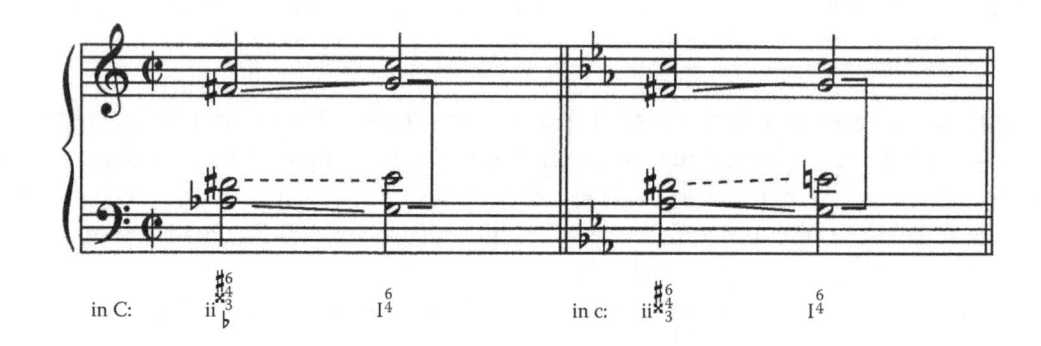

EXAMPLE 3.94 The augmented sixth/doubly augmented four chord illustrated in C Major on the left and c minor on the right. Note that in minor the resolution will still be to the major tonic triad.

The augmented sixth chords are admittedly difficult to keep track of, and students have many systems to assist with remembering them. You may note that the French sixth contains the elements of a whole tone scale commonly associated with French impressionistic composers. The German sixth and the augmented six/doubly augmented four chord sound (on most keyboards) like dominant sevenths. The Italian sixth contains only three discrete pitches.

Review

- Augmented sixth chords are characterized by the interval of the augmented sixth found between the bass and the altered root.
- The three common augmented sixths are called, inexplicably, the Italian sixth (It[6]), French sixth (Fr[6]), and German sixth (Gr[6]).

Harmony: Note(s) with Note(s)

- These three chords all resolve to a dominant or dominant seventh chord.
- In the process of resolution, the augmented sixth interval expands to form an octave, the root of the following chord.
- Although originally evolving in minor modalities, these chords work equally well in major.
- A related chord, the augmented six/doubly augmented four appears to be an enharmonically spelled German sixth, but its chief identifying characteristic is that it resolves to the major tonic six-four.

Related Exercises

In the following examples, each pair of chords consists of an augmented sixth chord and its resolution. (You may assume that all examples are notated in a minor key.) Give the harmonic analysis of each chord in the pair. If a chord is a French, German, or Italian sixth, you may use Fr^6, Gr^6, or It^6, respectively.

Extending the Notion of Stacked Thirds

Eleventh and Thirteenth Chords

Just as ninth chords were created by adding a third to a seventh chord, composers in the nineteenth century added a third to ninth chords to create eleventh chords and, later, added thirds to elevenths to create thirteenths. This process of "thirding" existing chords ran its course at this point because the addition of another third to a thirteenth would produce a fifteenth, a pitch exactly two octaves above the root and, thus, not unique.

By the time elevenths and thirteenths became a part of the standard harmonic vocabulary, few theorists—and even fewer composers—used any sort of inversion symbols for these chords. Much like ninth chords, eleventh and thirteenth chords were identified as shown in Examples 3.95 and 3.96.

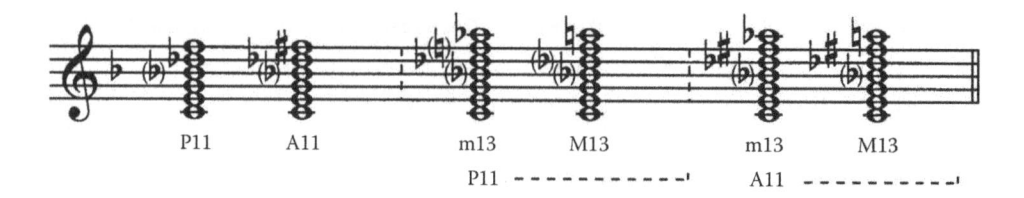

EXAMPLE 3.95 Eleventh and thirteenth chords built on dominant minor ninths in F Major. From left to right: perfect eleventh, augmented eleventh; perfect eleventh with a minor thirteenth; perfect eleventh with a major thirteenth; augmented eleventh with a minor thirteenth; and augmented eleventh with a major thirteenth.

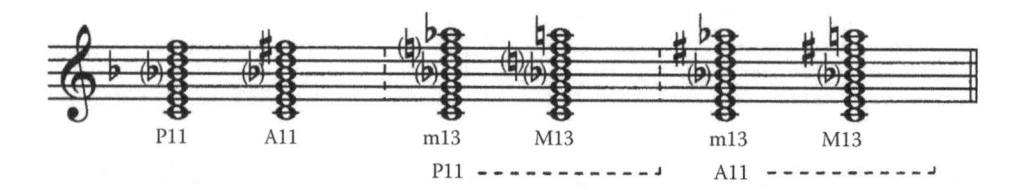

EXAMPLE 3.96 Eleventh and thirteenth chords built on dominant major ninths in F Major. From left to right: perfect eleventh, augmented eleventh; perfect eleventh with a minor thirteenth; perfect eleventh with a major thirteenth; augmented eleventh with a minor thirteenth; and augmented eleventh with a major thirteenth.

Because complete eleventh and thirteenth chords contain six and seven pitches, respectively, often too few voices or instruments are available to perform all of these notes. Therefore, some notes of the prototypical chord are omitted from the score. Composers usually do not omit the root or "highest" pitches (i.e. the eleventh or thirteenth). The resulting chords are often, therefore, difficult to identify.

To make a complex situation even more obscure, these chords (as with all chords in modern usage) may be used with any pitch distribution desired. Thus, for example, any of the six or seven pitches may function as the bass.

> Added pitches are often shown as +4 or +6. This use of the plus sign is not related in any way to the abbreviation for the augmented triad. However, confusion is certainly possible. In an effort to clarify, the +4 or +6 is routinely placed within parentheses as done here.

> Often called "fake book" notation. See p. 198 and Appendix XI, pp. 395–6.

Added Pitches

In advanced harmonic textures, composers may choose to add pitches to any triad or seventh chord regardless of the function (or non-function) of the base chord. Often the only possible analysis of such chords becomes "tonic triad with an added sixth" or "subdominant triad with a sharp (raised) fourth" because more logical (tradition-based) explanations are elusive at best. These chords may be thought of as being hybrids in that they are composed of standard triads or sevenths plus freely selected additional pitches that create new harmonic colors.

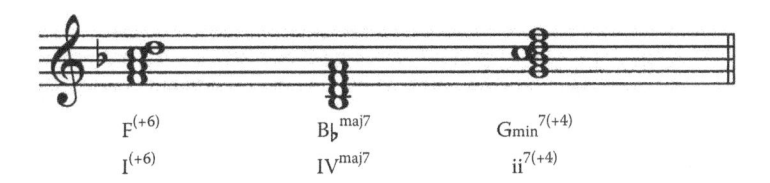

EXAMPLE 3.97 Some hybrid or coloration chords. From left to right (in F Major), a tonic triad with an added sixth, a subdominant triad with a major seventh, and a supertonic seventh with an added fourth. (The upper system of abbreviations used to identify these chords is frequently encountered in jazz or pops instrumental parts and lead sheets.)

Among the more commonly added pitches are what might be described as non-functioning sevenths. These sevenths are often added to chords that are functioning in tonally stable roles—such as tonics, subdominants, or submediants—and not intended to create the sort of harmonic tension that demands resolution.

Here is the standard blues progression in F Major with added sevenths and other pitches to create a richness of color not obtainable with the use of triads alone.

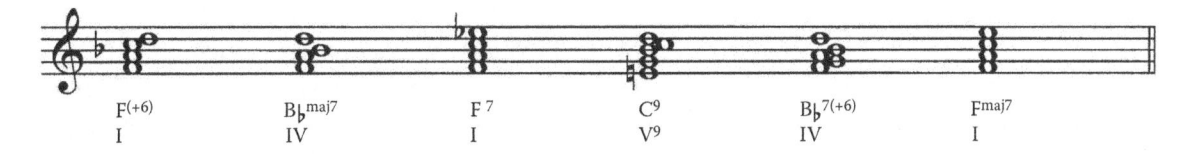

EXAMPLE 3.98 A series of chords that could form the basic progression for a blues in F Major. From left to right, F with an added sixth (tonic), B-flat with a major seventh (subdominant), F with a minor seventh (tonic), C ninth (dominant ninth), B-flat with a major seventh plus an added sixth (subdominant), and F with a major seventh (tonic).

Under-Thirding

In an effort to explain chords with added pitches, some theorists/composers have introduced the concept of under-thirding. Under-thirding is based on the concept that because triads were historically expanded by adding thirds *above* the fifth, might they not also be expandable by adding thirds *below* the root? Thus, a C Major triad could become an a minor-minor seventh or a C Major triad with an added sixth, depending on the use made of the chord in its context.

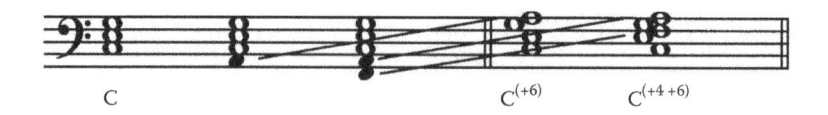

EXAMPLE 3.99 Beginning with a C Major triad and creating "new" chords by successively under-thirding the original chord. Assuming that C remains the root, the results are a C Major triad with an added sixth and a C Major triad with both an added sixth and an added fourth.

In fact, this expansion of the set of pitches from which any given chord may be drawn resulted in a situation at the end of the nineteenth and beginning of the twentieth centuries in which the concept of tertian harmony was called into question. Composers seeking new harmonic worlds threw out much of the old system and sought new ways to organize pitches, resulting in the twelve tone and serial systems among others. (See p. 125, Example 3.14.)

By the twentieth century, the complexity (or simplicity) of the system had developed such that, to paraphrase Vincent Persichetti in his book *Twentieth Century Harmony*, "Any note may follow any note and any note may be sounded with any note. Any chord may follow any chord and any chord may be sounded with any chord …"

Fake Book and Lead Sheet Notation

Fake book or lead sheet symbols are a form of tablature used to communicate chords to performers without having to write out all the specific pitches. These notations are—first and foremost—practical. They are used by working musicians who need to be able to sight read accurately, even when the lighting is dim and the surroundings are distracting. In these circumstances (unlike academic analyses discussed and provided in this book), clarity far outweighs pedantic accuracy! Thus, chord spellings are simplified and often, by theoretical standards, may be adjudged "inaccurate."

The symbols themselves consist of up to four parts: the chord's root, the chord's quality, and (sometimes) the bass note, and (perhaps) some added pitches. Here is an example: B♭ ^{maj7}. The pitch name (B♭) tells performers that they are to play a B-flat Major triad (B♭-D-F). The small ^{maj7} tells them to add to that basic chord the pitch a major seventh above B-flat ♭, which is A.

> If the bass is not specified, the root may be used as the bass pitch.

> The bass pitch may be written below the chord symbol: $\frac{B^7}{G}$

If the desired chord is a B-flat Major/minor seventh, then the symbol used would be B♭^{7}. The B-flat Major triad would be simply B♭, and the b-flat minor triad would be B♭ min.

If it is necessary to specify the bass note that needs to be played *with* the chord, the specific bass pitch is given after a slash after the chord symbol. Therefore, B♭^{maj7}/C would tell the performer to play a B-flat Major triad with the addition of a major seventh (A-natural) while sounding a C-natural in the bass. In this system of notation, it is easy to specify a bass pitch unrelated to the prevailing chord.

Sometimes numbers are added to a chord to communicate the addition of pitches outside the chord itself. Therefore, B♭6 would specify a B-flat Major triad with an added sixth above the root (i.e. a G.)

The following examples provide some of the more common fake book symbols. All illustrations use chords with a B-flat root.

EXAMPLE 3.100 The symbol on the left tells the performer to play a B-flat seventh over a G in the bass. The musical example on the right is one possible realization.

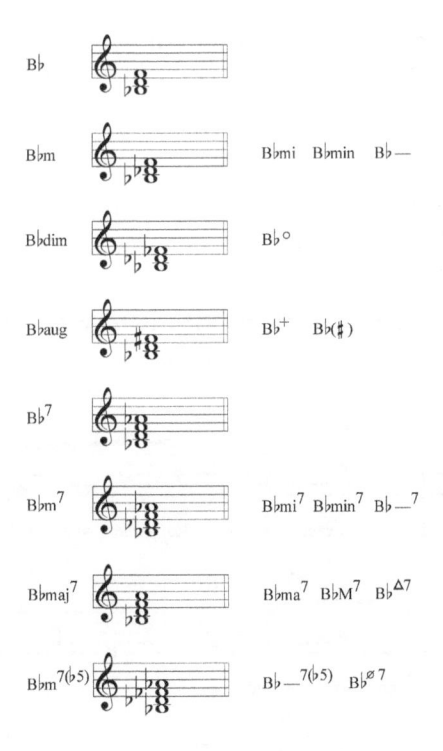

EXAMPLE 3.101 Some fake book symbols. Left column shows the usual symbol used. Next column shows the pitches specified (may be played in any octave with any distribution). Right columns show alternate symbols that may be encountered.

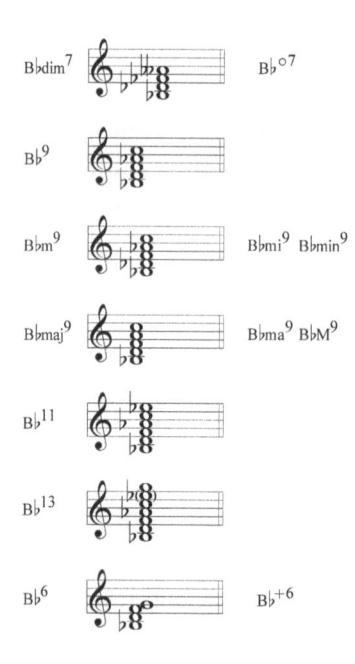

EXAMPLE 3.102 Additional fake book symbols. Left column shows usual symbols used. Next column shows the pitches specified (may be played in any octave with any distribution). Right column shows alternate symbols that may be encountered. It should be noted that in the B-flat eleventh, D (the third) is frequently omitted, and in the B-flat thirteenth, the E (the eleventh) is also omitted.

Some alternative notations shown above—B♭+, B♭–, B♭–7, B♭–7(♭5)—may create confusion because the plus sign (+) might be thought to indicate an added pitch and the minus sign (–) could even be mistaken for a random pen stroke. Also, the ○, ø, and Δ are not universally used nor understood.

When writing lead sheets, the normal practice is to write out the melody on the staff (usually in treble clef) with chord (fake book) symbols above. The results look much like this:

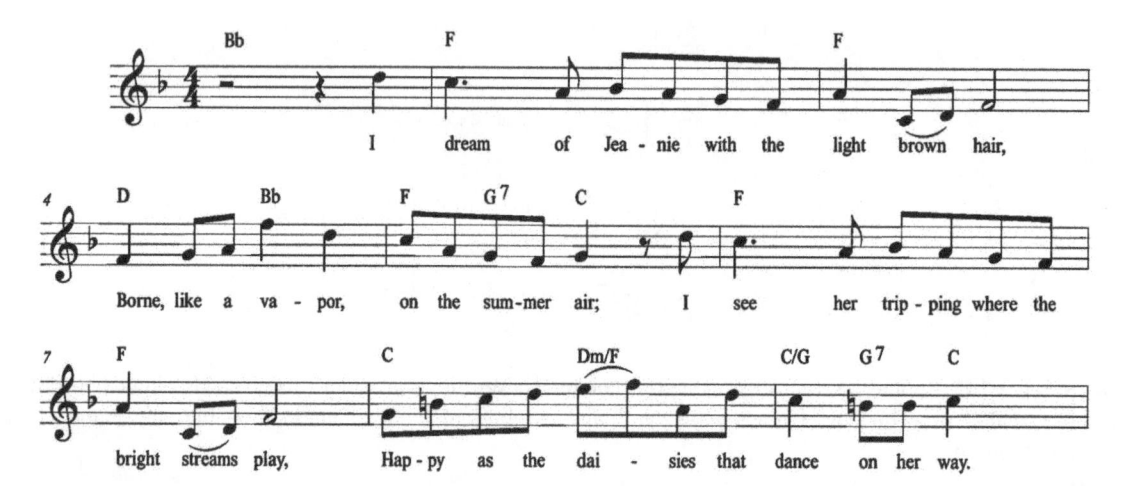

EXAMPLE 3.103 A lead sheet for Stephen Foster's "Jeanie with the Light Brown Hair."

Less Traditional Chords

The Tristan Chord

Other chords that are often referred to or encountered in writings about music are not simple, logical extensions of Rameau-based triadic structures. Composers created these chords for particular purposes.

One of the oldest of these is the ***Tristan chord***, created by Richard Wagner (1813–1883) for use in his music drama *Tristan and Isolde* (first performed in 1865). The effect of the Tristan chord involves both the initial chord and the harmonic changes that follow as shown below.

EXAMPLE 3.104 The Tristan chord, shown in the box. Analyzed as a type of seventh chord, it would be a minor triad (G-sharp, B, D-sharp) plus a diminished seventh (G-sharp to F-natural) in third inversion (not a common-practice seventh). It progresses to a dominant seventh built on E.

The Tristan chord has had an influence on composers since the opera's initial performance and is often found occupying a significant position in various compositions of the late nineteenth and early twentieth centuries. The harmonic language of the opera with its incessant creation of harmonic tensions followed by resolutions, which themselves contain new tensions, addressed the dramatic content of the opera, and revolutionized the harmonic language of Western music from that time forward.

The Mystic Chord

The ***mystic chord*** is the creation of Alexander Scriabin (1872–1915) and was used in his *Prométhée* and is therefore sometimes called the ***Promethean chord***.

EXAMPLE 3.105 Scriabin's mystic chord is a chord built from fourths of various sizes. From the bottom, an augmented fourth (C to F-sharp), a diminished fourth (F-sharp to B-flat), another augmented fourth (B-flat to E), and two perfect fourths (E to A and A to D).

The "Super" Dominant

The ***super dominant seventh chord*** is a convention dominant seventh with its fifth lowered, producing a dissonant chord that possesses both a leading tone and a Phrygian second. Here is an example with a typical resolution.

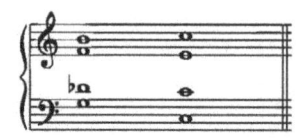

EXAMPLE 3.106   A super dominant seventh resolving to tonic in C. The leading tone and the flatted supertonic both resolve to tonic. The subdominant resolves to the mediant, and the dominant leaps to tonic. Thus, the usual final chord has a tripled root and no fifth.

The super dominant seventh chord is enharmonically a French sixth chord, but the harmonic progression is that of an altered dominant to tonic rather than an altered supertonic to dominant.

Review

- The practice of creating ever more dissonant chords by adding thirds above a preexisting chord structure was extended to include not just ninth chords but also elevenths and thirteenths.
- Chords containing more pitches than the number of available voices or instruments may be written with some pitches omitted. Usually, the root and the upper pitches in the stack are present.
- Since the nineteenth century, all chords may be written in any "inversion" and with any desired pitch distribution.
- Beginning in the latter part of the nineteenth century, the color of chords was frequently modified by adding additional pitches that were not part of the basic stack of thirds.
- Efforts to create a rationale for these newer chords produced the concept of under-thirding, the mirror image to the historic practice of stacking thirds.
- Working musicians have evolved fake book notation, which is direct and easy to understand. With minimal complexity, the bass voice and the harmonic content are communicated while leaving the exact voicing to the performer.
- From time to time, composers have created special chords that have caught the fancy of others. Among these are the Tristan chord of Wagner and the mystic chord of Scriabin.

Harmony: Note(s) with Note(s)

Related Exercises

§ These examples include ninths, elevenths, and thirteenths but are limited to only four voices. You may assume that the root is present as is the ninth, eleventh, or thirteenth as needed. Identify the following incomplete complex chords by writing the name of the root on the line provided together with a 9, 11, or 13 as appropriate.

§ You are provided with some of the usual fake book representations for chords. On the staff below each lead sheet or fake book chord, write the pitches implied by the chord symbol.

Dm   B♭   F°7   Am   Em7   Cdim   A7   Gm7(♭5)

part 4

Melodies in Harmony

1. Part Writing

For over 200 years, an important pedagogy for theory instruction has been ***part writing*** or ***voice leading***. The procedure is founded upon three primary conditions. First, it is based on ***contrapuntal*** practices. Second, it uses ***four voices***: soprano, alto, tenor, and bass. And third, it assumes the (tertian) triadic harmony of Western common-practice music.

Part writing, as we know it, dates primarily from the seventeenth and eighteenth centuries, but its procedures find a basis in compositional practices of the fifteenth and sixteenth centuries and its principles continue to influence composers into the twenty-first century.

Few likely situations exist where part writing ability could be considered essential, but the *knowledge* of part writing will prove valuable in the analysis of most Western music written since about 1600 CE.

Counterpoint

Counterpoint is the result of two or more ***independent*** and *equally significant* musical lines being performed at the same time. In the common-practice context, these lines fulfill certain melodic *and* harmonic expectations. These include establishing and maintaining harmonic frameworks, responding appropriately to one another, and ***preparing*** for, achieving, and ***resolving*** dissonances.

An important characteristic that each vocal line must possess is "singability." To achieve *this*, lines are written primarily with conjunct motion. Whatever disjunct motion they may possess usually consists of easier-to-sing melodic intervals, such as major and minor thirds, perfect fourths and fifths, and, primarily in the bass, perfect octaves.

> Even instrumental lines may tend to be more effective when structured to be singable.

The style of the music will determine the harmonic framework for a contrapuntal composition. For much of this music, the framework is the tonic-dominant and/or tonic-subdominant axis that is established as the structural basis. All harmonic motion proceeds from and returns back to this foundation.

> This was historically identified as **First Species Counterpoint** in *Gradus ad Parnassus*, a famous pedagogical treatise written by Johann Joseph Fux in the early eighteenth century.

> This is true in duple meters. In triple meters, second species CP consisted of three notes against each CF note. A brief, highly superficial explanation of the species is: Third species counterpoint was four against one (or six against one in triple meter), and fourth species was syncopation against the CF. Fifth species admitted more dissonances, added dotted notes, and integrated all of the species. Although many exceptions exist, the use of four voices for part writing has been fairly standard since the fifteenth century.

Note Against Note

The voices may relate to one another in a variety of ways. One of the fundamental relationships is simply note against note. In this relationship, for each note in a given voice (called the *cantus firmus*, abbreviated *CF*), a corresponding note exists in the other voice (the counterpoint, or *CP*).

Under the seventeenth-century concepts captured in this system, all intervals between the two voices had to be perfect consonances, which meant unisons, octaves, and fifths. *Second species* counterpoint, on the other hand, consisted of two notes in the CP for (almost) every note in the CF. Second species also admitted certain dissonances.

Species counterpoint is a contrapuntal study beyond the scope of this book, but the student will find that certain principles included in that pedagogy undergird common-practice part writing.

The Four Voices

A great amount of Western music is written for the human voice. Due to range and color characteristics, voices have traditionally been divided into four general quality/ranges (although many voices do not readily allow themselves to be so easily classified due to unique properties). The four classes are *soprano*, the higher women's and children's voices; *alto* (*contralto*), the lower women's and children's voices; *tenor*, the higher men's voices; and *bass*, the lower men's voices. This vocal distribution is often abbreviated to *SATB*.

The pitch ranges for each voice type, assuming untrained singers, are as follows:

EXAMPLE 4.01 The commonly accepted ranges for the four voice parts. From the left, soprano, alto, tenor, and bass. The whole notes indicate the normal range, while the stemless quarter note heads indicate pitches occasionally encountered or specified.

The literature contains many exceptions to the above ranges and, of course, trained singers will have much wider ranges than these. Many amateur singers may be able to sing only a portion of these ranges.

Voice Leading

As mentioned above, an alternative name for the study of part writing is the study of ***voice leading***. This is due to the importance associated with the control and planning of the motion of each voice relative to the other(s) as the music unfolds over time. Voice leading is concerned with following (or avoiding) the melodic tendencies discussed earlier, controlling the smoothness (or angularity) of the harmonic progressions, creating stylistically appropriate relationships between and among all of the voices, and doing all of this in a manner that leads to successful performance.

The four types of ***voice motion*** are ***contrary motion***, ***similar motion***, ***oblique motion***, and ***parallel motion***.

EXAMPLE 4.02   The four types of voice motion. From left to right, contrary motion, similar motion, oblique motion, and parallel motion.

With contrary motion, each voice, or line, moves from the initial pitch to the following pitch by going in the direction opposite to the direction of the other voice. If one line moves up, the other will move down.

In similar motion, both lines move in the same direction, but the interval transversed by one line is larger than the interval transversed by the other line. Oblique motion occurs when one line moves up (or down) while the other line remains on (repeats) the same pitch.

Parallel motion is a special case of similar motion and occurs when both voices move in the same direction *and* by the same amount. When this happens, the interval between the two lines does not change.

Clearly, the type of motion can be determined only between two voices at a time. In a texture with more than two voices, different types of motion will (usually) be observed among different voices.

Review

- Western music theory instruction has been based on part writing or voice leading for hundreds of years.
- Part writing is a contrapuntal art that assumes four separate voices: soprano, alto, tenor, and bass (SATB).
- Counterpoint is the result of two or more independent and equally significant musical lines being performed at the same time.

- When two independent lines are compared, the movement of one line relative to the other may be described as creating contrary motion, similar motion, oblique motion, or parallel motion.
- The intervallic content of each line will be primarily conjunct motion along with some easily sung intervals, such as major and minor thirds and perfect fourths and fifths.

Related Exercises

§ In the following examples, draw a line to connect the pitches moving in conjunct motion. Note the example provided.

§ In these examples, circle all pitches moving in disjunct motion and draw a line to connect the circles. Note the example provided.

§ Describe the motion between the two given voices by writing the correct term: parallel (or P), contrary (or C), similar (or S), or oblique (or O) on the lines provided between the notes.

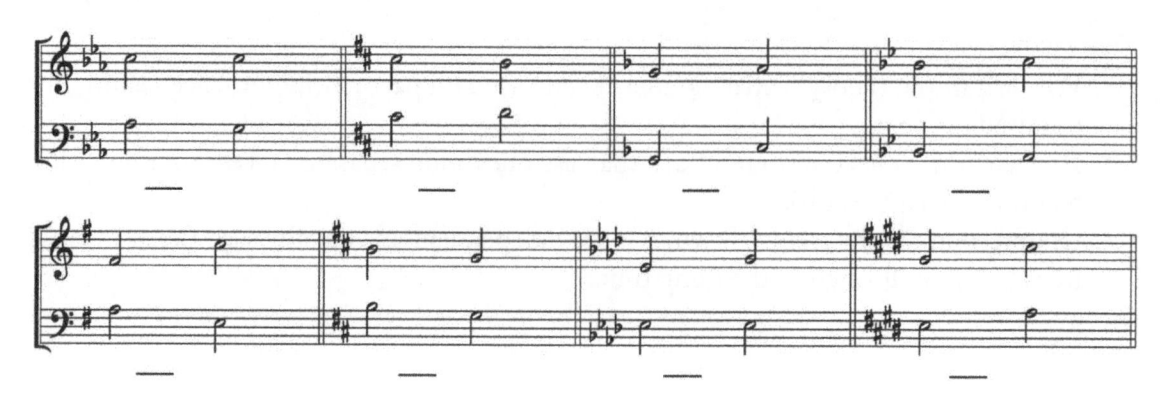

Parallel Fifths and Octaves

No other principle of music theory seems to be as widely known as this: "Avoid parallel fifths and parallel octaves." Yet ever since this was first communicated in a fourteenth-century treatise, composers have only somewhat heeded the admonition. Few modern students have understood why this particular motion has been discouraged. Indeed, most musicians realize that a standard practice of orchestrators and arrangers has been to double melodies, bass lines, and other melodic structures at the octave, thereby, obviously, creating parallel octaves.

To make sense of these principles, it may be helpful to examine them in the specific context of first species counterpoint. In writing first species counterpoint, not only must only consonances appear at each point (note), but also these consonances may not be achieved through *parallel fifths* or *parallel octaves*!

EXAMPLE 4.03   Traditionally avoided voice motion: on the left, parallel fifths; on the right, parallel octaves.

The discouragement of parallel octaves *in contrapuntal writing* is intended to preserve the independence of the lines. Independence is *necessary* for true counterpoint. When two lines, separated by a perfect octave, move together in the same direction thus remaining an octave apart, the upper line loses its unique identity and becomes (to the human ear) a harmonic of the lower voice (i.e. its second partial). From this point of view, the upper voice is lost as a separate contrapuntal component, and the texture is temporarily reduced by one voice. This is not a desirable event when trying to achieve a continuing four-voice texture.

The reason to avoid parallel fifths may seem less clear. A similar acoustical argument can be made because the effect of sounding two pitches a P5 apart is often the generation of a **resultant pitch** an octave below the lower of the two pitches. Clearly, if two contrapuntal voices are sacrificed to the generation of a single voice, the texture will sound as though it now has three, not four, voices. But another argument is that parallel fifths sound more like characteristics of many folk or traditional music rather than elements appropriate to such creations as are envisioned for counterpoint. Whatever the reasons, most composers outside the academy are fairly cavalier about these "rules," even though *extended* passages of parallel fifths or octaves in contrapuntal music remain rare.

> This is a common device used on pipe organs to generate lower notes when, for whatever reason, pipes of the correct length cannot be installed. Achieving this resultant pitch requires correct tuning of the fifth and adjustment of each pipe's timbre to that of the other.

> An early style of two- or three-voice performance, organum, involved various parallel motions, especially fourths, fifths, and octaves. It is conceivable that the avoidance of parallel fifths and octaves represented at one time an active effort to produce newer sounds.

The Four-Voice Texture

The study of part writing requires working in a four-voice environment, which, though it may look and sound to a novice as being chordal, is indeed contrapuntal.

EXAMPLE 4.04 An example of a four-voice texture as regularly used by seventeenth- and eighteenth-century composers for scoring of hymns.

The above example is typical of a very basic, four-voice texture. Although written on only two staves, the specific content of each voice is made clear by the use of stem directions. The upper staff in the treble clef contains the soprano and alto lines with the upward stems indicating the soprano part and the downward stems indicating the alto line.

The lower staff, written in the bass clef, contains the tenor and bass parts. In a manner similar to the higher voices, the tenor line is identified through the use of upward stems and the bass line with downward stems.

Spacing

A careful examination of Example 4.04 will show that the vertical spacing between the voices changes throughout the excerpt. This vertical characteristic is called the *spacing* or *position* and is usually described as *open position* or *close position* (sometimes *closed position*).

In determining the vertical spacing, only the top three voices are considered. The bass line is traditionally seen as being independent of the other three. Observe the first chord in the example. Here, the soprano has a B, the alto has a D, and the tenor has a G. These three pitches form a G Major triad.

But these pitches are not written as a stack of thirds. Spaces are left between the adjacent voices into which components of the G Major triad could be placed. Between the soprano's B and the alto's D is a G that is not sounded. And between the alto's D and the tenor's G is a B, also not sounded. This chord is an example of *open position* because chord tones are skipped between voices. (Another way of defining open position is by determining the interval between the soprano and the tenor. If the interval is greater than an octave, the voices are said to be in open position.)

Looking at the second chord in the second measure of Example 4.04, you see an F-sharp in the soprano, a D in the alto, and an A in the tenor. You cannot insert any chord tones between these pitches. This is an example of *close position*. Also note that the interval between the tenor voice and the soprano is a major sixth, certainly less than an octave. Although more of a detail than a critical principle, identifying the type of spacings used in four-part, part-writing examples is considered a reasonable observation to make.

Open Score

The next example uses exactly the same music from Example 4.04, but it is written in what is called *open score*. In this example, each voice has its own staff. In open score, the alto may be written either in the treble or alto clef. Likewise, the tenor may be written either in the tenor clef, the bass clef, or, as here, the treble clef an octave higher than it is to be sung (indicated by the 8 below the clef). Rarely, the soprano might be written in the older soprano clef (a C clef with middle C on the lowest staff line) instead of treble clef. The bass is always written in bass clef.

EXAMPLE 4.05 The same four voices shown in Example 4.04 here presented in open score formant.

Pitch Assignments and Doublings

Examining the above examples, either Example 4.04 or 4.05, you should be able to identify each chord by indicating its root via a Roman numeral and its inversion through the use of inversion symbols when required. However, two items might seem curious to the observant reader.

First, most of the chords contain only three unique pitches (i.e. they are triads), yet all chords have four notes: one for each voice. (And one of the chords has only two unique pitches distributed among the four voices.) These items are highlighted in Example 4.06 below. The *harmonic analysis* of the example is also provided.

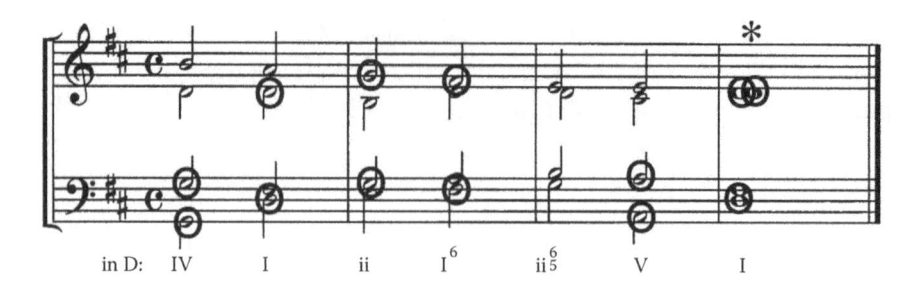

[Musical example: four-part harmony in D major with chord analysis: IV, I, ii, I⁶, ii⁶₅, V, I. An asterisk (*) marks the final chord.]

EXAMPLE 4.06 The same four-part example as shown before, now with its harmonic analysis provided and all doubled pitches circled.

In Example 4.06, the circled pitches are duplicates. An important choice that the composer makes when creating a four-voice texture is determining which pitches are to be ***doubled***. *In all triads used in four-part writing, one pitch must always appear in two separate voices.*

In the initial subdominant chord in the above passage, the duplicated pitch is G, the root of the chord. In the second triad, the tonic chord, the duplicated pitch is D, again the root. The third chord, supertonic, has the third (G) doubled, while the tonic six also has the third (F-sharp) doubled.

The fifth chord, the supertonic six-five, is a seventh chord. No doubling is required because each voice is assigned a unique pitch. The following dominant chord has the root (A) doubled.

The final tonic chord, marked with the asterisk (*), has *three* voices assigned to the root, while only the tenor provides the third. The fifth is omitted! A study of four-part writing examples will show that this incomplete triad is not unusual. It is especially common, as seen here, in a final, tonic chord that is preceded by the dominant triad or dominant seventh chord.

Selecting which Pitch to Double

Because each triad consists of three pitches—the root, the third, and the fifth—which of these pitches should be doubled? There are several ways to determine the appropriate answer.

One approach suggests that the best pitch to double is the root with the fifth being the second choice. Yet in the example above, the third was doubled in two of the chords.

Another approach to the question of which pitch to double was suggested by Walter Piston. In his approach, Piston identified each degree of the scale as being either tonal or modal (see Part 2, p. 100). The tonic, subdominant, and dominant scale degrees are tonal degrees while the mediant, submediant, and leading tone are modal. (Remember that these latter scale degrees are altered to produce either the major or the minor modality.) The supertonic is considered to function either way. Thus, instead of choosing the doubled pitch based on its position in the triad, the selection is determined by the function of the pitch within the scale.

In Example 4.06, all of the doubled pitches (except for the tonic six chord) are tonal degrees. The pitches used are D, G, and A (i.e. the tonic, subdominant, and dominant, respectively). Thus, the Piston guideline seems to account for all but one of the doubles, while the first approach accounts for only two of the doublings.

The choice of which note to double eventually depends on the interaction of *all* the part-writing guidelines *and* the composer's sense of style and sound. Remember, too, that these choices are predicated on an effort to make the result singable.

> In early nineteenth-century and older instrumental music, doubling decisions, especially in the winds, were often driven by the pitch limitations of the instruments.

Review

- Voice motion in contrapuntal style avoids parallel fifths and parallel octaves because either type of motion may cause the momentary loss of a voice.
- Part writing is usually notated on two staves with the upper staff using the treble clef and the lower staff using the bass clef.
- In this two-staff arrangement, the soprano is notated with stems up and the alto with stems down, both on the upper staff. The tenor is notated on the lower staff with stems up and the bass on the same staff with stems down.
- As an alternative to a two-staff score, the voices may be written in open score with each voice assigned to its own staff. The soprano on the top staff (in either the soprano or treble clef), the alto on the second staff (in either the alto or treble clef), the tenor on the third staff (in either the treble clef, sounding an octave lower, in the tenor clef, or in the bass clef), and the bass in the lowest staff (notated in the bass clef).
- When the upper three voices possess chord tones that are as close together as possible, the spacing is said to be close position.
- When the spacing is such that chord tones are skipped between the three upper voices (or when the interval between the soprano and the tenor exceeds an octave), the voices are in open position.
- When all three pitches of a triad are distributed among the four voices, one of the pitches in the triad will have to be doubled.
- Doublings may occur at the unison, the octave, the fifteenth (two octaves apart), or at the twenty-second (three octaves).
- In selecting the pitch to be doubled in a triad, preference is given to the root or the fifth of the triad and/or to those pitches that are the tonic, subdominant, or dominant in the immediate tonality.
- In certain cases, the root of the triad may be tripled and the fifth omitted. This is most likely found at the end of the piece or at the end of a section of the piece.
- When a triad possesses a tripled root, the chord is *probably* a tonic triad that was preceded by the dominant triad or the dominant seventh chord.

Related Exercises

§ Rewrite this two-staff rendition of a four-part texture onto the open score provided below. (Try singing each of the four parts in a convenient octave.)

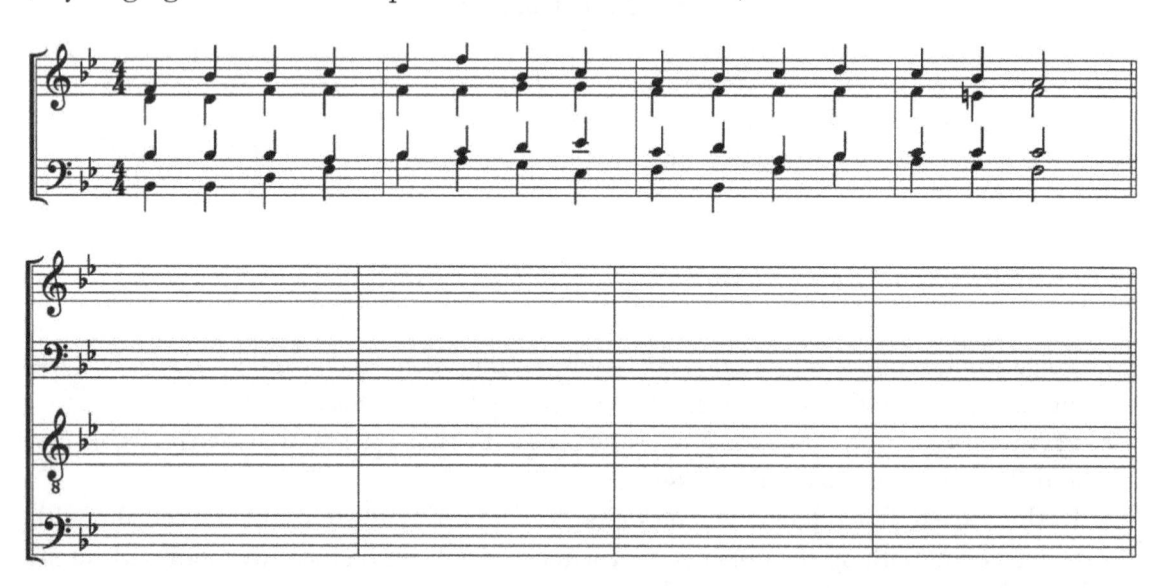

§ Condense the open score notation provided onto the two-staff system. Watch the stem directions. (Again, sing each of the four parts.)

§ In each of the following four-voice examples, describe the spacing as open or close. Write your answer on the line provided under each chord.

§ In the following harmonic patterns, circle the doubled (tripled) pitches. On the line below the chord, write the scale degree of the doubled (tripled) pitch. If no pitches are doubled, leave the line blank. (If no doubled [tripled] pitches occur, what might that tell you about the chord?)

2. Creating the Harmonic Structure

The Tonic-Dominant Axis and the Harmonic Framework

By the process of creating part-written scores, composers also establish the harmonic framework of the piece. In common-practice period music, the three important harmonic anchors or goals are overwhelmingly the tonic, the dominant, and the subdominant. Other slightly less frequently encountered goal tonalities are the submediant and the supertonic. Why these particular goals are most likely to form the landmarks of our harmonic geography is primarily a matter of conjecture based on such observations as the structure of the preexisting modal system, the nature of the harmonic series, the evolution of harmony in Western music, and other historic, musical, physical and/or psychological insights.

Examining much common-practice music will reveal that harmonic patterns regularly progress from tonic to dominant and back, or from tonic to subdominant and back. Often, some combination of the two is observed. When exceptions are encountered, alternative goals are frequently the relative minor (submediant), supertonic, or, especially in a minor modality, the relative major (altered mediant).

> German theorist Hugo Riemann (1849–1919) proposed a theory of functional harmony in which all chords are identified as being of the tonic class, of the dominant class, or of the subdominant class.

Traditionally, theory texts have based their presentation on the tonic-to-subdominant-to-dominant-to-tonic progression as fundamental. A few authors (notably, Richard Franco Goldman [1910–1980]) have replaced the subdominant with the supertonic (the *modal* dominant of the dominant) in the pattern identifying the subdominant as an *altered supertonic*.

Either argument has its merits, but the movement from tonic to dominant and back forms the harmonic foundation upon which the vast majority of common-practice music has been constructed. For composers working in the style, the establishment of this axis may seem both essential and obligatory.

The Bach-Style Chorale

The examples most often selected in theory texts to illustrate part writing are Bach, or Bach-style, chorales. We will examine one of his harmonizations to see what he did to flesh out the original melody. We will focus our attention for now on the basic harmonic selections made to harmonize the melody.

Here is the melody to be examined:

EXAMPLE 4.07   Hymn tune known to Bach both as *Befiehl du deine Wege* and also as *O Haupt voll Blut und Wunden*.

As customarily notated, the pitches with fermatas over them represent cadence points, the ends of lines of poetry. Whether the fermatas are merely phrase indicators or are intended to be performed is debated. Their presence helps the performer identify the tonal goals within the melody.

Given the task of creating a harmonization for this chorale melody, what would the process be? What chord might be used to harmonize the first pitch? Because the final pitch is

Melodies in Harmony

the same as the first pitch, must the two be harmonized the same? Actually, there are many possibilities. And Bach himself used more than one approach. (In Bach's chorale harmonizations, the melody is usually but not always assigned to the soprano voice.)

In our example, the melody begins and ends on E. In fact, the melody has some properties very similar to those found in ancient melodies in the Phrygian mode. It may even trace its origins to a medieval plainchant, but we may harmonize it in either a major or a minor context as well as a historic modality.

Because the E may be the root, third, or fifth of a triad—and the first triad could be any of the four types, there are twelve triadic options for harmonizing the first pitch:

A Major, C Major, E Major,
a minor, c-sharp minor, e minor,
a-sharp diminished, c-sharp diminished, e diminished, *or*
A-flat Augmented, C Augmented, E Augmented.

While the choice of the initial triad may be limited by the desired character or style of the following harmonization, the final arrival at tonic needs to be supported by a stable chord (not by a diminished or augmented triad). Most likely, the final chord will also not be a minor triad because Bach usually ends with a major triad, even when the piece itself is in minor. Thus, the likely final chord will be A Major, C Major, or E Major.

The various cadence points are, in order, E, A, and the repeat of E and A. These are followed by C, E, B, and E. If we think of the piece as being in C Major, the likely cadence chords could be tonic and subdominant (or submediant) in the first, repeated section and then tonic, submediant (or tonic), dominant, and finally tonic. Here are some possibilities.

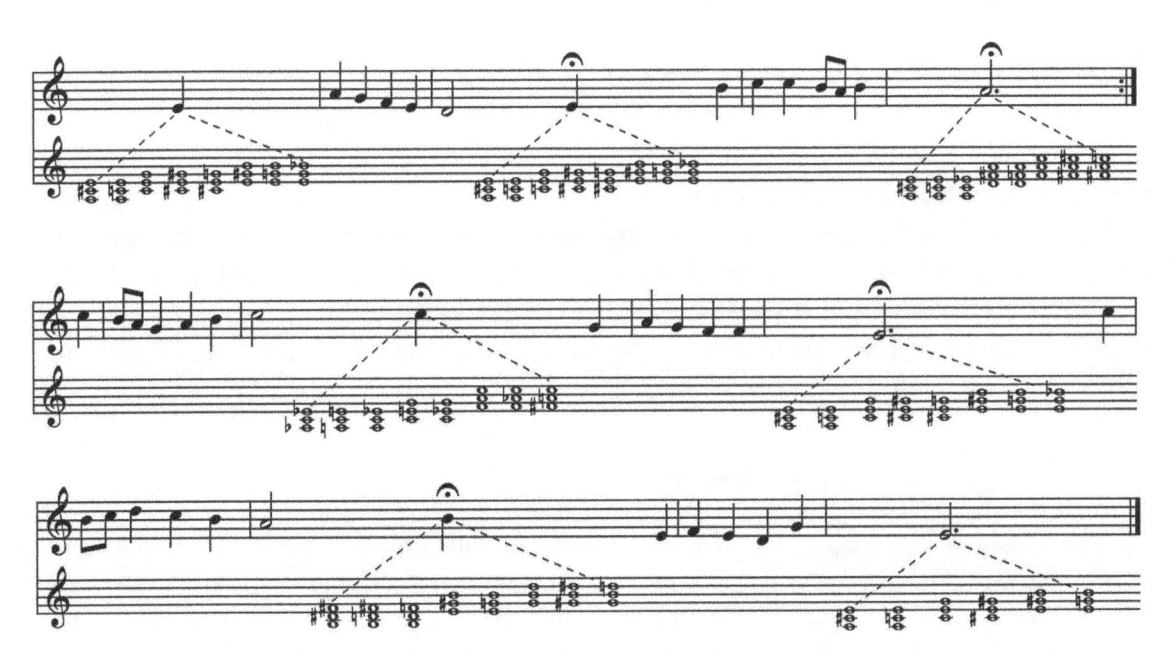

EXAMPLE 4.08 *O Haupt voll Blut und Wunden* (upper staff) with suggested alternatives for the first chord and each of the six cadence points (shown on the lower staff).

The Bass Line

For many composers, an early part of the process of setting a melody is the creation of an appropriate bass line. The bass line is second in importance only to the melody when it comes to establishing the character, flow, and style of the piece. Bass lines tend to have certain features, although all bass lines may not display all features.

Movement by Fourths, Fifths, and Octaves

Whether the bass is to be provided by an instrument or a voice, leaps of fourths and fifths (as well as octave jumps) are both characteristic and effective. Not all pitches so connected are roots or fifths of the chords but do often correspond to the tonal degrees of the scale.

Stepwise Motion

Bass lines frequently employ stepwise motion with and without chromatic pitches. In some styles of music, chromaticism in the bass is avoided, but in other styles, even very old styles, chromatic bass lines are expected. (See "Ground Bass" in Part 5, p. 322.)

Outlining of Triads (Or Seventh Chords)

Frequently, bass lines outline triads or seventh chords, either ascending or descending. The outlined triads may not correspond directly to the harmonic content of the moment but will usually be related to the primary chords of the tonal center.

Repeated Pitches

A variation of the idea of octave leaps is the repeated pitch. This may result from a desire to create a slow harmonic rhythm or for dramatic effect. In many cases, a series of repeated bass notes is called a pedal. (See Part 4, p. 245.)

The speed of the bass line assists in setting the harmonic rhythm and has a strong impact on the feeling and effect of the resulting music. The reader is encouraged, if not already familiar with the impact of the bass line, to listen especially carefully to bass lines in a wide variety of music. In many instances, the bass line alone may seem to define the style and character of the sounds.

> In the occasionally encountered common-practice piece that seems to deny the tonic-dominant framework, this avoidance specifically serves to acknowledge the fundamental influence of the dominant-tonic structure.

Review

- In the process of harmonizing a chorale melody, the composer will establish a clear tonic-dominant foundation upon which to base the harmonic choices.
- To create a four-part harmonic setting of a melody, the tonality and modality must be determined.

Melodies in Harmony

- The important harmonic structures that are heard at cadence points within a chorale harmonization are the tonic, dominant, and subdominant. Also heard, but less likely, are the submediant and the supertonic. Other harmonic goals are rarer.
- In the common-practice style, major and minor triads are consonances, while any other chords are, to various degrees, unstable (i.e. dissonant).
- The pitches of the melody are usually voiced as members of concurrently sounding triads or seventh chords.
- Cadence points are, by their very nature, likely to be consonants, thus triads.
- All other melodic pitches may be harmonized with consonant or dissonant chords.
- The purpose of the part-writing style is to create harmony from four simultaneous, easily sung melodies.
- The bass line is second only to the melody in importance, imparting style and character to the music.
- Bass lines tend to move in fourths, fifths, and octaves by outlining triads, in ascending or descending lines (either diatonic or chromatic), and using repeated pitches.
- The speed of the bass line helps determine both the harmonic rhythm and aesthetic of the music.

Related Exercises

§ In each of the chorale excerpts, locate the cadences. Mark the movement of each *voice* (soprano, alto, tenor, and bass) by connecting occurrences of conjunct motion with lines and by drawing a circle around those pitches displaying disjunct motion. Place a box around the root of each chord and write the *quality* of each chord on the line provided below.

Rejoice and Sing

Johann Hermann Schein
(1586-1630)

God and Man

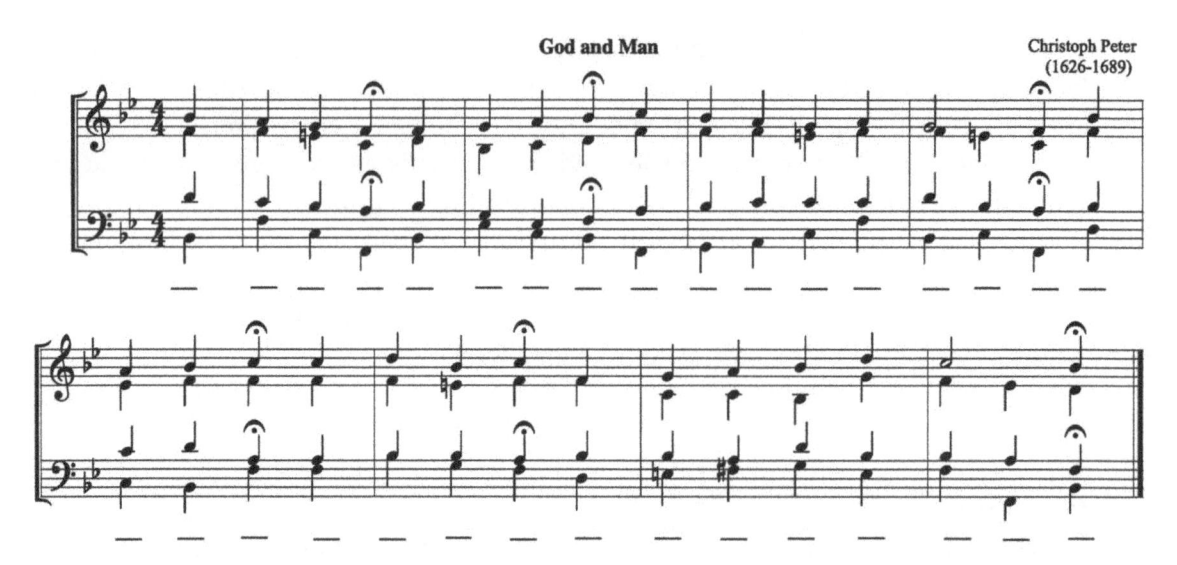

Christoph Peter
(1626-1689)

§ In the following harmonized excerpts, circle the root of each chord. On the line above each chord, write "O" if the chord displays open voicing or "C" if it displays close voicing. (If you aren't sure, write an "x.") Then, on the line between the chords, identify the *melodic interval* found between the successive pitches of the *bass* voice.

The Harmonization

Here is one of J.S. Bach's harmonizations in the key of C of *O Haupt voll Blut und Wunden*.

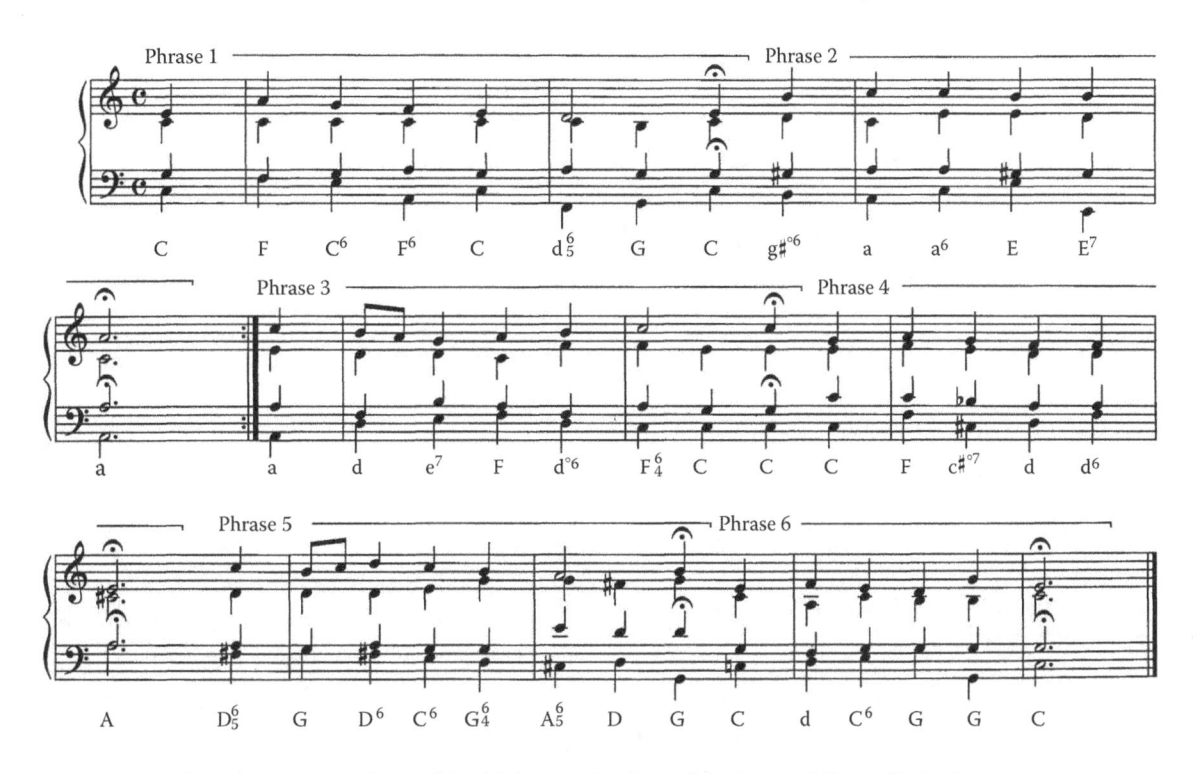

EXAMPLE 4.09 The essence of one of Bach's harmonizations of *O Haupt voll Blut und Wunden*.

When examining Example 4.09, you should note that the starting and ending chords are C Major as are the chords found at the first and third fermatas (i.e. the first and third harmonic goals). The chord at the end of the repeated section is an a minor triad, the relative minor to C Major.

The remaining goal tonalities are A Major at the end of the fourth phrase and G Major at the end of the fifth. G Major is the dominant of the central tonality, C. The A Major chord is, for the moment, more difficult to explain. The final C Major at the end represents the return to the home key of C.

> The version of the chorale melody and harmonization provided here is an adaptation by the author from Bach. It is intended to facilitate this initial presentation and is certainly not an attempt to "improve" upon Bach's definitive creation.

The First Phrase or Passage

Because these tonal goals are the important mileposts along the way, it should be informative to see how Bach manages to get the listener from one to the next.

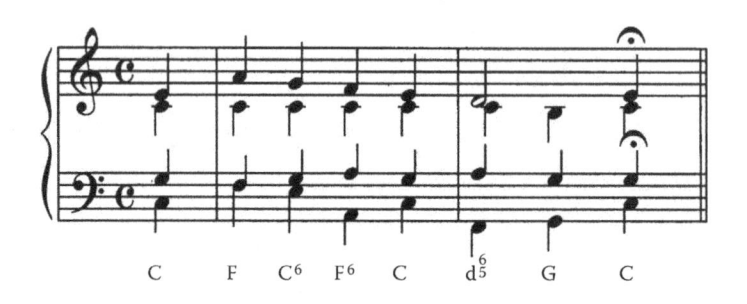

$$\text{C} \quad \text{F} \quad \text{C}^6 \quad \text{F}^6 \quad \text{C} \quad \text{d}^6_5 \quad \text{G} \quad \text{C}$$

EXAMPLE 4.10   Phrase 1 of Bach's harmonization.

> The D half note in the melody must be analyzed both as a part of the d minor-minor seventh chord and as a component of the following G Major chord because it sounds during both chords.

The first phrase fulfills the task of establishing the tonal center, the tonic. It begins and ends with the tonic triad and has two other tonic triads on the third and fifth notes. The subdominant F Major chord (on notes two and four) and the dominant G Major chord immediately before the C Major chord at the end of this excerpt reinforces that C Major is tonic. This dominant is preceded by the supertonic seventh (the d minor-minor seventh chord), creating a very recognizable (imperfect) authentic cadence.

Next, let's turn our attention to the voice leading. The alto line is notable because it consists of repeated middle Cs until the appearance of the dominant chord when it moves down a semitone to the B and then returns to C. The line is easy to sing, and it illustrates Bach's preference to *keep common tones in the same voice.*

The tenor line is slightly more complex but still moves only stepwise. Starting on the dominant pitch, the tenor moves to the subdominant, back to the dominant, up to the submediant, back to the dominant, again up to the submediant, and finally back to the dominant for the last two chords.

> When a large leap occurs (i.e. a leap of a fourth or greater), a voice frequently changes direction after the leap, which is a common practice in writing vocal parts. (Older counterpoint guidelines dictated that there should never be more than two successive leaps—of any size—in the same direction.)

Typical of many bass lines, this one incorporates larger leaps than those found in the upper voices. Starting on the tonic, it leaps upward a perfect fourth (an easy interval to sing) to the subdominant and then moves down a semitone to the mediant. Now the bass leaps down a perfect fifth to A, goes up a minor third to C, and then leaps down a perfect fifth. Even though the motion consists of several leaps, the pitches are relatively easy to hear because they form two diatonic triads: a minor and F Major. From the low F, the line steps up to G, the dominant and then, following the tendency of the dominant, leaps up to the tonic.

The Second Phrase

The second phrase is harmonized this way:

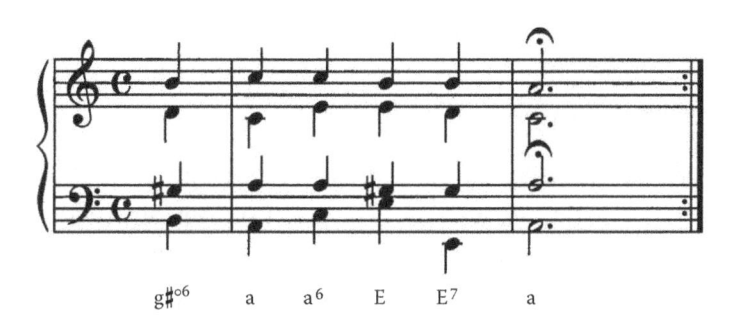

EXAMPLE 4.11   Phrase 2 of *O Haupt voll Blut und Wunden*.

In light of the assertion that this chorale harmonization is in the key of C Major, this passage may seem difficult to explain until we recognize that a minor is both the relative minor to and also the submediant of C Major. What Bach has chosen to do in this passage is to move briefly from C Major to a minor. The a minor pitch center is reinforced with E Major, the dominant of a minor (the fourth and fifth chords), as well as the g-sharp diminished triad, the leading tone triad in a minor, on the first note. Coming across the passage in Example 4.11 in isolation, you would easily see it as a passage in a minor.

Also, notice that the a minor chord immediately after the g-sharp diminished triad is not complete and consists of only the root and the third (each doubled). And the a minor chord at the cadence point consists of three roots and a third, thus lacking the fifth.

Examining the individual lines, beginning with the alto, you will note that the only pitches involved are C, D, and E and that the only leap is an upward major third. The tenor begins on a chromatic G-sharp (which was preceded by a G) and simply alternates between this pitch and A. The bass begins on a B (which was preceded by C) and moves down a step to A and then moves upward, outlining the a minor triad. From there, the bass line drops an octave to E and returns by an upward leap to the root of the a minor triad.

In these first two passages of the chorale harmonization, the voices move in easy-to-sing intervals and, for the most part, keep common tones within the same voice. And also a diversity of motion occurs between the voices with oblique, contrary, similar, and parallel motions all in evidence.

The Third Phrase

EXAMPLE 4.12 Phrase 3 of *O Haupt voll Blut und Wunden*.

This third phrase of our example begins with all voices sounding the same pitches with which the preceding passage had ended. The harmonic progression thus begins with an a minor triad and is followed by a d minor chord, an e minor-minor seventh, an F Major triad, a b diminished triad, an F Major triad, and a repeated C Major triad. The cadence is obviously on C but is approached by the subdominant F, creating a plagal cadence. All of the chords in this passage relate either to the tonic, C, or to the subdominant, F.

The first a minor chord is submediant in C Major. The d minor chord is submediant in F Major (and its root is a perfect fourth above the root of the a minor chord). The e minor-minor seventh is built on the leading tone to F and immediately moves to F. The b diminished triad is a leading tone seventh to C, which, although it doesn't follow immediately, *is* the tonal goal of the passage. The following second inversion F Major (subdominant) triad is followed by the tonic chord, creating a plagal cadence.

The alto line continues to move in a very narrow pitch range, going from E down a step to D, which is repeated, before going down another step to C. From C, the line leaps up a perfect fourth to F and then changes direction, stepping down to an E, which is repeated.

The tenor voice leaps from A down a major third to F and then leaps up a tritone (augmented fourth) to B—the first difficult interval to sing in the piece! It is made easier to hear (and thus, to sing) by the tenor's B being a whole tone above the initial A as well as functioning as the leading tone to the eventual goal, and tonic, C. The B is followed by a change of direction stepping down to A, followed by another major third leap down to F, this time followed by a return to A and a downward step to G.

The bass line is a little less angular in this passage having only one larger leap, a perfect fourth, from A up to D followed by an ascending scale fragment to F, from where it leaps back down a minor third to D and steps down to C where it remains into the cadence.

During the first beat of the first full measure of this third phrase, the soprano melody has two pitches, B and A. In the process of doing an analysis, this fact would of course add some complexity. In the analysis described above, the B was ignored. One may ask why this was done.

Melodies in Harmony

All analyses involve certain assumptions on the part of the analyst. One such assumption that has been in use in this discussion, though not before stated explicitly, is that the harmonic rhythm is a series of quarter notes with a chord change of some sort occurring on *almost* every quarter note.

Using this assumption, only one chord would be expected to be defined during the first beat of this third phrase. That means that it may be a d minor chord (if the B is ignored) or a b diminished chord (if the A is ignored). You may also realize that if the B and the A were both included in the chord, it would be a b half-diminished seventh chord. But because these two pitches are not sounded simultaneously, this latter interpretation should seem a stretch.

> This is a topic that is discussed in the section on "Non-Harmonic Tones" (p. 233). For the time being, the pitch is being ignored to facilitate the current, simplified discussion. *It would not be ignored in a more thorough approach.*

At this point in the presentation, there is no indisputably correct answer. It is easy to argue that the d minor tonality supports the following F Major chord, as was done. Or, conversely, it would be easy to argue that the b diminished chord anticipates the soon-to-follow b diminished triad (on the fourth beat of the measure) and that the b half-diminished seventh would be a very strong preparation for the eventual cadence on C Major.

Each of these interpretations possesses logical reasons to support its validity. However, this current presentation of the analytical process is only intended as an introduction to the processes of harmonic analysis. At this stage of the presentation, some complexities have been avoided.

The Fourth Phrase

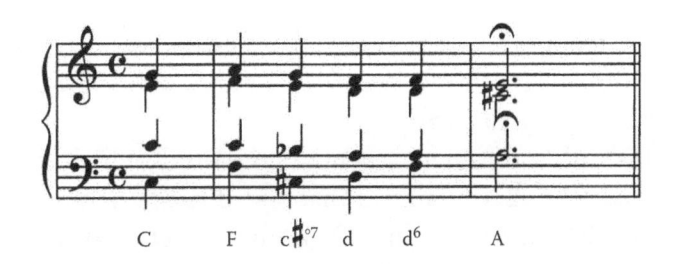

EXAMPLE 4.13 Phrase 4 of *O Haupt voll Blut und Wunden.*

If this passage had ended with an a minor triad, then the logic would be as follows: Beginning with the C Major triad that ended the previous passage, the harmony goes back to F Major and then on to d minor, the relative minor to F Major (i.e. the submediant of F Major). This tonality of d minor is preceded, on the second beat of the full measure, by a fully diminished seventh chord on C-sharp, the leading tone seventh to d minor. D minor would then be heard as the penultimate chord in a plagal cadence on a minor.

That interpretation is valid. But at the time of Bach, it was frequently the practice to change cadential minor triads into major triads. This altered minor triad, called the Picardy third, was not restricted to final cadences. It happens here.

> The D, F, and A pitches form a d minor triad, and the C-sharp is both the leading tone to the root of this triad as well as an upward chromatic modification of the first C. These factors can make the diminished fourth much easier for the basses to sing than might seem obvious.

The alto voice begins on E, moves upward by step to F, back down stepwise through E to D, and eventually down, chromatically, to C-sharp. The tenor begins with repeated Cs then moves down chromatically to B-flat and on to A. The bass has the more irregular line and the more difficult interval. It begins on C, leaps up to F, and then changes direction and makes a modestly awkward leap down to C-sharp. From there, it steps up to D, leaps to F, and then leaps to A.

The Fifth Phrase

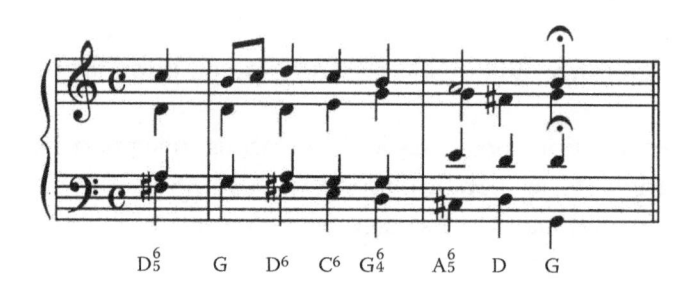

EXAMPLE 4.14 Phrase 5 of the analysis.

It has been helpful throughout this process to look at the end of a passage before beginning the analysis. This procedure is recommended. *The harmonic goal goes a long way toward determining the path that the composer will take.*

Example 4.14 begins with a dominant seventh chord on D, which is the dominant of the upcoming G Major goal. The A Major triad that ended the fourth phrase should be heard as the dominant of this initial chord. This D six-five is followed by G Major, D Major, C Major, and a G Major six-four. The final four chords of this passage, beginning with this G six-four, form an imperfect cadence on G with the dominant seventh on A replacing the supertonic (or supertonic seventh).

The A is heard as the dominant of the dominant of G. The following chord is the dominant itself, and the final cadence chord is G Major. Because the piece is in C Major, this cadence on G Major is an example of a half cadence.

All of the voices obtain their starting pitches for this passage from the A Major chord in the prior excerpt. The alto simply resolves the C-sharp leading tone to D, the tenor has a common tone and so stays on the same pitch, and the bass, which here has the greatest challenge, descends a minor third to the F-sharp, not really a difficult interval, but it's made even easier because the resolution of this F-sharp is on the upcoming Gs.

The alto line repeats the D, then steps up to E, and leaps up a minor third to G. The alto then repeats the G, goes down a minor second to F-sharp (the leading tone to G), and returns to G at the cadence point. The tenor line moves stepwise down to G, up to A, and then back down to repeated Gs before making the second largest leap we have seen so far in this harmonization, a major sixth up to E. Here, the line changes direction and steps down to a repeated D.

> The upward major sixth may look like a difficult interval, but for most experienced singers it is fairly easy because they can think of it as a leap from the dominant to the mediant (i.e. the fifth and third, respectively) in the overall tonality of C Major (the tonic triad).

The bass line moves from F-sharp up to G (the natural goal for the leading tone) and then sings a descending D Major scale from the subdominant (G) to the C-sharp, the leading tone to D. From there, the bass resolves to D and leaps downward to the current goal, G.

Looking ahead, we have determined that the composition will eventually cadence in the original tonality, C Major. Thus, this cadence on G represents a dominant preparation.

The Final Phrase

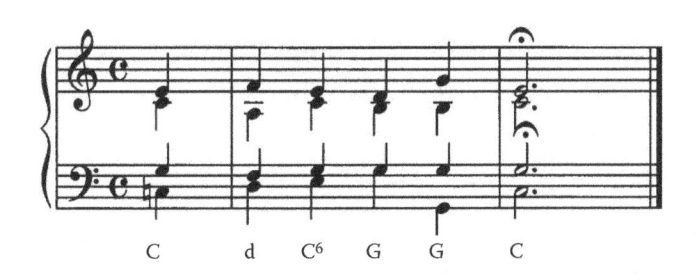

EXAMPLE 4.15   Phrase 6 of *O Haupt voll Blut und Wunden*.

In this final passage, the harmony begins with the C Major triad followed by d minor, another C Major chord, two G Major chords, and the final C Major triad. Clearly, this is an authentic cadence ending as it does on the tonic and uses the d minor triad as a supertonic preparation for the dominant G Major. Also note that the next-to-last chord is (somewhat unexpectedly) incomplete, consisting of three roots and a third.

Even though this is the final cadence, Bach chose to make it imperfect rather than altering the final melodic pitch from the mediant to the tonic to create a perfect cadence. He retains the original melody.

We can see that each of the voices moves in very singable manner. The alto begins on middle C, leaps down a minor third to A, returns up a minor third to C, steps down to B, which is repeated, and then resolves back up to C. The tenor steps down to F and then steps back up to G, which is repeated through the final chord. The bass line steps up from C through D to E, then leaps up a minor third to the dominant, G, leaps down an octave, and resolves on the tonic.

As simple as the voice leading is in this final phrase, the singers seem to have a bit of a challenge as they go from the last chord in Example 4.14 to the first pitches of this final excerpt. The soprano, alto, and tenor must all leap downward a perfect fifth while the bass leaps up a perfect fourth.

But the chord under the fifth fermata is the dominant triad, and the following chord is tonic. There is hardly a more conventional progression than dominant to tonic. Only the octave would be considered easier to hear and sing than the perfect fifth and perfect fourth.

In Summary

Understanding the harmonizing of a melody to be a series of discrete steps, the process requires first deciding what the tonal goals will be. This is followed by constructing a bass line and writing vocal lines that will connect each of these goals in a singable and musically satisfying manner while generating chords that are stylistically appropriate. The choices made will reflect the aesthetic ideals of the composer, time, and musical style.

In this Bach example, most of the chords are diatonic triads drawn directly from the tonic scale. Those chords that fall outside this set are chords that include chromatic pitches that function as the leading tone to some scale degree *other* than tonic. The lone exception is the B-flat used to create the c-sharp fully diminished seventh chord that prepares a d minor triad. But this is not exotic; it is still a leading tone chord.

A Harmonic Analysis of the Chorale

In Example 4.16 below, we see a summary of the tonal goals we identified in this harmonization of *O Haupt voll Blut und Wunden*.

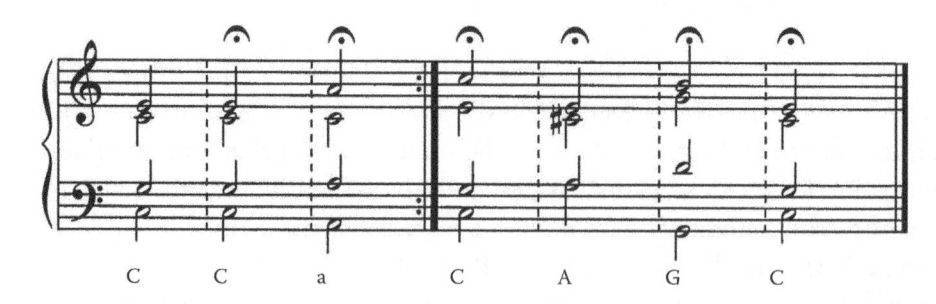

EXAMPLE 4.16   The chords used at the beginning and at each cadence point in J.S. Bach's harmonization of the chorale *O Haupt voll Blut und Wunden* discussed above.

After examining Example 4.16, it should be easy to understand Example 4.17, in which the chord names are now replaced with the Roman numerals traditionally used for harmonic analysis.

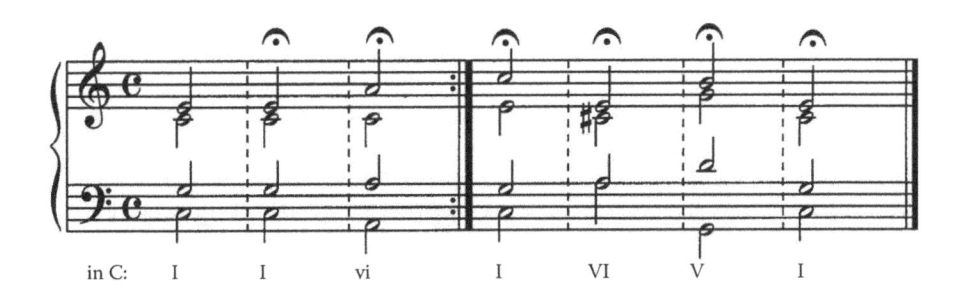

in C: I   I   vi   I   VI   V   I

EXAMPLE 4.17 The same information provided in Example 4.16 but now expressed in a functional, harmonic analysis.

In Example 4.17, the fourth fermata shows a major quality triad with a submediant root. Not all theory texts or instructors would recommend this notation. Alternatives would be vi♯ or VI♯ (with the sharp in each case indicating an altered submediant triad—that is, a raised third—which of course would identify the expected minor triad as having been transformed into a major triad).

> The sharp placed to the right of the analysis symbol indicates a raised third in the triad. This is derived from figured-bass writing where a single sharp, placed above the bass, indicated that the third above the bass should be raised.

The first alternative symbol could be used in a system using upper- and lowercase Roman numerals. The second alternative symbol would be found in a system where only uppercase Roman numerals are used. A third alternative would be to indicate a temporary change of key to A (major or minor) between the third and fourth fermatas. Such a brief key change is a temporary tonicization. (It could be argued, though, that this passage is too brief to justify any—even temporary—change of key.)

Concluding the Process

The following example shows the complete Bach harmonization of *O Haupt voll Blut und Wunden* analyzed with Roman numerals. Note the secondary relationships being indicated such as $\frac{V^7}{V}$, which would be read as the "dominant seventh of the dominant."

EXAMPLE 4.18 A complete, functional analysis of Bach's harmonization of *O Haupt voll Blut und Wunden*.

Review

- An approach to the harmonic analysis of a piece of music is to identify each triad or seventh chord that sounds at each cadency point by type, quality, and inversion.
- Through that process, the harmonic foundation (key and modality) of the piece is uncovered.
- With the harmonic goals in mind, every chord used leading up to each cadence point should be analyzed by type, quality, and inversion.
- Next, at each cadence point, the type of cadence must be determined.
- If the harmonization leads to a momentary tonal center, not clearly related to the tonic of the piece, this *may be* identified as temporary tonicization.
- Working within the key of the piece, convert each chord description into an appropriate Roman numeral indicating the functional analysis of the chord.
- The first chord and/or the printed key signature are never assurances of the actual key of a piece of music. Only examination of the pitch content of the whole piece will determine the tonal center.

Melodies in Harmony

Related Exercises

§ For both of the following examples, determine the key of the chorale and locate and label the type of every cadence. Then provide a harmonic analysis. On the line provided under each chord, place the correct Roman numeral for the chord within the key together with the inversion symbols.

in ____ : __ __ __ __ __ __ __ __

__ __ __ __ __ __ __ __ __

__ __ __ __ __ __ __ __ __

in ____ : ____

3. Non-Harmonic Tones

Chord Tones versus Non-Chord Tones

Almost every pitch in every voice of the harmonization we studied of Bach's *O Haupt voll Blut und Wunden* was a component of the triad (or seventh chord) sounds at that moment. All of these pitches may be considered ***chord tones***. In triadic harmony, chord tones are, by definition, consonances. Note, too, the harmonic rhythm of the example: It moves in quarter notes until the cadence chords.

> The sevenths added to triads to produce the various seventh chords were originally not considered chord tones. Initially thought of as dissonances—adding instability to the harmony—the author chose to include them as components of a harmonic entity and, by that process, defined all of the pitches as chord tones.

The chorale examined above is a simplified version of Bach's work. Example 4.19 shows the *second* phrase of the simplified harmonization, now presented in Bach's chosen key of D Major, on the left, and as Bach scored it on the right.

EXAMPLE 4.19 The second phrase of Bach's harmonization of *O Haupt voll Blut und Wunden*. On the left, the simplified version; on the right, Bach's original.

In Bach's harmonization, we find additional pitches that do not to fit into our harmonic analysis. These extra pitches are not components of the chords we have identified and, when the passage is played, may sound mildly or strongly dissonant. These pitches are called ***non-harmonic tones***.

Non-harmonic tones are controlled dissonances with specific names and identified by three properties:

- The manner in which the dissonance is ***prepared*** (the ***preparation***).
- The ***location*** of the dissonance relative to the harmonic rhythm.
- The manner in which the dissonance is ***resolved*** (the ***resolution***).

At times, it may be valuable to observe whether the dissonance is chromatic or diatonic.

It is *always* important to observe in which voice the dissonance occurs, but that is not a factor in naming the dissonance. When doing a harmonic analysis, the non-harmonic tones are identified (eliminating them from consideration as chord tones) before the chords are analyzed.

The *preparation*, sometimes called the approach, of a dissonance refers to what occurs in the voice that sounds the dissonance *immediately before* the occurrence of the dissonance. Basic questions to ask are: Is the *dissonance* approached by step or by skip (leap), or is the preparation pitch the same pitch as the dissonance? If the preparation pitch differs from the dissonant pitch, does the preparation lie above or below the dissonance?

The *location* of the dissonance refers to its rhythmic character. There are primarily two choices: On the beat (i.e. accented) or before (or after) the beat (i.e. unaccented). The answer relates to the occurrence of the dissonance relative to the harmonic rhythm. The "beat" (accent) occurs when the harmony changes or when a chord is revoiced.

The *resolution* refers to the chord tone that arrives to resolve the tension of the dissonance. Does the voice containing the dissonance move up or down to this resolution? Is the resolving pitch a step or a leap away from the dissonance, or are the dissonance and the chord tone the same pitch? Is the resolution on a weak or strong beat?

Here is the second phrase of the chorale with the non-harmonic tones circled and numbered for identification.

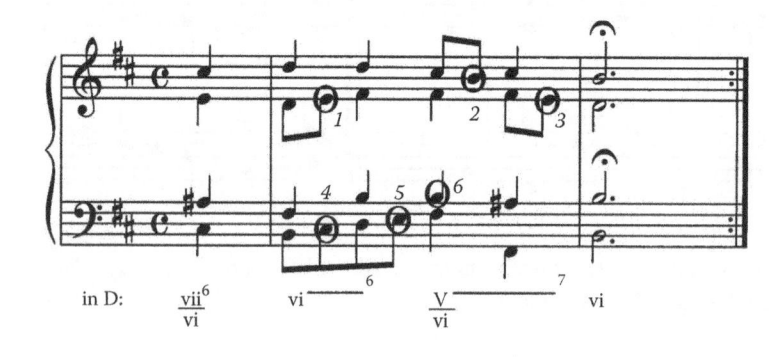

EXAMPLE 4.20 Phrase 2 of Bach's actual harmonization of *O Haupt voll Blut und Wunden*.

The non-harmonic tones shown in Example 4.20 are of four types. Most of them are passing tones (1, 4, and 5). One (2) is a (lower) neighboring tone, and another (6) is a suspension. The fourth type (3) is actually a special type of passing tone.

Passing Tones

The ***passing tone*** is a very ancient non-harmonic tone. Looking at Example 4.20, the E in the alto voice (1) is a passing tone, and so are the C-sharp and E (4 and 5) in the bass voice. As indicated in the analysis given, the prevailing harmony at this point is the submediant triad in root position (first beat) and first inversion (second beat). Thus, the C-sharp and Es are obviously not components of the triad and are, therefore, dissonances within this chord.

By definition, a passing tone is *a non-harmonic tone that is approached by step (conjunct motion) from a chord tone and resolves by step to another chord tone without a change in direction.* Examining the alto line reveals that the D on the first beat moves upward by step to the E and then moves up by step to the F-sharp, which, like the D, is also a chord tone.

To be more detailed in our description, it is a *diatonic, ascending, unaccented passing tone.*

Diatonic because E is a part of the D Major *scale* (but, of course, not of the b minor chord)

Ascending because the preparation, D, is lower than the dissonance, E, and the resolution, F-sharp, is higher than E, and

Unaccented because it occurs on the second half of the first quarter note of the measure in a passage in which the chords are changing on each quarter note.

Non-harmonic tones that occur at the same time as the chords change are described as ***accented***. Events that occur in between chord changes are ***unaccented***.

The non-harmonic tones (4 and 5) are also passing tones. Like the one described in the alto voice, they, too, are diatonic, ascending, unaccented passing tones.

Passing Sevenths

The other non-harmonic tone circled in the alto voice, the note E on the second half of the fourth beat (3), is another sort of passing tone but one that sometimes gets a special name: the ***passing seventh***.

Three hundred years ago, the seventh chord was not as ubiquitous as it is now. The dominant seventh chord actually evolved through the figure seen here: a dominant triad with one of the voices moving, via a passing tone, from the root to the seventh above the dominant and then resolving as the third of the following (tonic) triad. Initially, the pitch heard in this moving line would have been understood as a *passing tone*. Later, as the figure became more common, it was identified as a passing seventh.

Today, most musicians would simply say that the dominant triad changed into a dominant seventh on the second half of the fourth beat (as shown in the harmonic analysis below the example). Circling the E to call attention to its passing tone heritage is usually optional depending on for whom the analysis is being done.

Neighboring Tones

The circled B on the second half of the third beat in the soprano voice (2) is a ***neighboring tone*** (sometimes called an ***auxiliary***). Neighboring tones, like passing tones, are very old embellishments and also involve only stepwise motion. With neighboring tones, the preparation *and* the resolution are the same pitch, while the dissonance is either a step above (an upper neighbor) or a step below (a lower neighbor) as shown here. Neighbors may be accented or unaccented and may also be diatonic or chromatic. This example is a diatonic, unaccented lower neighbor.

Suspension

The final dissonance circled in Example 4.20 is on the third beat in the tenor voice (6). This is a **suspension**. Almost as ancient as passing tones and neighboring tones, the suspension *always* occurs on a strong beat, and the preparation tone is *always* the same tone as the dissonant tone. With a suspension, a chord tone sounds past the change in harmony and becomes dissonant with the arrival of the new chord. It then resolves, usually downward by step, to a chord tone. Note that the tenor's B on the second beat serves as the preparation, the B on the third beat is the dissonance, and the A-sharp on the fourth beat is the resolution. Often, the preparation tone is tied into the suspension. Because this example is rearticulated, some authors and theorists may identify it as a *struck suspension* or as an *articulated suspension*. (Piston and others have also identified these rearticulated suspensions as forms of *appoggiaturas* [q.v.] and not as suspensions.)

Cataloguing Dissonances

Theorists may not always agree on the appropriate name for every dissonance and/or how these non-harmonic tones should be grouped. For the purposes of this book, these categories and names will be used.

Passing Tones

The following example shows diatonic, unaccented passing tones.

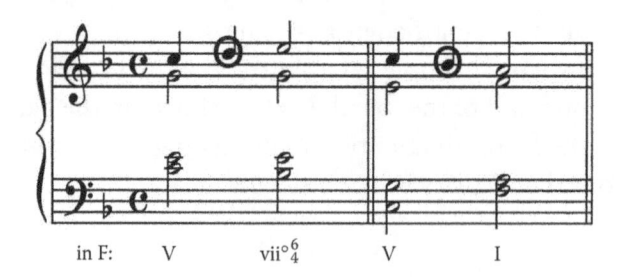

in F: V   vii°$^6_4$ V   I

EXAMPLE 4.21 On the left: a diatonic, *ascending*, unaccented passing tone; on the right, a diatonic, *descending*, unaccented passing tone.

There are also unaccented, chromatic passing tones that either ascend or descend.

[musical example: in F: V IV V IV⁶]

EXAMPLE 4.22 On the left: a chromatic, ascending, unaccented passing tone; on the right, a chromatic, descending, unaccented passing tone.

Passing tones may also be accented. The example below shows accented, diatonic passing tones ascending and descending.

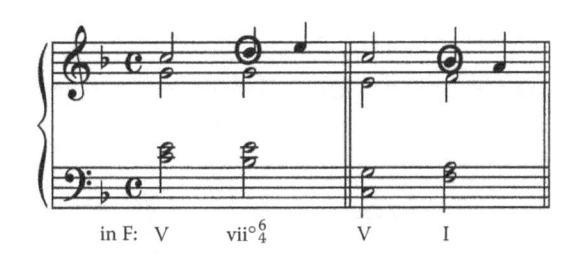

[musical example: in F: V vii°⁶₄ V I]

EXAMPLE 4.23 On the left: an accented, ascending, diatonic passing tone; on the right, an accented, descending, diatonic passing tone.

And, finally, ascending and descending passing tones may be both accented and chromatic as shown in Example 4.24.

[musical example: in F: V IV V IV⁶]

EXAMPLE 4.24 On the left an accented, ascending, chromatic passing tone; on the right, an accented, descending, chromatic passing tone.

Passing tones may fill in a partial scale between two chord tones as shown below. In these situations, the structure may be clearly a series of passing tones, even though some members of the pattern are not actually dissonant.

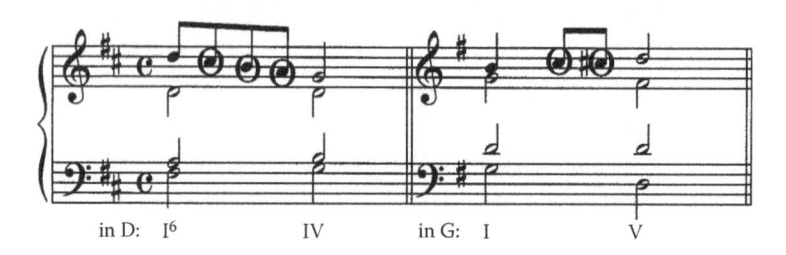

in D: I⁶   IV   in G: I   V

EXAMPLE 4.25 Multiple passing tones. On the left, the movement of the soprano from D down to G is filled in with diatonic passing tones. (Many would omit the A from the set of passing tones because it *is* a chord tone.) On the right, chromatic passing tones filling in between the B and the D.

Neighboring Tones (Auxiliary Tones)

Neighboring, or auxiliary, tones are approached by step and resolved by step but in the opposite direction. They may be upper neighbors or lower neighbors, chromatic or diatonic, and accented or unaccented. Here are illustrations of various neighboring tones:

in F: V   I⁶   V   I⁶

EXAMPLE 4.26 On the left, a diatonic, unaccented upper neighbor; on the right, a diatonic, unaccented lower neighbor.

Here are examples of unaccented, chromatic neighboring tones.

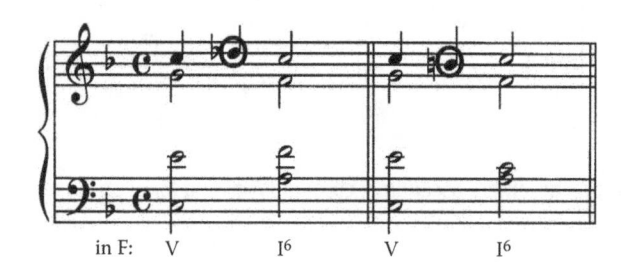

in F: V   I⁶   V   I⁶

EXAMPLE 4.27 On the left, a chromatic, unaccented upper neighbor; on the right, a chromatic, unaccented lower neighbor.

Like passing tones, neighboring tones may be accented. Below are examples of accented, diatonic neighbors.

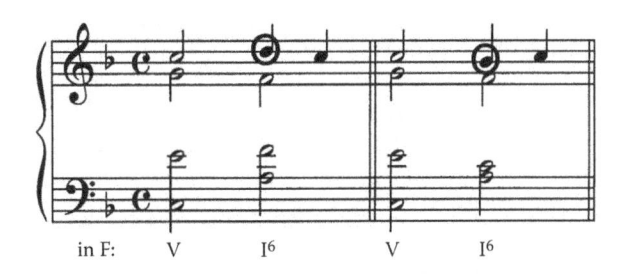

EXAMPLE 4.28 On the left, a diatonic, accented upper neighbor; on the right, a diatonic, accented lower neighbor.

And there can be accented, chromatic neighbors, such as shown below.

EXAMPLE 4.29 On the left, an accented, chromatic upper neighbor; on the right, an accented, chromatic lower neighbor.

Whether a composer chooses to use diatonic or chromatic passing tones and neighboring tones depends on the style and period in which the music is written.

Double Auxiliaries

A figure often found at important cadence points is the ***double auxiliary*** (or double neighboring tones), which may look like the following examples:

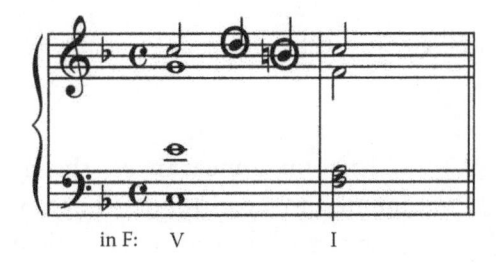

EXAMPLE 4.30 An example of an "incomplete" double auxiliary (or double neighboring tone) with a chromatic lower neighbor.

The double auxiliary may of course use only diatonic pitches.

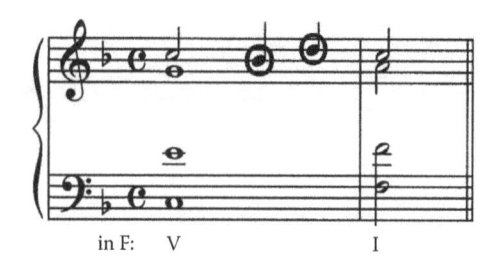

EXAMPLE 4.31 An incomplete double auxiliary using diatonic neighboring pitches.

The double auxiliary may be incomplete or complete. Complete versions include a return to the initial pitch in the middle. (Not all references make the distinction between complete and incomplete versions.)

EXAMPLE 4.32 A complete double auxiliary with a chromatic upper neighbor.

The non-harmonic pitches included in the double auxiliary may be diatonic or chromatic.

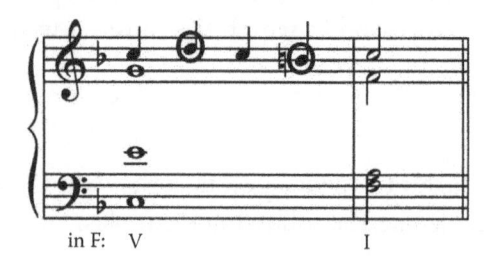

EXAMPLE 4.33 A complete double auxiliary with a chromatic lower neighbor. There are other possible variations, too.

> A trill is an ornament added to a pitch for purposes of coloration, emphasis, or as a means of sustaining the pitch. The notation is and the execution is typically .

In some appearances, the figure might even be ornamented to a greater degree than those shown above, such as by the addition of a trill on the last, non-harmonic pitch.

Anticipations

The preparation for an anticipation is a chord tone. The anticipation itself is *almost always* unaccented (i.e. it appears on a weak beat). The resolution occurs when the following chord arrives, by definition, on a strong beat. Here are examples:

EXAMPLE 4.34 Anticipations. On the left, the resolution of the dissonance occurs when the anticipated pitch is reattacked on the chord change (third beat). On the right, the dissonance is tied into the chord of resolution.

A series of anticipations with the non-harmonic tone tied into the resolution pitch, as shown in Example 4.35, is a familiar musical figure.

> Probably descended from the fourth species counterpoint of the fifteenth and sixteenth centuries.

EXAMPLE 4.35 A series of anticipations, each tied into the resolution pitch.

Appoggiaturas

The appoggiatura is almost always approached by leap (usually upward) and resolved by step (usually in the opposite direction). It is *always* accented. Here are examples:

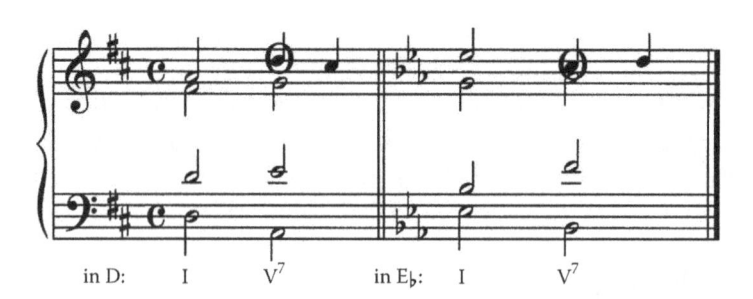

EXAMPLE 4.36 Appoggiaturas. On the left, the classic example approached by leap upward and resolved by step downward. On the right, less typical example approached by leap downward and resolved by step upward.

See also *accented suspension*, *articulated suspension*, or *struck suspension* in the next section.

> Some avoid use of the term struck suspension because striking is a percussive effect and these figures are descended from vocal traditions. Yet certainly, when performed on a piano, the term struck has much justification.

> Students are encouraged to convert all printed suspensions that are notated as dotted notes into tied notes so that the figure is not inadvertently overlooked in the analysis. Thus this: is rewritten as this: .

Suspensions

A suspension is prepared as a chord tone. The chord then changes, but the suspended tone remains, creating a dissonance upon the arrival of the new chord. It is therefore an accented dissonance. The resolution is usually downward by step occurring after the strong beat.

However, in some situations, the suspended note is not held over from the prior chord but is reattacked simultaneously with the chord changes. Some call this a *struck suspension, accented suspension,* or an *articulated suspension*. Others classify the latter figure as a type of appoggiatura.

EXAMPLE 4.37 On the left, a suspension created by the use of a tie. Second from the left, the same figure notated by the use of a dotted note illustrating that *suspensions are often easily overlooked* as you read the music without hearing it. Third from the left, what some would identify as a struck or articulated suspension. Note that the C is reattacked on the third beat. Far right, the same figure as the one immediately preceding it except the C is held *into* the third beat and not reattacked.

In describing suspensions, clarifying numbers are often added. Thus, in Example 4.37, the first and second illustrations would be identified as **four-three suspensions** because the dissonance is a fourth above the bass while the resolving pitch is the third. In a similar manner, the two illustrations on the right would both be called **nine-eight suspensions** (or perhaps **two-one suspensions**).

Échappées and Cambiatas

These non-harmonic tones are *never* accented. You may tell them apart by keeping in mind the direction of motion toward and away from the dissonance. It is perhaps also helpful that another common name for an *échappée* is **escape tone**.

The échappée is approached by step and resolved by leap. This is due to the "escaping" nature of this non-harmonic tone. The movement from the chord tone (preparation) to the escape tone is *opposite* to the melodic direction from the pitch of preparation to the pitch of resolution. This initial movement "escapes" from the melodic direction, hence the name. The échappée is *always unaccented*.

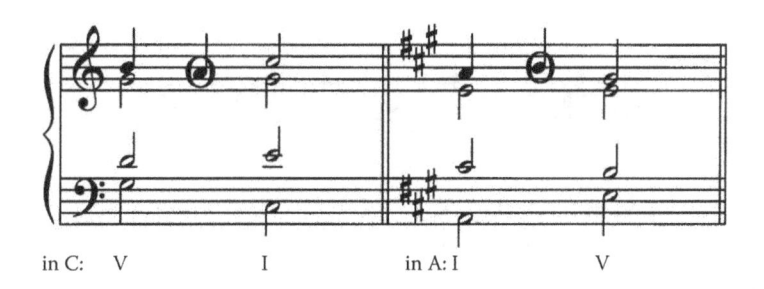

EXAMPLE 4.38   On the left, an échappée that occurs within an ascending melodic line. On the right, an échappée that occurs within a descending melodic line. In either case, the échappée is approached by step and resolved by leap. Either type involves a change of direction, and neither are accented.

Another non-harmonic tone that is never accented is the ***cambiata***. To an extent, a cambiata is the opposite of an escape tone because it is always a leap followed by a step. In the case of this non-harmonic tone, the initial motion from the preparation pitch is a leap to the pitch one step *beyond* the resolution tone followed by a stepwise movement back to the pitch of resolution.

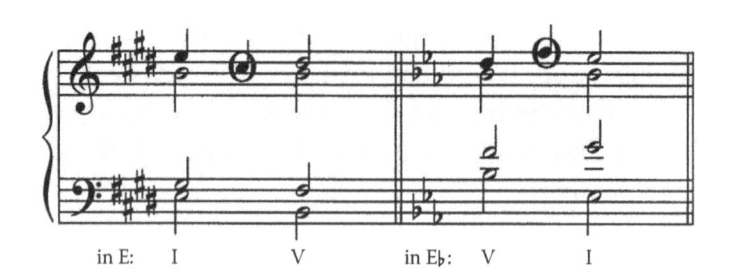

EXAMPLE 4.39 On the right, a cambiata within a descending melodic line. On the right, a cambiata within an ascending melodic line. Both are approached by leap and resolved by step. Both involve a change of direction, and both are unaccented.

Nota Cambiata

Information on non-harmonic tones often mentions the ***nota cambiata***. The definition of this figure is not consistent. In fifteenth- and sixteenth-century counterpoint, a five-note figure usually had dissonant pitches for the second and fourth pitches and consonant pitches on the first, third, and fifth pitches.

EXAMPLE 4.40 An example of the historic five-note construction usually called *nota cambiata*. This is a species counterpoint construction rarely encountered in common-practice music.

However, the term has also been applied to complete double auxiliaries, such as those shown earlier in Examples 4.32 and 4.33, and to unaccented non-harmonic tones approached by skip and resolved by step without a change of direction. The latter are shown below.

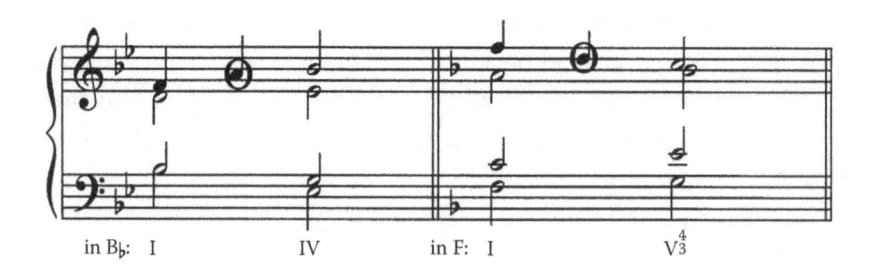

EXAMPLE 4.41 On the left, what some identify as a nota cambiata within an ascending line. On the right, the same within a descending line.

Pedal Point or Pedal

One particular non-harmonic tone is usually easily recognized. But going strictly by the definition of "non-harmonic tone," it does not always seem to qualify. This is the ***pedal point***, sometimes called simply a ***pedal***.

The pedal has no predictable preparation and no standard resolution. It is sometimes completely consonant with some or all of the concurrently sounding pitches. Its more obvious characteristic is that it is sustained for an extended period of time independent of the other pitches sounding at the time.

> Another, less common name for this figure is *organ point*. It is not, however, a *pedal tone,* which is a term sometimes used for the fundamental partial of a wind or brass instrument.

The pedal is frequently the lowest pitch present (but is usually not analyzed as the bass of the various chords above it). It may also be the highest pitch, in which case it may be called an *inverted pedal* (or an *inverted pedal point*).

Pedals are usually identified by the degree of the scale sounded, such as a *tonic pedal* or a *dominant pedal*.

In traditional music, pedals are frequently found in the form of drones, such as the tonic/dominant drones associated with Scottish bagpipes.

EXAMPLE 4.42 Two examples of pedal point. On the left, in the bass, from Bach's c minor fugue from *The Well-Tempered Clavier.* On the right, in the treble, from *Herzliebster Jesu* by Johannes Brahms. Both are examples of tonic pedals.

> This timpani pedal is infamous because the initial performance was ruined when the drummer drowned out the whole ensemble because he mistook the subtle, underlying rhythmic figure to be a very loud kettledrum roll.

Pedal point can be found in non-sustained forms, too. An example would be the timpani's repeated D under the double fugue in the 3rd movement of Brahms's *Ein Deutsches Requiem*.

Free Tones

When all other explanations fail to identify a non-harmonic tone, it may be an example of a free tone. Several writers have used this term, but very few clear examples are found in the literature.

in D: V^7 I

EXAMPLE 4.43   An unlikely musical construction. The term *free tone* might be used to describe it.

Non-Harmonic Tones in Harmonic Analysis

Because non-harmonic tones are not found in the consonant chords of a functional, harmonic analysis, they are identified and then omitted from consideration as the analysis progresses. The identification is executed by circling the non-harmonic tone and writing an abbreviation next to it. Some of the commonly accepted abbreviations are these:

Passing tone	PT
Accented passing tone	>PT
Upper neighboring tone	UN
If accented	>UN
Lower neighboring tone	LN
If accented	>LN
Auxiliary	Aux.
Appoggiatura	App.
Suspension	Susp. (or Sus.)
Accented (or struck) suspension	>Susp. (or >Sus. Or App.)
Anticipation	Ant.
Échappée (or escape tone)	Ech. or ET
Cambiata	Cam.
Pedal tone	Ped.

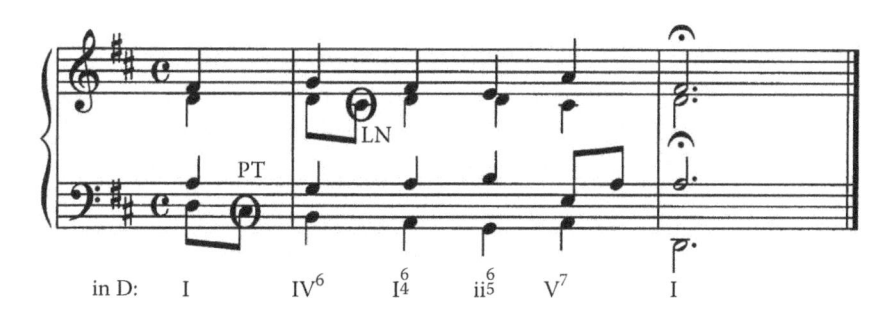

EXAMPLE 4.44 A passage from Bach's harmonization of *O Haupt voll Blut und Wunden* showing a harmonic analysis with circled and identified non-harmonic tones.

Review

- In the contrapuntal part-writing style, dissonances are systematically introduced in carefully structured contexts and are referred to as non-harmonic tones.
- Non-harmonic tones are identified by the manner in which they are approached and how they are resolved.
- Non-harmonic tones may be further distinguished as being either diatonic or chromatic and as being stressed (accented) or unstressed (unaccented).
- Non-harmonic tones include passing tones, neighboring tones (or auxiliaries), anticipations, appoggiaturas, suspensions, échappées (or escape tones), cambiatas, nota cambiatas, pedal points, and free tones.
- Certain non-harmonic tones are always accented: suspensions and appoggiaturas.
- Certain non-harmonic tones are never accented: échappées, cambiatas, and some forms of nota cambiatas.
- In doing harmonic analyses, the ability to identify non-harmonic tones will facilitate the correct analysis of the underlying chord structure.

Melodies in Harmony

Related Exercises

§ In the following examples, various non-harmonic tones are illustrated. Identify each by circling the non-harmonic tone(s) and writing its description on the line provided. If appropriate, state whether it is accented or unaccented and/or diatonic or chromatic.

§ Copy each example on the staves provided below and *add* the specified non-harmonic tone. There often will be more than one correct solution.

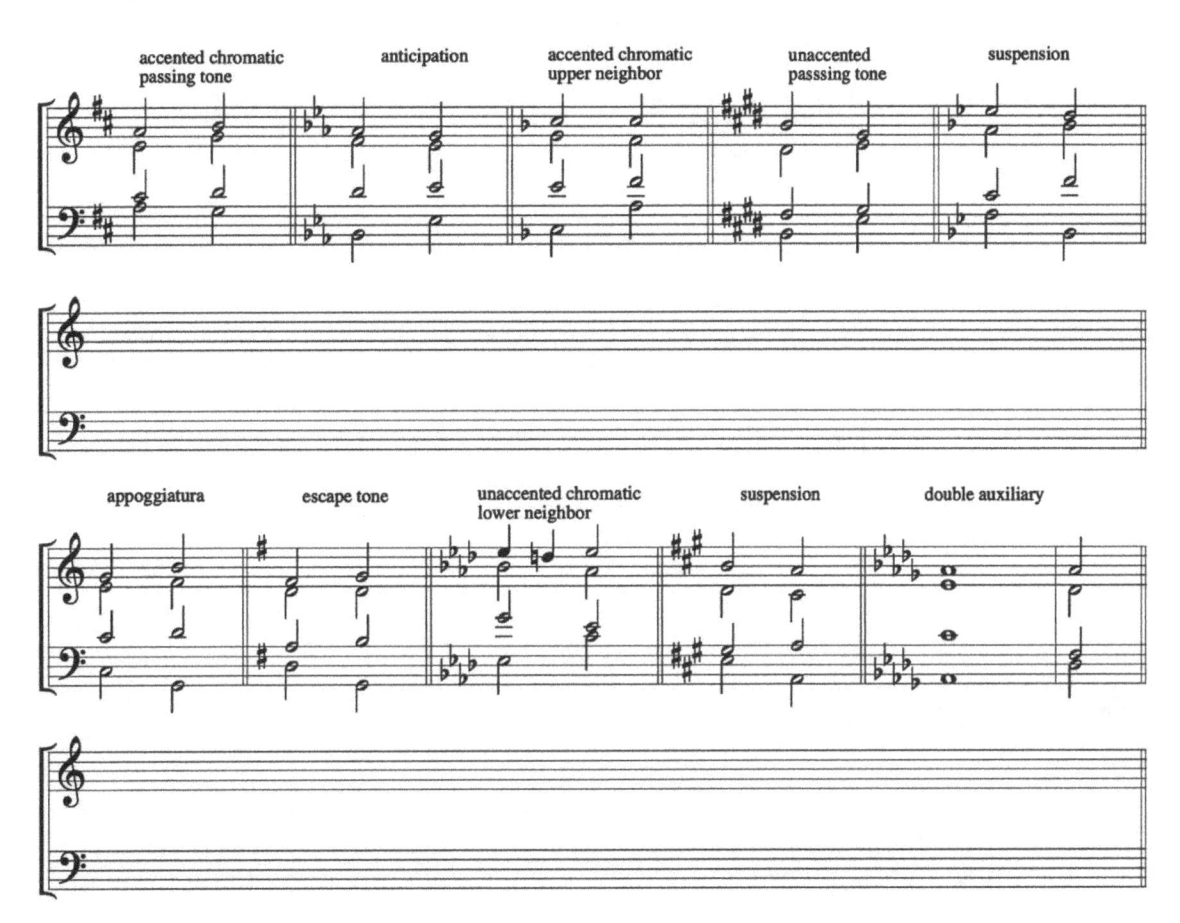

Another Chorale Harmonization

Here is another Bach harmonization of *O Haupt voll Blut und Wunden* that differs from the initial example by being both an alternative harmonization and complete with non-harmonic tones. (It is suggested that this analysis be compared with the one in Example 4.18 on p. 230.)

EXAMPLE 4.45 Analysis of alternative harmonization of *O Haupt voll Blut und Wunden* by Bach. The tenor's lower neighbor and bass's passing tone in measure 9 are chromatic. The >UN in measure 1 might be identified by some as an >Susp.

4. Analyzing Later Styles
Beyond the Four-Part Style

The four-part style, exemplified by the Bach chorales examined above, forms the basis for many of the procedures and terminology used in harmonic analysis today. But much time has passed since Bach's day, and many different types of music have appeared on the scene only to be "replaced" with even newer styles. Later styles of music require slightly modified approaches to harmonic analysis. For example here is a minuet written by Wolfgang Amadeus Mozart (1756–1791) in about 1786 (at least 50 years later than the latest of the Bach chorales).

EXAMPLE 4.46 A minuet from the first act of the opera *Don Giovanni*, here scored for piano.

To analyze this Mozart piece, we will need to modify some principles we have accepted. The first clear difference is that, by choice, the Mozart example is an instrumental piece. This means that it does not need to take into consideration the limits of the human voice. Thus, we can expect larger leaps and melodic intervals that may be difficult to sing.

Here, too, is a harmonic rhythm more varied than that seen in the selected Bach chorales. Certain harmonies may last for a measure or longer. This means that it will not be necessary to place an analysis symbol under every beat.

There is no assumption as to the number of lines that might be present, and they need not be equal. We will also find places where there are too few pitches to create a triad.

Incomplete Triads and Sevenths

> Augmented fifths expand; diminished fourths contract.

When writing for only two lines, composers imply a triad by using only two pitches. When a major or minor triad needs to be implied, the better choice is to use the root and the third. When an augmented or diminished triad needs to be implied, the frequent choice is to use the root and the fifth together with the anticipated resolution. If a seventh chord needs to be implied, the only, but ambiguous, choice is to write the root and the seventh.

If the composer must represent a seventh chord using three pitches, the triad will be implied, as described above, and the seventh will be assigned to the third voice. For more complex chords, such as ninth chords, the fifth *and* seventh may be omitted, but other substitutions are also found.

Arpeggiated Chords

> Named for the composer Domenico Alberti, early eighteenth century, who is said to have used it frequently. Although primarily a keyboard figure, for reasons stated above, it is sometimes found in wind and string writing, perhaps to evoke a keyboardesque effect.

When examining instrumental music, vertical "blocks" of pitches that form clearly defined triads or sevenths may not always be found. Frequently, composers arpeggiate the chords as a way either to create a particular texture or to sustain the harmony on an instrument that possesses little sustaining capability. An example is the Alberti bass.

This figure, familiar from much keyboard music, is merely a repeated rhythmic pattern that is formed from a complete triad. The true Alberti bass figure is lowest pitch, highest pitch, middle pitch, highest pitch.

EXAMPLE 4.47 On the left, an Alberti bass accompaniment as might be found in harpsichord or piano music. On the right, arpeggiated chords but not truly an Alberti bass.

Melodies in Harmony

When analyzing a piece with arpeggiated chords, much of the information that we seek to determine the nature of the specific chord structure is included in the arpeggiated accompaniment. We can generally omit most inversion symbols because a feature of such bass figures is that the lowest pitch is constantly changing. (When it is necessary to include the inversion, the lowest pitch in each chord grouping is usually selected as the bass.)

Review

- Although the compositional practices of the Bach-style chorales form the basis for much of music theory's terminology and practices, later music (and instrumental compositions) requires modified understandings of these procedures.
- Melodic lines in instrumental writing frequently use large, and what would be vocally awkward, leaps.
- The harmonic rhythm may show greater variety than we found in Bach chorales.
- Chords will often be incomplete and may be presented in an arpeggiated manner.
- The number of lines present may not remain constant.

Related Exercises

§ You are given four melodic lines. Which lines seem to be clearly instrumental? Why? Which lines are more likely vocal? Again, why? In your view, what causes some lines to be ambiguous? (Does trying to sing the excerpt help you decide?)

§ Examine each of the following excerpts. Which ones do you hear as most harmonically "simple," and which seem more harmonically "complex"? What are the reasons for your choices?

Analyzing Mozart's Minuet

The first quality that needs to be determined in any harmonic analysis is the key of the composition. By examining the Mozart work, it is easy to decide that it is in F Major.

It is fairly clear, too, that the phrases of the piece are each two bars long, with a cadence on the second beat of every other bar (except bars 8 and 16, where the cadence chord is on beat one). Also, the cadence chords (most of which are incomplete triads) in order are F Major, F Major, C Major, C Major (repeat sign), F Major, F Major, F Major, and, finally, F Major. Together with the key signature and the initial chord, these cadence tonalities (i.e. tonic and dominant in F Major) offer overwhelming evidence of an F Major piece.

Important observations in this arrangement are that the bass line (left-hand part in the bass clef) never has more than one pitch at a time and that the right hand, the upper staff, sometimes possesses one pitch and sometimes three pitches but usually two pitches at a time. The density of

> The example was selected for clarity. You should never expect the tonal center to be this clear and obvious.

the sonority may vary from one to as many as four notes played simultaneously. *That* is certainly unlike four-part style (and was probably chosen by the unknown arranger to make this transcription easier for a less experienced pianist to play).

EXAMPLE 4.48 A harmonic analysis of the *Minuet* from *Don Giovanni*.

The first two measures are analyzed as tonic, even though most of the time there is no tonic triad sounding. The left hand outlines the complete tonic triad in the first measure and plays the root and the third of this chord in the second. During these same two measures, the right hand plays primarily the third and the fifth of the tonic with just a brief (a sixteenth note) tonic pitch. Taken together, the listener clearly hears F Major. The complete triad is produced, between the two hands, on the first beat of the piece and on the "and" of the second and third beats of the second measure.

Except for the dominant six-four in measure 7 and the tonic six-four in measure 15, inversion symbols are not used. The second beat of the first measure has the third in the bass, and the third beat of the same measure has the fifth in the bass. Some may wish to mark these as inversions, but there seems to be no harmonic impact from this arpeggiation, thus they are omitted. In the second measure, the melodic/rhythmic movement in the left hand to the third of the chord on the third beat also seems inconsequential.

The second pair of measures clearly forms a dominant seventh to tonic progression (authentic cadence), even though at no time does the third measure display a complete C Major-minor seventh chord due to the arpeggiations taking place in both hands. So the harmonic structure of the third measure can comfortably be identified as dominant seventh and the harmonic structure of the fourth as tonic.

The next pair of measures (5 and 6) is a secondary dominant with a cadence on the dominant. Measure 5 consists only of a G Major-minor seventh chord (the dominant of C Major, which is *the* dominant in F Major), and this chord is complete and in root position. The resolution is in measure 6 on the dominant triad, which is presented both as an incomplete and complete triad.

Measures 7 and 8 bring the first half to a close with a cadence on the dominant (A composition that ends its first half on the dominant is said to be in **open form** and is characteristic of pieces in binary form. [This piece is an example of that common form. See the discussion of forms in Part 5, p. 301.]) in measure 8. There is very clearly a cadence formula in these two measures with the first beat of measure 7 being the subdominant of the dominant, the second chord is the dominant in second inversion, and the third beat is G, the dominant of C Major.

The second half of the piece begins on the dominant seventh but cadences quickly (measure 10) on the tonic. Again, in measures 11 and 12, this harmonic pattern is repeated, although the melodic (right hand) material differs. In these four measures, the left hand plays the root and the fifth of the chord (measures 9 and 11) or outlines the triad (measures 10 and 12). Both measures 10 and 12 begin in the left hand as though we were going to hear an Alberti bass, but the last beat in each bar does not follow the pattern.

The four concluding measures introduce a harmonic shift (in measure 13) when the subdominant harmony is presented for the first time followed by the tonic (measure 14). Then, in measures 15 and 16, we get the same authentic cadence pattern that was heard in measures 8 and 9 except the tonal center has now returned to the tonic, F Major. The cadential tonic six-four appears in the middle of measure 15.

Review

- In the Mozart example examined above, it was found that the phrases were all two bars in length.
- The first half ended with a cadence on the dominant creating an open form.
- The piece ended with a parallel cadence on the tonic.
- Except for two measures, the harmonic rhythm was very slow moving with each functional chord lasting for a full measure.
- Only in the penultimate measures of the first and last halves of the piece did the harmonic rhythm move as quarter notes.

Related Exercises

§ Study this composition using the same step-by-step processes as were used to understand the structure and character of the Mozart piece (p. 255).

Friedrich Kuhlau

5. Nineteenth-Century Analysis

Although the Mozart example was different from the earlier Bach examples, it may seem like a close relative to the next piece, a prelude by Frédéric Chopin (1810–1849), a Polish composer and virtuoso pianist who lived most of his life in France. This is primarily due to the shared instrumental style.

The Mozart piece is a simple dance. The prelude is a solo piano work; part of a set of compositions created by Chopin about fifty years after the Mozart minuet.

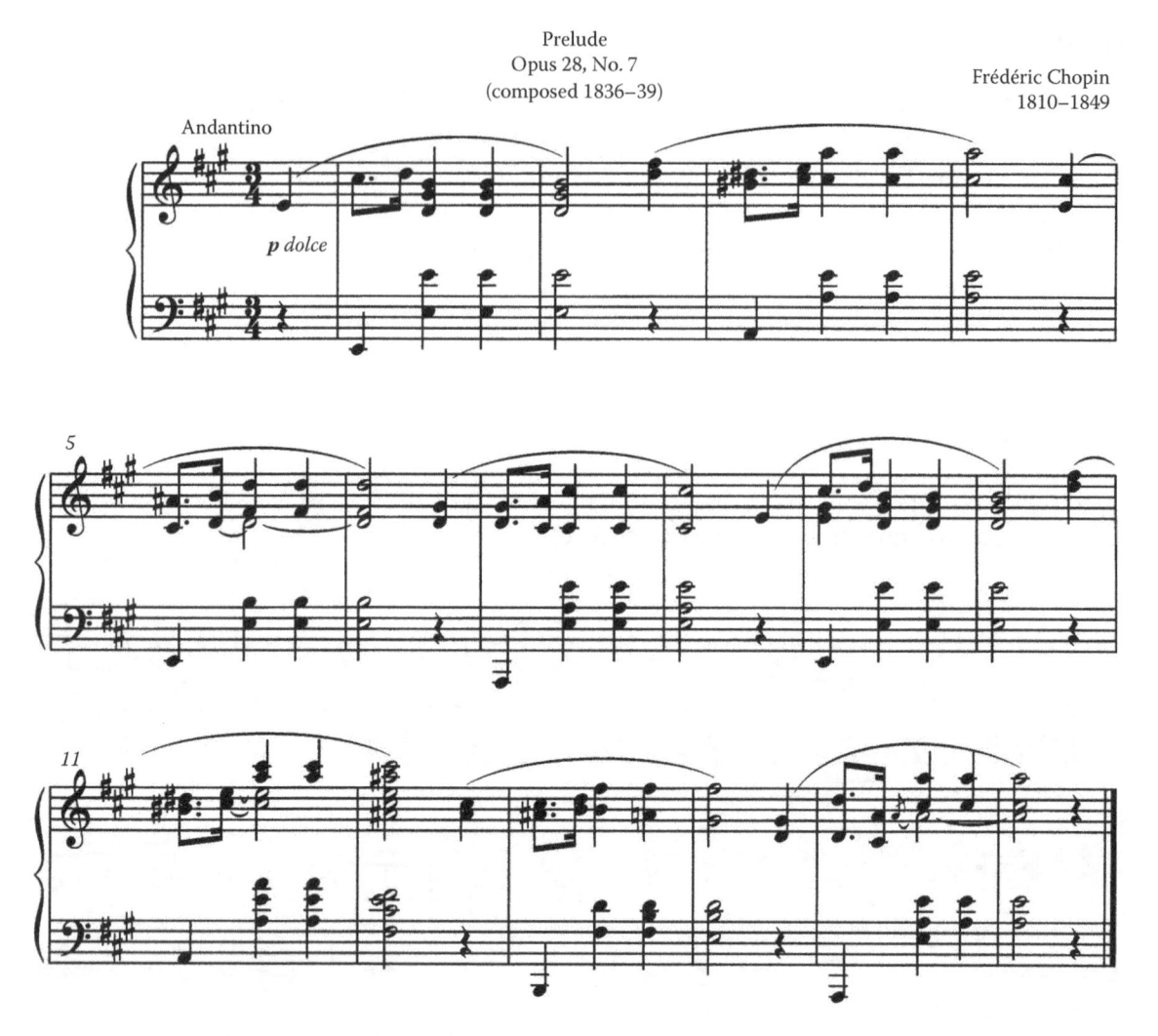

EXAMPLE 4.49 Chopin's Prelude in A Major. One of a set of twenty-four preludes Chopin wrote using the twelve major and twelve minor keys.

An element of the Chopin piece that may catch the reader's eye is the chord on the downbeat of measure 12, which contains nine notes. The reach in the right hand is a minor tenth, which is impossible for some performers to span. The addition of the intervening notes only adds to the difficulty. The left hand spans an octave, but again the C-sharp and E in the middle create physical performance problems for some. If you like, try to play both the right hand and the left hand chords to understand the challenges.

Another item that may be observed is the repeated rhythmic pattern that begins with a quarter note pickup followed by a dotted eight-sixteenth figure on the down-

> Chopin was said to have possessed very large hands. The performance alternative for pianists with smaller hands is to "roll" or arpeggiate this chord, which is acceptable in the style.

beat, followed by two quarter note chords and a half note chord on the next downbeat. Against this, the left hand plays what might be described as an "um-pah-pah" bass line composed of a single downbeat note and two quarter note after-beat chords leading to a half note on the next downbeat.

Note that the downbeat after each pickup always includes an accented non-harmonic tone. Most of these non-harmonic tones are appoggiaturas, but a few appear to have irregular resolutions. (The expected form of an appoggiatura is a leap followed by a step in the opposite direction.) The appoggiaturas in measures 1 and 9 are approached by an upward leap but seem to be resolved by an upward step. However, the D sixteenth note, while a chord tone, is not the resolution. These two appoggiaturas resolve downward on the following B.

Likewise, the appoggiatura in measure 15 is approached by an upward leap and resolved by a downward step (moving into an inner voice) on C-sharp (again on the second beat). The non-harmonic tones that are not appoggiaturas are articulated suspensions.

> If the sixteenth note Ds in measures 1 and 9 are not included as part of a dominant seventh chord, then they are escape tones. The sixteenth note A in measure 15 is a chord tone.

The key of the piece is A Major; Chopin's title tells us that. If you did not know the key, an examination of the piece reveals an A Major key signature, a final cadence on an A Major chord, and the chords used in the piece: E Major (dominant) and A Major (tonic). These all define A Major. However, the prelude begins with the dominant chord.

Notice also that the number of pitches used on each beat varies from one pitch (the pickups to measures 1 and 9) up to the nine pitches in the chord in measure 12. Other features are a grace note in measure 15 and tied notes that are to be played in the same hand as is also playing articulated notes (the right hand in measures 5, 6, 11, 15, and 16). All of the pickups may be analyzed either based on the two pitches (if present) or from the prevailing harmony.

Listening to the piece reveals a very slow, deliberate harmonic rhythm but still a harmonic complexity not heard in this book's earlier examples.

The climax of the piece, on the downbeat of measure 12, is not only the moment of greatest density but also the first secondary dominant in the piece and a significant tonal distance from the tonic. Notice, too, the use of the dominant ninth chord both in measure 5 and measure 14.

Chopin manages to make the initial tonic cadence, in measures 7 to 8, sound much like a half cadence by resolving it in second inversion. He thus saves the root position tonic cadence for the last chord of the piece where ultimate stability is required.

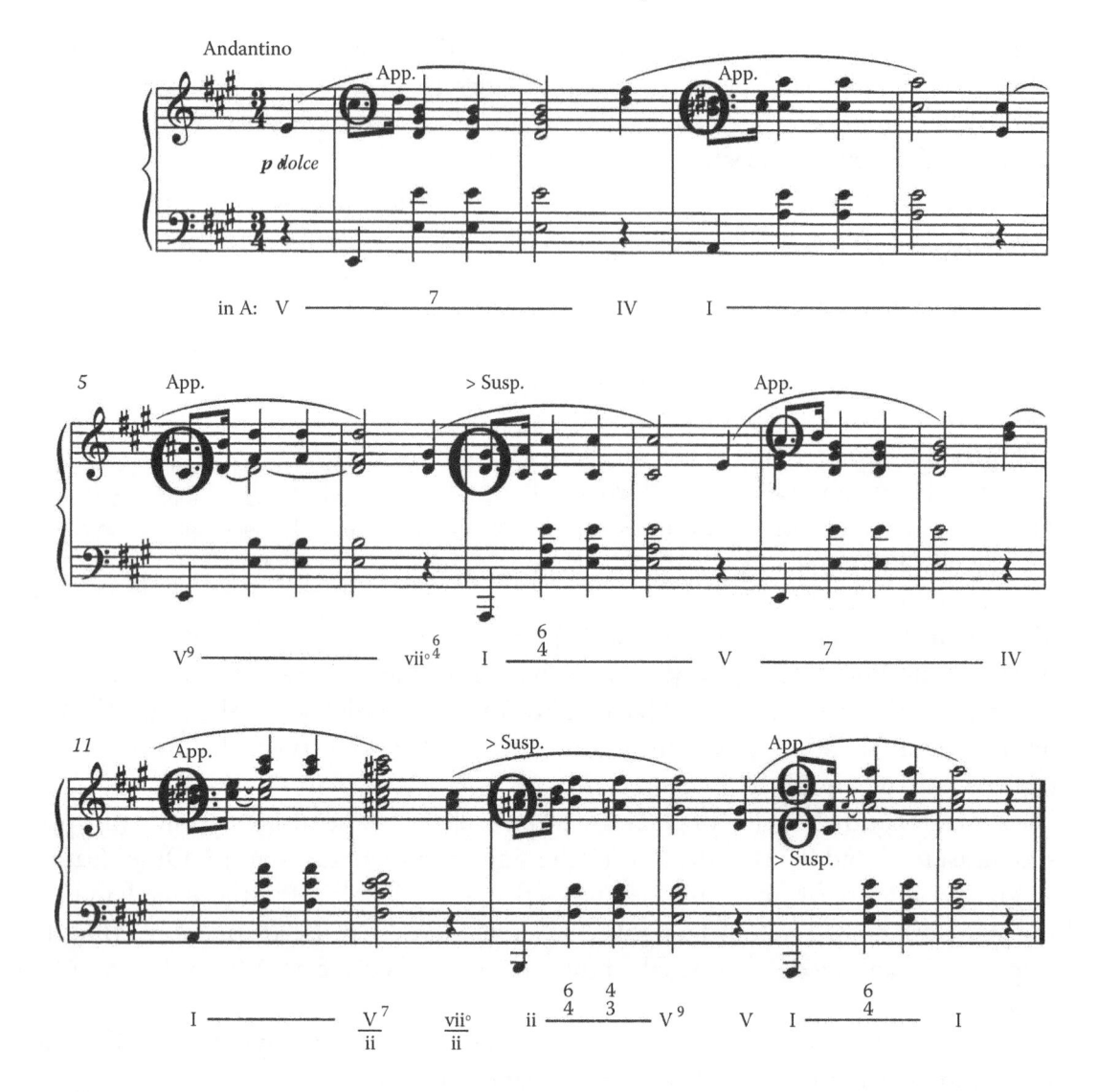

EXAMPLE 4.50 An analysis of Chopin's Prelude No. 7.

A Second Chopin Analysis

The Prelude in c minor from Chopin's Opus 28 has long been a favorite, and its harmonic progression has even been used in jazz and popular music compositions. Upon first glance, it may seem to resemble a Bach chorale with its harmonic rhythm that moves in quarter notes throughout. However, its harmonic language and chord voicing is definitely a product of the nineteenth century.

EXAMPLE 4.51 An analysis of Chopin's Prelude No. 20.

An Overview of the C Minor Prelude

It is easy to see why this prelude is in c minor. From the combination of the key signature, initial and final chords, there really is no doubt. You will also notice that the second system and the third system are, except for the dynamics and the extra measure that ends the piece, identical. Thus, we need to analyze only the first two systems.

As with the A Major prelude, the c minor prelude features the same rhythmic pattern in each measure of the right hand throughout the piece: two quarter notes, dotted eighth note followed by a sixteenth note, and one quarter note. Only the ending measure differs. The left hand plays quarter notes throughout.

The first system begins with a measure that establishes the tonic key with a tonic, subdominant, dominant-seventh, tonic progression. This pattern is an example of

> Readers who know this prelude from other sources may notice that in some editions, the upper staff of the first system is written in the bass clef. In measure 3, the highest pitch on the fourth beat has sometimes been given as E-natural, not E-flat. An E-natural would of course change the final chord of the measure from c minor to C Major.

a conventional authentic cadence. (Note that the F in the sixteenth note figure would have been a passing seventh in an earlier time.)

The second measure duplicates the first measure harmonically but now in the key of the submediant: A-flat Major. The third measure moves back to the subdominant, and the fourth measure cadences on the dominant. (If the last beat of the third measure is a C Major triad, the analysis of the third measure ends on the dominant of the subdominant. See sidebar on p. 261.) All chords in this first system are in root position.

The second system returns to the tonic. A distinctive descending chromatic bass line begins on the third beat of measure 5 and continues into measure 6. The harmony is conventional at first: tonic, submediant, and dominant. But on the fourth beat of measure 5, there is a, perhaps surprising, g minor chord.

One explanation for this minor dominant triad looks to the descending melodic minor scale, which, in c minor, would contain a B-flat. Any triad built on the dominant pitch in descending melodic minor would indeed be a minor triad. A second explanation would be that Chopin simply altered the G Major triad to produce the chromatic bass line.

Measure 6 begins with the supertonic seventh of the dominant followed by the French sixth chord in c minor that has its standard resolution to the dominant. On the fourth beat, the seventh is added to the dominant leading to the tonic on the downbeat of measure 7.

Measure 7 is almost the same as measure 1 with the tonic, subdominant, dominant becoming dominant-seventh, cadential pattern. And measure 8 appears, at first, as though it will mimic measure 2. But there is a critical difference.

The first two chords of measure 8 are identical to the first two chords of measure 2, but (due to the changed last half of measure 8) they function differently. In measure 2, the A-flat Major triad was seen as the submediant of c minor, and this was reinforced by the typical authentic cadence on A-flat that Chopin chose for the harmonic content of the measure.

In measure 8, the cadence's goal is c minor. Working backward, the third beat is the dominant seventh chord in c minor, which leaves the explanation of the second beat (the D-flat Major triad) as the Neapolitan (sixth) in c minor. (Because the Neapolitan chord in measure 8 is not in first inversion, the use of the term *Neapolitan sixth* may seem inappropriate (although many prefer to retain that name). The inversion symbol is placed in parentheses. The A-flat chord on the first beat is the dominant of the Neapolitan.

Non-Harmonic Tones

Chopin maintains the dotted eight and sixteenth note pattern on the third beat throughout the prelude. Most of the time, the dotted eighth note is the non-harmonic tone and, obviously, accented.

In the first measure, the G is a passing tone (between A-flat and F), but the E-flat is an articulated suspension. In measure 2, both the E-flat and the C are accented passing tones. In measure 3, the G is an appoggiatura being approached by an upward leap and resolved by a downward step. In measure 4, the B-natural is also an appoggiatura.

In measure 5, the dotted eighth A-flat is an articulated suspension, but the dissonant F-sharp sixteenth note is a cambiata (approached by leap beyond the note of resolution and resolved by step in the opposite direction). It is, of course, unaccented. In measure 6, the non-harmonic tones are the sixteenth notes (A-natural and C), which are unaccented passing tones. In measure 7, there are no non-harmonic tones. And, in measure 8, the E-flat dotted eighth note is an accented passing tone.

Review

- In performing music, additional stress or weight is often given to dissonances, and the eventual resolutions of these dissonances are less likely to be stressed. Analysis allows the performer to know where these stresses may or should appear.
- Whether by intent or intuition, composers tend to build logical structures within their compositions.
- The harmonic foundation of a piece of music provides the basis to which all melodic and rhythmic elaborations are anchored.
- The objective of analysis is to inform the performance of the music; it is not in and of itself a goal.
- The purpose of any analysis of a piece of music is to gain a better understanding of its construction and how to better perform it.
- There is never a "correct" analysis. Every thoughtful view yields unique insights.
- The more sophisticated the composition, the more diverse analyses are possible.

Related Exercises

§ Examine each of the following two Chopin preludes. Provide a harmonic analysis for each.

- In Prelude No. 6, why are measures 7 and 8 totally unlike any others measures in the piece? Explain the role of measures 14 through 22. What specific harmonic structures does Chopin use to establish the tonal center? What is the harmonic rhythm of the piece? How does having the melody in the bass impact chord inversions?

Prelude
Opus 28, No. 6
(composed 1836–39)

Frédéric Chopin
1810–1849

Melodies in Harmony

- In Prelude No. 9, how can you explain the tonality of measure 8? Try to discover how Chopin establishes and changes the tonal centers. What is the harmonic rhythm found in this composition?

Prelude
Opus 28, No. 9
(composed 1836–39)

Frédéric Chopin
1810–1849

part 5

Textures, Structures, Techniques, and Forms

1. The Textures of Music

The word *texture* has quite different meanings in the various arts. In music, **texture** refers to the total effect of the interactions between and among melody, rhythm, timbre, and harmony. Terms used to classify some of the more commonly encountered musical textures include ***monophony, homophony,*** and ***polyphony*** along with ***heterophony*** and ***cacophony***.

Monophony

Monophony is music that consists of a *single line* performed either by a single voice or by many voices. We differentiate the two by calling the single voice (or instrument) a ***solo*** line (this could be an unaccompanied saxophonist performing on the street corner or a cantor intoning a psalm). Whenever more than one singer (or instrument) performs a single line, we call the result a ***unison*** (for example, the first violin section of a symphony orchestra or the congregation responding to a priest's solo voice).

EXAMPLE 5.01 The top line is to be played or sung by a single performer; the lower line by everyone (*tutti;* Italian for "all"). The texture in this example is monophonic, but the first two measures are an example of a solo texture, and the last two are an example of unison.

When the music consists of more than one melody, the texture may be identified as ***homophonic*** or ***polyphonic***. Both categories have variations.

Homophony

Homophonic music exists in two primary incarnations: ***rhythmic unison*** (sometimes termed ***homorhythmic***) and ***melody with accompaniment***. In rhythmic unison, the melody and its accompanying harmony proceed together in time, much like the typical performance of "My Country 'Tis of Thee" and certain types of *barbershop* or harmonized singing. Even though the primary melody may be found in only one of the voices, while the other voices provide harmony, all voices move with much the same rhythm. The Bach chorale harmonization studied in Part 4 is an example of homorhythmic music.

> Although we understand that Bach's harmonizations were based on contrapuntal practices, listeners will usually perceive the result to be a rhythmic unison.

> In Western music, many pieces in all genres have the melody placed in the highest voice. This is called **treble dominant melody** and is no doubt due to the fact that the human ear is more sensitive to higher pitches.

In contrast, a folk singer singing a song while strumming chords on her guitar or a pianist playing a piece with a melody in one hand and broken chords in the other are each performing music consisting of a melody and accompaniment. In melody and accompaniment, the melody is predominant while the accompaniment is clearly secondary.

EXAMPLE 5.02 The Mendelssohn excerpt is an example of rhythmic unison with the melody consisting of the highest pitches. The Boieldien excerpt is an example of melody (upper staff) and accompaniment (lower staff).

Polyphony

Another important class of textures is ***polyphony***. Music is described as polyphonic when two or more voices are present and the voices (melodies) are equal, or close to equal, in importance. In a polyphonic texture, the lines are presented in such a manner as to make it difficult for the listener to determine which line(s) is primary in importance and which is subordinate.

Polyphonic textures are regularly created by the use of contrapuntal writing techniques. A familiar example of a polyphonic texture is the singing of a round, such as "Are You Sleeping?" After all four groups have begun singing in turn, it is difficult to determine which of the groups is the more important voice. They all sound equally significant, but clearly several (in this case four) separate melodies vie for our listening attention.

EXAMPLE 5.03   A Bach invention in a minor with two related but separate lines. From the point of view of the listener, each line is equally important.

Below is *Frère Jacques* ("Are You Sleeping?") showing how in this piece every line is the same, but, due to each beginning at a different point in time, the effect as heard by the listener is of four equal, independent lines.

EXAMPLE 5.04   Four equal and identical voice lines beginning in succession and creating an imitative polyphonic texture.

Combined Textures

In many pieces, we may hear a primary melody that is obviously the most important line, but at the same time other melodies seem to be, to varying degrees, important from time to time. This is an example of music with a somewhat polyphonic texture. For example, the Sousa march "Stars and Stripes Forever" displays this complex sort of texture at the end of the Grandioso when we hear the brass countermelody, the piccolo descant solo, and the rest of the ensemble with the main theme plus the harmony, bass line, and rhythmic accompaniment.

Heterophony and Cacophony

We encounter other textures, more common perhaps in traditional and folk music, from time to time. One of these is **_heterophony_**, which is characterized by two or more almost simultaneous performances of the same (usually melodic) material but with differing presentations or variations occurring at the same time. It would be like a crowd singing the national anthem before a game or certain jazz improvisations involving two or three players performing the same melody simultaneously but each with his/her own subtle differences of tempo, rhythm, and/or ornamentation.

EXAMPLE 5.05   Assuming the upper line is the intended melody that, in a performance, is played exactly as written by some while others produce the second or third line.

A final textural term is **_cacophony_**, which usually means that the sounds seem to have little or no organization or logical structure. (It is a term that is most likely used pejoratively to dismiss music that is too complex or unfamiliar for the listener.)

Certain pieces, written in specific genres or formalized styles, may use only one or two textures. An example would be a hymn tune where the verse is performed by a solo voice without accompaniment and the refrain is sung with a guitar accompaniment of strummed chords. The piece just described would be a solo texture (monophony) followed by melody with accompaniment (homophony). However, very few large pieces of music display only one type of texture throughout. And, even if they seem to do so, the details are often such that the piece is not an unambiguous example of the texture in question.

Review

- The term *texture* is used in music to describe the existence of, and the relationships among, various layers and figures that make up the complex soundscape.
- Monophony is a one-line melody that may be performed by one voice or instrument (solo) or two or more voices or instruments (unison).
- Homophony comes in two forms: rhythmic unison in which two or more voices and/or instruments each have a different melody but all share the same rhythm, and melody with accompaniment in which one or one group of voices or instruments performs the melody while the other(s) creates clearly subservient rhythmic/harmonic figures.
- Polyphony is produced when two or more voices or instruments create melodically and rhythmically independent lines of virtually equal character that compete for the listener's attention.
- Heterophony describes two or more voices or instruments performing almost, but not literally, identical lines, and cacophony describes two or more voices or instruments performing with no discernable relationship to one another.

Related Exercises

§ The following compositions and fragments represent various musical textures. Examine each excerpt and decide what texture best describes the example: monophonic (solo or unison), homophonic (rhythmic unison or melody with accompaniment), or polyphonic.

Andante — **Den lieben langen Tag** — German Folksong

§ Study the music provided. Notice that each excerpt may exemplify several different textures. Match the various sections of each example below to the correct term: *monophonic* (solo or unison), *homophonic* (rhythmic unison or melody with accompaniment), or *polyphonic*. For example, the first two measures of "Swing Low, Sweet Chariot" are clearly unison (monophonic).

Swing Low, Sweet Chariot
Spiritual

Swing Low Sweet Char-i-ot, Com-in' for to car-ry me home!
Swing Low Sweet Char-i-ot Com-in' for to car-ry me home. I
looked o-ver Jor-dan and what did I see? Com-in' for to car-ry me home? A
band of an-gels com-in' af-ter me, com-in' for to car-ry me home.

D.C. al Fine

Fantasia in C minor
W.A. Mozart

Adagio.

Invention in A minor   J.S. Bach

2. Fundamental Structures

Simple Melodic Forms

Any set of two or more pitches arranged one after another forms a melodic gesture or line. Potentially, millions of lines are possible, but in Western music, certain organizational patterns seem to occur with regularity. Among these are ***call and response*** and the closely related ***antecedent-consequent*** structures. These responsorial structures are at least as old as the Psalms.

In these structures, an initial melodic idea (a ***phrase***) is stated—perhaps by a single voice (***solo***). Then that phrase (or a contrasting phrase) is stated—perhaps with many voices (***unison***).

The difference between the initial statement (the call) and the response may be only that a single voice states the initial melody while another voice (or a group of voices) responds with the same melody. The ubiquitous "Sound Off" associated with military drills is an example.

Here is the pattern found in "Sound Off" as revealed in the words:

Sergeant:	"I had a gal in Tennessee."	**Initial statement**
Troops:	"I had a gal in Tennessee."	**Repeat of statement**
Sergeant:	"She said she would wait for me."	**Altered statement**
Troops:	"She said she would wait for me."	**Repeat of altered statement**

Sometimes the response is altered, either deliberately as part of the form or accidentally due to imperfections in performance (***heterophony***). Again, "Sound Off" provides an example of a deliberate, and in this case, "traditional" alteration.

Sergeant:	"Sound off!"	**Third statement**
Troops:	"One, two…"	**Slightly altered response**
Sergeant:	"Sound off"	**Altered third statement**
Troops:	"Three, four."	**Slightly altered response**
Sergeant:	"Cadence, count!"	**Fourth statement**
Troops:	"One, two, three, four, one, two…three, four!"	**Greatly altered response**

Here is the music for "Sound Off."

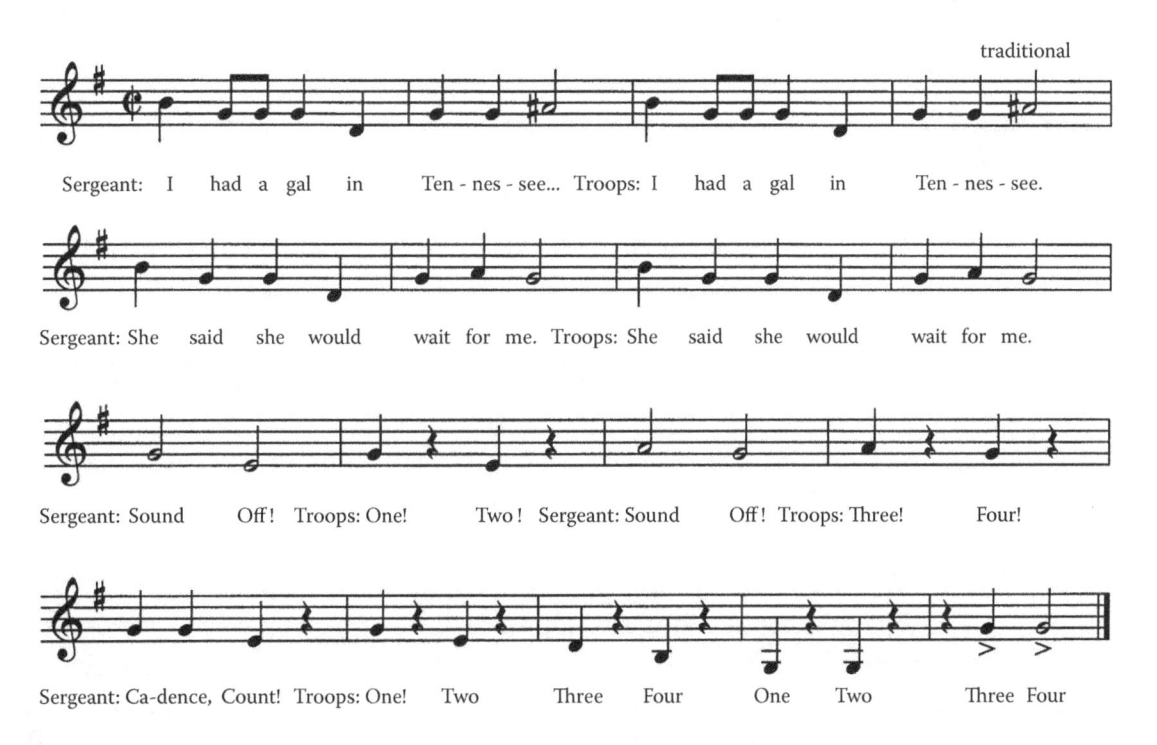

[Musical notation with lyrics:]

Sergeant: I had a gal in Ten-nes-see… Troops: I had a gal in Ten-nes-see.
Sergeant: She said she would wait for me. Troops: She said she would wait for me.
Sergeant: Sound Off! Troops: One! Two! Sergeant: Sound Off! Troops: Three! Four!
Sergeant: Ca-dence, Count! Troops: One! Two Three Four One Two Three Four

EXAMPLE 5.06 An example of call and response in a familiar army drill song, "Sound Off."

Antecedent-Consequence Phrases

The antecedent-consequent form is like the latter portion of "Sound Off" with an initial phrase followed by a seemingly inevitable completing phrase. After the sergeant barks out "Cadence, count!" we expect the song to be completed by the response of the drilling soldiers.

When an initial melodic line (***antecedent***) seems incomplete, it is usually because it ends on a degree of the scale other than tonic. Frequently, the last pitch of this unfinished phrase is the dominant or supertonic and forms a melodic half cadence. The completing (*consequent*) phrase almost always ends on tonic creating a melodically complete, full, or authentic cadence.

More complex musical structures, like folk songs, usually have several phrases. Some of these phrases will be very similar, and others will be contrasting phrases. An example of this sort of song is the venerable "Home on the Range."

EXAMPLE 5.07 A traditional cowboy song "Home on the Range."

Here are the words with, at the end of each line, an analysis of the associated melodic structure:

Oh give me a home where the buffalo roam, Where the deer and the antelope play.	**A**
Where seldom is heard a discouraging word, And the skies are not cloudy all day.	**A'**
Home, home on the range. Where the deer and the antelope play;	**B**
Where seldom is heard a discouraging word, And the skies are not cloudy all day.	**A'**

The first antecedent or phrase, ending with the word "play," is incomplete. It ends on the supertonic, and so the music cannot end there. The second (consequent) phrase is very much like the first but ends on the tonic, thereby logically and musically completing the section.

The third phrase is a contrasting phrase beginning with new material ("Home, home on the range") while ending with the familiar melody ("Where the deer and the antelope play"). Not only does the third phrase contrast with the first two, but it also ends on the supertonic, compelling the listener to expect a fourth, more final phrase. The fourth phrase is identical to the second phrase, and because it ends on the tonic, the song now sounds complete.

> There are other formal structures used for songs.

This melodic structure is sometimes called *song form* and can be represented as *A A' B A'* where A and A' indicate similar melodic materials and B indicates contrasting material. Note that the letter A is assigned to the first phrase encountered. Thus, the next phrase is identified with an added prime (') to show that, even though the material is almost identical, the phrase is different, in this case because it ends on the tonic.

Review

- Simple melodic forms include the call response and the **AABA** song form.
- Melodic lines are by their nature monophonic but may be distinguished by the number of voices or instruments performing.
- When an initial melodic phrase that seems incomplete is followed by another phrase that seems to complete the melody musically, we have antecedent-consequent phrases.
- Melodic patterns may be identified as identical, similar, or different.
- Melodic patterns may repeat or may return after intervening material has been heard.
- Melodic phrases end with some form of cadence.

Related Exercises

§ Examine these melodies. Label the cadences and determine which phrases are antecedent and which are consequent.

§ Each example presents a phrase fragment and three other fragments. Identify each of the "other" fragments as being *identical*, *similar*, or *unlike* the initial fragment. Write your answer on the lines before the fragments.

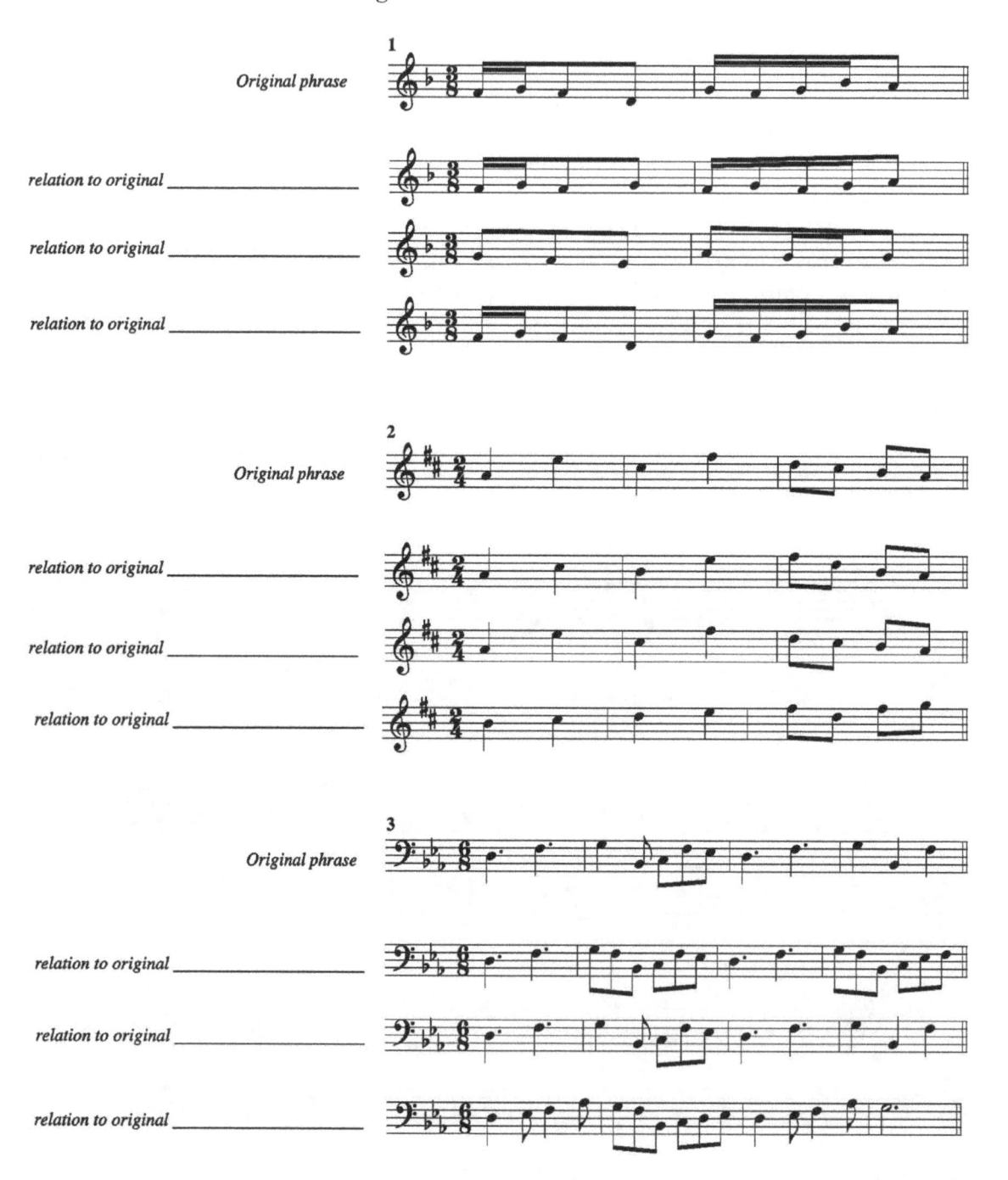

Original phrase

relation to original _____

relation to original _____

relation to original _____

Original phrase

relation to original _____

relation to original _____

relation to original _____

Original phrase

relation to original _____

relation to original _____

relation to original _____

Elided, Truncated, and Prolonged Phrases

Since about the eighteenth century, popular, folk, and many art songs have tended to be formed with ***balanced phrases*** like the ones discussed above. What's more, the overwhelmingly favorite phrase length seems to be four bars or, at least, even multiples of two bars.

> In some sources, a period is understood to be made up of two phrases, and a section is two periods. However, not all musicians will use the terms this way.

Careful observation will reveal many, many pieces of various types that consist of sixteen or thirty-two bars per ***section*** and sections composed of eight- or sixteen-bar phrases. A ***period*** made of two phrases of equal length (in terms of number of beats) is said to possess balanced phrases.

However, to avoid obviousness and monotony, many composers like to work unbalanced phrases into their compositions. This is often done for dramatic effect or to create variety and interest. It can also be used for purposes of surprise and humor.

When a phrase is shortened from its expected length, the phrase is said to be ***truncated***.

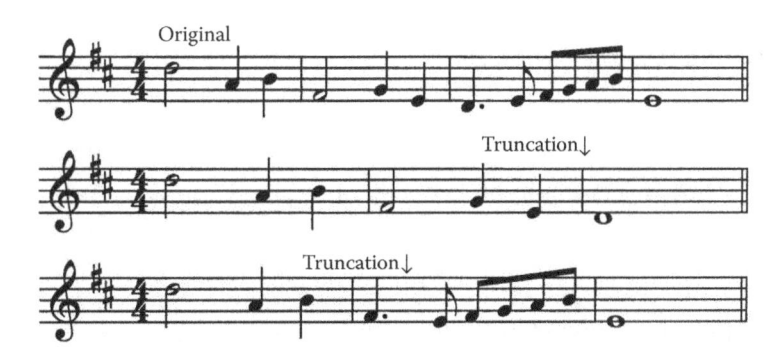

EXAMPLE 5.08 An original phrase and two examples of truncated phrases.

When a phrase is lengthened beyond its expected length, the phrase is said to be ***prolonged*** or elongated. The prolonging of a phrase may be accomplished through the repetition of material or through the use of additional material. Here are examples:

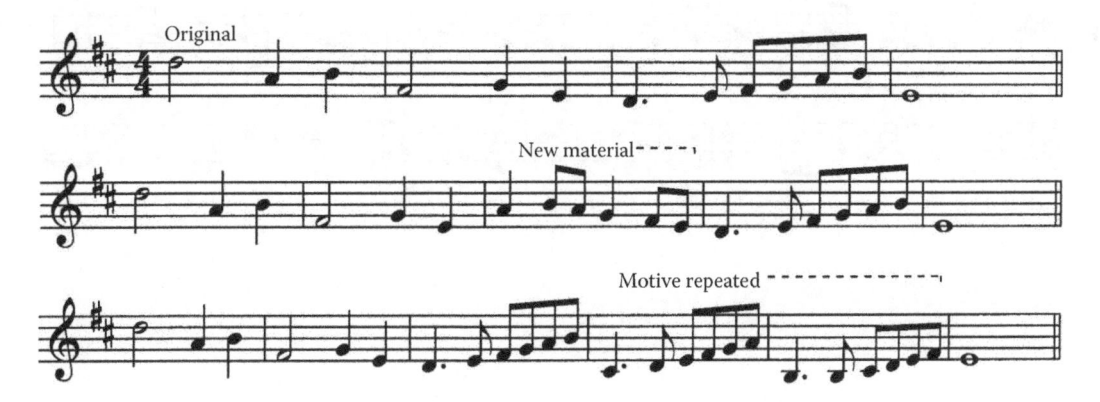

EXAMPLE 5.09 The original phrase and two prolonged phrases. Top, the original phrase. Middle, a phrase prolonged through use of additional materials. Bottom, prolongation through the repetition of a motivic figure.

Two phrases are said to be *elided* if the ending of the initial phrase becomes the beginning of the second phrase. As with truncated phrases and prolonged phrases, the elision is usually most effective after the listener has experienced balanced phrases so that the changed phrase length offers an unanticipated contrast. Example 5.10 shows a pair of elided phrases:

EXAMPLE 5.10 Two phrases that have been elided.

Review

- Balanced phrases of from four to sixteen measures (or other multiples of two) have been common in Western music since the eighteenth century.
- For purposes of variety, expression, surprise, and listener interest, phrases may be truncated, prolonged, and/or elided.

Related Exercises

§ For each of the following melodic phrases, identify the example as being *balanced* or *not balanced*.

§ Identify each of the following phrase pairs as being an example of a *truncated*, *prolonged*, or *elided* phrase.

More Complex Melodic Forms

Melodic structures can be more complex than those illustrated above. Adding a **chorus** or **refrain** is one means of making a song more complex. Often, we hear songs with refrains in which a basic melody, perhaps in an AABA form, is repeated—sometimes with subtle changes with each repetition—and in which each repetition is followed by a recurring, contrasting melody. An example familiar to most Americans is "The Battle Hymn of the Republic."

EXAMPLE 5.11 "The Battle Hymn of the Republic."

In "The Battle Hymn of the Republic," we find the following structure:

Mine eyes have seen the glory of the coming of the Lord;	**A**
He is trampling out the vintage where the grapes of wrath are stored;	**A'**
He hath loosed the fateful lightning of His terrible swift sword;	**A**
His truth is marching on.	**B**

Glory, glory, hallelujah!	**C**
Glory, glory, hallelujah!	**C'**
Glory, glory, hallelujah!	**C**
His truth is marching on!	**B**

"The Battle Hymn of the Republic" possesses two more-or-less equal sections. The first, sometimes called the *verse*, is composed of four phrases. The first and third phrases are identical musically and thus are marked **A** above. They both end on the tonic. The second phrase is melodically very similar, yet it begins a step higher and ends lower on the dominant. It is marked **A'**. The final phrase also ends on the tonic but is very different musically (consisting of even quarter notes with none of the dotted rhythms that dominate the first three phrases) and is marked **B**.

The second part of the song, the *refrain*, is also made up of four phrases. Again, the first and third phrases, marked **C**, are identical (including the same words) with both ending on the tonic. The second phrase, marked **C'**, differs in that it begins a step higher and ends on the mediant. The final phrase, **B**, is identical to the final phrase of the verse (including words) and its return helps tie the verse and chorus together.

In a performance of "The Battle Hymn of the Republic," each time the verse is performed a different set of words is sung. However, each verse is followed by the refrain in which the words do not change.

> The word setting of the verse of "The Battle Hymn of the Republic" is said to be ***strophic***, which means that the same music is repeated but different words are used.

When listening to various pieces of music (of all styles and genres), you should attempt to identify the melodic structure of the piece. What elements are repeated? What items change? Is there a return? And never forget that in songs the words are critical elements of equal importance to the pitches and the rhythms in determining the structure.

Bar Form

Another less obvious form encountered in music is the ***bar form*** represented as **AAB**. An example in this form is the old Welsh hymn "CWM Rhondda." Here, the two **A** sections are each composed of two phrases: an antecedent phrase and a consequent phrase.

The first two-bar phrase, which ends on the supertonic (a half cadence) and shows mainly conjunct motion, is identified as **a** while the second two-bar phrase, which ends on the tonic, features more disjunct motion and is quite different rhythmically so is identified as **b**.

The second section has the same first phrase **a** as the first section, but its consequent phrase has more conjunct motion while retaining the same rhythm as the second phrase of the first section and ends on the tonic. Thus, it is identified as **b'**.

> Some authors would prefer to identify the contents of these two measures as motives.

The third, **B**, section of the hymn tune has four phrases. The initial two phrases are one measure each and consist of an ascending line in measure 9 that is repeated immediately (in measure 10) a step higher. These are identified as **c** and **c'**, respectively.

The remaining four measures consist of a contrasting figure **d** (mm. 11–12), which begins and ends on the dominant, and **d'** (mm. 13–14), which begins on the dominant and ends on the tonic.

EXAMPLE 5.12 The traditional Welsh hymn "CWM Rhondda."

Thus, the form of "CWM Rhondda" phrase by phrase is **abab'cc'dd'** but section by section may be understood as **AA'B.**

Review

- More complex songs may have multiple sections, including verses, choruses, and refrains.
- Complex songs may be analyzed at larger and smaller levels of detail.
- Larger levels are usually indicated by capital letters and smaller levels by lowercase letters.
- Songs composed of two similar large sections followed by a contrasting large section are in bar form (AAB).

Related Exercises

§ Do a formal analysis of each of these compositions. Use uppercase letters to represent the primary sections. Be sure to take any repeated sections into account as you do your analysis.

A Bach harmonization. What formal structure does this piece display?

Ermuntre Dich, mein schwacher Geist

Johann Schop (*c.* 1644)
harmonized J.S.Bach (1685-1750)

A simple piece by Robert Schumann. What is its structure?

Melody

Robert Schumann (1810-56)
from Album for the Young

Another piece by Robert Schumann. What role does the modality of the sections play in creating the form of the piece?

3. Melodic Manipulation

An Overview

Examining the music for "The Battle Hymn of the Republic," you may note that the composer repeatedly uses this rhythmic figure throughout the piece:

EXAMPLE 5.13 A rhythmic motive used in "The Battle Hymn of the Republic."

This is a rhythmic *motive* that helps define this particular composition. Music inevitably has unifying material. A large-scale melody or a small *gesture* (or motive) may provide the common link within the various parts of the work. In "The Battle Hymn of the Republic," one of the unifying elements is this familiar rhythm.

Textures, Structures, Techniques, and Forms

Structuring compositions so that the component parts (melody, harmony, phrases, motives, and/or sections, etc.) possess musical materials related by pitch content, melodic shape, and/or rhythmic content is the essence of music composition. Composers consciously (or intuitively) use particular devices to create their music, and these techniques may be easily understood.

> We have already seen in the Chopin preludes discussed in Part 4 how certain rhythmic and/or pitch patterns create a unifying character for a piece.

The Original

Suppose this is our *original* idea:

EXAMPLE 5.14 A musical phrase that will be used as the basis for the following examples.

Retrograde

A fundamental compositional device is to reverse the order of the notes. The composer recasts the original so that the last pitch and duration come first, the next to last come second, and so on. This *variation* is called the *retrograde*.

EXAMPLE 5.15 The retrograde of the original theme.

Because our original possesses both pitches *and* durations, one element may be reversed but not the other. This is an example of *pitch retrograde*:

EXAMPLE 5.16 The original theme in pitch retrograde; the rhythm is identical to the original rhythm, but the order of the pitches is reversed.

And this illustrates ***rhythmic retrograde.***

EXAMPLE 5.17   The rhythmic retrograde of the original theme.

Inversion

Another device is ***inversion*** in which the original melody is turned upside down.

EXAMPLE 5.18   The inversion of the original theme. Compare this version to the original given in 5.14.

Where the original melody went up in pitch, the inversion goes down and by the same amount. Where it went down, the inversion goes up. Thus, an ascending third becomes a descending third, and a descending fourth becomes an ascending fourth.

> Unfortunately, older sources use the term *mirror* to mean *any* inversion of a melody. Therefore, the term *mirror* may easily be misunderstood.

The process produces a built-in variation. The initial melodic interval in the original is an ascending *minor* third, but in the inversion it becomes a descending *major* third. (This is not a true mirroring of the original.) For this reason, the sort of inversion shown above is often called a **tonal inversion** because *exact* mirroring of the original is sacrificed to retain the original tonality.

In order to produce a true mirror of the original, each inverted interval would have to match exactly the size of the original interval. Using the original theme, a true ***mirror*** (or ***real***) ***inversion*** would be this:

EXAMPLE 5.19   The real inversion of the original theme.

However, you may have noticed in Example 5.19 that the process of creating the real inversion has changed the key of our theme from C Major to A-flat Major. (This version of the theme is often called a ***mirror.***)

Retrograde/Inversion

All compositional devices may be combined. A composer may simultaneously invert and retrograde a theme. We have three types of retrograde: (complete) retrograde, pitch retrograde, and rhythmic retrograde. And we have two types of inversion: tonal inversion and real inversion. Thus, six types of retrograde/inversions can be generated.

EXAMPLE 5.20 Retrograde/inversions. From the top, (1) the retrograde of the tonal inversion; (2) the pitch retrograde of the tonal inversion; (3) the rhythmic retrograde of the tonal inversion; (4) the retrograde of the real inversion; (5) the pitch retrograde of the real inversion; and (6) the rhythmic retrograde of the real inversion.

Transposition

Transposition may be used to alter the tonal center without affecting the intervallic shape of a piece. It is also used to accommodate the needs of different voice ranges or instruments. However, another type of transposition results when the composer shifts the original melodic idea up or down *within the key* of the original.

For more information on this sort of transposition, see Appendix V, p. 356.

As with tonal inversions, this sort of transposition alters some of the intervals, making them in some cases a semitone larger or smaller than in the original. This produces an altered version of the original. For this reason, some theorists describe this process as *tonal transposition*. Other authors have termed the process *transmutation*, and still others call it *modal transposition* or a *modal shift*. None of these terms is especially widely used. There seems to be no universally embraced term for this very common process.

Tonal transposition can provide seven different versions of the original and, depending on the nature of the original, each of them may prove to possess unique intervallic structures.

EXAMPLE 5.21 Here is the original theme beginning on each scale degree of the original key, C Major. Compare the intervallic content of each version.

When a melodic theme is tonally transposed successively upward (or downward), a *sequence* is produced. Here are two examples:

EXAMPLE 5.22 On the left, an ascending sequence. On the right, a descending sequence.

Sequences quite often involve harmonic as well as melodic materials.

A chord, like a melody, may be shifted up or down the scale within the same key or may be shifted up or down while retaining its composition regardless of key. Examples are given below.

EXAMPLE 5.23   On the far left, a series of chords within the same tonality being shifted upward and, left of center, being shifted downward. Note how the structures of the chords change. On the right, a chord shifted successively upward while retaining its original structure and, on the far right, again a chord, with a fixed configuration, being shifted downward.

The process of shifting the harmony upward or downward within a key has been referred to as *planing* or *diatonic planing*. The shifting of a fixed chord structure, upward or downward, has also been simply called planing or *harmonic planing*.

Augmentation and Diminution

Another device frequently employed by composers is to lengthen the duration of some or all of the notes in the original theme. This is called *augmentation*. Thus, our original theme, through augmentation, could become:

> Diatonic planing is a frequently found characteristic of pandiatonicism, a term that refers to a harmonic language that includes only chords constructed from the pitches of a diatonic and usually major key.
>
> The opening to the second act of *La Bohème* is a familiar example of diatonic planing. *La Bohème* was composed by Giacomo Puccini (1858–1924), an important composer of Italian opera.

EXAMPLE 5.24   Two different augmentations of the theme. Above, each duration is doubled in length. Below, all durations are increased but by varying amounts.

Augmentation will occur when the durations are lengthened, as shown above, or *when the tempo slows down*. Composers use both approaches to create the sense of temporal elongation associated with augmentation.

The opposite of augmentation is *diminution*; the shortening of the durations of a theme.

Here are two examples of diminution:

EXAMPLE 5.25 Top, the original theme diminished by reducing each duration by 25 percent. Bottom, a diminution formed by making all durations sixteenth notes.

As a practical matter, certain conceivable diminutions might prove to be so rapid as to be impossible to perform.

As with augmentation, theoretically an infinite number of diminutions are possible, and the effect may be created either by reducing durations or by increasing the tempo.

Some Twentieth Century Techniques

Composition with Twelve Tones

As originally conceived by Arnold Schoenberg between circa 1916 and 1923, the tone row was an ordered series of all twelve chromatic (keyboard) pitches arranged (without duplications or omissions) so as to avoid having any three successive pitches form any of the four (major, minor, augmented, or diminished) triads. Tone rows do not necessarily have durations associated with the individual pitches. But, when the row possesses a rhythmic identity, all of the manipulations given above and following may be used.

In twelve-tone composition, all octaves of a given pitch are equivalent (i.e. interchangeable). This is known as **octave equivalence**.

In the following discussion, we will continue to use the original theme given in Example 5.14 but will treat it as if it were a **tone row**. With the advent of twelve-tone composition, several procedures were developed that are variants on traditional compositional operations.

Traditionally, musicians have thought of diminution and augmentation in terms of duration. But in the twentieth century, composers consciously applied the concepts to pitches, too. Here is an example of **pitch augmentation** applied to the original theme:

EXAMPLE 5.26 In this example, each successive interval has increased by an additional semitone.

And this is an example of *pitch diminution*.

EXAMPLE 5.27 Every interval is reduced by a semitone (minor seconds become unisons).

Creating Chords

By collecting the pitches found in the original theme into groups of three or four, various standard and exceptional chords could be produced. American composer and teacher Kenneth Gaburo (1926–1993) called this process **density**, or the creating of a **density structure**. The decisions made below are purely arbitrary. The composer could use any other grouping as desired.

With this operation, the intention is to create harmonic structures that are intrinsically related to the melodic material. By reversing the process, it would be possible to create a melodic line from a series of chords.

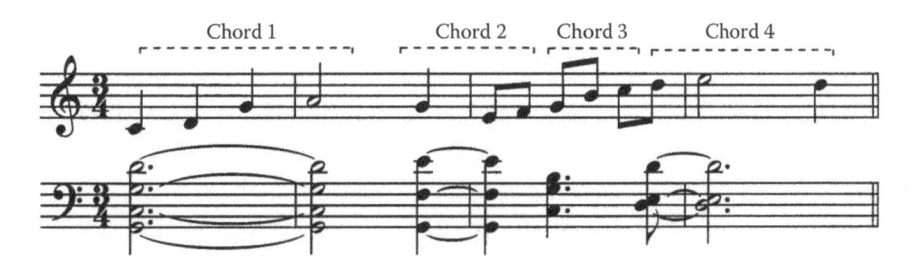

EXAMPLE 5.28 Top, the original melody, and, bottom, some of the chords that might be formed from the melody. Other groupings could be selected, such as choosing the first three melodic pitches to form the first chord.

In the above example, the duration of each chord corresponds to the duration from the attack of the first pitch included in the chord until the release of the last note in the chord. This was an arbitrary choice.

The chords could be performed *secco* (short) by being sounded very briefly only at the moment that the initial chord tone was sounded. Or a rhythmic pulse could be assigned to the chord within the time span during which it might have sounded.

Using the same material as Example 5.28, here are secco chords along with the original melody.

EXAMPLE 5.29   Using secco chords.

The chords created in Example 5.28 could also be treated rhythmically. Here is such an example.

EXAMPLE 5.30   The original melody with chords (in the bass clef) given a rhythmic figuration.

> The number of possible permutations is obtained by multiplying 5 times 4 times 3 times 2 times 1, which is known as 5 factorial and is written 5!. If we started with 9 items, there would be 9! permutations or 362,880 discrete combinations.

Permutations

Another manipulation found in twentieth century compositional styles (and not foreign to earlier composers) involves *permutations*. Permutation is the reordering of an element. For example, the numbers 1, 2, 3, 4, 5 could be rearranged as 2, 4, 5, 3, 1, or 3, 2, 4, 1, 5, or any of the other 117 possible permutations. Any sonic property may be permuted. Pitch is an obvious choice, but certainly durations, dynamics, articulations, and instrumentation could be manipulated.

For some composers, *cyclical permutations* have a certain appeal. In cyclical permutations, the ordering of the elements remains fixed, but the starting element changes. Here are the cyclical permutations of the whole numbers 1 through 5:

      1, 2, 3, 4, 5
      2, 3, 4, 5, 1
      3, 4, 5, 1, 2
      4, 5, 1, 2, 3
      5, 1, 2, 3, 4

With five objects to be arranged, there are five cyclical permutations.

Applying the cyclical permutation process to our original theme, we get thirteen permutations. Here are numbers two through seven (remember the original is a permutation and would be counted as the *first* permutation).

EXAMPLE 5.31 Six of the thirteen possible cyclical permutations of our original theme. Some pitches are placed in a different octave to keep the result on the staff.

In Example 5.31, the rhythmic order remained fixed; only the pitches were permuted.

> The numbers above each note identify its order in the original theme.

Other Uses for Numbers

The Golden Mean

When planning a composition, composers make many decisions. One of the first is the instrumentation (i.e. for whom or for what ensemble the piece is to be composed). But another important decision is the form of the piece. Composers are never obligated to use a standard form. Nor is the composer obligated, if using a standard form, to retain all of the usual properties of the form.

Another concern to be addressed has to do with the proportions built into the finished composition. The composer may trust his/her sense of time and drama to guide him/her or may look elsewhere for an appealing model. One such model some composers have used is the ***golden mean*** or ***golden section***.

> The more accurate name golden section implies the visual arts roots of the concept.

The golden mean is a ratio, drawn from the visual arts, thought to achieve a desirable balance between two related but differently sized objects. It can be summed up as:

The length of A (shorter distance) is to B (longer distance) as B is to the sum of A and B.

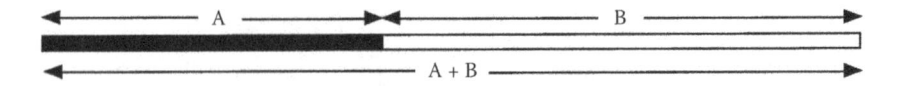

EXAMPLE 5.32   The visual proportions provided by the golden mean.

Calculation of the relationship between A and B shows that A is about 61.8 percent of B, and that means that B is about 61.8 percent of A+B.

Fibonacci Numbers

Composers have used *fibonacci numbers* to identify, for example, the location of a climactic moment in a composition. The fibonacci series is an ordered set of numbers, beginning with 1 and 2, such that each number in the series is the sum of the two preceding numbers: 1, 2, 3, 5, 8, 13, 21, 34, 55, 89…n.

The composer might use this series to determine that a composition, which lasts 89 bars for example, should have its climax on the bar 55. Obviously, there are many other ways to use such values and other numeric patterns.

> Bach's name numerically equals 14 (B=2, A=1, C=3, H=8, thus 2+1+3+8=14). It is said that 14 plays a structural role in many of Johann Sebastian Bach's themes and/or forms.
>
> Readers who are particularly interested in relationships between numbers and music may wish to study Joseph Schillinger's system of music composition and/or Milton Babbitt's writings on music.

Numerology

Using numbers to contribute to the design and construction of a piece of music is not new or unusual. Bach was influenced by numerology, and Mozart is credited with a minuet for which the performer determines the order of the measures by rolling a die. Twelve-tone and serial music have their obvious debt to numbers, and *alleatoric* music frequently uses chance procedures, based on mathematical operations, to determine outcomes.

Extraction

The original theme can be used as a source from which to generate two (or more) independent lines that will work with each other in a contrapuntal relationship. In this *extraction*—also likely a Gaburo-generated term—process, much as in the creation of density structures, the composer is free to choose which of the original pitches to assign to each voice. Here is one example:

EXAMPLE 5.33 Top, the original theme with the pitches to be extracted and placed into the lower voice circled. Bottom, a new, two-part, contrapuntal passage thus created.

As with the chords created from the original theme in Example 5.28, the two lines may be expressed as sustained pitches or with various lengths and ornamentation as shown in Example 5.34.

EXAMPLE 5.34 Variations on contrapuntal structures created by extraction: Top, staccato lines. Bottom, lines in which pitches are ornamented by trills, repeats, grace notes, and varied lengths.

Now that two new themes have been created through the extraction process, the composer may again begin using *each* of these as a new original theme and subjecting each to any or all of the modifications and variations laid out above. All of the compositional devices can be freely intermixed.

Summary

By combining all of the above compositional devices in many different ways, an incredibly large number of variations on an original musical line can be generated. What this means is that a composer need never be found short of musical material. But simply because a variation grows out of an original idea—even a brilliantly original idea—not all of these variations may prove to be musically useful or attractive. No matter how many variations of a theme *can* be produced, the challenge is, and always has been, to select and combine those particular variants that produce the most effective art.

Review

- Retrograde means that the pitches and the rhythms are reversed.
- Rhythmic retrograde reverses the rhythm but not the pitch order.
- Pitch retrograde reverses the pitch order but not the rhythm.
- Themes may be inverted (turned upside down) in order to obtain additional materials.
- There are two types of inversions: tonal and real.
- A tonal inversion remains in the key or modality of the original theme.
- A real inversion reverses the direction of each melodic interval, and each interval retains its exact size.
- The term *mirror* is frequently used to describe either type of inversion. However, a few theorists restrict the use of *mirror* as a synonym only for a real inversion.
- The retrogrades discussed above can also be applied to both types of inversions creating six additional variations.
- These variations are the retrograde of the tonal inversion, the pitch retrograde of the tonal inversion, the rhythmic retrograde of the tonal inversion, the retrograde of the real (mirror) inversion, the pitch retrograde of the real inversion, and the rhythmic retrograde of the real inversion.
- Augmentation and diminution are manipulations of a theme's durations and/or intervals.
- Rhythmic augmentation increases the duration of the pitches.
- Rhythmic diminution reduces the duration of the pitches.
- Pitch augmentation increases the intervals between the pitches.
- Pitch diminution reduces the intervals between the pitches.
- Composers use a technique variously called transmutation, tonal transposition, modal shift, or modal transposition to create additional versions of a theme each beginning on a different scale degree.
- A repeated series of themes or theme fragments ascending or descending stepwise is called a sequence and may include harmonic material.
- The act of shifting a series of parallel chords upward or downward may be called planing.

Textures, Structures, Techniques, and Forms

- Chords can be formed from a given theme by grouping the melodic pitches together.
- These chords (densities) can be performed in many manners and styles.
- Additional lines and structures can be formed by permuting any of the components of the original material.
- Cyclical permutations offer a systematic means for rearranging the elements with which the composer is choosing to work.
- By extracting a second or third melodic line from the original melodic line, contrapuntal variations may be created.
- All of the composition processes may be applied in any combination and in any order to any musical ideas, original or derived.
- Composers have literally millions of options. The art is in the selecting from among all the many variants and combining those selected components into a composition.

Related Exercises

§ Given this compositional idea, determine how each of the five variants was created from the original. Write your answer on the line to the left of the example.

§ Always working from the given original, create the specified variants on the staves provided.

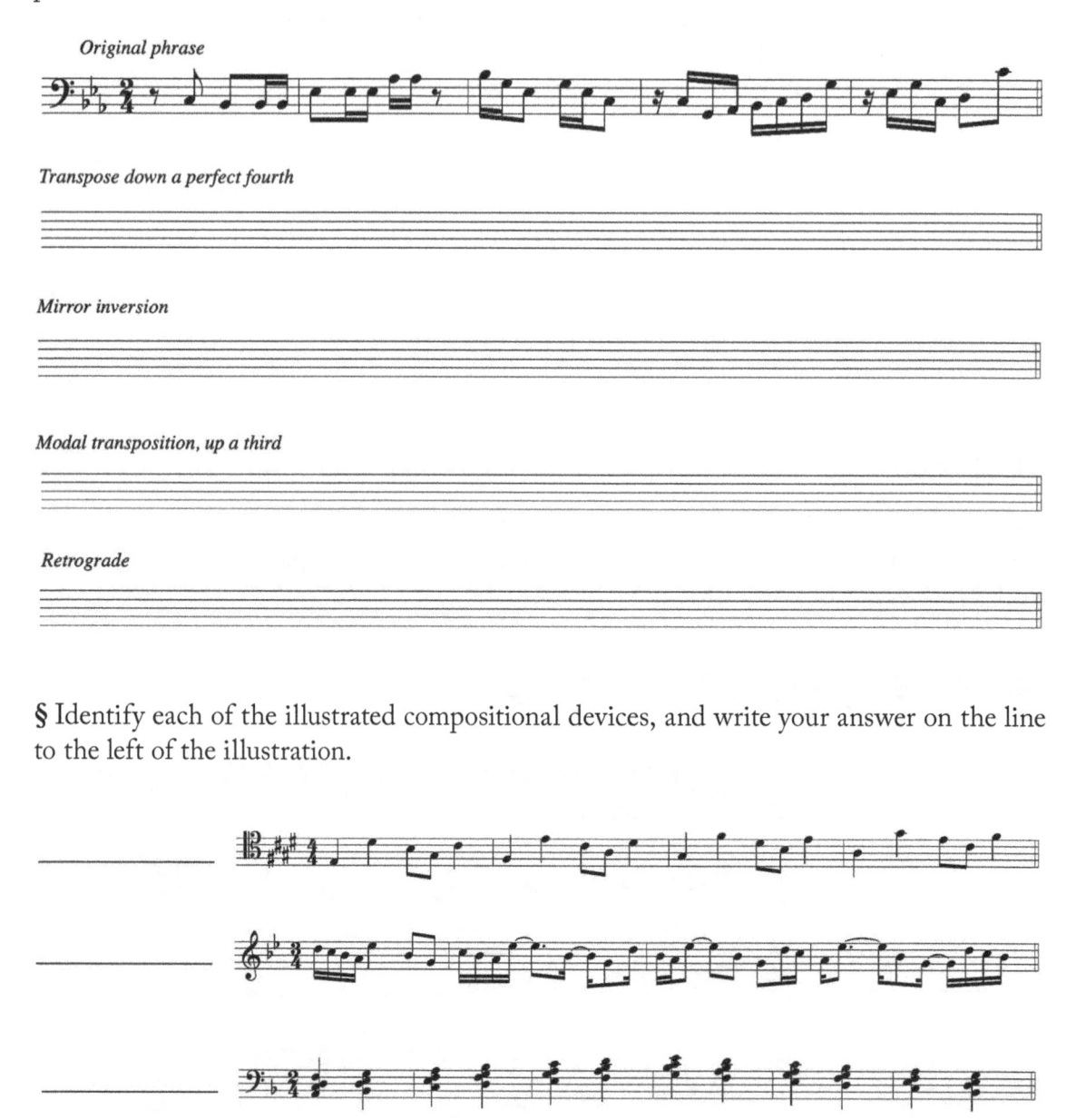

Original phrase

Transpose down a perfect fourth

Mirror inversion

Modal transposition, up a third

Retrograde

§ Identify each of the illustrated compositional devices, and write your answer on the line to the left of the illustration.

_____

_____

_____

§ In each of the following three derivations, the original phrase has been altered. On the lines to the left of each altered passage, describe how the passage was created.

Original phrase

4. Form

Microscopic versus Macroscopic Views

When approaching and analyzing any particular structure, musical or otherwise, the analyst may assume two fundamental perspectives. One is an up-close and detailed view often called *microscopic* analysis. The other is a broader but less detailed view called *macroscopic*. Analyzing a composition several times, each time from a different perspective along the micro to macro continuum, is always profitable.

This book has primarily focused on the microscopic view of music: beat by beat, note by note, chord by chord. In the following articles, the broader characteristics and the larger structures that one finds in musical expression will be discussed.

Larger Forms

For the purpose of formal analysis, music is often separated into one of two broad categories: *sectional* or *continuous*. Sectional music is marked by clear phrases and obvious cadences that audibly demarcate important structural points.

In contrast, continuous pieces may sound—especially upon first hearing—to have no (or few) clear cadences. They may sound as though the music was constantly flowing and evolving without clear or predictable goals.

Certainly, some compositions include elements of both. Our largest works, symphonies, operas, string quartets, etc. often exhibit a variety of formal structures.

Sectional Forms

Sectional pieces have clearly presented phrases and periods. What characterize these works of music are the establishment of a tonal center and the presentation of melodic and harmonic materials that are rhythmically directed in such a manner that cadences are inevitable.

> When graphing sectional pieces, letters are used in alphabetical order. A new letter is used when a new phrase or section arrives. A prime is added to indicate that a modification has occurred to an earlier phrase or section, causing it to be heard as being changed but clearly related to or derived from—the original.

Returns and Repeats

Because sectional music has clearly presented themes, they possess recognizable materials that the listener can remember and recall. Once presented, a phrase or section and its characteristic material may be repeated, repeated with changes, or replaced with new material.

A	**A**	Repeated
A	**A'**	Changed
A	**B**	Replaced

EXAMPLE 5.35   The formal options for a piece with two phrases or sections.

After the presentation of the second phrase or section, the composer has the following options:

1. If the pattern **AA** was selected, the original choices remain: repeat **A**, go on to a variation of **A** (**A'**), or create new material (**B**).
2. If the initial choice was **AA'**, then the options are to return to **A**, repeat **A'**, go on to another variation (**A"**), or create new material (**B**).
3. Had the choice been **AB**, the composer may return to **A**, create a variation of **A** (**A'**), repeat **B**, create a variation of **B** (**B'**), or write new material **(C).**
4. Stop. The composition is complete.

These various possibilities are graphed below

A	A	A
A	A	A'
A	A	B
A	A'	A
A	A'	A'
A	A'	A"
A	A'	B
A	B	A
A	B	A'
A	B	B
A	B	B'
A	B	C

EXAMPLE 5.36 The formal options for a piece with three sections.

> When a phrase or section is restated immediately after having been presented, the second presentation is called a repeat. When a phrase or section is restated after contrasting material has been presented, it is said to be a return.

There is little reason to continue with these illustrations because the logic should be obvious. Using this process and these terms, all sectional forms may be graphed.

Formal Conventions

In representing musical forms graphically, larger bold capital letters are usually used to represent the largest (most macroscopic) structures. Lowercase and script letters represent successively more microscopic details. The progression from largest section to smallest motive may look like this:

A A A **a** a *a*

EXAMPLE 5.37 From the left, largest formal unit to, on the right, smallest formal unit (macroscopic to microscopic).

This approach could, of course, be expanded to include even more levels of detail, but the above range of symbols is more than adequate for most analyses.

Review

- Microscopic and macroscopic express the level of detail being examined.
- Microscopic is more detail-oriented while macroscopic is broader.
- Sectional form music has an obvious phrase structure with clear cadences.
- Continuous form music has obscured cadences with hard-to-identify phrases.
- New material is music that has not been previously stated in the piece.
- A repeat occurs when musical material just presented is immediately restated.
- A return occurs when material is heard again after different material has been presented.
- A variation is an altered form of previously presented material.
- When graphically representing the form of a piece of music, letters are used in alphabetical order.
- The larger or bolder the letters, the more macroscopic the information.
- The smaller and more cursive the letters, the more microscopic the information.
- The initial musical unit encountered at any level is assigned the designation "A".
- Successive new material, at the same level, is identified by the next available letter.
- Repeated (or returned) material is identified by using the originally assigned letter.
- Varied material is identified by its initial letter plus an added prime for each variation.

Related Exercises

§ For each of the following pieces, create both a macroscopic and a microscopic analysis. Can you assign a particular form to each work, or do you find that they possess unique structures?

A Tyrolese folk song adapted for keyboard by Robert Schwalm

§ In your analysis, discuss the use of basic melodic structures (motives) in this composition.

Tyrolese Air

Robert Schwalm
(circa. 19th century)

Textures, Structures, Techniques, and Forms

An original composition by Robert Schumann

§ This piece is more complex than the two Schumann works you examined earlier. Compare his use of motives in this work with the use found in the Schwalm piece above.

Little Morning Hiker

Robert Schumann (1810-56)
from Album for the Young

A movement from a Sonatina by Muzio Clementi

§ This is formally a much more complex piece than the two above. Remember to account for all the repeats, and pay attention to any changes in the tonal center and/or the texture.

Binary, Rounded Binary, Ternary, and da Capo Forms

Among the frequently encountered sectional forms are the binary, rounded binary, ternary, and da capo forms. These appear frequently in songs, dances, symphonic movements, various instrumental concertos, and suites as well as stand-alone concert works.

Binary Form

Binary simply means that the piece divides into two main sections. Binary form is called an ***open form*** because typically the first section moves from the tonic key to another pitch center (most often the dominant). The second section then begins in this new tonality and moves back to the tonic. (If the initial tonality is minor, the second tonal area is usually the relative major.) In shorter pieces, the end of the first section may be simply a half cadence. In larger versions, the composer will modulate to the new tonal center.

In binary pieces, the materials used in the second section will likely be closely related to the initial musical materials. It is also likely that the two parts would be represented as

A followed by **A'**. (If these two parts are less closely related, then **AB** would be the formal description.) Commonly, both the first and second sections are repeated.

Graphically, on the macroscopic level, a binary composition would be represented this way:

$$\|: \quad \mathbf{A} \quad :\|: \quad \mathbf{A'} \quad :\|$$
$$ I-V V-I$$

EXAMPLE 5.38 A graph of binary form showing the usual repeats.

Rounded Binary Form

Rounded binary is a variation of binary form in which new material appears in the second half (i.e. AB) but with a return of the initial materials toward the end of the second section. This return is intended to "round" out the piece by providing a certain amount of closure for the listener brought about by the reappearance of the familiar "A" material.

This is a graphic representation of rounded binary that is at a more microscopic level than seen in Example 5.38.

$$\|: \quad \mathbf{a + a'} \quad :\|: \quad \mathbf{b + a''} \quad :\|$$
$$ I-V V-I$$

EXAMPLE 5.39 A graph of rounded binary form showing the return of **a** material in the second section after the new material.

Ternary (or Tripartite) Form

The typical ***ternary*** composition is known as a ***closed form*** because each of the three parts begins and ends with its tonic. In a ternary composition, the second section is set in its own key and is usually composed of new material rather than from material obviously derived from the first section. The graph of a ternary form in which the second part is set in the relative minor would be:

$$\|: \quad \mathbf{A} \quad :\|: \quad \mathbf{B} \quad :\|: \quad \mathbf{A} \quad :\|$$
$$ I-V-I \quad\; vi\text{--}\underline{V}\text{--}vi \;\; I-V-I$$
$$ \underline{vi}$$

EXAMPLE 5.40 Macroscopic view of a piece in ternary form, with the B section in the relative minor showing the most common repeat pattern.

Sometimes, the ternary form will have no repeats. However, because the third and first sections are quite often identical, composers may choose to use a *da capo* (*DC*) instead of writing out the return. These alternatives are reflected in the following graph.

$$\mathbf{A} \parallel \mathbf{B} \parallel$$

I –V–I *fine*   vi–V–vi   **DC** *al fine*
                  vi

EXAMPLE 5.41 Graphic representation of a piece in ternary form with no repeats but in which there is a da capo.

Some authors refer to the three-part form by such names as **arch form** or **bow form** derived from the fact that in such pieces the point of greatest tension and drama would typically be near the middle of the B section, creating a sound journey in the shape of a curved bow or an arch.

The Da Capo Aria

> An aria is a composition for solo voice. Aria da capo was used in opera from before the eighteenth century to well into the nineteenth century.

A variant on the ternary form is the ***aria da capo*** or ***da capo aria***. In this form, the initial A section is extended and includes sections for the orchestra and the singer. It usually has a modulation away from tonic and a return to tonic. The B section tends to be shorter but in a key other than tonic. The material is different from that of the A section, but because both sections are lengthy, some material might appear in both. At the conclusion of the B section, the music returns to the beginning (hence the da capo name) and the A section is reprised.

Here is a graphic representation of a da capo aria:

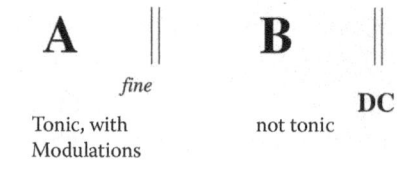

$$\mathbf{A} \parallel \mathbf{B} \parallel$$

fine   **DC**

Tonic, with   not tonic
Modulations

EXAMPLE 5.42 The graphic representation of a typical da capo aria.

Binary, ternary, and rounded binary forms were used for hundreds of years for dances and songs as well as for moments of various solo instrumental and orchestral works. Among the typical binary compositions are the minuet moments in classical symphonies where the minuet is usually written in binary or rounded binary and is followed by a ***trio,*** which is usually another minuet but one created from different melodic and harmonic materials, and then a da capo to the first minuet. The second minuet (the trio) is also usually binary, and it, too, may or may not be rounded.

> The term may have originally referred to a portion of a piece performed by only three players, but by the classical period (and ever since) it has been used to identify a contrasting section that is not necessary performed by fewer players. In marches, it is almost always characterized by a change of key, usually to the subdominant.

Review

- Binary form has two parts and is usually written as an open form.
- Open form means that the first section ends in a tonality other than the initial tonic key, most often the dominant.
- In rounded binary, the second section usually begins with new material but concludes with the return of the original material or a variation thereof.
- This return creates a sense of symmetry and "rounds" off the piece.
- Ternary form, sometimes called tripartite or three-part form, has three distinct sections and is usually written as a closed form.
- Closed form means that each section concludes with a cadence on the tonic of that section.
- In ternary forms, the middle section is usually in a key other than the initial tonic. The relative major, relative minor, and the dominant are typical choices.
- Also in ternary forms, the third section is frequently identical to the first section, and the composer may choose to use a da capo to achieve the return.
- Ternary form has also been called arch form and bow form.
- An aria da capo is a three-part form in which a portion of a libretto is set for solo voice and orchestra.
- In a da capo aria, the A section usually includes an orchestra introduction and at least two vocal sections with a modulation between them and a return to tonic before the next section.
- The B section of an aria da capo is in a key other than the tonic.
- At the end of the B section, the whole A section is repeated (i.e. da capo) to conclude the piece.
- The trio of a multipart composition is a contrasting section. It may include a reduction in the number of performers and a change of key, tempo, time signature, or instrumentation.

Related Exercises

§ Review your understanding of the materials presented by completing the following statements and questions.

When the first section of a composition in binary form ends in a tonality other than the initial tonic, it is said to be _____.

Compositions with three distinct sections are called tripartite, three-part, or _____ form.

Other names for ternary form are arch form and _____ form.

When a binary form ends with the return of the initial musical materials, it is called _____.

When a trio is present, what are some of its expected qualities? _____
_____

Song Form, Bar Form, Through-Composed

Song Form

The discussion of "Home on the Range" on p. 276 introduced the term *song form* as illustrated by a single line of music. When this line has accompanying material, the form is no less recognizable.

The traditional folk song or poplar song from the early part of the twentieth century is often in the form AA'BA'. These compositions tend to be about thirty-two measures in length and in performance are regularly repeated with variations including different lines of poetry. Harmonically, this would usually graph as follows:

$$\begin{array}{cccc} \mathbf{A} & \mathbf{A'} & \mathbf{B} & \mathbf{A'} \\ I-V & I-I & V-V^7 & I-I \end{array}$$

EXAMPLE 5.43   The graphic representation of a common song form piece.

In this form, the **A** section begins in the tonic and ends with a half cadence. The **A'** is a repeat of the **A** section material but ends with an authentic cadence. The contrasting **B** section may be in any related tonal center. (The dominant is frequently selected but so is the subdominant, the relative minor/major, the dominant of the dominant, and even the tonic itself.) This **B** section, often called ***the bridge***, ends harmonically in a way that will lead back to the original tonic and set up the return of the **A** material. Because the returning **A'** section ends the piece, its final cadence is almost always an authentic cadence.

Works in this form may also form subsections of larger compositions, such as *the theme* for a theme and variation or the trio of a march. Many songs, written for the musical theatre, use this form.

Bar Form

Bar form was discussed briefly on pp. 283–84. The graph for bar form is **AAB**. No particular harmonic structure is implied. In discussions of bar form, two German terms *Stollen* and *Abgesang* are found. The A section of the piece is called the Stollen, while the B section is the Abgesang. Many Lutheran chorales of the sort that Bach harmonized were written in bar form.

> The term is derived from the tradition of the German *Meistersingers* and originally referred to the manner in which a melody was generated from poetry or other sources.
>
> This reflects recent usage where *Stollen* is used both for the singular and plural. The original singular is *Stoll*.

Stollen   Stollen   Abgesang
A   **A**   **B**

EXAMPLE 5.44 An illustration of a piece in bar form. Other than ending on the tonic, little may be asserted about the harmonic structure.

Through-Composed

Music can be described as through-composed if no *obviously* repeated materials are used. Originally this term was applied to songs in which each verse was set to a different melody. There would of course also be no return. Since about the eighteenth century, there have been rather few examples of through-composed music. A through-composed piece has a graph that looks like this:

A   **B**   **C**   **D**   **E**   **F**   *etc.*

EXAMPLE 5.45 The graphic representation of a through-composed composition.

Review

- Song form is typically graphed as AA'BA'.
- A variety of other forms are found in songs.
- In the AA'BA' song form, the A' sections usually end on the tonic.
- The B section may or may not be in the same key.
- The B section is often called the bridge.
- The bar form is AAB.
- The A sections are called Stollen; the B section is called the Abgesang.
- There is no anticipated harmonic design.
- A through-composed piece will have no repetition of material and will graph as ABCDEF etc.

Related Exercises

§ Review your understanding of the materials presented by completing the following statements and questions.

What is the typical graphing of a piece in song form? _____
The B section may be referred to as the bridge or the _____.
The *Stollen* usually ends on what tonality? _____
A composition graphed as ABCDEF etc. is referred to as _____.

Large Sectional Forms

French Overture

A form we call the **French overture** appeared in the Baroque era. The name comes from its association with the French court where it was a model for overtures to opera or ballet performances.

The characteristic features are these:

- A slow, stately *introduction*, usually using dotted rhythms
- A second, faster section, often with a polyphonic texture
- A separate, concluding *coda* leading to the beginning of the
- production

> The word *coda* means "tail" in Italian and is an ending attached to a piece of music to bring it to a satisfying conclusion.

Its structure is said to have evolved because the king would often enter the theatre, fashionably late, interrupting the beginning of the event. To minimize the impact of the king's arrival, composers began to provide appropriately stately music for the royal party.

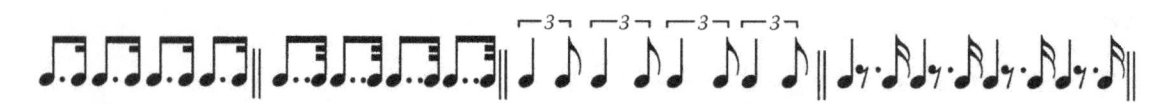

EXAMPLE 5.46 Typical "dotted rhythms" found in the introductions of French overtures.

The faster section that followed was the central part of the overture, and the coda at the end signaled the actual beginning of the opera or ballet.

The slow introduction followed by a faster middle and a dramatic coda was effective and became the norm for opera, ballet, and oratorio overtures well into the nineteenth century. Vestiges of the French overture can still be heard in the overtures for some twentieth century Broadway productions.

Introduction
Slow
(with dotted rhythms)

Body
Faster
(often polyphonic)

Coda
Dramatic
(faster or slower)

EXAMPLE 5.47   The outline of a French overture.

Rondo Form

Rondo form has often been used for the final movements of classical concertos. A rondo usually begins with the statement of a distinctive theme that returns throughout the movement. This theme is called the ***rondo theme***, the ***refrain***, or, simply, the ***rondo***. In between statements of the rondo theme, contrasting sections called ***episodes*** or ***couplets*** appear.

> The name *rondo* may have come from the medieval French poetic form called a ***rondeau***. These poems had refrains that recurred throughout. The terms *refrain* and *couplet* also come from poetic usage.

In its most basic form, rondo would be graphed as ABACADA etc. The initial A, the refrain, is followed by and alternates with contrasting sections (i.e. B, C, D etc.), the couplets. The movement usually ends with a final, perhaps embellished, statement of the rondo theme with or without a brief coda. The refrain is always in the tonic key. Couplets are usually not.

The couplets may be derived from the rondo theme or may represent new material. The contrasting section will never be simply a repetition of the rondo theme. Couplets that are minor modality versions of a major modality refrain and couplets that are major key versions of minor key refrains may be encountered. The immediate repetition of the refrain will occur only in instrumental concertos where the initial presentation of the rondo theme is provided by the orchestra and then repeated by the solo instrument or vise versa.

A   B   A   C   A   D   A
I   x   I   y   I   z   I

EXAMPLE 5.48   A basic rondo form graph. The I represents the tonic key while *x*, *y*, and *z* stand for contrasting keys.

Over time, various modifications were introduced so that today we have the ***two couplet rondo***, the ***variation rondo***, the ***sonata rondo***, or the ***truncated rondo***. One of the favorite variations, the two couplet rondo is graphed as ABACA.

In the variation rondo, each appearance of the rondo theme shows some alteration of its structure. Typical variations include the lengthening or shortening of the rondo theme or manipulations of the melodic and/or harmonic content.

The sonata rondo is usually constructed so that the rondo theme is in the tonic key and the first couplet, B, is in the dominant. (See also the article on sonata form on p. 318.)

The middle AC section shows a tendency toward becoming a *development* and the AB' return has the B couplet now in the tonic key. The final refrain may be omitted.

A truncated rondo most often will usually have the B couplet return after the C couplet without an intervening refrain: ABACBA.

Two couplet rondo	A I	B x	A I	C y	A I		
Variation-rondo	A I	B x	A' 	C y	A" 	D z	A''' (I)
Sonata-rondo	A I	B V	A x	C y	A I	B' I	(A) (I)
Truncated-rondo	A I	B x	A I	C y	B x or z	A I	

EXAMPLE 5.49 Two couplet, variation, sonata, and truncated rondos as they may be graphed. The rondo theme is most likely to be presented in the tonic key. The couplets, in all but sonata-rondo, may be in any key.

> In the Baroque period, the name rondeau was applied to dances that had an initial refrain which was repeated after each presentation of contrasting materials.

There is also a cousin to the rondo called the *ritornello form* in which the returning theme will likely appear in various keys.

Theme and Variations

In *theme and variations*, the first material presented will often be the theme. Composers tend to select the theme from among hymn tunes, folk songs, or other fairly small homophonic pieces. Often the theme is familiar to most listeners, but it may also be an original composition by the composer or an obscure piece that the composer feels will lend itself well to a set of variations.

Following the performance of the theme, a series of other modified versions of the theme will be performed. In between each of these pieces, there may be a pause (silence), or the composer may indicate that two or more variations should be played as a continuous piece by allowing no space between them either by indicating *attacca* or by writing in such a way that one variation evolves into the next variation.

Each of these pieces may be called a ***movement***, but they are each usually called "a variation," often numbered: First Variation, Second Variation or Variation 1, Variation 2, etc.

In older versions of theme and variations, the variations immediately following the presentation of the theme are fairly similar to the theme and are definitely recognizable as being a variant on the theme. Later variations within the set may be less clearly related and show more modifications.

What a composer chooses to modify to create a variation is impossible to predict. Alterations are likely to include moving the melody into a different range; modifying the harmony; changing the modality; ornamenting the melody with various extra notes and non-harmonic tones; changing the rhythm from duple to triple (or the reverse); increasing the complexity of the accompaniment; and changing tone colors, tempo, and dynamics. In the classic theme and variations, the original theme and/or its harmonic structure and/or its rhythmic figurations remain fairly easy to detect within most variations.

Other theme and variations may not start with the theme at all. If the theme is well known, it may never be presented. Most jazz pieces are theme and variations. Typically, the theme is well known by the audience so the performers simply begin playing variations. They may precede the first variation (usually called a ***chorus***) with an introduction (***the head***) that may or may not be related to the theme. Typically, the *harmonic structure* of the theme *is* maintained throughout the piece but may be elaborated upon by the use of borrowed, substituted, and altered chords, and it may be subjected to a variety of rhythmic or modal alterations.

Successive choruses are usually played one after another with no break, and each will consist mostly of a soloist improvising against an accompaniment that may be no more than a piano, guitar, drums, or bass. Or the soloist may be supported by an ensemble that includes some or all of those instruments. The piece may end with a return to the introduction now modified to sound final. Or perhaps a different composed figure (***the tail*** or coda) will be used to conclude the piece.

From the middle of the nineteenth century on, theme and variations have been written that expand the initial style of variations to be less predictably structured and which have extended the notion of variation to become more like ***developments***. These variations may not share any strong similarities with the original theme, which may or may not be presented.

In some theme and variations, the variations precede the theme's presentation and seem to gradually coalesce into the theme out of many gestures and motives. While the classical theme and variations sound as though the composer were taking the source apart to see how it is structured, newer variations often sound as though the composer were reassembling the theme out of musical remnants.

Sonata Form

> Some musicians use the term Sonata-allegro when speaking of sonata form. This term dates back to a time when the first movement of a piece was likely to be fast and in sonata form. Since this association can no longer be assumed, this term is not recommended.

The term *sonata* has two meanings within any discussion of musical forms. It is a multi-movement composition for solo keyboard instrument (organ, piano, etc.) or for a solo instrument (violin, trumpet, flute, etc.) with keyboard accompaniment or a large work for an ensemble such as a string quartet. And it is a complex, formally structured movement used as the first or other movement of a symphony or instrumental sonata. To clarify that sonata is being discussed *as a form*, the term *sonata form* is used.

Sonata form probably evolved from rounded binary. Earliest examples of sonata-like pieces feature a modulation from the initial tonic to the dominant where the first part of the movement ends with a repeat to the beginning. The second portion begins in the dominant and has a return of original materials in the tonic key at the end.

As the sonata form evolved, some of these vestiges of rounded binary disappeared, and uniquely sonata characteristics were introduced. Near the end of the eighteenth century, the classic sonata form could be discerned.

Sonata Form Overview

The sonata form seems, graphically, to be more like a ternary form than its forbearer, the rounded binary form.

$$\|: \quad \underset{\text{Exposition}}{\mathbf{A}} \quad :\| \quad \underset{\text{Development}}{\mathbf{B}} \quad | \quad \underset{\text{Recapitulation}}{\mathbf{A'}} \quad \|$$

EXAMPLE 5.50   The macroscopic overview of sonata form.

Details reveal a sophisticated, multipart form that can be worked in many ways creating a musical structure that is most at home in a strongly tonal environment.

The Exposition

> Because the first bridge in the exposition usually moves from tonic to dominant (or relative major), it is often described as a *modulating bridge*.

The first section is called the ***exposition*** and is intended to present or expose the materials from which the bulk of the movement will be created. The initial melodic/harmonic idea is called the ***first theme*** and is presented in the tonic key. This is followed by a harmonically less stable section that modulates from the tonic to the dominant key. This transitional material is the ***first bridge*** and leads into a new melodic/harmonic presentation in the dominant (relative major or minor) called the ***second theme***.

The second theme may contrast with the first theme in more ways than just providing a new tonality. It is usually clearly different in character. If the first theme is angular and jagged (a lot of disjunct motion or dotted rhythms, for example), then the second theme will usually be more placid and thoughtful and possess more stepwise motion.

The second theme is followed by another transitional passage that connects it to the closing section. This connecting passage is called the *second bridge.* It does not modulate but leads into the final theme of the exposition, the *closing theme.* The closing theme cadences on the dominant, and then the exposition is repeated.

> Often a sonata will not have a full closing theme but merely a brief closing section to conclude the exposition.

The Exposition

First Theme	First Bridge	Second Theme	Second Bridge	Closing Theme :||
I	I–V	V	V	V$^{(7)}$

EXAMPLE 5.51 The section-by-section structure of a sonata exposition.

The Development

The second large section of the sonata movement is the ***development***. By its very nature, it is impossible to specify the development's structure in any but the most general terms. In the development, the composer works out the musical possibilities inherent in the materials (i.e., the first, second, and closing themes as well as the first and second bridge materials). In a typical development, this material or portions of it will be presented in many settings, including new tonalities and modalities, altered textures and varied rhythms, and instrumentation.

The themes and bridges may be recombined and restructured, and composers are free to introduce new materials. The development usually begins in the dominant but will travel though many keys before returning to a strong, dominant-seventh harmony that leads the listener to the last section of the movement.

The Recapitulation

The last large section of a sonata movement is called the ***recapitulation*** and is structurally identical to the exposition except for one significant change. The second theme and all the parts that follow are now in the tonic key.

A Recapitulation

First Theme	First Bridge	Second Theme	Second Bridge	Closing Theme ||
I				

EXAMPLE 5.52 A graph of the sonata recapitulation.

An Expanded and Modified Sonata Form

As the sonata evolved, changes took place in every aspect of the structure. Among the more common changes was the addition of an ***introduction*** and/or a ***coda***.

The introduction is frequently a slow section, often using materials found nowhere else in the sonata, which prepares for the exposition. The introduction is usually not included in the repeat of the exposition.

At first, a coda might be added to the end of the sonata's recapitulation to provide a convincing ending. But composers, like Beethoven, often expanded the coda to become virtually a second development ending with the final cadence.

Other alterations to the basic sonata structure were the addition of a ***codetta*** to end the exposition after the closing theme and the occasional use of a single melody to function both as the first and second themes. Sometimes a bridge-like section, called a ***retransition***, was added at the end of the development to prepare for the recapitulation.

> A codetta may be either a small, short coda or a coda-like figure used at the end of a section within a larger work rather than at the end of the work itself. Here it is used in the latter sense.
>
> This variant is found in some of Haydn's work who often relied upon the transposition of the theme to the dominant to achieve the first theme/second theme contrast.

Review

- The French overture begins with a slow introduction using dotted rhythms.
- The main section is usually faster and likely to be polyphonic.
- The overture ends with a coda that may be either fast or slow.
- Rondo form consists of an initial theme, called the rondo theme or refrain, and a series of contrasting themes, called couplets or episodes.
- The rondo theme is in the tonic key.
- The couplets are rarely in the tonic key.
- Modified forms of the rondo include the two couplet rondo, the variation-rondo, the sonata-rondo, and the truncated rondo.
- The rondo often forms the last movement of a classical instrumental concerto.
- The theme used in a theme and variations is usually a simple piece with a clear formal structure. It may be a folk song, a popular piece, or an original composition.
- In a classic theme and variations, each variation is a complete piece in itself with a form that closely follows the form of the original theme.
- Variations usually involve some of the following: changing the mode; elaboration of the melody or the accompaniment; changing the meter, tempo, or rhythmic accompaniment; and/or the changing of the instrumentation.
- Newer forms of variations often treat the variations as continuous components of a single movement.

- All aspects of the original may be altered, and the composer may choose not to use the structure of the original as a framework for the variations.
- The original theme may be totally omitted or may appear only at the end.
- Sonata form evolved during the eighteenth century.
- The three main sections to sonata form are the exposition, development, and recapitulation.
- The exposition consists of a first theme (in tonic), a first bridge (that modulates from tonic to the tonality of the second theme), a second theme (usually in the dominant or the relative major/minor), a second bridge, and closing material. It is usually repeated.
- The development features the working out of some of the potential of the musical materials found in the exposition. The end of the development leads back to the recapitulation, sometimes through a retransition.
- The recapitulation follows the development and uses the formal plan of the exposition, but the tonal center remains tonic.
- An introduction may precede the exposition, and/or a coda may follow the recapitulation.

Related Exercises

§ Review your understanding of the materials presented by completing the following statements and questions.

The first part of a French overture is of what relative tempo? _____ And what rhythms might be expected to be heard? _____

In a rondo, the rondo theme alternates with sections called _____ and _____.

Where might a rondo be expected? A rondo is frequently found as the final movement of a classical _____.

The three primary sections of a work in sonata form are the exposition, the _____, and _____.

The first bridge in the exposition usually serves to _____ _____.

What are some of the characteristic features of the development?
What is a retransition? _____

Continuous Forms

Continuous music is different from sectional in that it avoids easily separated phrases that end in clear cadences. In reality, most continuous pieces do have phrases, sections, and cadences but, because these points of rest are disguised, to the casual listener the music seems to not be separated. To the knowledgeable listener, the sections are discernable.

Ground Bass

> It may help if the bass line is not too complicated so that, once heard a few times, the listener's attention is drawn elsewhere.

A form that bridges the gap between sectional form and continuous music is the ***ground bass***. In the ground bass, a bass line is repeated many times, while upper lines, often contrapuntal, are superimposed. The bass line is sometimes called the ***ground***. Each repetition of the bass clearly marks the beginning of a new section, but because of the complexity of the upper lines, the moment of repetition is often obscured from all but the most diligent listeners.

When the composition is a lament or when the words deal with tragedy or grief, the ground bass will frequently be a descending, semi-chromatic line. Excellent examples are found in "Dido's Lament" from Henry Purcell's opera *Dido and Aeneas* and in the "Crucifixus" from Bach's B Minor Mass.

EXAMPLE 5.53 Top, the ground bass line from Purcell's "Dido's Lament." Bottom, the ground bass from the "Crucifixus" from Bach's B Minor Mass.

Passacaglia and Chaconne

The ***passacaglia*** and/or the ***chaconne*** in some forms may be related to the ground bass because either may be written using a ground. Here is a description that may apply to *either* form:

1. The piece is in triple meter.
2a. It is *either* a bass line repeated throughout against which variations are set, or
2b. It is a harmonic progression repeated throughout against which variations are set.
3. The variations change with each repetition of the bass line or harmonic pattern.

Historically, the names *passacaglia* and *chaconne* have been applied to both types of compositions. And some pieces conform to the above descriptions but bear neither name.

Examples, familiar to many concertgoers, include Bach's Passacaglia and Fugue in C Minor for organ, which is an example of the repeated bass line composition.

EXAMPLE 5.54 The repeating bass figure from Bach's Passacaglia and Fugue in C Minor.

And also the last movement of Brahms's Symphony No. 4 in E Minor with its repeated harmonic pattern. The Brahms's bears neither the name *chaconne* nor *passacaglia* but has been described as both.

EXAMPLE 5.55 The harmonic progression that underlies all of the final movement of Johannes Brahms's Symphony No. 4.

The repeat of the passacaglia or chaconne bass line is often, intentionally, obscured by the complexity of the overlying lines and counterpoint. The slow-moving harmonic pattern's repeats also become easily covered by the more complex and intricate contrapuntal materials that are usually the focus of the listeners' attention. Thus, its sectional quality is at times difficult to discern.

Review

- The ground bass is a repeated bass line over which other music is composed.
- The material placed above the ground may be contrapuntal or homophonic.
- In vocal or instrumental music dealing with grief or any type of lament, the ground is often a line that descends in a chromatic or semi-chromatic manner.
- The terms *passacaglia* and *chaconne* are used equally by composers to describe two different forms.
- The common elements are that the passacaglia and the chaconne are in triple meter, and the basic pattern, as with the ground bass, is repeated throughout the composition.
- The repeated pattern of a passacaglia or chaconne may be a bass line or a series of chords.

Related Exercises

§ Review your understanding of the materials presented by completing the following statements and questions.

A melody, stated and repeated in the lowest voice, is called a _____ bass.
In chromatic form, it may be used in Baroque and latter works about _____.
A composition in triple meter frequently built on the sort of bass referred to in the question above may be a _____ or a _____.
As an alternative to the repeated bass, compositions may have a repeated _____.

Imitation

Most music that we perceive as being continuous is often polyphonic. Though it is possible to write homophonic music that is continuous, such compositions are rare. Knowledge of polyphonic constructions is helpful in understanding continuous forms.

Although not restricted to polyphonic music, *imitation* by its very nature creates a contrapuntal texture. In imitation, a musical idea is stated by a voice (or group of voices) and is repeated but by another voice (or group of voices). The initial statement is called the **Dux** (from the Latin for "leader"), and the imitating line is called the **Comes** (from the Latin for "follower").

EXAMPLE 5.56 An example of imitation. The melody to be imitated, *Dux*, is presented here in the upper voice. The imitation, *Comes*, follows two bars later in the lower voice.

It may be helpful to identify the interval at which the imitation occurs. There are two intervals of interest: the pitch interval between the two lines and the time interval between the two entrances.

> Or eight beats, or two whole notes apart.

In Example 5.56, the pitch interval is the octave, and the distance between the entrances is two measures. The instant that the imitation begins (here, on the first beat of the third measure) is called the ***point of imitation***.

Imitation need not be ***strict***. It may be free imitation as seen in Example 5.57.

EXAMPLE 5.57 An example of free imitation.

Canons and Rounds

When a voice presents an extended melodic idea that is imitated, in total, in another voice while the first voice continues the initial melody, we have **canon**. Canon involves two (or more) voices in imitative counterpoint. A canon involves a single musical line *being followed* in time by at least one, carefully defined version of itself. The pitch and rhythmic relationships between canonic lines are precisely defined. *Canon* means, literally, a list of rules.

Historically, many canons were not written out but rather the *Dux* was notated and the rules for creating the *Comes* were given in words or code. Often the rules were a puzzle for the performers to solve creating what was called a riddle canon.

Types of Canon

The Round

A familiar, simple canon possesses a single melodic line being imitated (usually three or four times) at the unison (or octave) and with each successive entrance occurring at the same time interval as the preceding one. When all have entered, the first voice may repeat the melody while the other voices continue to follow.

This very special type of canon is a **round**. Rounds are said to be **infinite canons**. Most of us are familiar with rounds such as "Row, Row, Row Your Boat" and "Are You Sleeping?" Even though all rounds are canons, not all canons are rounds.

EXAMPLE 5.58 A familiar round. Numbers indicate where each successive voice should enter. The first voice begins at 1. When the first voice arrives at 2, the second voice begins at 1. When the first voice arrives at 3 and the second is at 2, the third voice begins at 1, and so on. This is a four-voice round.

Mirror and Crab Canons

Mirror canon is a canon involving two performers each reading the same music but upside down to each other. One performer reads from the upper left corner while the other musician, sitting across from the first, reads from the upper left corner (which is the lower right corner to the first performer). Thus, what is the top system for the first performer is the bottom system for the second. If played correctly, the performers will end up together (in the opposite corner from where they began), and the counterpoint will work out all the way through. (The mirror canon is written such that the *Comes* is the retrograde-inversion of the *Dux*.) In **crab canon**, also called **cancrizans**, the *Comes* is the retrograde of the *Dux*. The above are finite canons because they are not designed to be repeated.

Other Canons

Composers may write canons such that the *Comes* begins at some interval higher or lower than the *Dux*. The canon may involve two or more voices that start together, but each performer is provided with a different duration (proportion) for all of the notes, thus creating a ***mensuration canon***. The *Comes* may be the inversion of the *Dux*.

The following illustrate some of the different types of canon that may be encountered.

A mirror canon in which the Comes is the inversion of the Dux.

EXAMPLE 5.59   A mirror canon.

A crab canon in which the Comes is the retrograde-inversion of the Dux.

EXAMPLE 5.60   A crab canon.

Canon at the fifth occurs when the Comes is a fifth above the Dux, independent of the exact octave notated.

EXAMPLE 5.61   Canon at the fifth.

Canon at the third occurs when the Comes is a third above the Dux, independent of the octave.

EXAMPLE 5.62 Canon at the third.

Review

- Imitation occurs when a melody (the *Dux*) presented in an initial voice is restated but in a second voice (the *Comes*). Imitation may be exact or free.
- Canon is a contrapuntal procedure that, by using specific criteria, creates an imitation of the melody in one voice by a melody in another voice.
- Canons are described by the time interval between the beginning of the *Dux* and the statement of the *Comes* in terms such as double whole note or three eighth notes.
- Canons are described by the pitch interval between the first pitch of the *Dux* and the first pitch in the *Comes* such as at the octave or at the fifth.
- Canons are also described by the rules applied to the *Dux* that generate the *Comes*, such as a mirror canon, a mensuration canon, a modulating canon, or a crab canon.
- Imitation that does not follow canonic rules is called free imitation.
- A canon that has a definite ending is called a finite canon.
- A canon at the unison (octave) that is infinite is called a round.

Related Exercises

§ Review your understanding of the materials presented by completing the following statements and questions.

When a melody (called the _____) is presented in an initial voice and then imitated (the _____) in a second voice, we have canon.
A canon is often described by the interval between the _____ and the _____.
A canon at the unison with no definite ending is called a _____.
A cancrizans is _____.

How to Write a Round

Historically, rounds have been fun to sing and are fairly easy to compose. The approach is straightforward. First, write (on a staff) the initial line (*Dux*) of the round, the portion from the beginning up to the entrance of the second voice. Then, on the staff below, write a simple CP to work with the music on the first staff.

Then, on a third staff, write a second contrapuntal line to work with the first two lines. At this point, you have a three-part round. If you want a four-part round, simply compose a fourth line to work with the first three.

Here is a three voice round, attributed to Beethoven, written in the manner suggested.

EXAMPLE 5.63 A three-part round. The music on the top staff is composed first. Then the music on the second staff is added to go with the top staff. Finally, the music on the third staff is written to fit with the first two.

When the round is completed, it may be copied out as a single line of music with numbers indicating when each singer (or group of singers) is to enter. Obviously enough copies need to be produced so all the singers have music to follow. This is how the Beethoven round would finally appear:

EXAMPLE 5.64 The round from Example 5.63 as written for performance.

Inventions

No one except J.S. Bach seems to have ever written inventions. References are made to two-part and three-part *inventions*, but Bach called his three-part inventions *sinfonias*.

> The fifteen inventions and fifteen sinfonias date from the early 1720s. The Baroque period in music is generally considered to be from 1600 to 1750.

These pieces are excellent examples of seventeenth and eighteenth century counterpoint and have been used to develop keyboard skills and as contrapuntal models since the Baroque period. The name *invention* comes from an important property that is shared by all of these works: the use of *invertible counterpoint*.

Invertible counterpoint means that two lines written one above the other in a contrapuntal relationship may later in the work be reversed so that the lower line appears *above* the original upper line yet the counterpoint will still work. This means, for example, that an original interval of a perfect fifth between the two lines will become a dissonant perfect fourth upon inversion and in this configuration will resolve correctly.

Two-part inventions regularly contain two themes or motives. One or both may be presented in one hand, while the other hand introduces its material with a different temporal ordering. As the piece progresses, the themes are interchanged and the tonality altered, producing invertible counterpoint.

Here is Bach's F Major invention:

EXAMPLE 5.65 Bach's Invention in F Major. Motive one (the ascending eighth-note pattern) is presented by the right hand in measure 1 and imitated in measure 2 in the left hand while the second motive (descending sixteenth notes) is introduced in the right hand.

Review

- Inventions and sinfonias are two- and three-part keyboard pieces written by J.S. Bach.
- The sinfonias are sometimes called three-part inventions.

- These pieces feature invertible counterpoint, which means that two musical lines that contrapuntally function correctly with one above the other will also function correctly when the lower line is played above the original upper line.
- The inversion may occur at the octave and other intervals.

Related Exercises

§ Review your understanding of the materials presented by completing the following statements and questions.

Two- and three-voiced (part) keyboard pieces with invertible counterpoint written by J.S. Bach are called _____ and _____.

The term *invertible counterpoint* means that the two line are be written so that _____ _____.

Another term for a three-part invention (the term that Bach used) is _____.

Ricecare

A brief mention is made here of the **ricecare** (also *ricecar*), an instrumental piece from the fifteenth century related to the vocal motet. It was highly contrapuntal and is of special note to us because it is an important precursor of the fugue. The quality that leads to this conclusion is this: Ricecares featured a well-characterized thematic figure that was presented throughout the piece in imitative counterpoint.

This thematic figure, because of its strong pitch and/or rhythmic qualities, was usually heard clearly within the contrapuntal texture. It would be tossed about among the instruments and would appear at various pitches and in various modalities. The term ricecare was later applied to academic fugues written in the late eighteenth century after fugue (as a vital musical form) had somewhat faded.

The Fugue

> The base of the word *fugue* is *fuga*, which means "flight" as "to flee."

The fugue, as we know it, is a product of the Baroque era appearing in the 1620s. (The word *fugue* had earlier been applied to all imitative music.) However, for modern students, the basic definition and structure of fugue is invariably associated with J.S. Bach, even though his contemporary Georg Fredrick Handel and many other composers of that time and earlier also wrote significant fugues.

A fugue is an imitative, contrapuntal piece in which a single (usually) theme, the **subject**, is introduced in a single voice followed by entrances of the same theme in other voices until all voices have entered. The number of voices may be as many as six—or sometimes more—but the most common number is three to five.

The successive entries alternate the pitch level of the theme. The first, third, and fifth voices state the theme in the tonic. The second, fourth, and sixth voices state the theme in the dominant. This latter, transposed version of the subject is called the ***answer***. If more than six voices are included, the pattern of alternating subjects on the odd-numbered entrances and answers on the even-numbered entrances will continue.

> However, Bach himself created exceptions. The C Major fugue in *The Well-Tempered Clavier* has the unusual pattern of subject, answer, answer, subject.

The fugue will typically have two main parts, the ***exposition*** and the ***body***. In the exposition, each of the voices presents its version of the theme (either subject or answer) and provides counterpoints, called ***countersubjects***, to the successive voices as they enter. The exposition usually ends on either a tonic or dominant chord at which point the body begins.

The body of the fugue will consist of ***entries*** of the subject or answer and, between the entries, ***episodes***. The body may end with a coda to conclude the fugue.

Here is a diagram of a typical fugal exposition for a four-voice fugue:

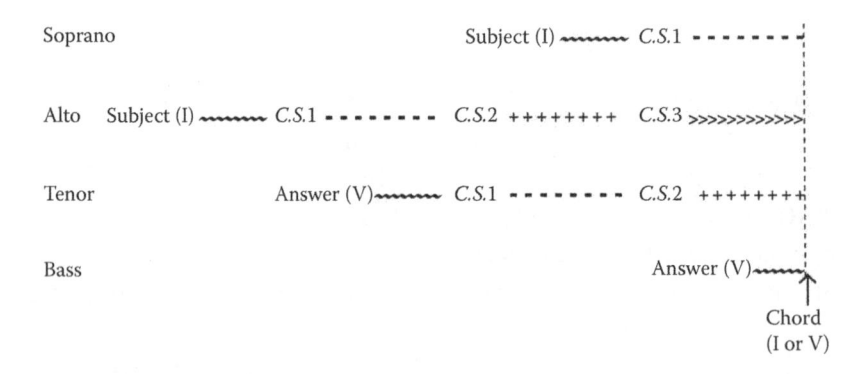

```
Soprano                                          Subject (I) ~~~~ C.S.1 - - - - - - -

Alto     Subject (I) ~~~~ C.S.1 - - - - - - C.S.2 +++++++ C.S.3 >>>>>>>>>>

Tenor                   Answer (V) ~~~~ C.S.1 - - - - - - C.S.2 +++++++

Bass                                             Answer (V) ~~~~
                                                            ↑
                                                          Chord
                                                          (I or V)
```

EXAMPLE 5.66 Diagram of a four-voice fugue's exposition. The subjects are in the tonic (I), the answers in the dominant (V). C.S. stands for countersubject. Countersubjects with the same number tend to be composed of similar material, but each countersubject is written so as to support the subject or answer that is currently being performed.

The Subject

The subject of the fugue may take many forms but often will have what may be described as a ***head*** and a ***tail***. The head will usually have distinctive characteristics that enable the listener to spot its appearance easily. The tail will be more utilitarian in nature, leading into the countersubject.

> Some writers have specified the order in which the voices should enter. In practice, such orderings do not appear to have been widely adhered to.

Here is a familiar Bach fugue subject:

EXAMPLE 5.67 The subject from Bach's Fugue in G Minor from *Book One of the Well-Tempered Clavier*. Note the head and the tail.

The Answer

To determine the answer of the fugue, given the subject, it would seem only necessary to transpose the subject up a fifth (or down a fourth) to put it into the dominant. However, there are many exceptions. It has been observed that Bach often altered his answers under certain circumstances. Below is the actual answer he used with the subject given in Example 5.67 and also the answer that he theoretically might have used:

EXAMPLE 5.68 Top, Bach's answer to the subject used in the Fugue in G Minor from *Book One of the Well-Tempered Clavier*. Bottom, the literal transposition of the subject. Notice the differences.

The lower line in Example 5.68 is what would be called a ***real answer***: the exact transposition of the subject. The upper line is a ***tonal answer***: an answer that has been modified.

Theorists have observed that Bach tends to prefer tonal answers and that tonal answers are typically created under certain circumstances.

- If the opening interval of the subject is from the tonic pitch to the dominant pitch, or the reverse, Bach usually writes a tonal answer.
- If the fugue subject modulates, the answer will usually be tonal.
- If the subject emphasizes the dominant pitch, the answer will usually be tonal.

Below are four original subjects, which, according to the principles cited above, would require tonal answers.

EXAMPLE 5.69 This fugue subject begins with a leap from dominant to tonic. Its answer should begin with a leap from tonic to dominant.

The following subject begins with a leap from tonic to dominant. As with the dominant-to-tonic leap, in the usual practice, this would require a tonal answer.

EXAMPLE 5.70 This subject begins with a leap from tonic to dominant. Its answer should begin with a dominant-to-tonic leap.

The subject given in Example 5.71 has an emphasized dominant (A), which requires a tonal answer.

EXAMPLE 5.71 This subject emphasizes the dominant. The answer would emphasize the tonic.

If a subject modulates, its real answer would modulate even further away from the initial tonic, and this would make the third (tonic) entrance impossible. Thus, the answer to a modulating subject would need to be tonal in order to modulate back to the original tonic key.

EXAMPLE 5.72 This subject modulates. The answer would need to return to the tonic key.

The Countersubjects

To create the countersubjects in a fugue, the composer may use materials found in the subject or may write original counterpoint to the answer. In either case, the counterpoint is usually invertible and stylistically similar to (and complementary to) the nature of the subject.

As the exposition unfolds and additional countersubjects are created, each of them may be given a distinctive character. In very complex fugues, especially if the number of voices increases to six or more, some of the later appearing countersubjects may be found to be simple and sparse.

Episodes

In a Bach fugue, the episode is a portion of the piece that does not contain a statement of the subject or the answer. Usually found in the body of the fugue, an episode may appear in the exposition if the composer is altering the time interval between entrances.

Episodes are contrapuntal, composed of material taken from the subject, answer and/or the countersubjects. They often feature material presented *sequentially* and are likely to contain invertible counterpoint.

EXAMPLE 5.73   Two examples of typical episodes taken from the g minor fugue.

The Body

The body of the fugue begins at the chord that ends the exposition and consists of *entries* (or *statements*) of the subject or answer and, in between these, *episodes*. The body may end with a coda to conclude the fugue. The body of the fugue, like the development in sonata form, is impossible to predict. The composer is free to introduce statements of the subject or the answer in any desired tonality. Episodes fill the time between statements and between other episodes.

When thoroughly discussing or analyzing a fugue, statements are described as "an entrance of the subject in a particular key (or scale degree)" or "an entrance of the answer on a particular scale degree (or in a certain key)." In fugues with real answers, the distinction between the subject and answer obviously cannot (and need not) be made.

Special Fugal Features

Several musical events may be found in fugues but need not be present. Among these are *stretto*, pedal point, a coda, a delayed entrance within the exposition, augmentation, diminution, a *counter exposition*, and even the appearance of a second subject.

Stretto is the term used to describe entrances of subjects and/or answers that occur *before* a previous entrance has been completed. Example 5.74 shows a fugue subject and the beginning of its answer. On the second system is a possible stretto as a statement of the subject (it could have been an answer) appears before an earlier statement has been completed.

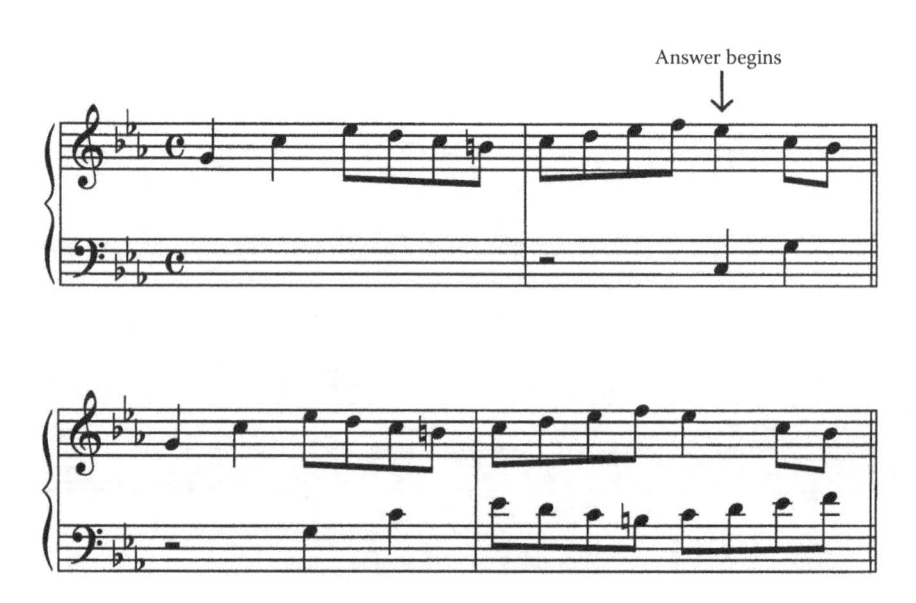

EXAMPLE 5.74 Top system, a fugue subject with an arrow showing the location of the appearance of the answer. Lower system, the sample subject now subjected to stretto.

Augmentation and diminution refer to the slowing down or speeding up of the subject or answer by using longer or shorter note values, respectively. Here is an example of augmentation.

EXAMPLE 5.75 The same subject found in Example 5.74 shown in augmentation.

Shortening the note values produces diminution, as shown in Example 5.76.

EXAMPLE 5.76 The same subject found in Example 5.74 shown in diminution.

Counter Exposition

A counter exposition is much like the exposition, described above, but it occurs *within the body* of the fugue. All the voices may drop out and then reenter one at a time, or the counter exposition may grow out of the counterpoint of the body with no hiatus in any voice. In a counter exposition, the subject and answer are the same as those originally presented in the exposition, but the ordering of entrances may change.

Pedals and Codas

Pedal point is typically either on the tonic or the dominant and is found in the body of the fugue, usually occurring near the end of the body. A coda for a fugue, as with other forms, is an ending attached to bring the piece to a suitable close. It may include one final statement of the subject or answer.

Delayed Entrance within the Exposition

Not infrequently within the exposition the composer will delay one of the voices' entrance beyond the time interval expected, thus making the eventual appearance of that voice something of a surprise. (This may happen earlier but is more often encountered with the entrance of the last voice.) The delay may be facilitated by the use of a short episode within the exposition.

Double and Triple Fugues

In a few large and complex fugues, the composer may use two subjects, or even three, thereby producing what is called a ***double fugue*** or ***triple fugue***, respectively. Usually the second subject is introduced using a complete, new exposition within the body of the fugue that, unlike a counter exposition, is built totally on a new subject.

This new exposition follows the plan of a typical fugal exposition, but, at its conclusion, the following portion of the body will almost always utilize materials from both the first and the second expositions in any way the composer may choose. Rarely, this process may be carried out a third time producing a triple fugue. There have been quadruple fugues composed, too.

Another use of the term *double fugue* is as the description of a fugue in which each entrance of the subject (and answer) during the initial (and only) exposition utilizes two simultaneous voices written in counterpoint to each other. Thus, in this type of double fugue, the subject and the answer are each presented as two separate but interdependent lines throughout the exposition. Sometimes, the two parts of the subject or the answer are identified as **subject a** and **subject b** and **answer a** and **answer b**.

An Exemplary Fugue

Many theorists choose the following fugue as a good example of a Bach fugue. No fugue will exhibit all of the characteristics discussed in this article but this three-voice, c minor fugue is well known, typical of the form, and easily analyzed. Here, with annotations, is that fugue.

The exposition begins with the subject presented in the alto voice followed by a tonal answer in the soprano. (Why is the answer tonal?) Then a surprise as the third entrance is delayed by an episode *within the exposition*. This is followed by the subject, again, entering in the bass. The exposition ends on the tonic six-three chord on the downbeat of measure 9 where the body begins with an episode.

> In the analysis of a fugue, if no tonality is specified for a statement of the subject or answer within the body of the fugue, it may be assumed that the statement is in its original tonality.

In measure 11, the soprano enters with the subject transposed to the relative major, E-flat. Another episode follows, in measures 13 and 14, and the answer returns in measure 15 in the alto. In measures 17 through 19, there are two consecutive episodes followed by a statement of the subject in the soprano in measure 20.

Measures 22 through the first half of 26 contain a series of three episodes. After the third beat of measure 26, the bass enters with the subject, and upon the completion of this statement, measure 28, there is an eighth note's worth of silence before the coda. A tonic pedal appears on the third beat of measure 29 in the bass as the soprano begins the final statement of the subject.

This is a keyboard fugue. Even in fugues written for the keyboard, Bach is usually quite strict about using no more pitches at any point than the number of voices. The only exception is in the coda where he often seems comfortable giving the performer fuller chords during the final cadence (see mm. 29–31).

Fugue 2 in C minor
from
The Well-Tempered Clavier; Book 1

J.S. Bach

EXAMPLE 5.77 Bach's Fugue in C Minor from *The Well-Tempered Clavier*.

Review

- The ricecare was a fifteenth-century instrumental composition related to the vocal motet, which served as a precursor to the fugue.
- The ricecare featured much imitation based on a highly recognizable figure that would appear frequently within the piece.
- The fugue as it is now known appeared around the 1620s.
- A fugue is an imitative contrapuntal form with clear formulas for its construction.
- The main theme of the fugue is called the subject and is presented at the beginning in a single musical line (voice) in the tonic key.
- The answer is the subject transposed to the dominant and follows the subject in a second voice.
- While the second voice presents the answer, the first voice provides invertible counterpoint, called a countersubject, to the answer.
- The third voice enters with the subject while the first and second voices provide countersubjects.
- The process, alternating answers and subjects, continues until all voices have entered, in which case the exposition is complete.
- Answers that are exact transpositions of the subject into the dominant are called real answers. Altered answers are called tonal answers.
- A tonal answer may be appropriate when the subject modulates, stresses the dominant, or begins with a tonic-dominant or dominant-tonic leap. Otherwise, real answers are used.
- The section following the exposition of the fugue is called the body.
- The body of the fugue will contain statements of the subject and/or the answer on various pitches. In between these statements will be episodes.
- Episodes are created from materials drawn from the subject, the answer, and the countersubjects.
- An episode will feature invertible counterpoint and may often use its material sequentially.
- Other features sometimes found in the body of the fugue include stretto, augmentation, diminution, and pedal point.
- Stretto occurs when a second (or third) statement of a subject begins before the initial statement has concluded.
- Augmentation occurs when the subject is stated in longer note values, and diminution occurs when the statement is in shorter note values.
- A pedal point is the sustaining of a single pitch in one of the voices over several measures. The pitch selected is usually the tonic or the dominant.
- The body may conclude with a coda.
- Composers have written double fugues with two subjects and two expositions or in which both the subject *and* the answer consist of two contrapuntal lines presented together.

Related Exercises

§ Review your understanding of the materials presented by completing the following statements and questions.

A fifteenth-century instrumental precursor to the fugue was the _____.
The initial melodic idea stated at the beginning of a fugue is called the _____.
In what ways is the answer related to this initial statement? _____.
What is a tonal answer? _____.
A fugue is usually divided into two primary large sections, the exposition and the _____.
When a voice enters sooner than expected, especially after the exposition has been completed, we have _____.
The contrapuntal materials presented by the first voice while the answer is being stated is called _____.
Diagram the exposition of a four-voice fugue.

part 6

Appendices
Appendix I

Systems for Identifying Pitches

When discussing music or writing about musical topics, it often becomes necessary to specify a particular pitch in a particular octave. It would be desirable if everyone used an agreed-upon system. Unfortunately, there is no single system, but several systems have evolved over time that satisfy different needs.

The chart below illustrates seven pitch identification systems that have been developed. Each of these, except for the Piano and MIDI systems, separate the pitch spectrum into different octaves. Each octave begins with the pitch C and ends with the pitch B.

One of the oldest is given first. This system is based on pipe organ practice in which pitches are identified by the length of the open pipe needed to produce a particular C. Thus, the lowest C usually found on an organ (a pitch with a frequency of about 16 Hz) is produced by a thirty-two-foot long pipe, and all the pitches from that C upward to the next B are said to be in the thirty-two-foot (32') octave. Beginning the next octave with the 16' C, all the pitches up to the next B are said to be in the 16' octave. This continues with the length of each successive octave's C being half the length of the preceding octave's C. Thus, the D above middle C would be the 2' D.

> MIDI stands for Music Instrument Digital Interface, which is a protocol published in 1983, for allowing electronically controlled musical instruments to communicate with computers and/or other electronically controlled instruments.

> It has long been known that halving an open pipe raises the pitch of the pipe by an octave. Thus, the piccolo is about half the length of a flute, and a tenor trombone is twice as long as a B-flat trumpet.

Another traditional naming system is that used by the famous German scientist Hermann Helmholtz (1821–1894), who carried out extensive research in acoustics. In this system, the 32' C is identified as C2, while the next (16') C is C1. The octave above C1 is C, and the next higher octave is c. Middle C is then identified as c^i, and the C above middle C is c^{ii}. In this system, the D above middle C is d^{ii}. This system is at best awkward and, for many, difficult to remember.

A third system that has some similarities to the Helmholtz system is also from the pipe organ tradition. In this "second organ" system, the 32' C is called CCCC, the 16' C is CCC, and the 8' C is CC. The C in the staff bass clef (sometimes called tenor C or TC) is C, and middle C is c^1. The octave above middle C is c^2 and so on. The D above middle C in this system is d^1.

A system called USA Standard starts with C_0 for the 32' C and proceeds logically enough to C_1, an octave higher, C_2 an octave above that, and so on. Some of the earliest sound software written for microcomputers used this system where the D above middle C would be D4.

Written without the subscript.

Sometimes a system used in piano building is encountered where the usual lowest piano pitch, A, is identified as A_1, and the C above that (16' C) is identified as C_4. In this system, the numbers correspond *to the piano keys*, counted from the bottom A so that the last C on the keyboard is C_{88}. D_{42} would identify the D above Middle C in this system.

A system that had some use with mainframe-based music software, like MUSIC 4BF, is known as octave point pitch class. In this system, the octave location is given by a number from 0 to 9 followed by a period (point) in turn followed by the pitch coded as 0.00 for C, 0.01 for C-sharp, 0.02 for D, and so on chromatically up to 0.11 for B. If a pitch, such as the quarter tone between F-sharp (0.06) and G (0.07), were needed, the pitch class would be 0.065. In octave point pitch class, middle D would be 4.02.

The newest system, MIDI, dates from 1980 and begins its numbering (typically for digital systems) with a 0, which is assigned to the 64' C (an octave below the 32' C). Each octave begins with a multiple of 12 so that 32' C is 12, 16' C is 24, 8' C is 36, and so on. Middle D is 62.

The following chart illustrates and compares these systems.

1st Organ	32'	16'	8'	4'	2'	1'	1/2'	1/4'	1/8'	1/16'	1/32'
Helmholtz	C2	C1	C	c	c^i	c^{ii}	c^{iii}	c^{iiii}	c^v	c^{vi}	c^{vii}
2nd Organ	CCCC	CCC	CC	C	c^1	c^2	c^3	c^4	c^5	c^6	c^7
USA Standard	C_0	C_1	C_2	C_3	C_4	C_5	C_6	C_7	C_8	C_9	C_{10}
Piano	—	C_4	C_{16}	C_{28}	C_{40}	C_{52}	C_{64}	C_{76}	C_{88}	—	—
8va . Pitch-class	0.00	1.00	2.00	3.00	4.00	5.00	6.00	7.00	8.00	9.00	—
MIDI	12	24	36	48	60	72	84	96	108	120	—

EXAMPLE 6.01 Chart showing various standard systems used to identify Western pitches.

Appendix II

The Harmonic Series

The important intervals in our Western music, and indeed in most music, are the octave, the perfect fifth, and the perfect fourth. In seeking why this is so, we need to look at a basic phenomenon of physics: the vibration modes of the string, the open pipe, and the closed pipe. In each of these vibrating systems, a harmonic series is generated.

The open pipe and the string display the similar characteristics in that, when caused to vibrate, each produces a standing wave. This wave is twice the length of the string or pipe. This pitch is known as the ***fundamental*** pitch of the string or pipe.

> In a closed (stopped) pipe, it is four times the length of the pipe.

Increasing the vibration speed, the next standing wave to appear is the one that vibrates at twice the frequency of the first. Another attempt to increase the vibration speed will produce a third standing wave with a frequency that is three times as fast as the initial vibration.

In fact, this pattern continues (theoretically infinitely) producing frequencies that are four, five, six, seven, … through n times the initial frequency. These frequencies are known as ***partials*** or ***harmonics*** and are illustrated by the harmonic series:

> The stopped pipe, found in pipe organs and instruments of the clarinet family, produces only the odd-numbered partials.

EXAMPLE 6.02 The harmonic series of a string or pipe that produces a fundamental pitch of C_2 (65.406 Hz) up through the thirty-second partial. Notes with black heads are not in tune with Western temperaments. The arrows indicate whether the partial's pitch is too sharp (upward) or too flat (downward) to be useful in most Western music.

Note that the second partial (harmonic) is an octave above the fundamental, while the third partial is a fifth above the second partial. Continuing up the harmonic series, the fourth partial is two octaves above the fundamental and also a perfect fourth above the third partial.

Since these partials are the initial ones encountered, it is believed that they are, therefore, the easier ones to hear. We also know, from research done by Hermann Helmholtz, and others, that the frequencies of each of the

> Some of us have learned to call the partials "overtones." There is nothing wrong with this term, but the terms *harmonic* or *partial* have been chosen for this book because a direct correlation exists between the number of the partial and the multiplier of the frequency. (The first overtone is, unfortunately, the second partial; the second overtone is the third partial, etc.)

partials are equal to the frequency of the fundamental multiplied by the *number of the partial*. Thus, the second partial, an octave, is twice the frequency of the fundamental, and the third partial is three times the fundamental and also 3/2 times the frequency of the second partial. In other words, the ratio of the frequency of the upper note of a perfect fifth to the frequency of the lower note is 3:2.

Following the system, we find that the fourth partial, the upper note of a perfect fourth interval, vibrates four times for every three vibrations of the third partial, the lower pitch of the perfect fourth. Therefore, the vibration ratio of the perfect fourth is 4:3.

Some theorists and authors have used the harmonic series to explain the *historical evolution* of harmony from fifths and fourths to thirds because, as the reader will note, the distance from the fourth partial to the fifth partial is a major third (5:4 ratio) and from the fifth to the sixth is a minor third (6:5 ratio). This association likely has some truth to it, but no one has been able to demonstrate an irrefutable relationship. Continuing up the harmonic series, other intervals are fairly quickly encountered that are not a part of our Western music vocabulary. If there is an influence, it is limited.

The harmonic series is also used by some as a basis for tuning systems calling the intervals produced between the adjacent pitches in the harmonic series *just* intervals and proposing a system of tuning called ***just intonation*** based on these intervals and their ratios. It is an attractive idea and may, too, have some validity but is not the universal solution that many of its proponents may have once believed.

> Historically, musicians have been attracted by the ratio for the major triad (6:5:4) found in just tuning. However, the audible and musical superiority of this numerically enticing pattern has never been demonstrated. See also Appendix III, "Tuning and Temperament."

The problems with the harmonic series as a basis for our tuning become especially bothersome with the seventh, eighth, ninth, and tenth partials. We note that the interval between the sixth and seventh partials is a minor third. But it is one that is so small (7:6) as to be, historically and practically, useless. And the interval between the seventh partial and the eighth partial (8:7) is a whole tone that is much too wide for our tastes.

> Intonation is the extent to which a musical performance is in (or out of) tune.

The whole tone between the eighth and ninth partials (9:8) is acceptable and is, indeed, what natural brasses use to obtain these pitches. These same instruments can also use the whole tone between the ninth and tenth partials (10:9). But surely both of these major seconds cannot be *the* correct size because they involve two different ratios.

> It is not insignificant that the harmonic series produced by actual wind instruments and, to a slightly lesser degree, strings shows greater variability between the tunings of the partials relative to each other and the fundamental than the theoretical model suggests.

The extent to which these intervals are useful to us is based on taste and tolerance. Elementary school music ensembles do not usually play with the precision necessary to demand a 9:8 major second (or a 10:9 major second) rather than the alternative. But a professional string quartet does. And, in that situation, differences can be aurally jolting.

So while it may be true that the first three intervals generated by the harmonic series are, for the most part, excellent tuning examples for the octave, the fifth, and the fourth, the fourth and fifth intervals—the major and minor thirds—are not as easily accepted. For many, the 5:4 major second seems a bit too small while the 6:5 minor second seems somewhat too large. The bottom line is that as with other musical dimensions, *intonation*, too, is a matter of taste.[1]

Appendix III

Tuning and Temperament

Of all the important tonal relationships that have been introduced and used in this book, the tonic-dominant and tonic-subdominant associations remain among the most widely recognized and oldest of musical structures. This is due in part to the need for tuning instruments with multiple strings. The octave is the easiest interval to tune, but since most cultures recognize the equivalence of all pitches with a frequency ratio of 2:1 (or some multiple thereof), the octave provides no new "notes" for a tuning system.

However, the 3:2 and 4:3 frequency ratios are equally easy to tune, and each produces recognizably different tones because each creates a useful interval: the perfect fifth and the perfect fourth, respectively. Most string instruments are tuned, primarily, as a series of fourths or a series of fifths. The guitar is of the former type, while the violin is of the latter.

EXAMPLE 6.03 On the left, the pitches to which the guitar's strings are usually tuned (sounding an octave lower). On the right, the pitches to which the violin's strings are tuned (sounding as written). Tuning the guitar requires the tuning of a series of perfect fourths, up to G, then a major third, and a final perfect fourth. (The top string is also two octaves above the lowest string.) The violin is tuned through the use of a series of perfect fifths.

Pentatonic Tuning

A fairly extensive pitch system can be created by extending either the tuning by fifths or the tuning by fourths concept to obtain the pentatonic scale (used by many cultures over the centuries).

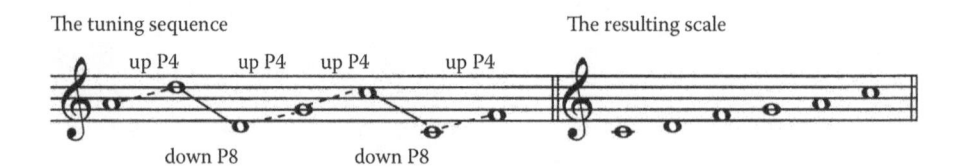

EXAMPLE 6.04 A typical pentatonic scale showing, on the left, a tuning process for achieving the pitch content, which is illustrated on the right. Additional octaves could be generated, as in other tunings, by tuning up or down an octave or two from this central octave.

However, trying to continue this tuning pattern to create Western music's twelve-pitch system creates problems. The primary one is the ***Pythagorean comma***, so named because it was first identified by the sixth-century BCE Greek mathematician, Pythagoras.

> In the study of acoustics, other commas may be encountered. The term *comma* means the result of an action or, as in this case, of a measurement.

What Pythagoras discovered, and what has proven to be a problem for Western musicians ever since, was that attempting to produce an accurate tuning for all twelve pitches found within the octave on our modern keyboards by tuning a series of perfect fifths or perfect fourths results in the final pitch being so out of tune as to be useless.

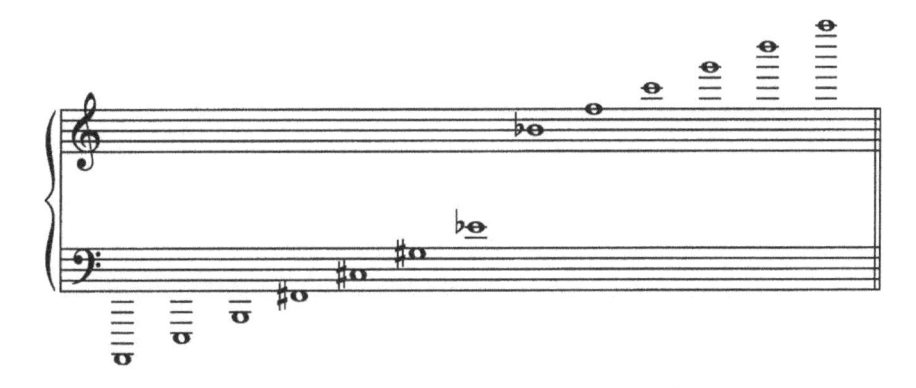

EXAMPLE 6.05 Tuning all twelve notes using ascending fifths. Starting with the lowest A on the piano (on the left) and continuing to the highest A, on the right, seven octaves higher.

The piano's lowest A is 27.5 Hz, and by multiplying that number by 1.5, the frequency of the E a perfect fifth above it can be calculated as 41.25 Hz. (The multiplier, 1.5, is the value of the perfect fifth's ratio, 3:2.) Using the same ratio to tune a series of fifths as shown in Example 6.05, the following table of frequencies is generated:

Pitch Name	Frequency (in Hertz)
A_0	27.5
E_1	41.25
B_1	61.88
$F\#_2$	92.81
$C\#_3$	139.22
$G\# (A\flat)_3$	208.83
$E\flat_4$	313.24
$B\flat_4$	469.86
F_5	704.48
C_6	1,057.19
G_6	1,585.79
D_7	2,378.68
A_7	3,568.02

> This calculation does not (and should not) take into account the "stretching" of octaves, used by piano tuners and necessitated by the vibrating characteristics of steel strings. Because both of the discussed tuning processes would be done using the same strings, the stretching would apply in both cases. It does not significantly affect the illustration.

Note the top A, where the tuning process ended. It is the aforementioned seven octaves above the lowest A. Using the absolutely accurate 2:1 ratio for tuning octaves, the frequency of the piano's highest A is calculated to be 3520.0 Hertz.

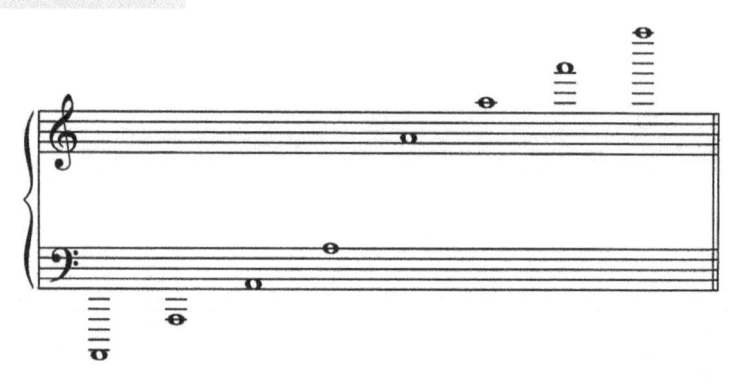

EXAMPLE 6.06 The eight pitches tuned, starting with the piano's lowest A, and tuning by octaves until seven octaves have been spanned. The values obtained, in Hertz, are shown below.

Pitch Name	Frequency (in Hertz)
A_0	27.5
A_1	55.0
A_2	110.0
A_3	220.0
A_4	440.0
A_5	880.0
A_6	1,760.0
A_7	3,520.0

The difference between tuning by fifths and by octaves is 48.02 Hertz (3,568.02 Hz minus 3,520 Hz) and is audible. It is about one-fourth of a semitone in size and is the Pythagorean comma.

Equal Temperament Tuning

An effort to build a keyboard that could produce all the required variations of pitches used in our musical system would generate an extremely large number of keys within each octave. (Depending on the precision of tunings required, the number of keys per keyboard octave could approach 80 keys!) Experimental keyboards have been produced but have proven to be both unwieldy and awkward. The alternative, for keyboards, has been to

> Keyboards have been made with split keys (especially the G-sharp/A-flat and D-sharp/E-flat keys) to provide improved tuning choices.

retain the "standard" twelve keys per octave and to "temper" the tuning (i.e. make compromises).

Today, the most pervasive temperament is what we call **equal-temperament tuning**. In this tuning, a single key is used to provide two or more pitches with different names. The pitches so assigned are said to be **enharmonic**. Thus, we use the same key to produce C-sharp and D-flat. By doing this, we limit the number of keys required per keyboard octave to twelve, but it also requires us to make all semitones the same size.

The mathematics behind this tuning system is fairly complex. The objective is to divide the Pythagorean comma equally among the twelve semitones available on the modern keyboard. As a way of discussing and comparing pitches and tuning systems, acousticians use a measurement called a **cent** (¢). The octave is divided into 1200¢, which means that (in equal-temperament tuning) each semitone is 100¢. Thus, in equal-temperament tuning, the perfect fifth is 700¢; however, a perfect (Pythagorean) fifth should measure 702¢.

> A cent is calculated as the 1,200th root of 2.0 (i.e. $1¢ = \sqrt[1200]{2.0}$).

> As a point of clarification, the *well-tempered tuning* celebrated in Bach's famous collection of preludes and fugues is *not* the same as equal-temperament. It is a modification of *meantone tuning*, which in some ways approaches equal-tempered but still leaves some intervals (and therefore some keys) harmonically "rougher" than others.

In order to minimize the problem of the Pythagorean comma, every perfect fifth is narrowed (and, concomitantly, every perfect fourth is expanded) so that, rather than a beat-less 3:2 ratio (or 4:3 ratio), you will hear, near the middle of the keyboard, about three to four beats every five seconds. An obvious characteristic of an equal-tempered keyboard is that all perfect fifths and perfect fourths are flawed, and the thirds are of the incorrect size; the major thirds end up being too wide, and the minor thirds end up being too narrow. But because these errors exist in every key, the tuning is usable. (No professional vocal or instrumental ensemble would tolerate such intonation, but the keyboardist has no choice.)[2]

Other Tuning Systems

Historically, many tuning methods have been tried in efforts to work around the conundrum of the Pythagorean comma. Among these are two broad types worth mentioning: meantone temperament and various well-tempered systems. Musicians who do historically informed performances need to be aware of these various solutions. The average theory student may find them to be simply curiosities or too arcane to bother with.

Meantone Systems

There are many meantone temperaments, including 1/4, 1/5, and 1/6 comma found in writings on temperaments but so are many other variants. The term *meantone* refers to the tone halfway between one pitch and the pure major third above. In meantone systems, this middle pitch (e.g. D between C and E) is exactly halfway between the two outer pitches. Meantone temperaments create pure thirds but sacrifice perfect fifths. In Pythagorean tuning, all fifths (but one) are perfect, while major thirds are much too wide. This flawed fifth is often called a "wolf" and is unusable.

Well-Tempered Systems

In meantone systems, there is always an unusable, wolf fifth. In well-tempered systems, there are thirds and fifths of differing sizes but no unusable intervals. This results in the phenomenon of each key possessing a unique quality or (perhaps) emotion. Just as there are many meantone systems, there are many well-tempered systems. Unlike meantone systems, well-tempered systems can play in all keys.

Tuning in Performance

While it is necessary to tune keyboard instruments before a performance, string players, wind players, and vocalists continue to tune every pitch as they perform. Thus, the final set of pitches used is the result of an active listening and selecting process that occurs throughout a performance. The establishment and maintenance of a temperament is not a decision made and adhered to in advance, as it must be for the tuning of keyboard instruments, but rather a dynamic exercise in excellence that is both challenging and all-consuming for the performers.

When music is performed by voices, or on non-keyboard instruments, semitones are not all the same size. Nor are all whole tones the same. In his respected book, *The Acoustical Foundations of Music*, John Backus reports that in scientifically controlled tests, live string performers tend to use Pythagorean tuning, including *larger than just* major thirds and *smaller than just* minor thirds.[3] During performances, tuning adjustments are constantly being made. (Tuning, like many aspects of music, is subject to interpretation.)

There is the additional musical need to "inflect" pitches that create specific harmonic motions, such as leading tones moving to tonics, and pitches that form augmented or diminished intervals. Because diminished intervals have strong tendencies to contract, it is more harmonically satisfying to compress the distance between the two pitches. On the other hand, because augmented intervals want to expand, the distance between the two pitches in an augmented interval will need to be increased. Note the following example:

EXAMPLE 6.07 On the left, a diminished fifth and its most likely resolution. On the right, an augmented fourth and its most likely resolution. Except when performed in equal-temperament, the diminished fifth is a smaller interval than the augmented fourth.

The ***diatonic semitone*** (between C and D-flat) is 10 percent smaller than the equal-tempered semitone found on keyboards. The ***chromatic semitone*** (C to C-sharp) is almost 15 percent larger than the equal-tempered semitone. Thus, the distance between the two pitches G and D-flat will be almost one-fourth of a semitone smaller than the distance between G and C-sharp, assuming that the frequency of the G is identical in both cases. This fact should reinforce the need for the composer/arranger to notate intervals and chords correctly, taking into account how each pitch is functioning, that is, in each case where the line (or chord) is progressing.

Appendix IV

The Circle of Fifths

The equal-tempered tuning of the keyboard has led many to use the concept of the circle of fifths—or the circle of fourths—to relate the various major and minor keys. This is a useful mnemonic device. (But it is important, especially in terms of correct notation, to remember that this circle should actually be a spiral.)

This is the circle of fifths as often presented:

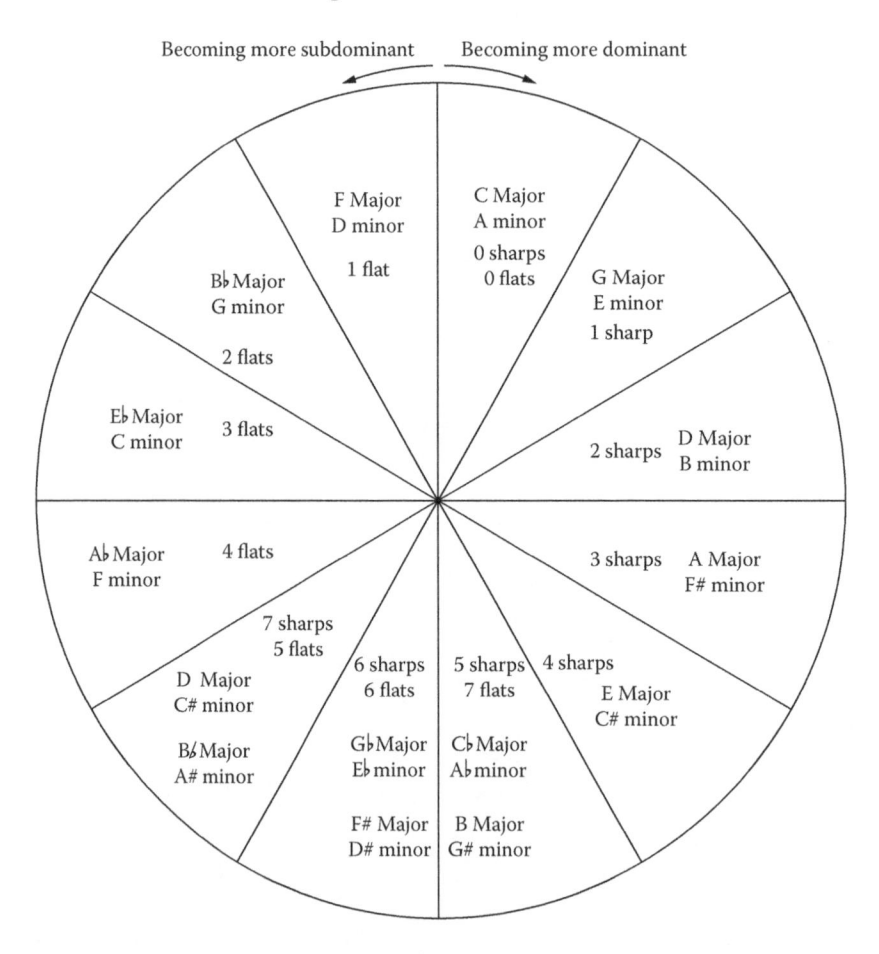

EXAMPLE 6.08   An illustration of the circle of fifths.

Note that traveling around the circle of fifths in a clockwise direction results in movement to an increasingly dominant tonality, while moving counterclockwise results in an increasingly subdominant tonality. And, due to the nature of our notational system, the counterclockwise direction produces the same result as using "the circle of fourths."

However, a problem with this circle concept is that it only works in equal-temperament tuning (or, with subtle differences, in well-tempered tunings). In all other circumstances, we should conceive of this as a ***spiral of fifths*** (or fourths) because—by specifying true, perfectly tuned fifths—we can never return to our starting pitch (see Appendix III). (And, therefore, in that case, the enharmonic equivalents given in the circle of fifths above are inaccurate.)

In the spiral of fifths, once we get to seven sharps, we would go on to eight, nine, ten, etc. sharps. These would represent the keys of G-sharp Major, D-sharp Major, A-sharp Major, etc.

Although the key signatures for these keys are not used in published music, the tonal centers designated by them can be specified (and sometimes are) by the use of accidentals.

Appendix V

Transposition

Most musicians accept the international tuning standard that A above middle C is tuned to a frequency of 440 Hz. It is also accepted that the piano, among other instruments, is tuned so that when the A above middle C is played, the pitch sounded vibrates at 440 Hz. This is referred to as ***concert pitch***. We have assumed this fixed tuning system throughout the book.

> Historically, the tuning standard has varied and has by no means been used by all musicians even within a given community at a given time.

When music is performed on an instrument not built in concert pitch, such as a *clarinet in B-flat*, the notation needs to be transposed to accommodate that instrument's key. In the case of the clarinet, it has historically evolved so that when the clarinetist sees a middle C notated and covers and uncovers the necessary keys and holes on the instrument to produce a middle C, the listener will hear a pitch, which on a piano or other concert-pitched instrument will be identified as a B-flat. The clarinet is described as a transposing instrument. Other familiar transposing instruments are the clarinet in A, the B-flat trumpet and cornet, the E-flat alto saxophone, the B-flat tenor saxophone, the B-flat bass clarinet, the E-flat baritone saxophone, the (French) horn (in F), and the alto flute in G.

> The orchestral trumpet and natural horn parts have been written in a variety of transpositions over the years as the result of the initial lack of valves on these instruments and then later, during the evolution of the procedures, for the use of valves. There were also, especially in the nineteenth century, varying opinions as to which fundamental and harmonic series provided the most desirable or characteristic sound for the instrument. This debate continues, to some extent, between the B-flat trumpet and the C trumpet, especially in orchestral music.

It is also necessary at times to transpose music from one voice to another. Songs written to be sung by sopranos are too high to be sung by altos and so would be transposed into a lower key. It is a value for anyone wishing to be musically literate to understand how to transpose, even though fluency at transposition is usually assumed to be needed only by composers, arrangers, conductors, and those performers who play transposing instruments such as horns, trumpets, and clarinets.

In its simplest form, transposing means to shift all of the pitches in a piece of music to a different tonic, and, concomitantly, all the other degrees of the scale are shifted the same distance. Because the B-flat clarinet will sound a *whole step lower* than a concert-pitched instrument, it is necessary to correct for this distance by notating the music for the B-flat clarinet a *whole step higher* than one wishes to hear.

Here is an example:

EXAMPLE 6.09 On the top, the desired passage to be heard as it is to sound (concert pitch). On the bottom, the same passage notated for performance by a clarinet in B-flat.

Note that the original (concert pitch) melody is in the key of G Major. Because it is necessary to write the B-flat clarinet part a whole tone higher, the clarinet will be notated in A Major, the key that is a major second above G Major.

Therefore, the key signature for the clarinet will be that of A Major (three sharps—two more than the original G Major), and each note will be written a whole step above the original. Thus, D becomes E, A becomes B, G becomes A, E becomes F-sharp, and so on.

Transposition by Interval

The transposition described above is fairly simple and many musicians, especially clarinet, trumpet, and horn players, can do it at sight. What they may be doing in the process is what is called transposition by interval. Many musicians find reading all the given pitches up or down a step as needed to be fairly simple, so that is what they do, adjusting the key signature, as explained.

Transpositions that are simple for the performer or arranger to execute can be done quickly at sight. Transpositions that are not so easy may require some time and effort to accomplish. Fortunately for many, software programs, such as Sibelius™ and Finale™, can do transpositions for us. It remains necessary to be able personally to transpose only when the transposition needs to be done at sight (such as having a clarinetist read and play an alto saxophone part).

Transposing by Function (Scale Degree)

Another way to accomplish the transposition of a passage or part is to understand the given material in terms of the function of each pitch. This approach can be especially helpful when the interval between the written pitch and the pitch that will have to be played is large or mentally awkward.

Here is a passage written for alto flute, a G transposition:

EXAMPLE 6.10   A passage written for alto flute (in G).

In order to play Example 6.10 on a piano (concert pitch), the interval of transposition will be up a perfect fourth. It is possible to simply read all pitches a perfect fourth lower but the process shown in Example 6.11 below may prove easier.

EXAMPLE 6.11   On top, the original alto flute part, but here all of the pitches are identified as a degree of the D Major scale (the key that the alto flute sees as tonic). Below, the same passage as it would be notated for piano with all of the degrees of the scale still identified but, of course, now in the key of A, the corresponding key for the piano. Thus, what was tonic in the original remains tonic in the transposed key. What was dominant is still dominant.

> Fixed *do* does not work for this purpose.

If using moveable *do*, the scale degrees, illustrated in Example 6.11, could be replaced with solfege syllables.

Using (Other) Clefs

Some theory instruction includes learning to read not just the treble, alto, tenor, and bass clefs but also the soprano, mezzo-soprano, and baritone clefs. One reason for this additional knowledge is to facilitate transposition. Here, for clarity's sake, are all seven clefs, each showing the location of middle C.

EXAMPLE 6.12 The seven clefs that may be encountered in music (and music theory classes). From left to right: treble clef, soprano clef, mezzo-soprano clef, alto clef, tenor clef, baritone clef, and bass clef. The placement of middle C is shown in each.

This is how transposition by clefs works.

We will start with a passage written in the treble clef for an instrument in B-flat, such as the clarinet (or the soprano saxophone, trumpet, flugelhorn, or cornet). All of these instruments sound a whole step lower than written. (The tenor saxophone and bass clarinet are also usually in B-flat but sound a ninth lower than written.)

EXAMPLE 6.13 A passage as originally written in the treble clef for a B-flat clarinet.

In order to play it on a concert pitch instrument, it needs to be written (or read as though it were written) a whole tone lower. Reading the original passage leaving the notated pitches on the same lines and in the same spaces as were given, but with the tenor clef replacing the treble, produces the following example:

EXAMPLE 6.14 The passage given in Example 6.13 but now showing the use of the tenor clef in place of the treble clef.

However, Example 6.14 has the incorrect key signature (it has not yet been changed), and it is an octave too low. In order to correct the key of the original (Example 6.13) for the concert-pitched instrument, two flats must be added to the key signature and, finally, the result must be played an octave higher to obtain the desired sounds.

EXAMPLE 6.15 The passage from Example 6.14 is now moved up an octave together with being provided with the correct key signature and required accidentals.

All the notational modifications shown in Examples 6.14 and 6.15 would, of course, be done mentally by the performer. Each step was shown here to illustrate the process.

When using clefs for the purpose of transposition, the following chart should prove helpful. Notice that the distance provided by the change in clef is in terms of generic intervals, not a specific one. The interval given will need to be modified by the use of a key signature applied to the original notation. That key signature will be determined by the exact relationship between the transposition (if any) of the original music and the transposition (again, if any) of the instrument upon which the music is to be performed.

	Music Written in Treble Clef	Music Written in Soprano Clef	Music Written in Mezzo-soprano Clef	Music Written in Alto Clef	Music Written in Tenor Clef	Music Written in Baritone Clef	Music Written in Bass Clef
When Read in Treble Clef		Sounds Up a 3rd	Sounds Up a 5th	Sounds Up a 7th	Sounds Up a 9th	Sounds Up an 11th	Sounds Up a 13th
When Read in Soprano Clef	Sounds Down a 3rd		Sounds Up a 3rd	Sounds Up a 5th	Sounds Up a 7th	Sounds Up a 9th	Sounds Up an 11th
When Read in Mezzo-soprano Clef	Sounds Down a 5th	Sounds Down a 3rd		Sounds Up a 3rd	Sounds Up a 5th	Sounds Up a 7th	Sounds Up a 9th
When Read in Alto Clef	Sounds Down a 7th	Sounds Down a 5th	Sounds Down a 3rd		Sounds Up a 3rd	Sounds Up a 5th	Sounds Up a 7th
When Read in Tenor Clef	Sounds Down a 9th	Sounds Down a 7th	Sounds Down a 5th	Sounds Down a 3rd		Sounds Up a 3rd	Sounds Up a 5th
When Read in Baritone Clef	Sounds Down an 11th	Sounds Down a 9th	Sounds Down a 7th	Sounds Down a 5th	Sounds Down a 3rd		Sounds Up a 3rd
When Read in Bass Clef	Sounds Down a 13th	Sounds Down an 11th	Sounds Down a 9th	Sounds Down a 7th	Sounds Down a 5th	Sounds Down a 3th	

EXAMPLE 6.16 Matrix showing the effect on the pitch sounded by reading music written in one clef and played in another clef.

The matrix provided in Example 6.16 can only be used correctly by knowing the intervallic relationship between the given music and the desired sound. Thus, if the given music is notated in the treble clef at concert pitch and needs to be performed on a clarinet in A (which sounds a minor third lower than written), then it can be read in soprano clef but with three sharps added to the originally notated key signature. (If the original key signature had two flats, the key signature to be used would be one sharp; + 3 sharps − 2 flats = 1 sharp). This formula results from the fact that A Major (the transposition tonality) has three more sharps than C Major (the concert tonality).

However, if the original were written in treble clef for horn in E-flat and is to be played on a horn in F, then the tenor clef may be used by adding two flats and playing the result an octave higher. That is because the E-flat horn is a major second below the F horn, but no clef provides a pitch shift of a major second. However, the ninth is an octave and a second, so you must correct for the "extra" octave. (The two added flats come from the fact that E-flat Major has three flats, but F has only one, so the resulting key signature needs the two "missing" flats.)

The reader might note that the process of correctly notating an E-flat part so that it can be played on an F instrument is the same process as notating a B-flat part so that it can be played on a concert-pitched instrument.

Appendix VI

All Major Scales in Four Clefs

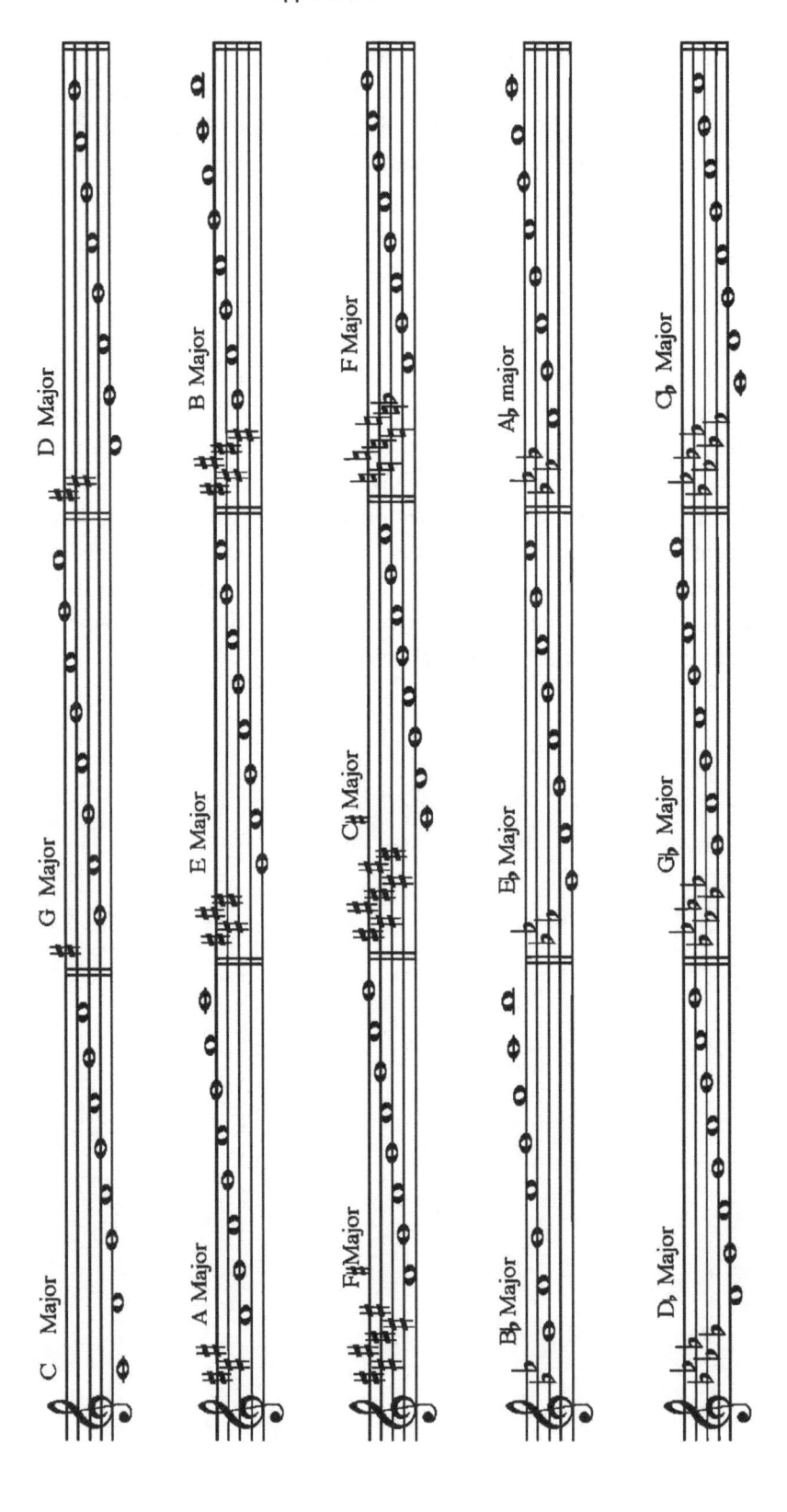

Appendices

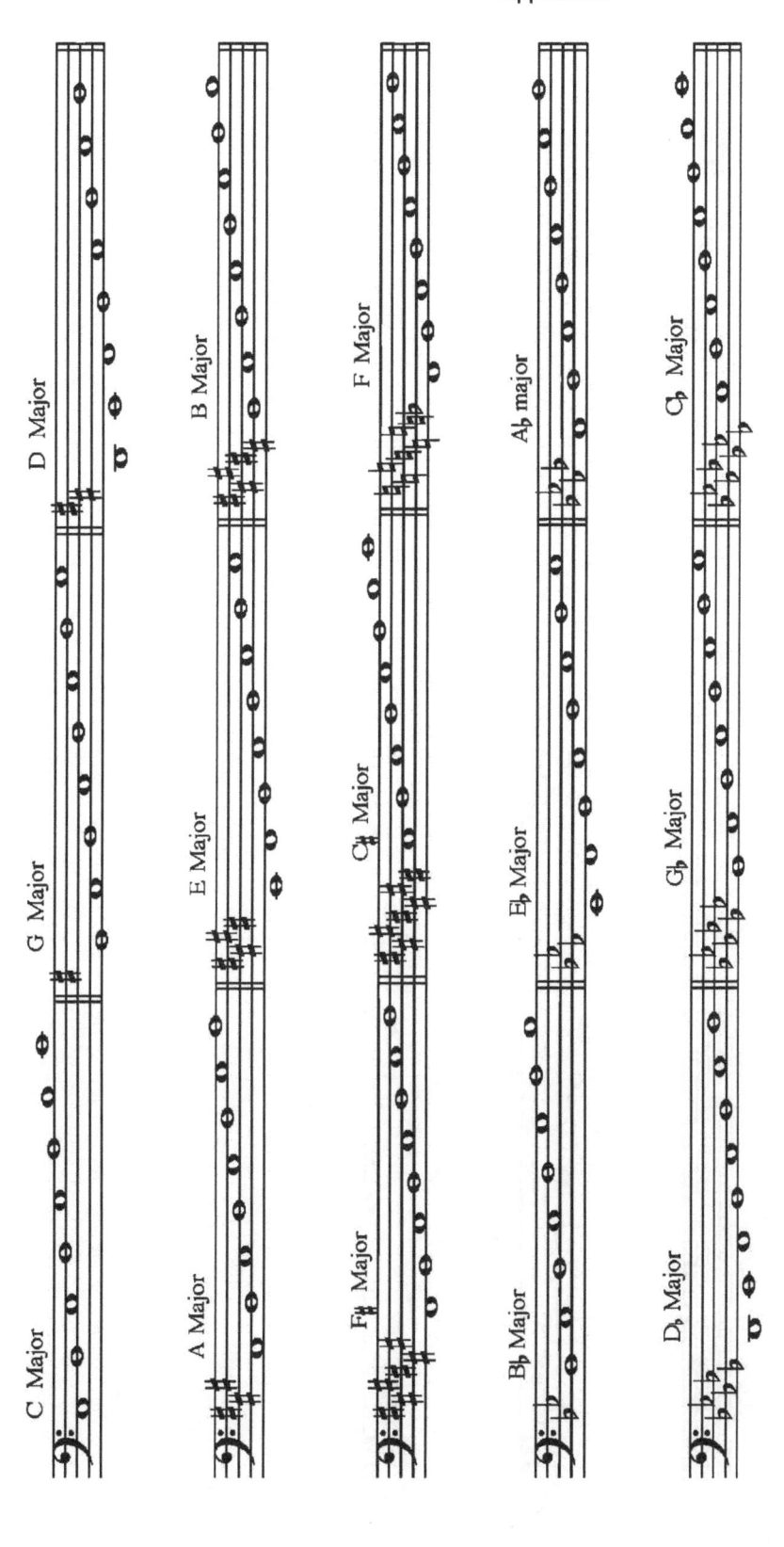

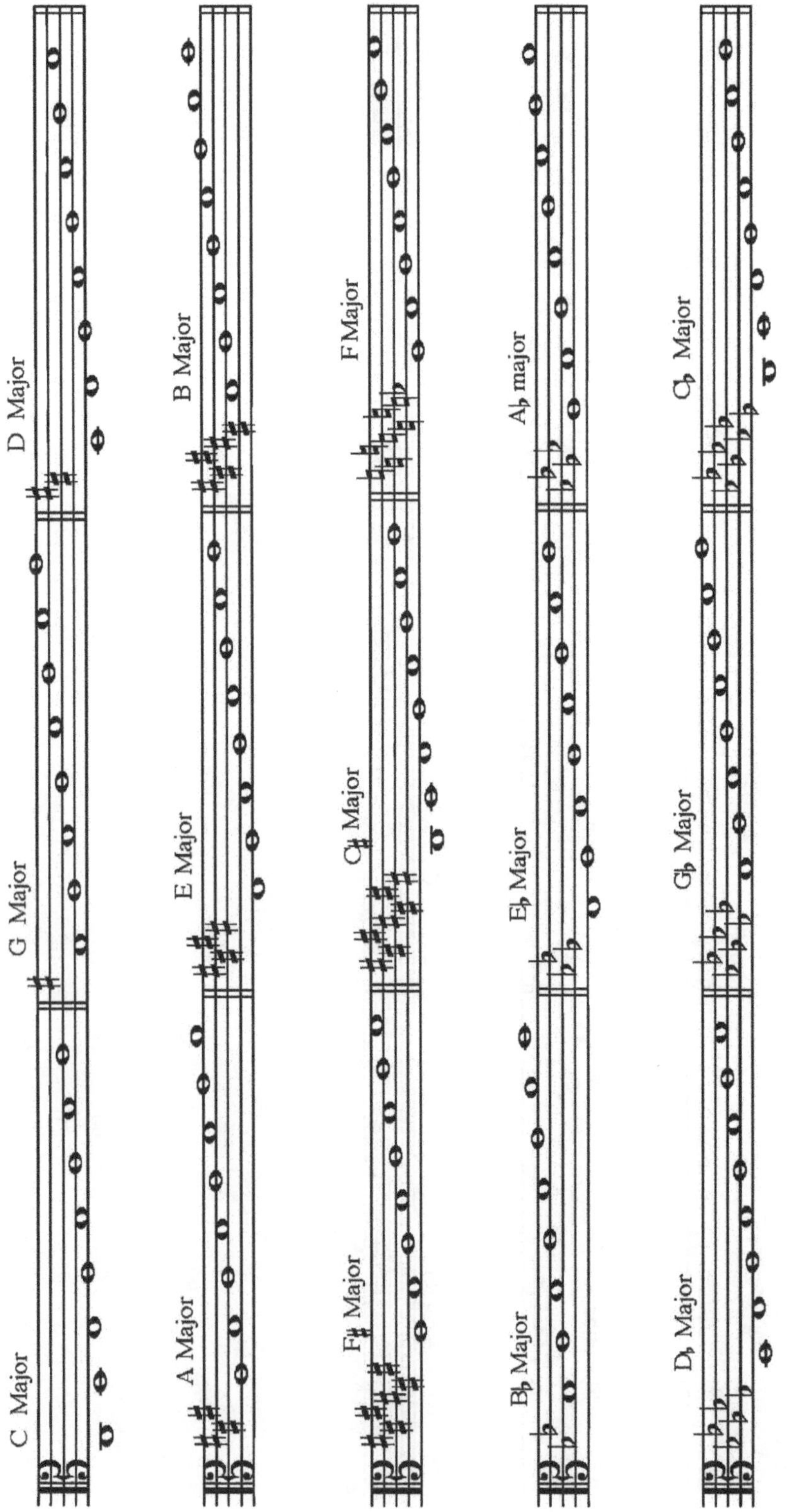
C Major
G Major
D Major
A Major
E Major
B Major
F♯ Major
C♯ Major
F Major
B♭ Major
E♭ Major
A♭ major
D♭ Major
G♭ Major
C♭ Major

C Major
G Major
D Major
A Major
E Major
B Major
F♯ Major
C♯ Major
F Major
B♭ Major
E♭ Major
A♭ major
D♭ Major
G♭ Major
C♭ Major

Appendix VII

All Minor Scales in Four Clefs

Appendices

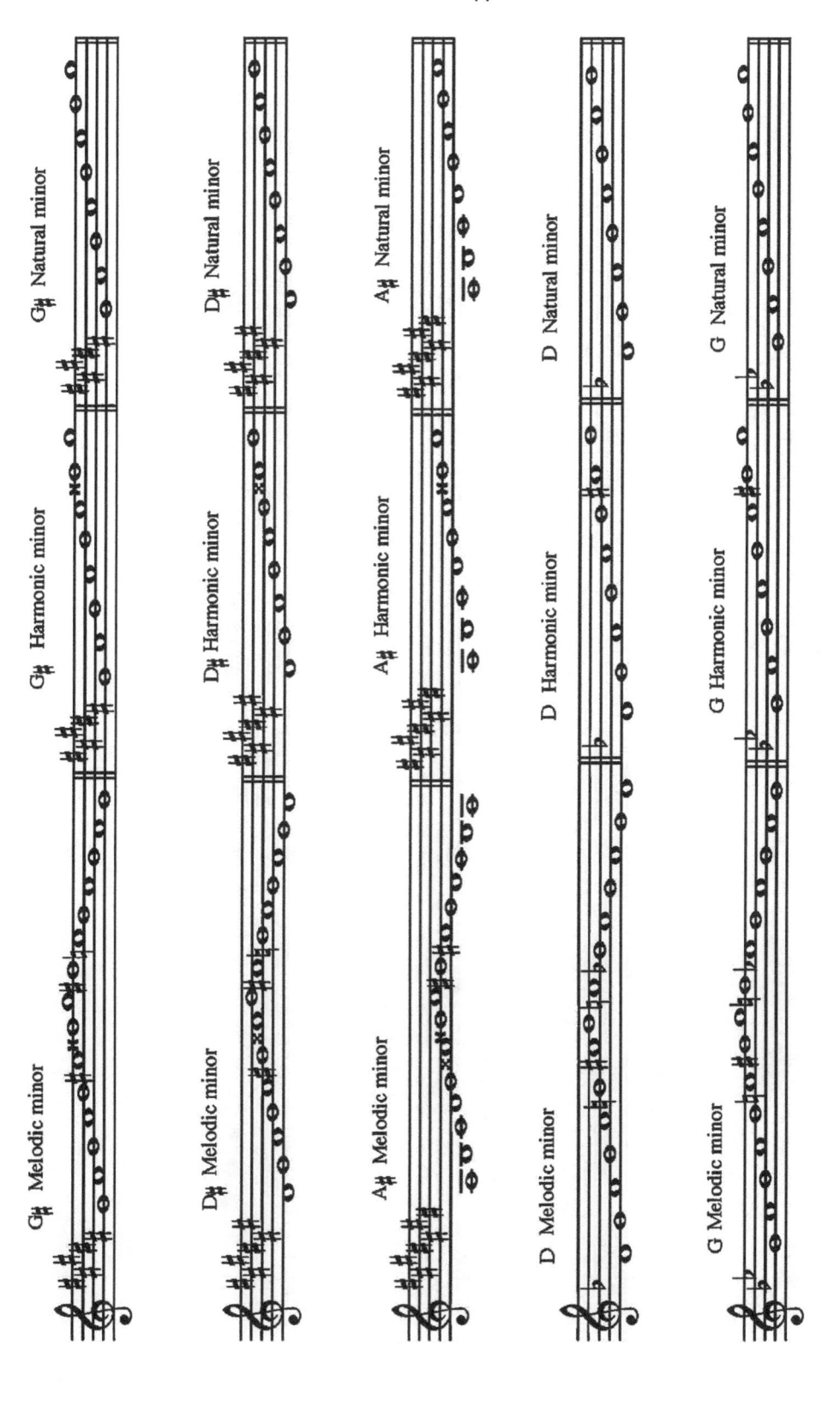

Appendices

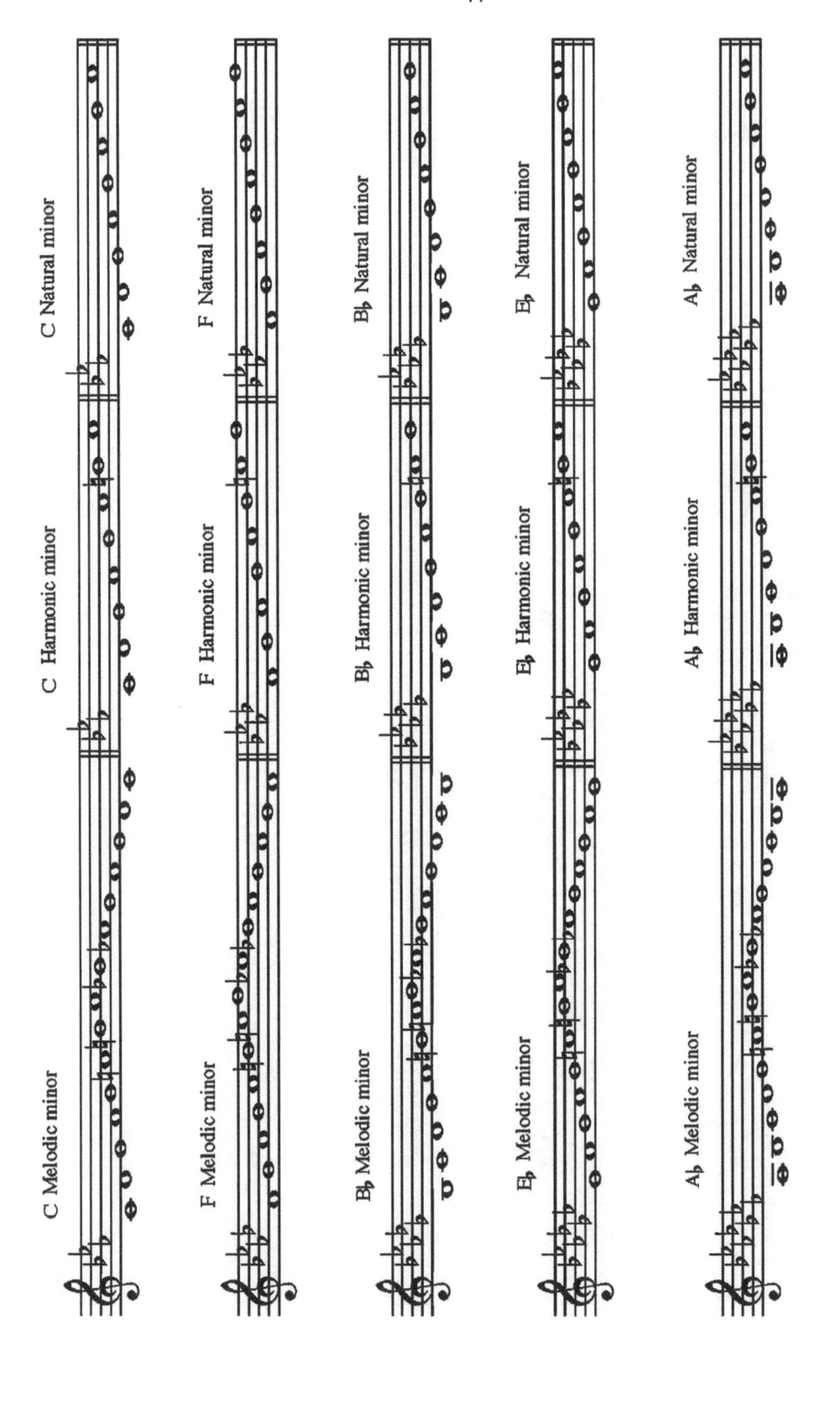

Appendices

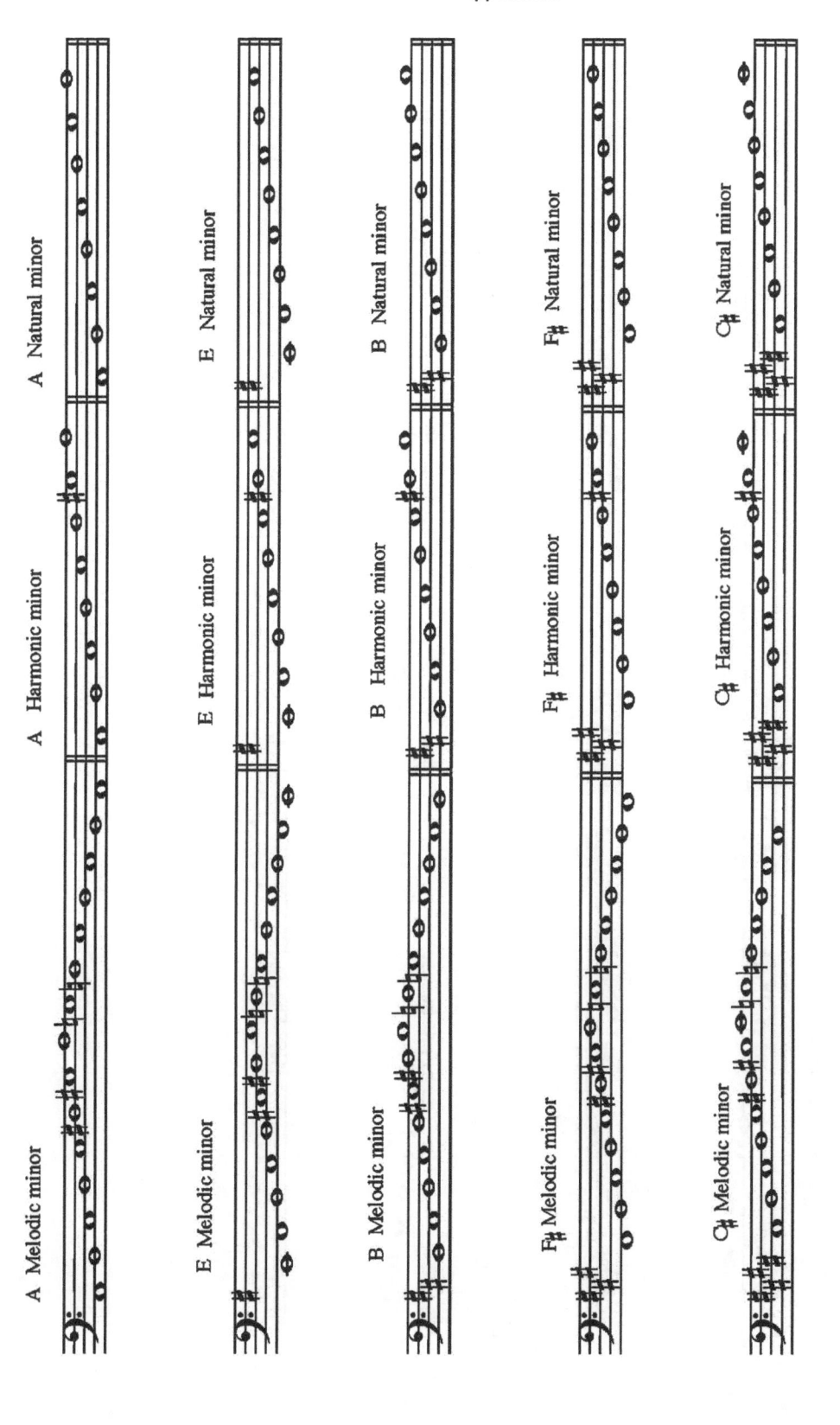

Appendices

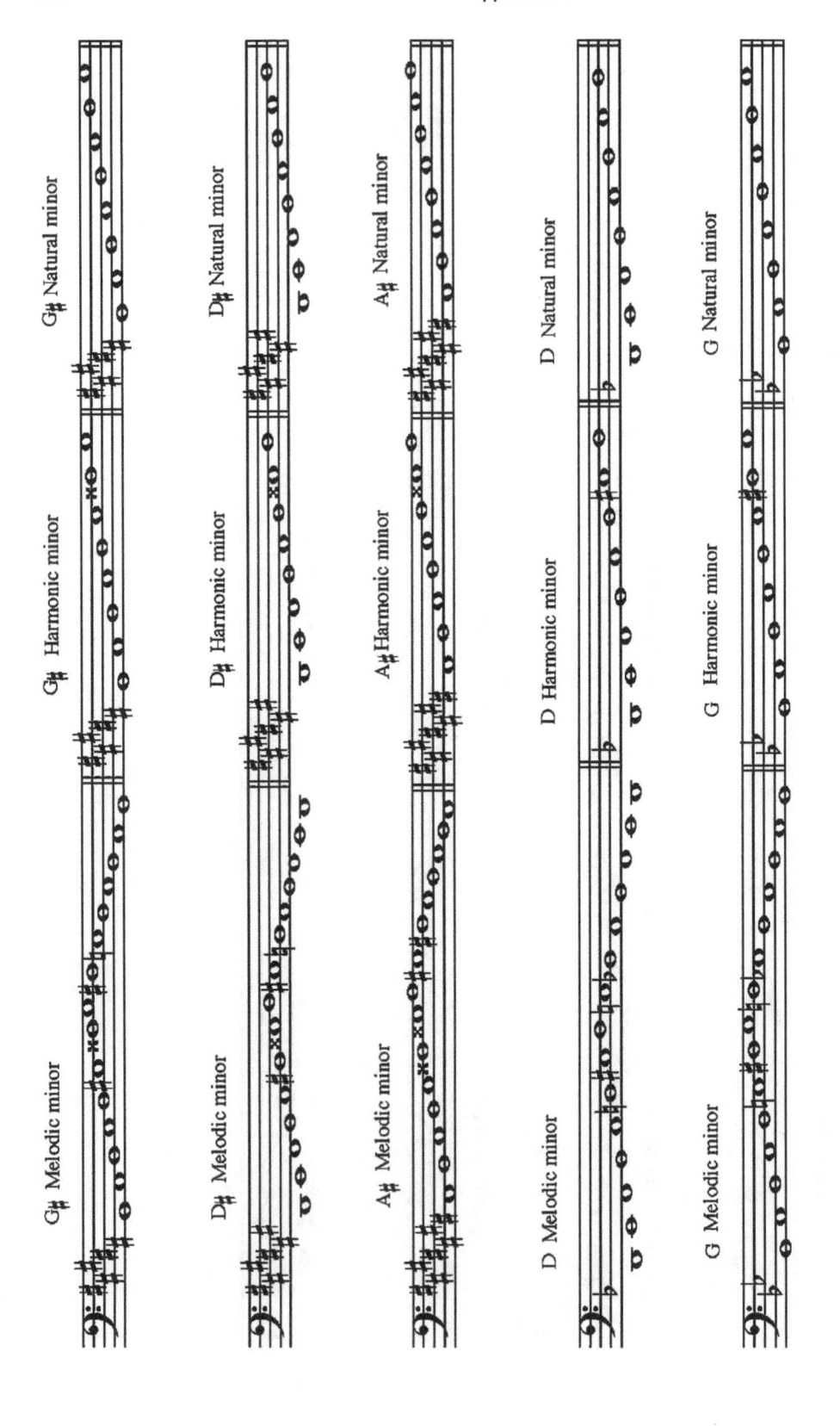

Appendices

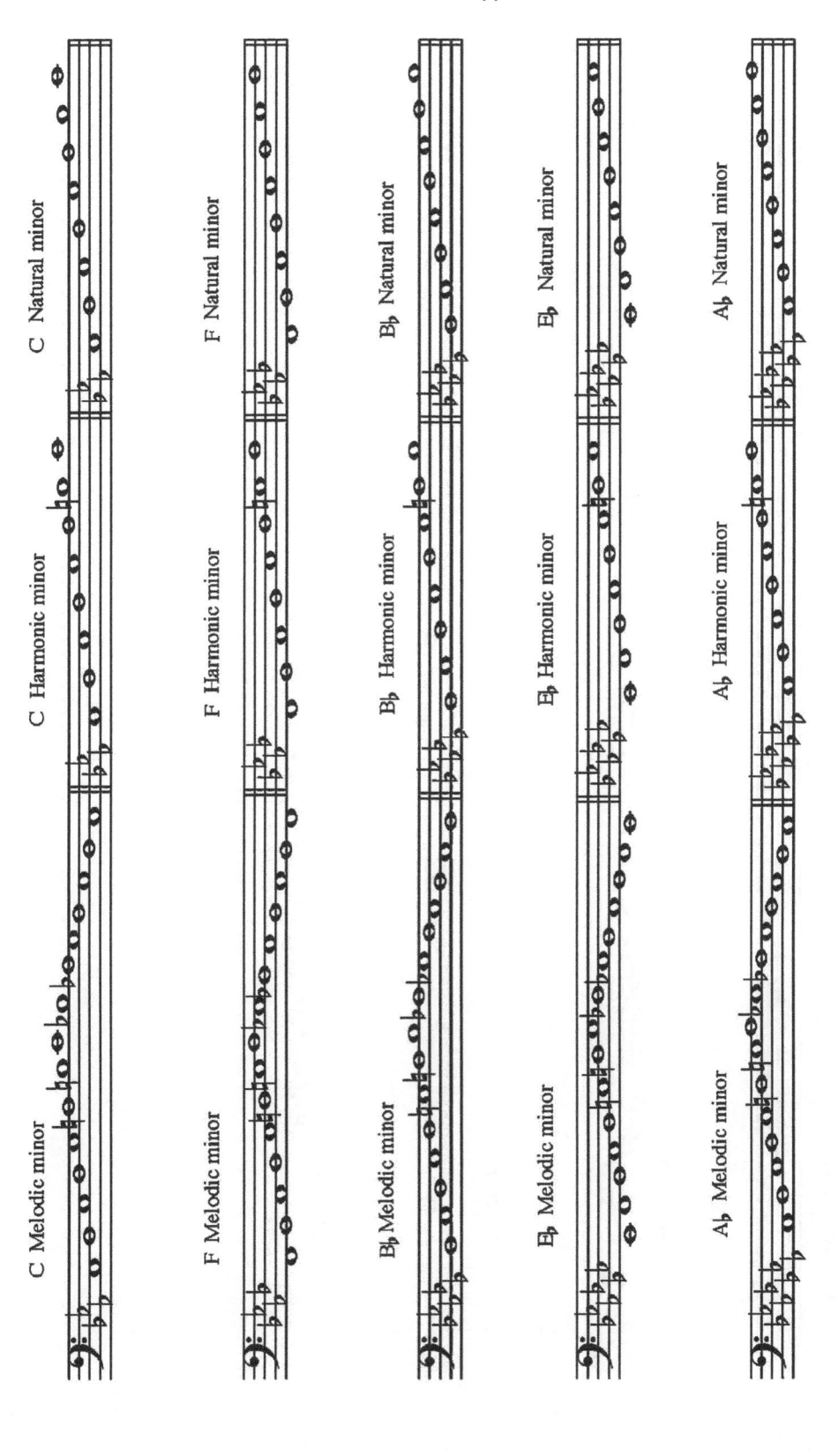

372 Appendices

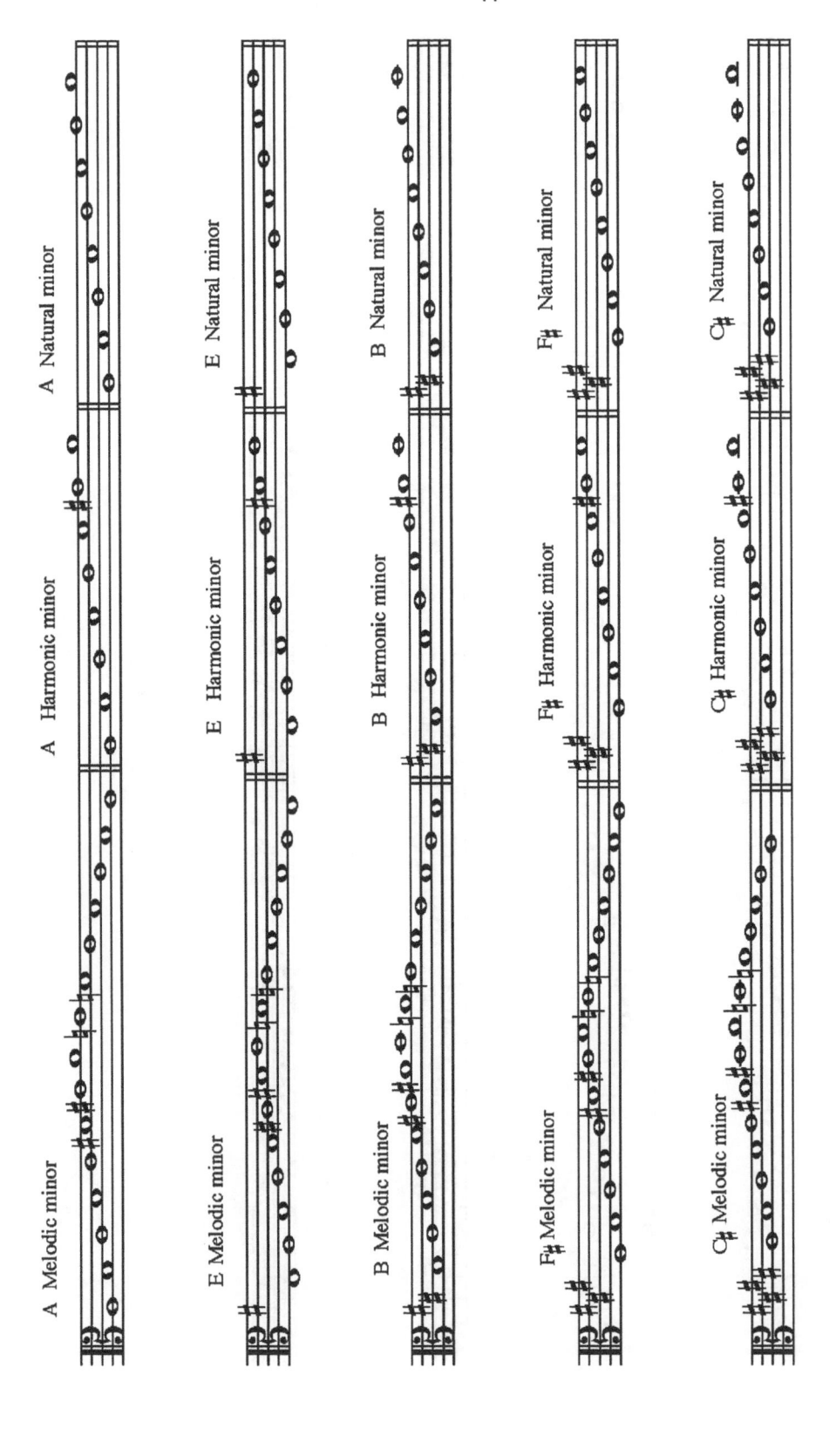

Appendices

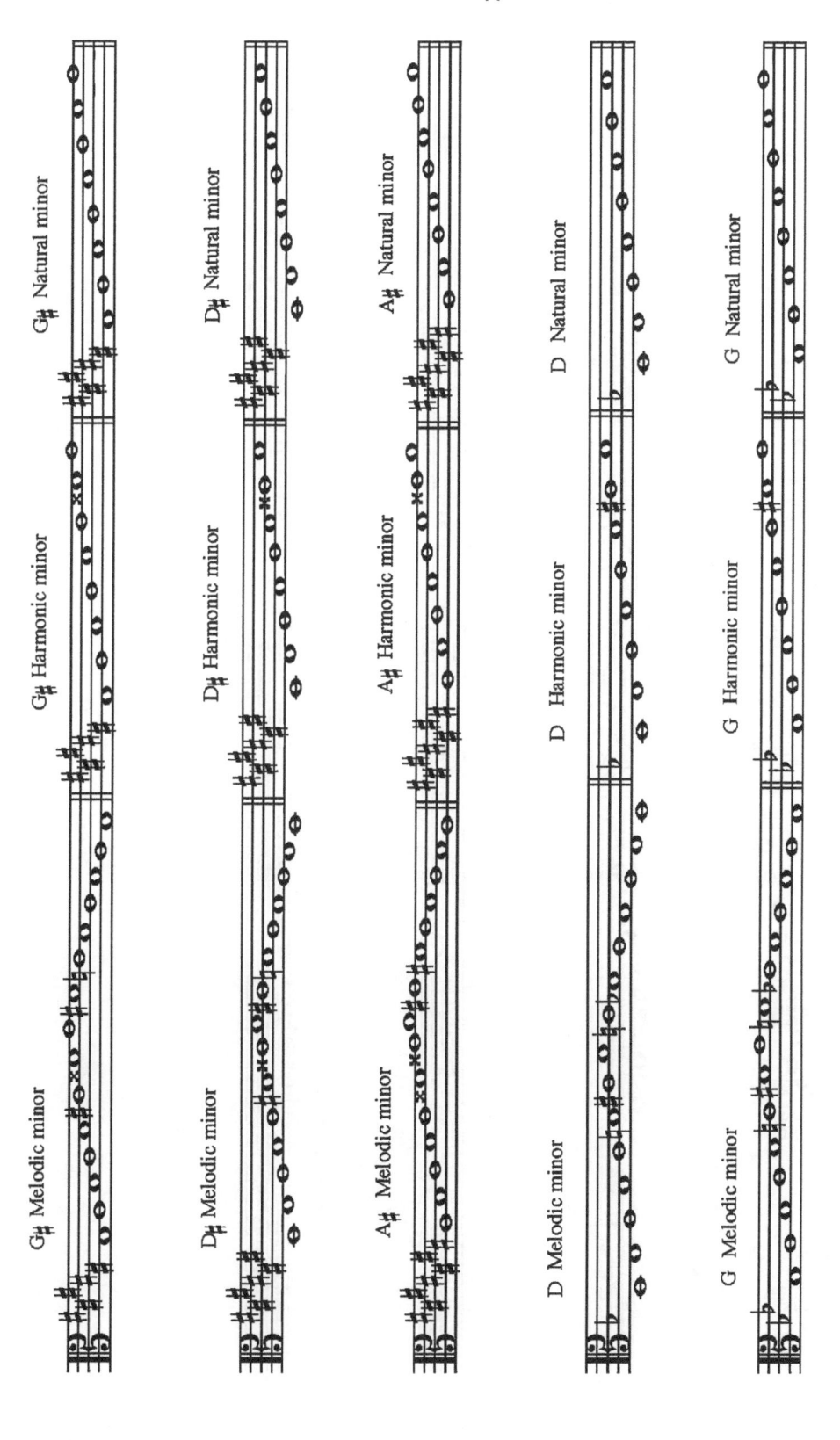

Appendices

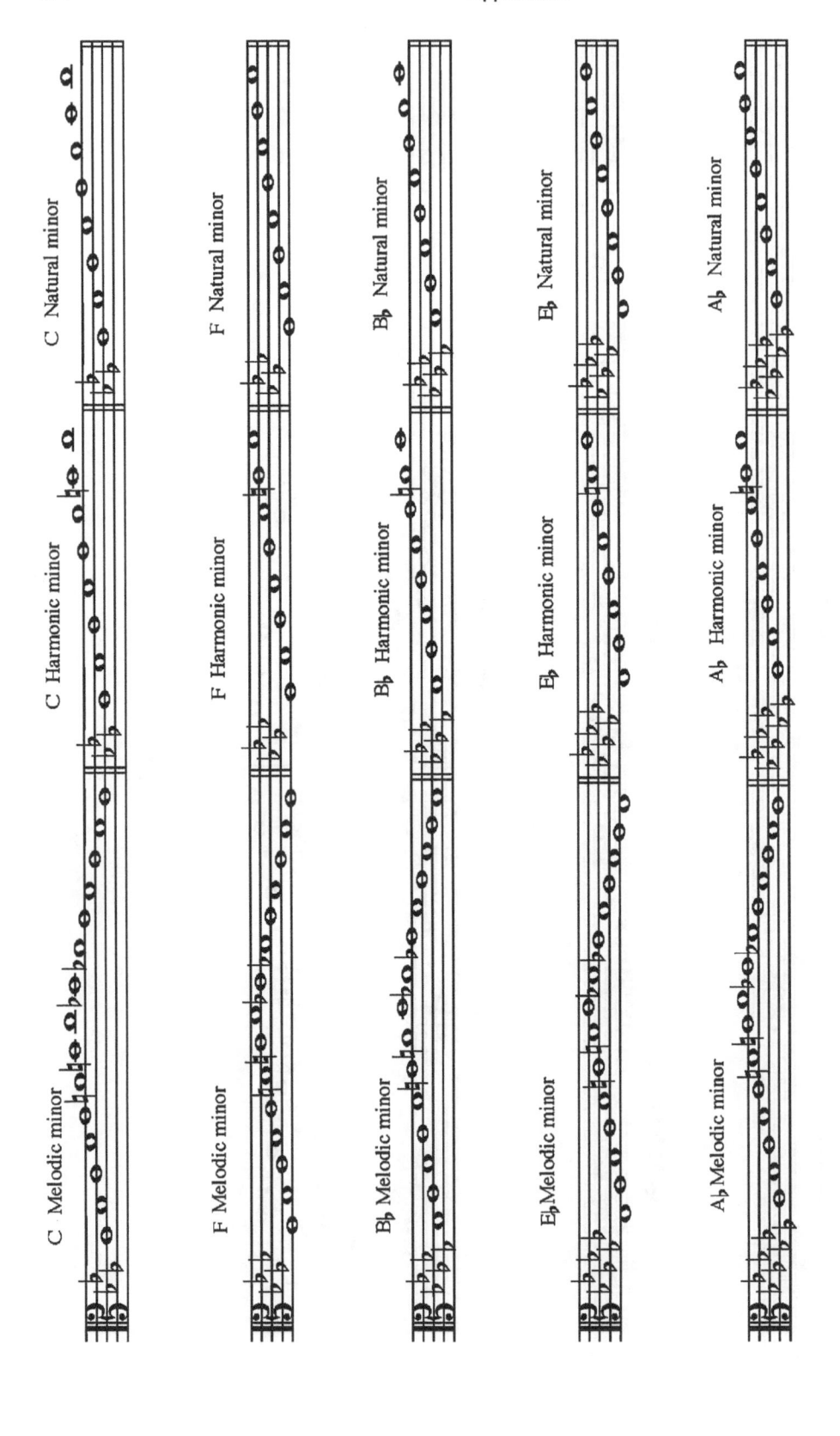

Appendices

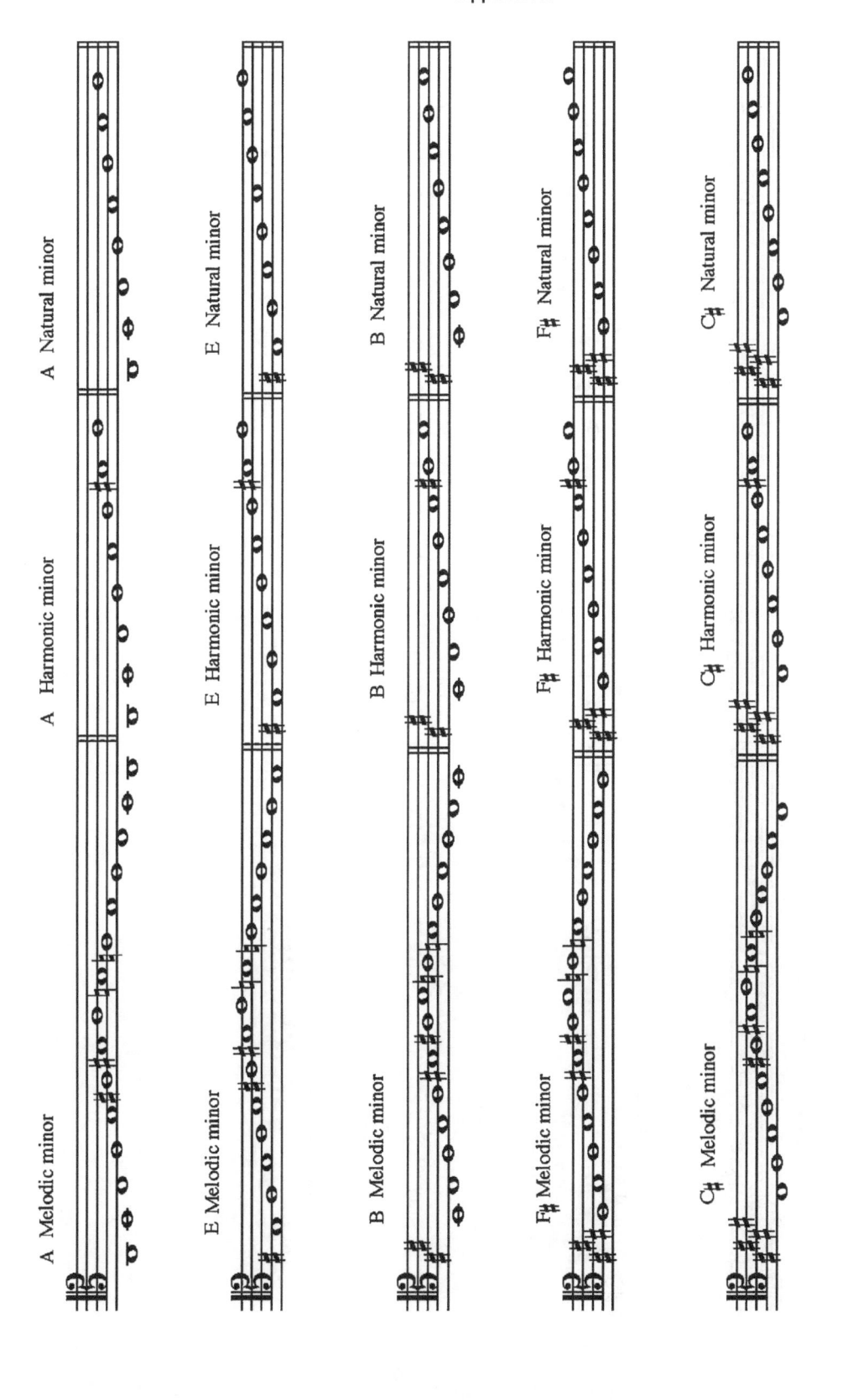

Appendices

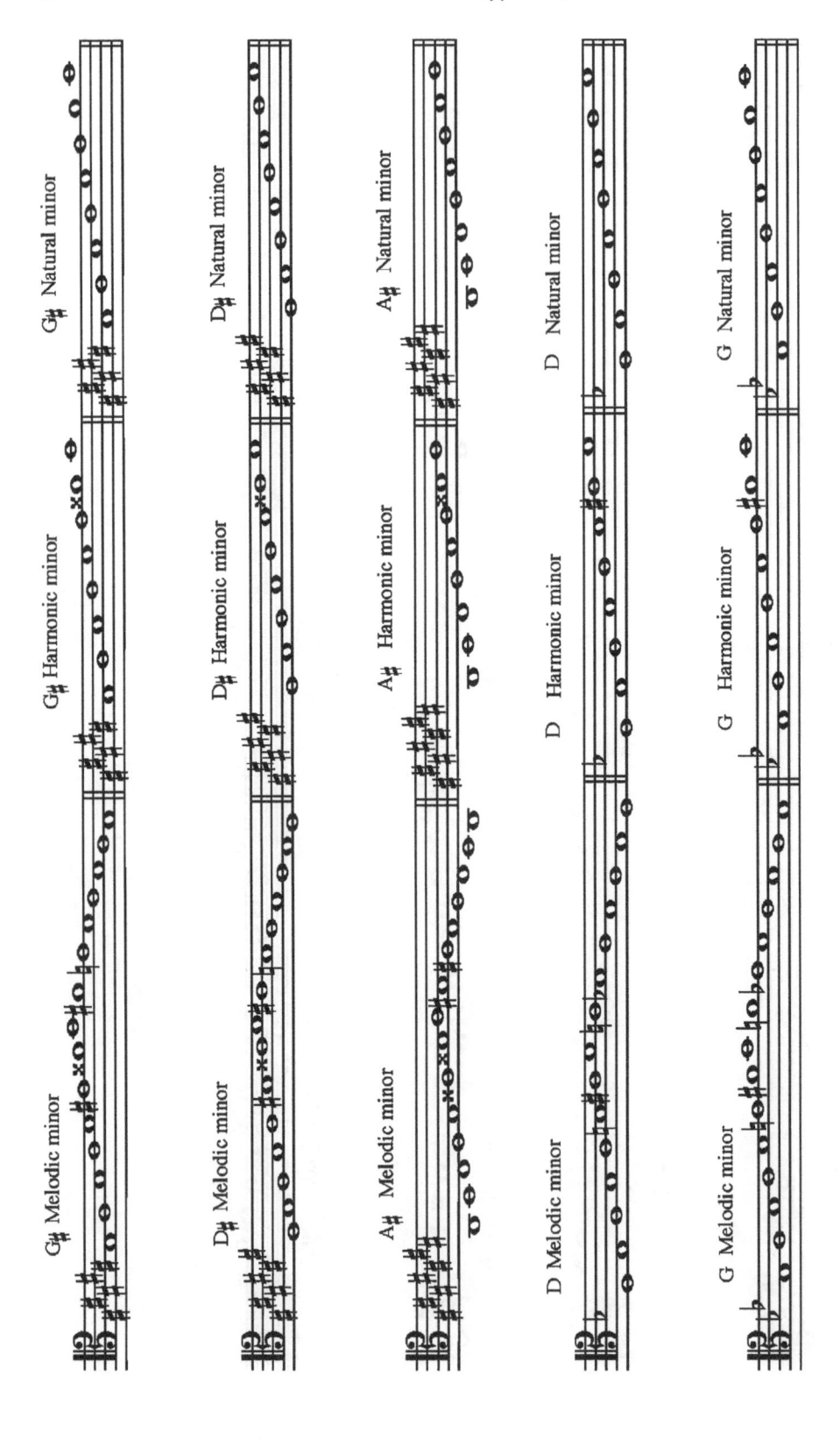

Appendices

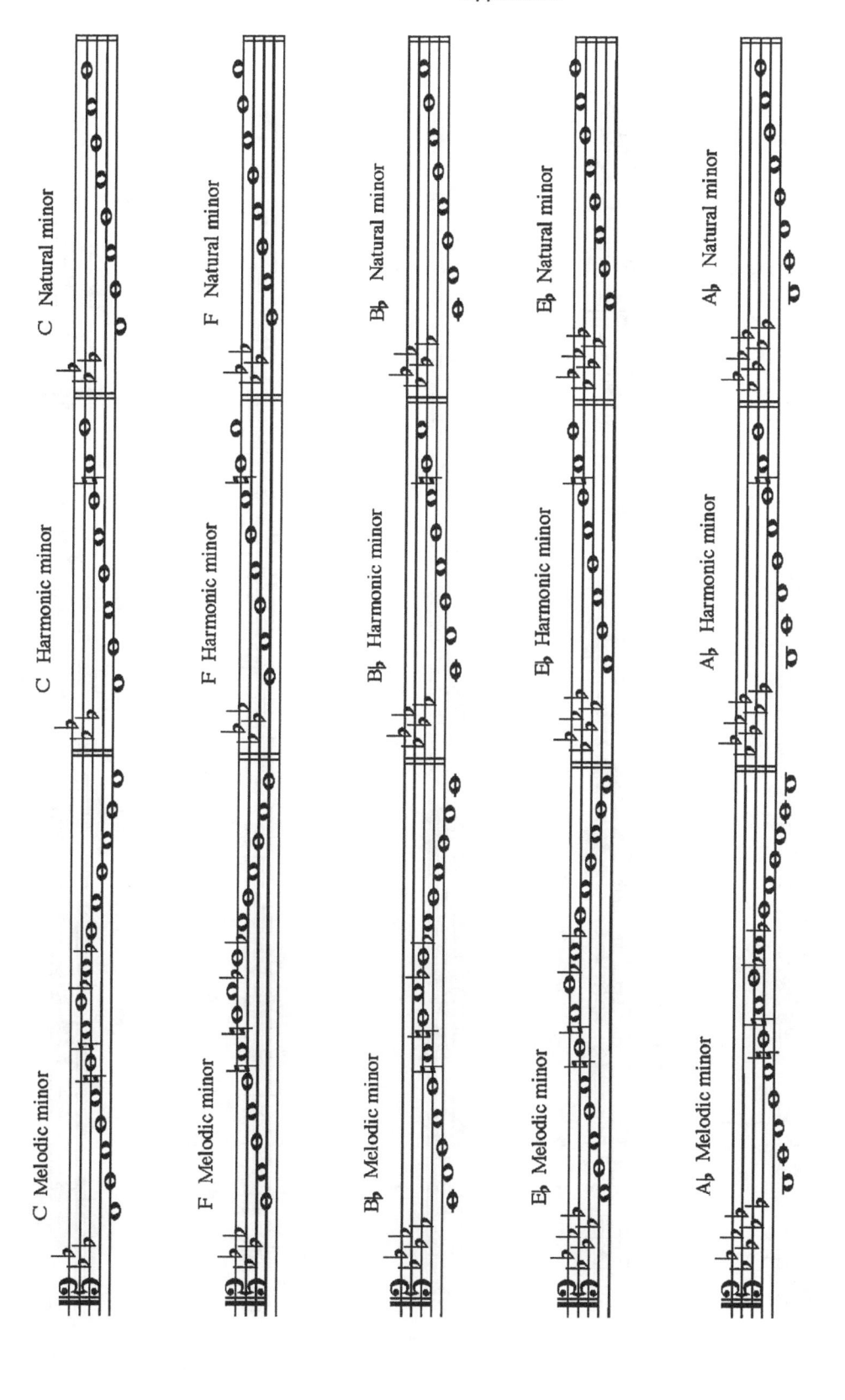

Appendix VIII

Inversions of All Triads on All Pitches in Two Clefs

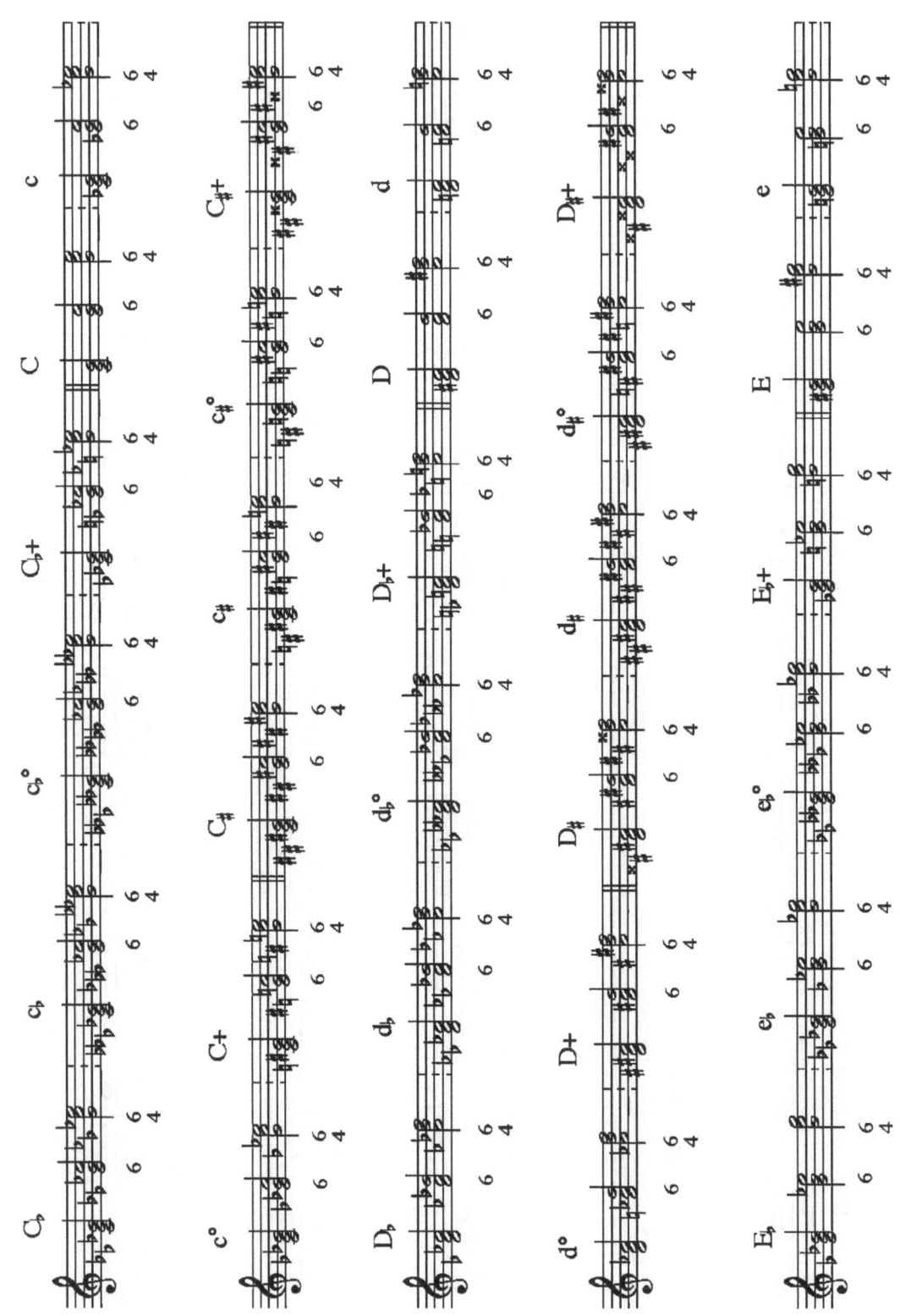

Appendices

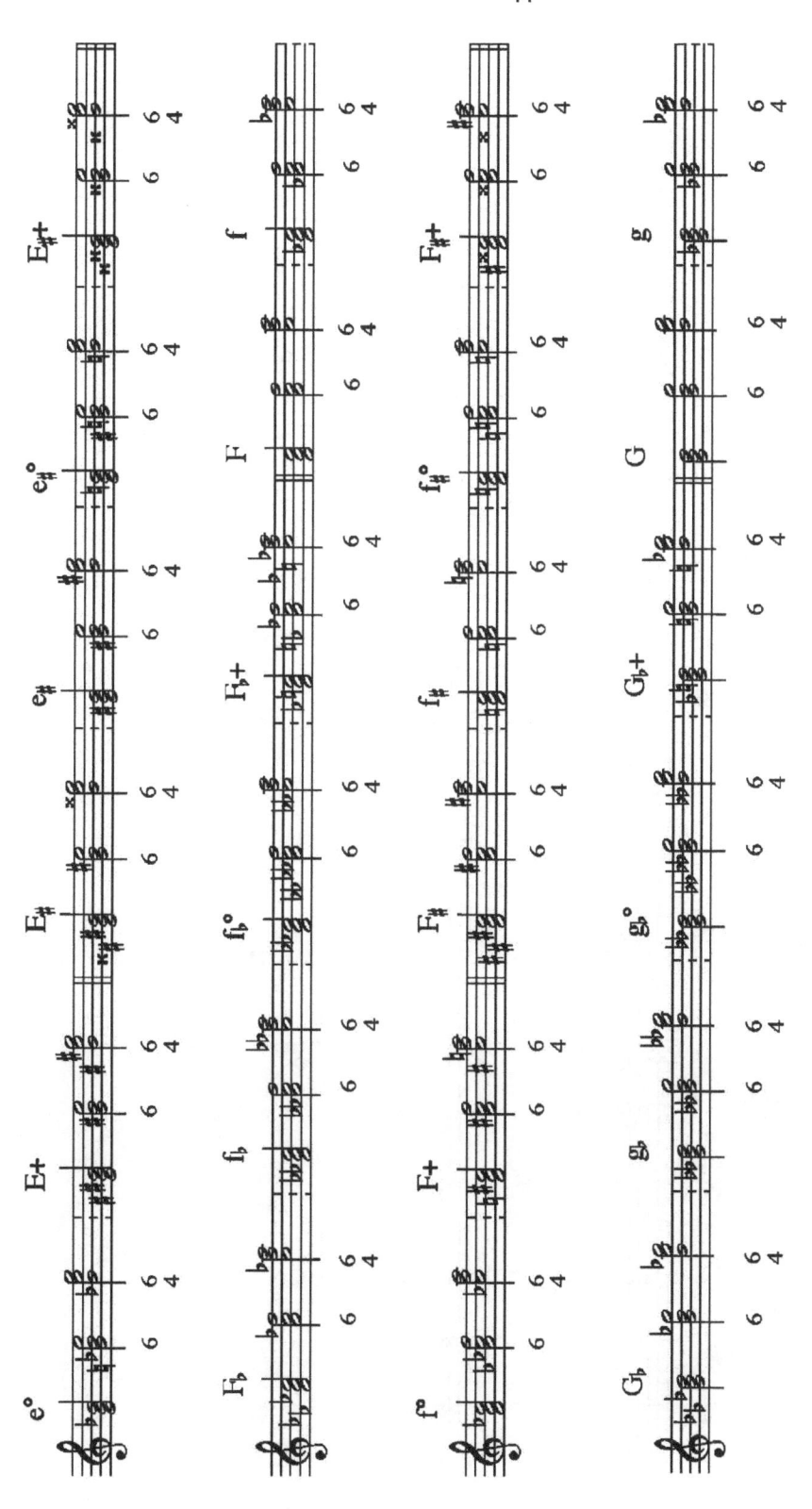

Appendices

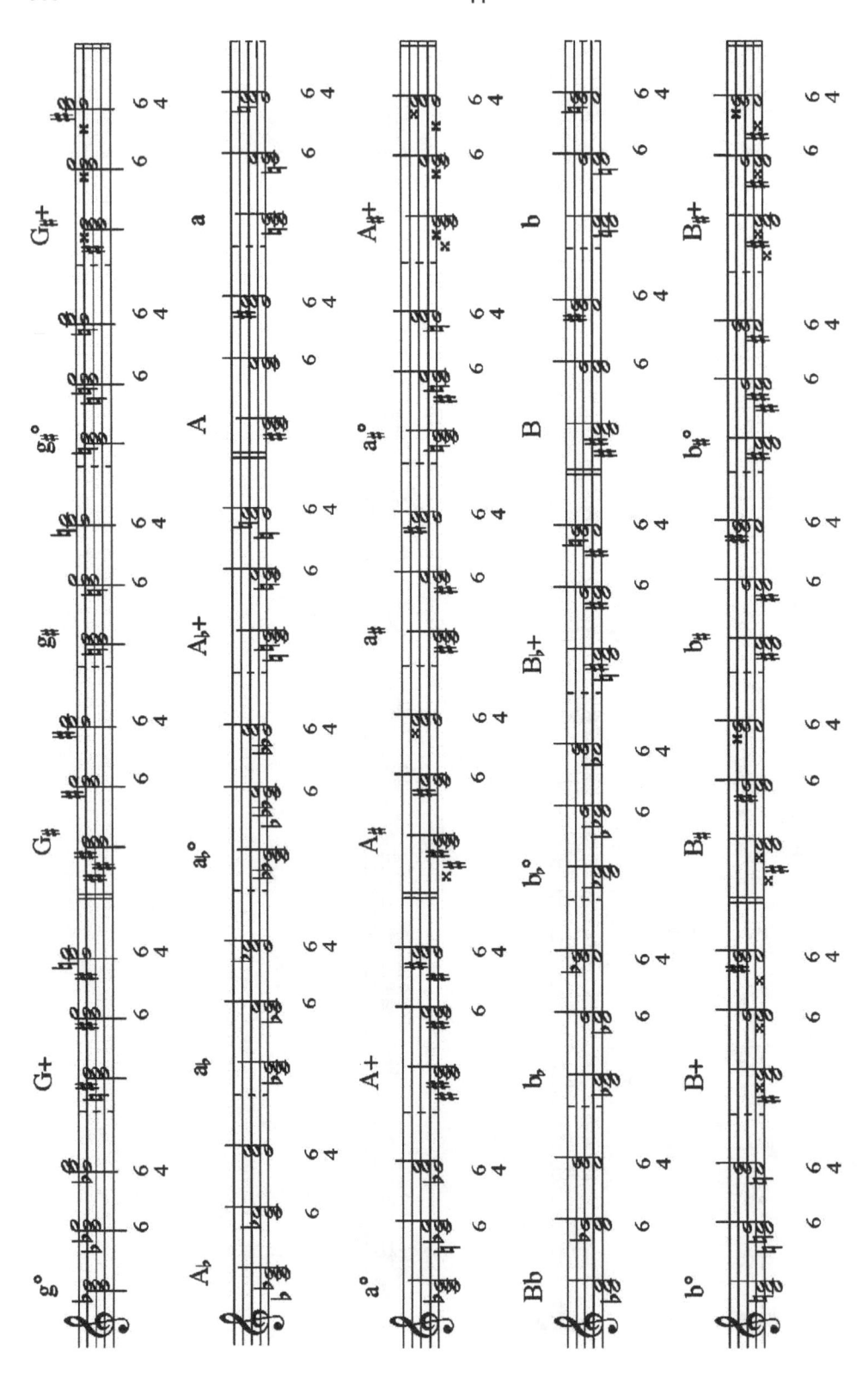

Appendices

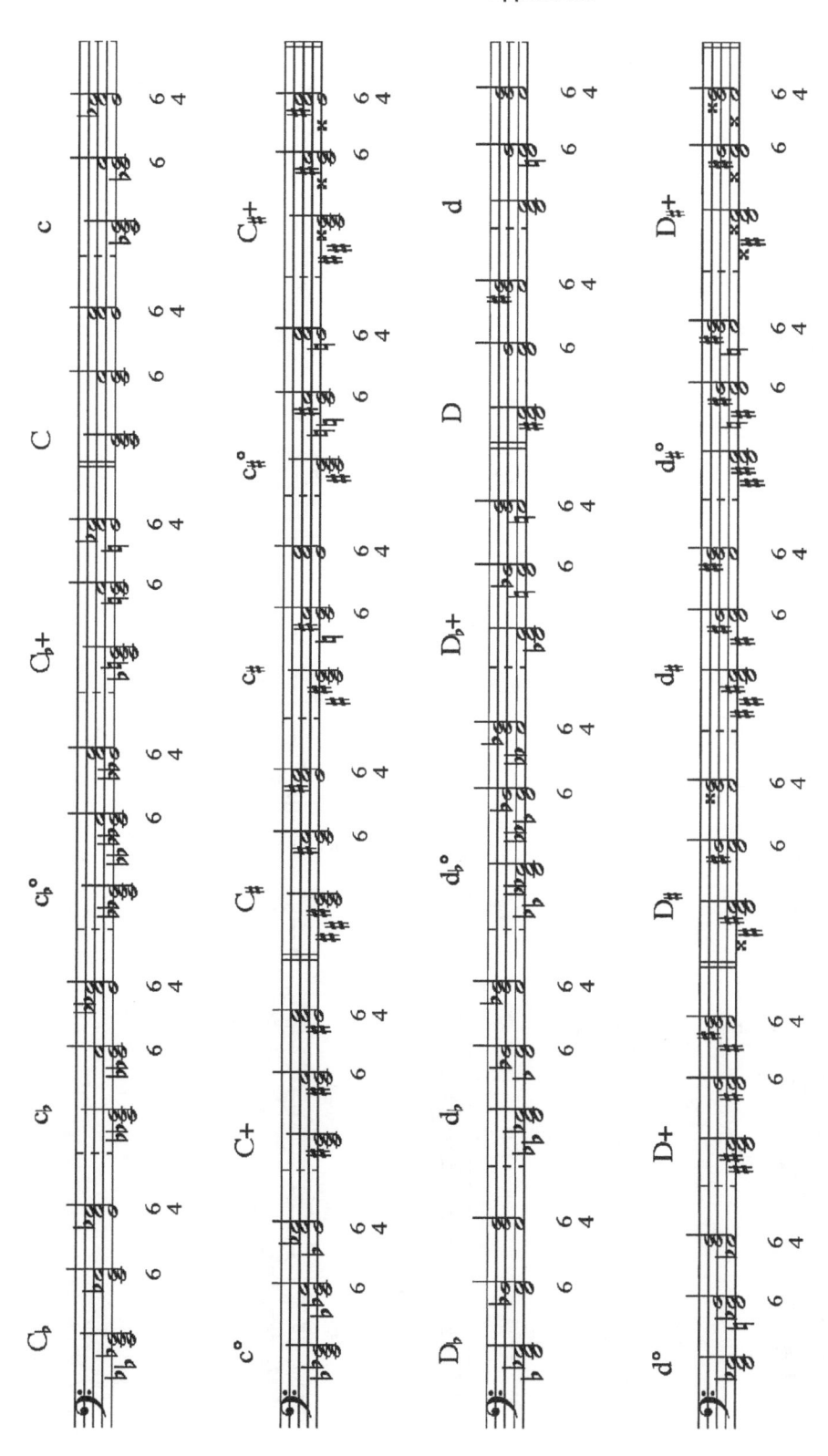

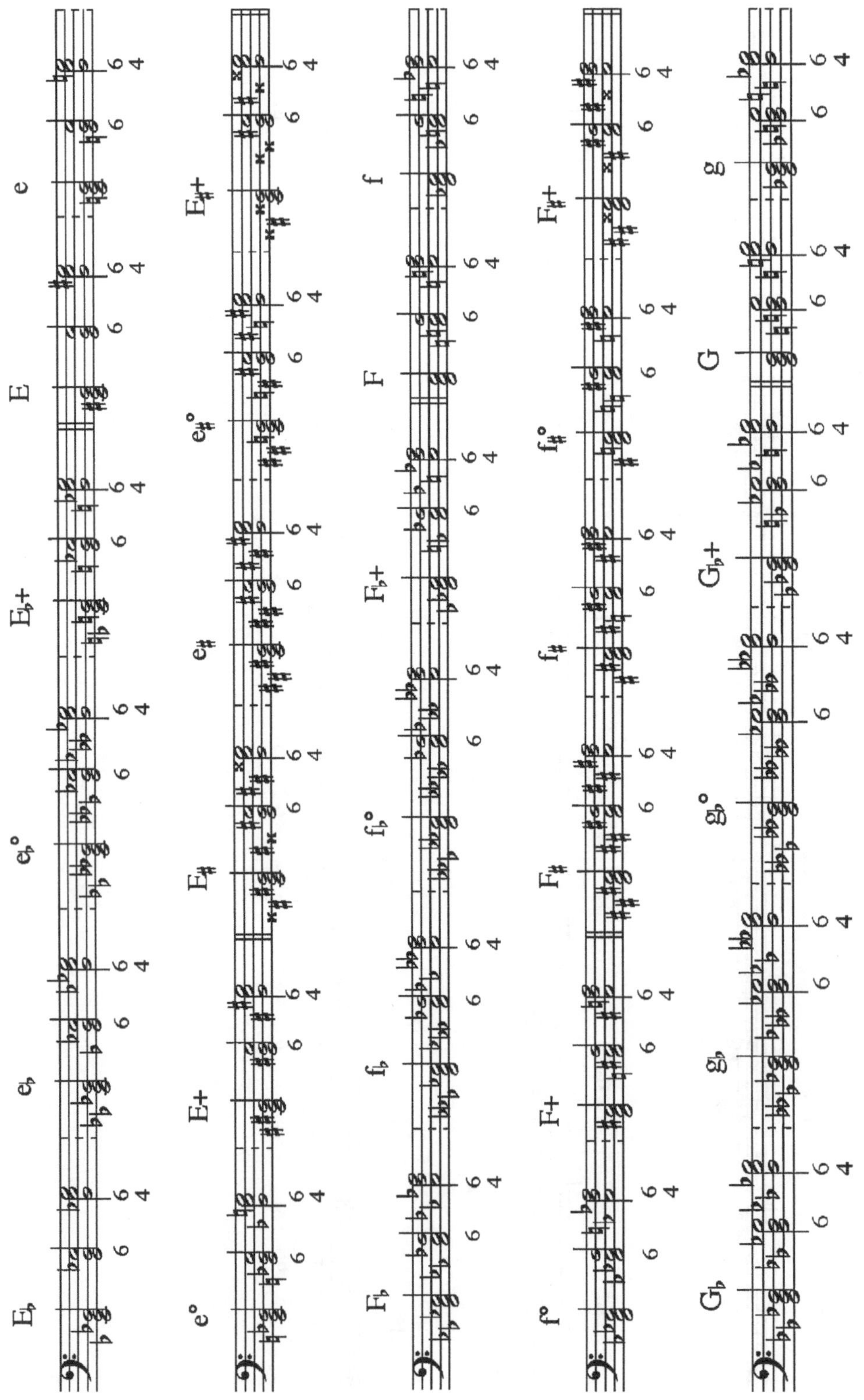
E♭ e♭ e♭° E♭+ E e
e° E+ E♯ e♯ e♯° E♯+
F♭ f♭ f♭° F♭+ F f
f° F+ F♯ f♯ f♯° F♯+
G♭ g♭ g♭° G♭+ G g

Appendices 383

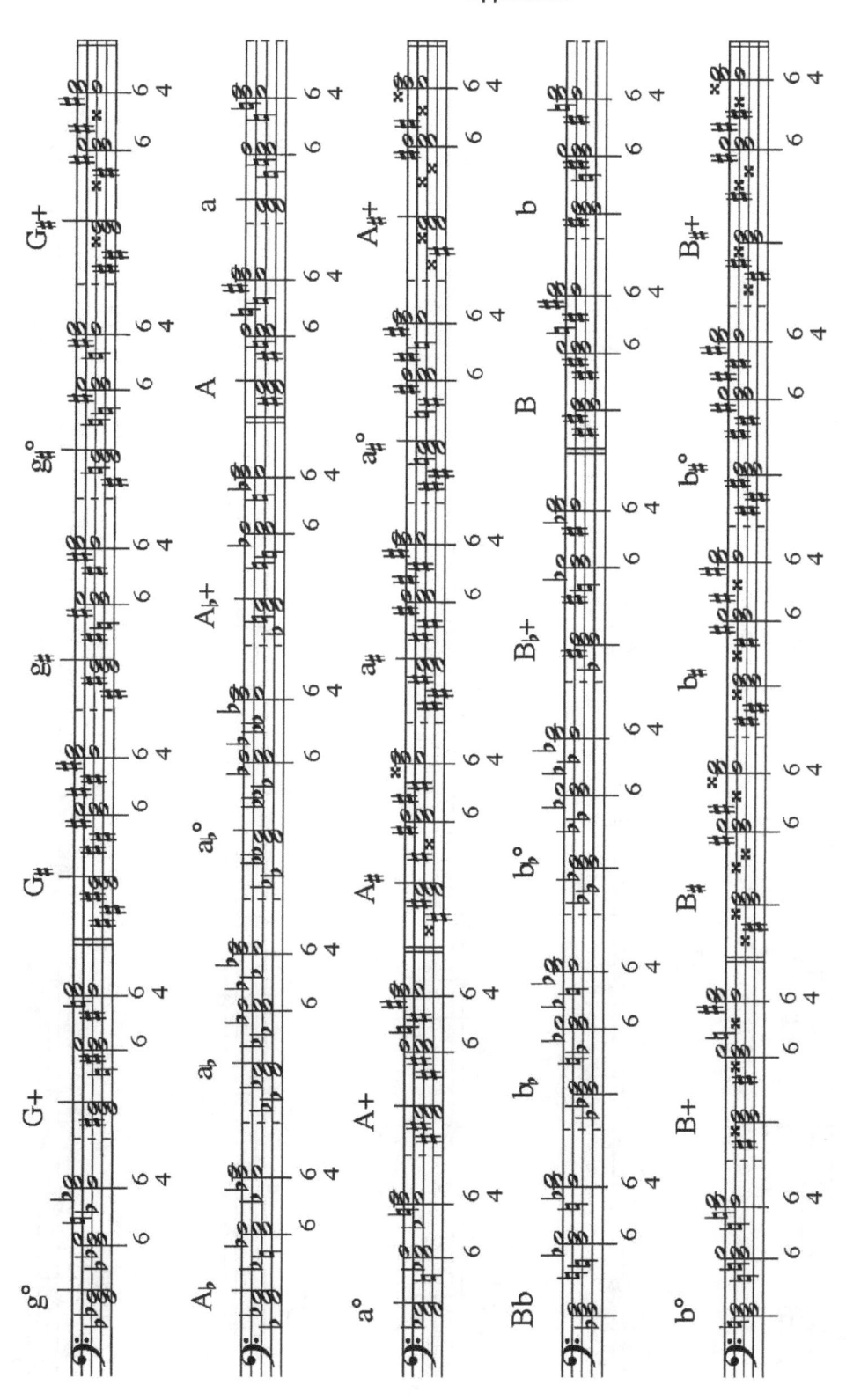

Appendix IX

Inversions of All Common Seventh Chords on All Pitches in Two Clefs

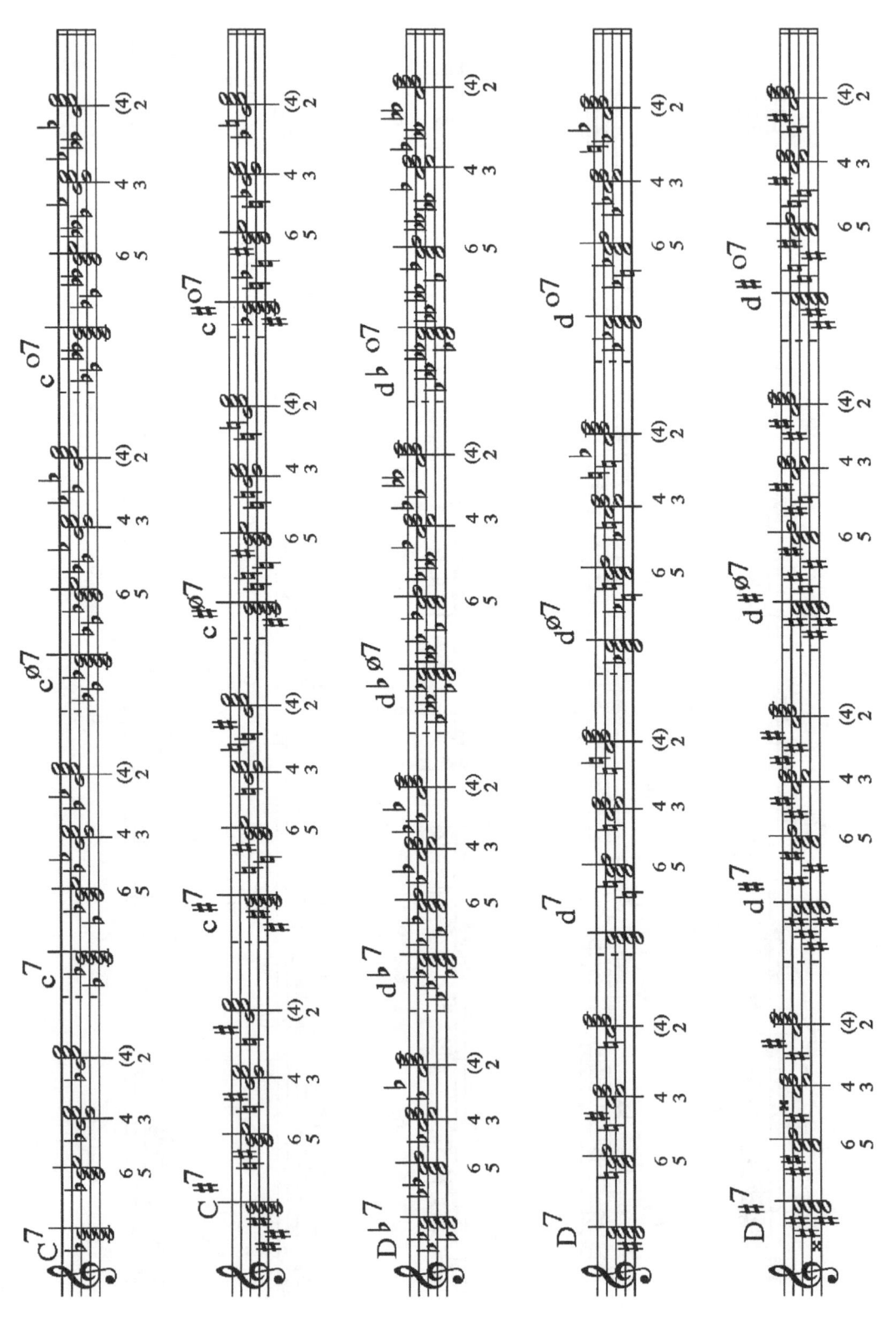

Appendices

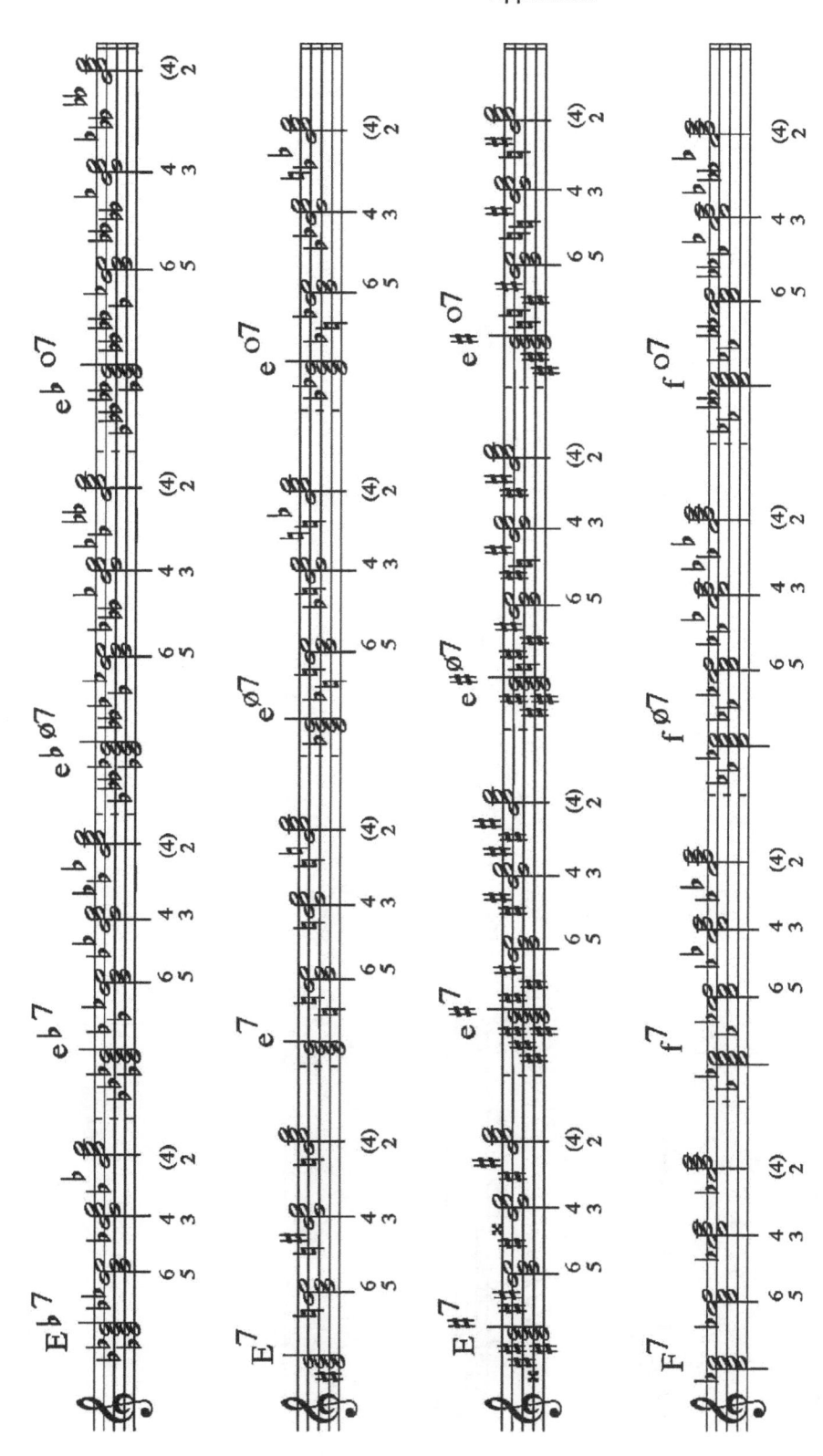

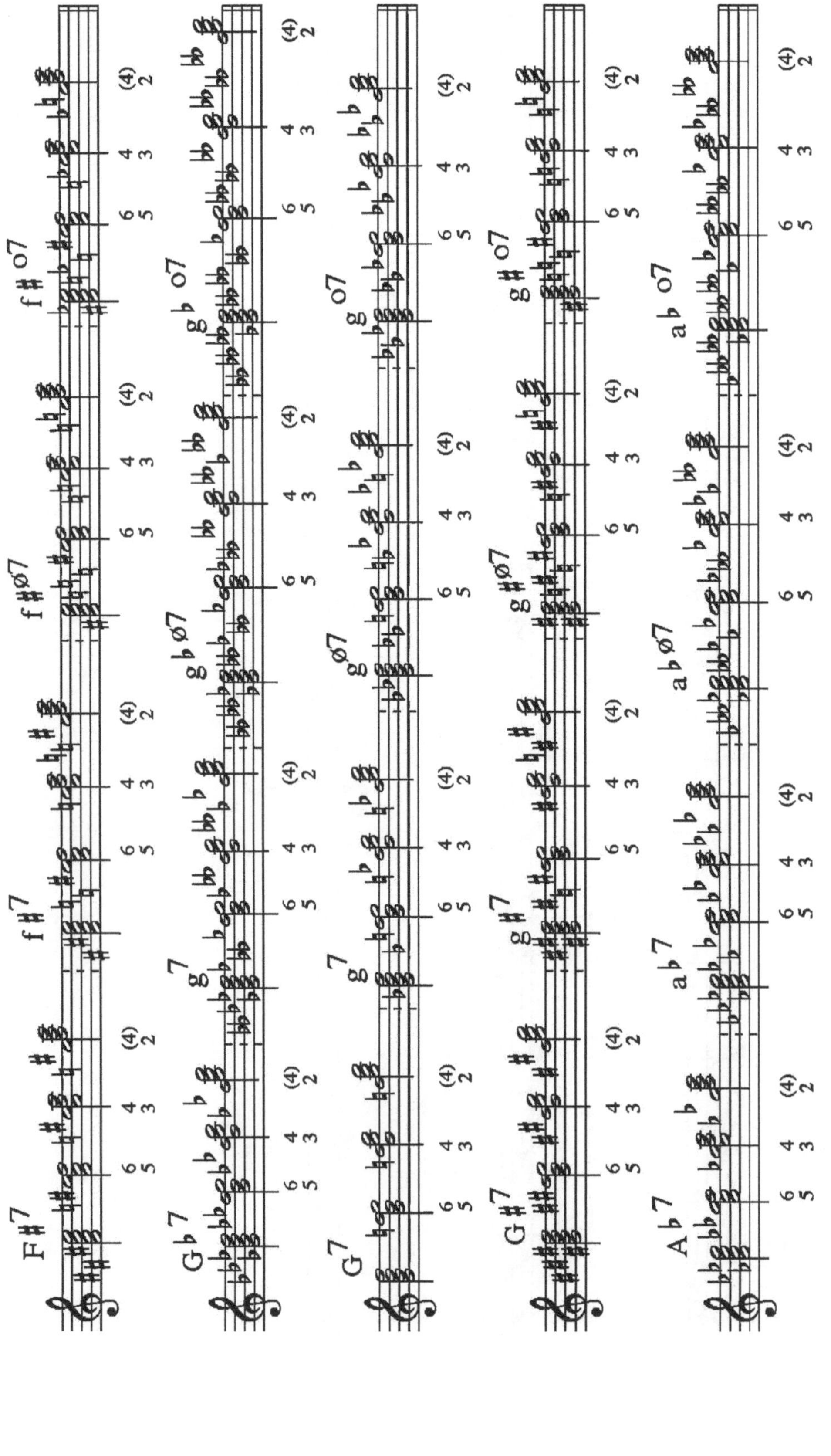
F♯7
f♯7
f♯ø7
f♯o7
G♭7
g♭ø7
g♭o7
G7
gø7
go7
G♯7
g♯7
g♯ø7
g♯o7
A♭7
a♭7
a♭ø7
a♭o7

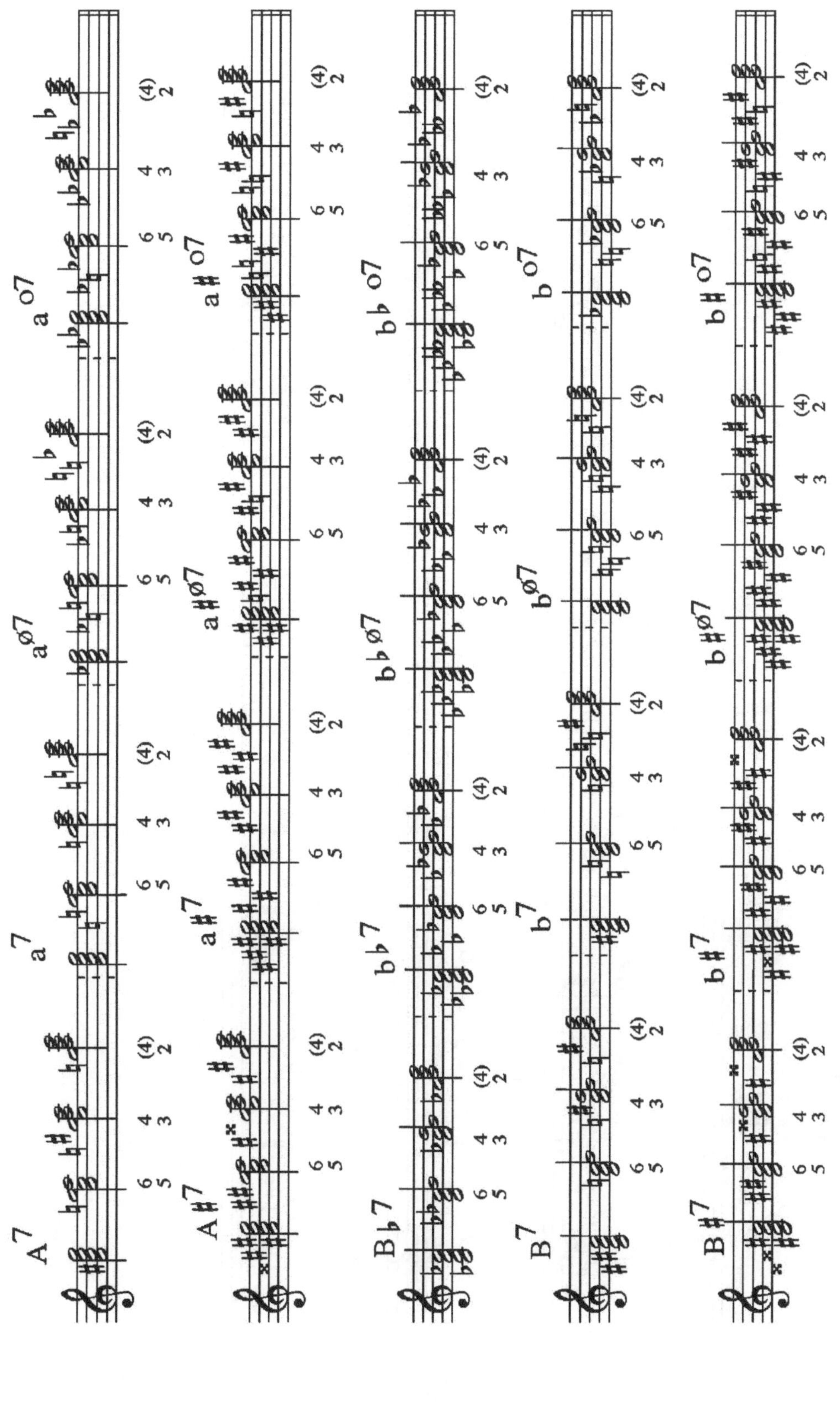
A7
a7
aø7
ao7
A♯7
a♯7
a♯ø7
a♯o7
B♭7
b♭7
b♭ø7
b♭o7
B7
b7
bø7
bo7
B♯7
b♯7
b♯ø7
b♯o7

Appendices

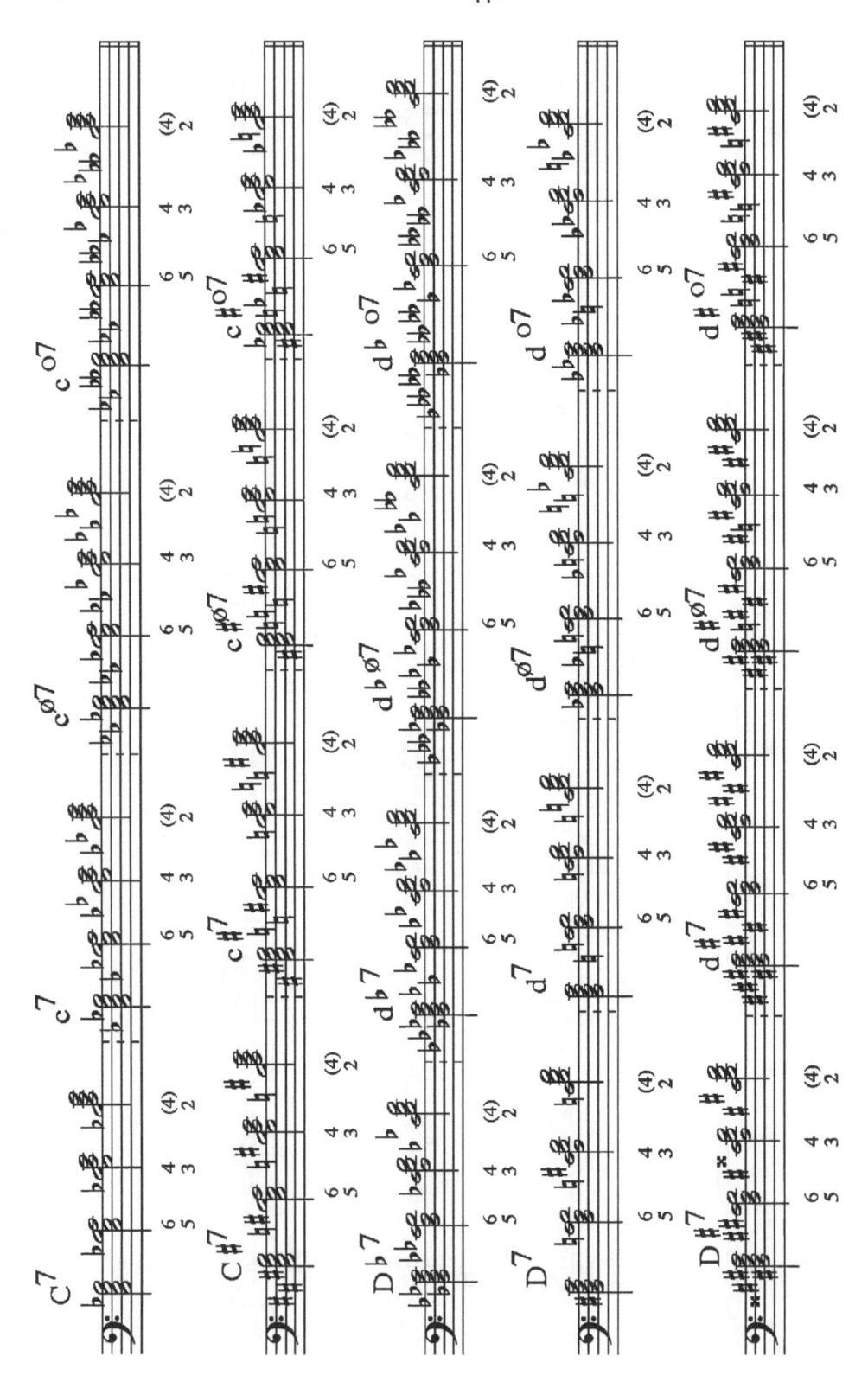

Appendices

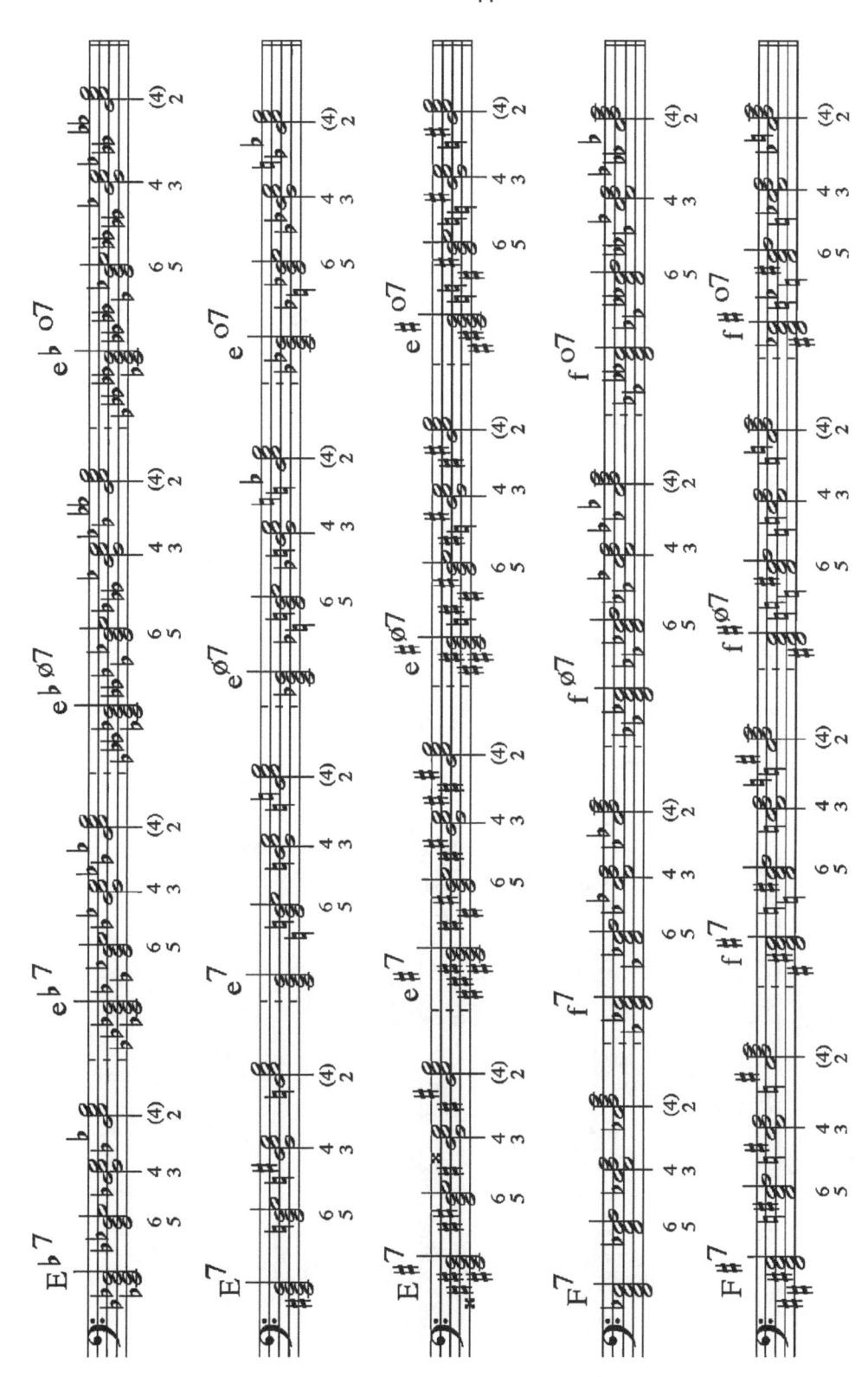

Appendices

Appendices

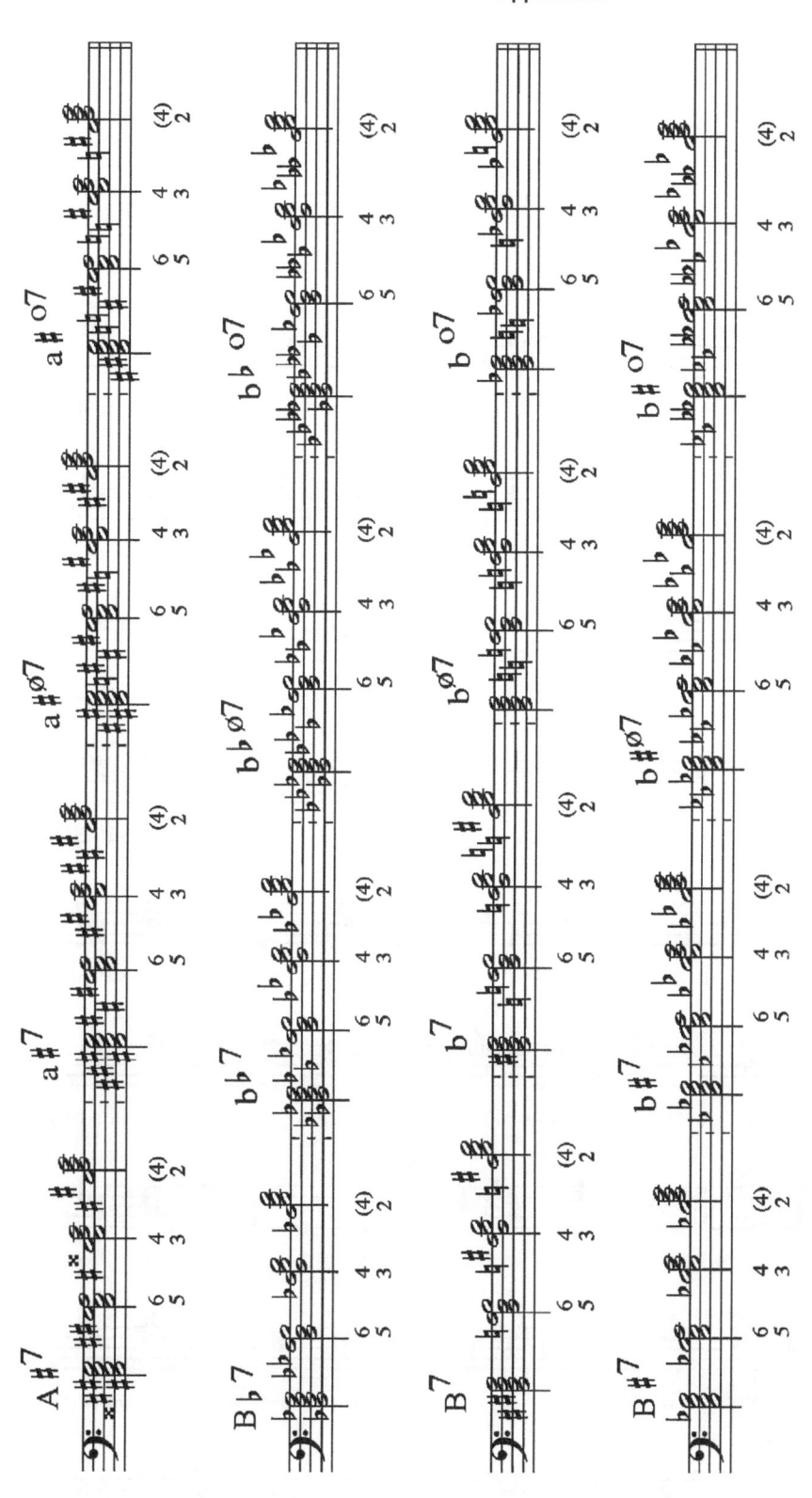

Appendix X

Primary Chords in All Major and Minor Keys in Two Clefs

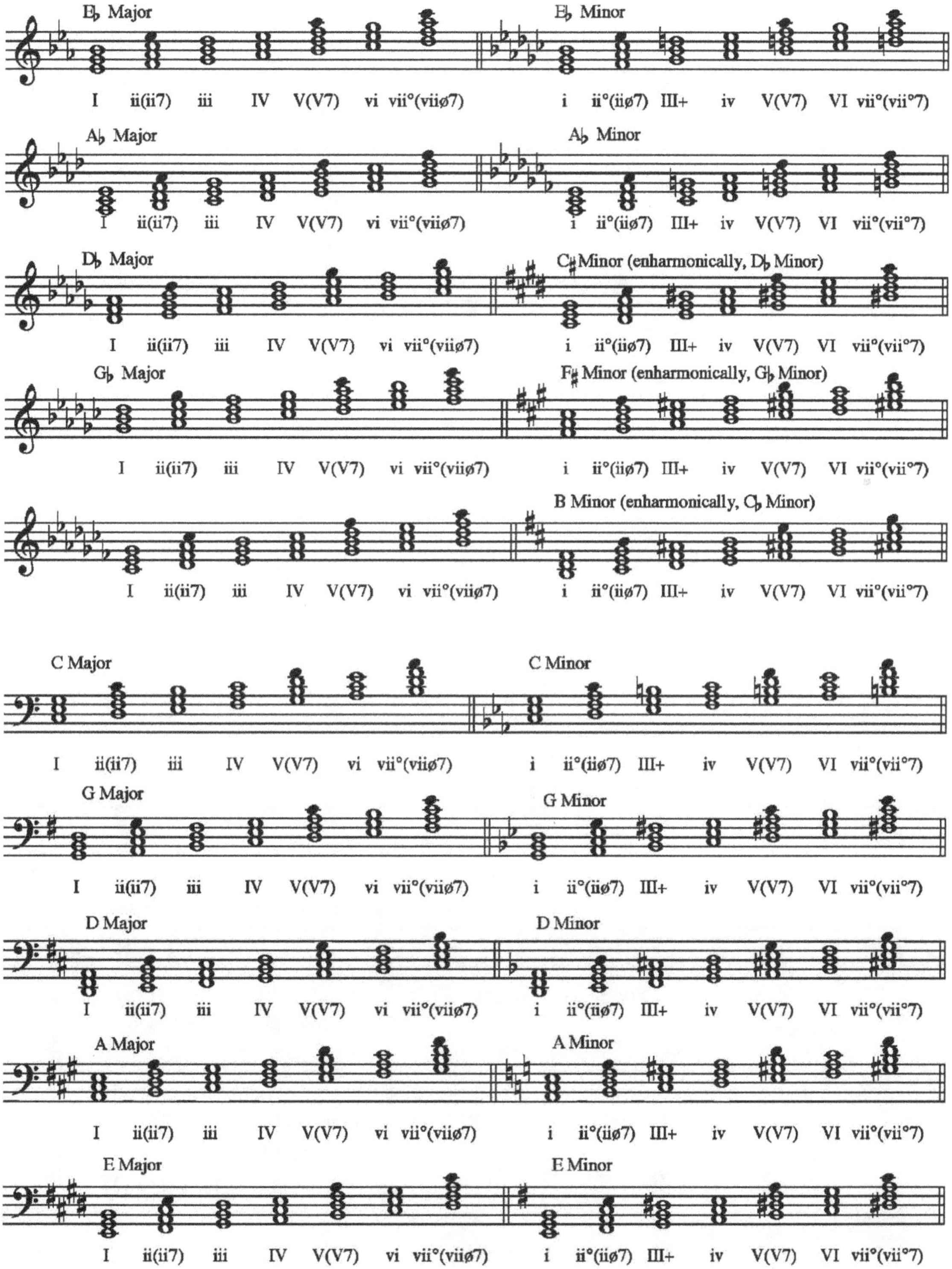
E♭ Major
I ii(ii7) iii IV V(V7) vi vii°(viiø7)
E♭ Minor
i ii°(iiø7) III+ iv V(V7) VI vii°(vii°7)
A♭ Major
I ii(ii7) iii IV V(V7) vi vii°(viiø7)
A♭ Minor
i ii°(iiø7) III+ iv V(V7) VI vii°(vii°7)
D♭ Major
I ii(ii7) iii IV V(V7) vi vii°(viiø7)
C♯ Minor (enharmonically, D♭ Minor)
i ii°(iiø7) III+ iv V(V7) VI vii°(vii°7)
G♭ Major
I ii(ii7) iii IV V(V7) vi vii°(viiø7)
F♯ Minor (enharmonically, G♭ Minor)
i ii°(iiø7) III+ iv V(V7) VI vii°(vii°7)
I ii(ii7) iii IV V(V7) vi vii°(viiø7)
B Minor (enharmonically, C♭ Minor)
i ii°(iiø7) III+ iv V(V7) VI vii°(vii°7)
C Major
I ii(ii7) iii IV V(V7) vi vii°(viiø7)
C Minor
i ii°(iiø7) III+ iv V(V7) VI vii°(vii°7)
G Major
I ii(ii7) iii IV V(V7) vi vii°(viiø7)
G Minor
i ii°(iiø7) III+ iv V(V7) VI vii°(vii°7)
D Major
I ii(ii7) iii IV V(V7) vi vii°(viiø7)
D Minor
i ii°(iiø7) III+ iv V(V7) VI vii°(vii°7)
A Major
I ii(ii7) iii IV V(V7) vi vii°(viiø7)
A Minor
i ii°(iiø7) III+ iv V(V7) VI vii°(vii°7)
E Major
I ii(ii7) iii IV V(V7) vi vii°(viiø7)
E Minor
i ii°(iiø7) III+ iv V(V7) VI vii°(vii°7)

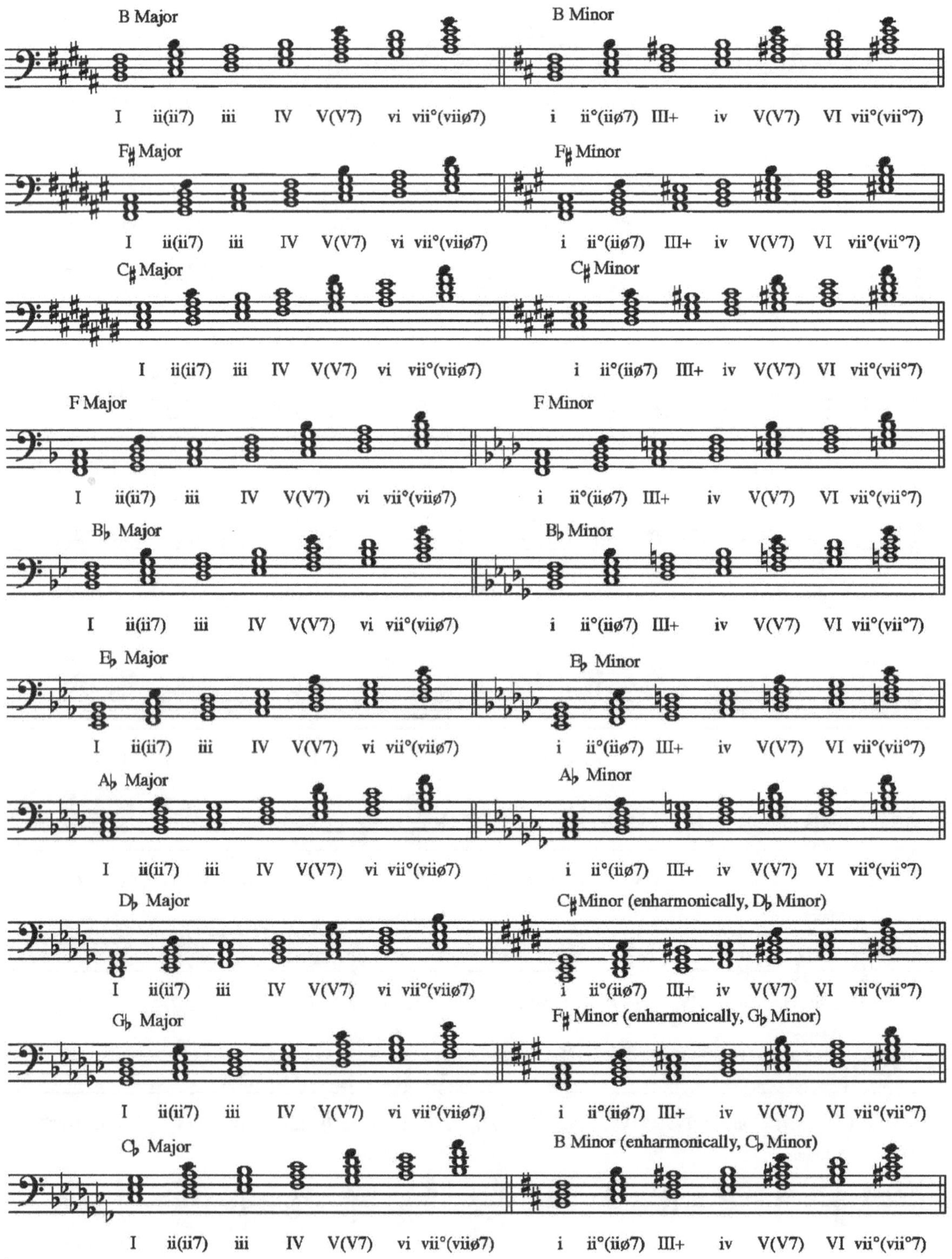

Appendix XI

Chord Symbols Used in Lead Sheet and Fake Book Notation in Two Clefs

Appendices

Notes

1. Additional reading on this line of thinking should include Harry Partch's *Genesis of a Music*.
2. Readers who wish to explore this topic further are referred to Thomas Donahue, *A Guide to Musical Temperament*, Lanham, Maryland, Toronto, Oxford: The Scarecrow Press, Inc., 2005.
3. John Backus, *The Acoustical Foundations of Music*, New York: W. W. Norton & Company, Inc., 2nd ed., 1977, p. 149.

Index

A

a 18
a coda 40
a fine 40
a tempo 19
Abgesang 313
Abide with Me 107
abbreviating triad inversions 191
abbreviating seventh chords 150
accent 21, 39, 40, 44, 47, 104, 234
accent, agogic 40
accent, dynamic 40
accent, metric 40
accent pattern 23
accent, tonic 40
accented lower neighboring tone (>LN) 246
accented non-harmonic tone 259
accented passing tone (>PT) 246
accented suspension (>Susp.) 246
accented upper neighboring tone (>UN) 250
accelerando 19
accidentals, correct usage 94
acoustic phenomena 115
active 105
active tones 102
adagio 18
added ninths 191
added pitches 196–98
added sixth 196
adjacent lines 49
adjacent spaces 49
advanced harmonic texture 196
Æolian mode 65–66
affrettando 19
agitato 19
Ah! vous dirai-je, maman 113
Alberti, Domenico 252
Alberti bass 252, 256
Algerian scale 111
alla breve 22
allargando 19, 39
alleatoric 296

allegro 17, 18
allegretto 18
allemande 35, 36
altered statement 274
altered subdominant 193
alto 4, 205–06, 210, 338, 358–60
alto clef 211, 364, 372–74
amateur singers 206
"Amen" cadence 171
America the Beautiful 107
anacrusis 21
analysis 116, 179, 260
analyzing later styles 251
analysis of Mozart minuet 255
analysis related to temporary tonic 179
analyst's assumptions 225
anapest 37
andante 18
andantino 18
animato 18
answer 332–35
antecedent-consequent phrases 274–75
antecedent phrase 283
anticipation (Ant.) 241, 246
applied dominant 175
appoggiatura (App.) 236, 241–42, 246, 259, 263
approach to non-harmonic tone 234
Arabian diminished scale 111
Arabian scale 109
arabic numerals 132, 145–46
arco 43
Are You Sleeping? 269, 325
aria da capo 310
Aria from *Rinaldo* 169
arpeggiate 258
arpeggiated chords 252–53
arpeggiations 256
arrangers 209
arsis 21
articulated suspensions 236, 259, 263
articulation 39, 104
ascending line 284
ascending major scale 104

ascending passing tones 235
ascending pitches 71
ascending sequence 290
Asian scale 111
assai 18
associating major and minor keys 92
attacca 316
auditory journey 159
augmentation 291, 335–36
augmented 56, 60, 116
augmented fourth (A4) 55, 63
augmented second in harmonic minor scale 84
augmented seventh (A7) 150
augmented sixth chord 192–93
augmented sixth/doubly augmented four chord 194
augmented triad 130, 149, 188, 217, 378–83
Auld Lang Syne 112
authentic cadence 105, 170, 173, 182, 222, 262, 276
authentic mode 62, 69
auxiliaries (Aux.) 235, 238–39, 246
Ave Maria (1889) 110
avoidance of resolutions 182

B

Bach, J.S. 167, 185, 210–11, 216–17, 221, 223, 226–28, 230, 233–34, 245–47, 249–51, 257, 268–69, 272, 274, 285, 296, 313, 322, 328–29, 331–33, 338–39
Bach chorale 216, 260
Backus, John 352
Balinese scale 110
ballet 36
bar 19
bar form 285, 313
bar lines 19
"barbershop singing" 268
baritone clef 5, 358–60
baroque era (*c*.1600–1750) 36, 159, 314, 316, 328
basic intervals 59
bass 4, 138, 205–06, 210, 338
bass clef 54, 210–11, 358–60, 363, 369–71, 382–83, 388–91, 393–94, 396
bass line 209, 218, 222, 170
bassoon 5
baton 45
Battle Hymn of the Republic 281–83, 286
beams 13
beating time 47
beat(s) 17, 28, 351
beats per minute (BPM) 19
Beethoven, Ludwig van 36, 320, 328
Befiehl du deine Wege 216

Believe Me, If All Those Endearing Young Charms 108
bells up 43
Benedicamus Domino 272
Berstein, Leonard 32
binary form 308
"bird's eye" 41
blues scale 110–11
blues, the 161
body motions 36
body of fugue 335, 338
Bohème, La 291
Boieldien, F.A. 268
bolero 35–36
bossa nova 35
bourée 35
bows 39
Brahms, Johannes 36, 245–46, 323
bravura 18
breath 39
breve 12–13, 15
bridge 312
brio 18
Buccheri, John 48
BWV 262 210–11
Byzantine scale 111

C

c clef 4
c major scale 71
C Minor Fugue from the *Well-tempered Clavier* 338–40
cacophony 267, 270
cadare 105
cadences 105–06, 170, 233
cadence formula 256
cadence in c major 225
cadence on the tonic 182
cadence points 216–17
cadences that do not sound final 170, 172
cadences that sound final 170
cadence tonalities 254
caesura (//) 41
call and response 274
calypso 35
cambiata (Cam.) 243–44, 246, 263
cancelation of accidentals 115
cancrizan 325
canon 324–25
canon at the fifth 326
canon at the third 327
cantus firmus (CF) 206
capitol letters 303

Index

cents (¢) 351
cha-cha 35
chaconne 322
changing 2 or more chord tones 164
changing inversion 164
change of direction 222
changes in tempo 18
children's voices 206
Chinese-Mongolian scale 110
Chinese scale 110
Chopin, Frédéric 257–265
Chopin preludes 287
chorale harmonization 167, 249, 313
chord alteration 186
chord borrowing 186
chord changes 154
chord quality 198
chord substitution 186
chord symbols 200
chord tones 233–34
chord voicing 260
chordal 210
chords 98
chords in all keys 392–94
chords, other 188
chorus 288, 317
chromatic 99, 233
chromatic inflection 1, 64, 192
chromatic scale 99–100
chromatic scale notation 100
chromatic semitone 352
chromatically 226
chromatically altered triad 184
church modes 62
circle of fourths 354
circle of fifths 161–62, 354
classical period (*c.* 1750–1810) 35, 40, 316
clef 4
Clementi, Muzio 307
climax 259, 296
close position 210
closed form 309
closed position 210
closing theme 318–19
coda 40–41, 314, 320, 335, 337
codetta 320
coloration 190–91, 240
coloration chords 197
colorings 160
combined textures 269
Comes 324–27
comma (,) 41
common practice era (*c.*1660-present) 71, 151, 205, 215

common practice part writing 206
common tones 23, 222–23
commonly usd seventh chords 151
complex sounds 117
complex wave 1
composition with twelve tones 292
compound intervals 31, 123
compound time 22–23, 48
con 18
con sordino 43
concert pitch 356
conducting 36, 44–45, 47
configuration 39
conjunct 52, 101
conjunct motion 51, 205, 283
conjunct tetrachord 71
consonances 116–17, 209, 122, 233
constructing minor scales using accidentals 93
consequent phrase 283
continuous forms 301, 316, 321
contralto 206
contrapuntal 210, 269, 322
contrapuntal materials 323
contrapuntal writing 209
contrary motion 207, 223
coordination of movement 34
Cope, David 122
correcting key signature 359–61
counter exposition 335, 337
counter melody 270
counterpoint (CP) 205–06, 327
countersubject 332, 334–35
counting time 25
couplets 315
courante 35–36
courtesy accidentals 94
crab canon 325
constructing a natural minor scale 88
crescendo (cresc.) 39
crotchet 12–13
crowd singing 270
Crucifixus from *B Minor Mass* 322
cut time 22
CWM Rhondda 283–84
cyclical permutations 294–95
czardas 35

D

da capo (DC) 40, 310
da capo form 308
dactyl 37

dal segno (DS) 40
dance 34
dance figures 35
Dances from Galanta 36
Danses: sacrée et profane 36
dashed bar lines 22
Debussy, Claude 36, 110
deceptive cadence 172
decibels 38
decrescendo (decresc.) 39
degree sign 145
degrees of scale 149
delayed entrance, in exposition 335, 337
demisemiquaver 13
Den lieben langen Tag 271
density structure 293
descending chromatic bass line 262
destination chord 176
descending pitches 71
descending sequence 290
development 317–19
"devil in music, the" 65
diabolus in musica 65
diatonic 233
diatonic passing tone 235
diatonic pitches 142
diatonic planing 291
diatonic semitone 352
Dido's Lament from *Dido and Aeneas* 372
diminished 56, 60, 116, 179
diminished-diminished seventh 154, 384–91
diminished fifths (d5) 56, 63
diminished-minor seventh 154, 384–91
diminished seventh 150, 153
diminished sevenths as pivot chords 183
diminished triad 126–27, 130, 149, 153, 217, 378–83
diminuendo (dim.) 39
diminution 291, 335–37
disjunct 52, 101
disjunct motion 51, 205, 283
disjunct tetrachord 71–72
dissonance 116–17, 122, 205–06
dissonant 157, 233
distorted 115
diverse sounds 117
divertimento 36
divided four beat pattern 46
division of beat 29, 32
do 71
dolce 18
dolore 18

dominant 96, 100–02, 105, 147, 152, 157, 170–72, 212, 215, 312
dominant chord 146
dominant chord, beginning with 259
dominant ninth chord 190, 259
dominant preparation 227
dominant seventh 153, 157–59, 174, 194, 256, 384–91
dominant six-four 256
dominant-tonic 205
dominant triad 159
dominant, of a tonicized pitch 179
Dorian mode 62, 69–70
Dorian 63, 68
dots 14
dotted bar lines 28
dotted eighths 25
dotted rhythms 314
double auxiliaries 239–40
double bass 5
double flats 94
double fugue 337
double sharps 94
double whole note 12–13, 15
doubled 147, 209, 211–12
doubling decisions 213
doubly augmented 60
doubly diminished 60
downbeat 21, 45
duple meters 21, 46, 206
duple pattern 46
duplets 30
duplicated pitches 147
durations 1, 12–13, 104
duration of each chord 161
Dux 324–27
Dvořák, Antonin 31
dyad 121
Dykes, John B. 272
dynamic balance 44
dynamics 38, 104

E

e 18
easy to sing 51, 223
échappée (escape tone; Ech. or ET) 243, 246
E-flat Piano Sonata 185
Egyptian scale 110
electronic alteration of tone quality 43
Eleventh Century 71
eleventh chords 195–96

elided phrase 279–80
elongated phrase 279
eighth note 12–13, 15, 28–29
eight note scales 111
Eighteenth Century 15, 125, 189, 205–06, 313, 331
Ein Deutsches Requiem 246
endings 41
enharmonic 351
enharmonic equivalents 9, 61, 355
enharmonic French sixth 202
enigmatic scale 111
entries 332
episode 315, 332, 335, 337–38
equal temperament tuning 351, 355
equal tempered semitone 353
equally significant lines 205
Ermuntre Dich, mein schwacher Geist 285
escape tone (see also échappée) 243, 259
espressivo 18
establishing the tonal center 222
even-eights 33
eventual resolution 182
evolution of the flat sign 8
experimental keyboards 350
exposition 318–19
exposition of fugue 332, 338
expanded melodic sources 108
expanded uses for seventh chords 174
extending stacked thirds 195
extracted pitches 297
extraction 296
eye contact 47

F

f clef 4
f sharp 72
fa 71
factorial 294
fake book 196
fake book symbols 147, 198–200, 395–96
false modulation 182
fandango 35
Fantasia in C Minor 273
fast 17
fermatas 41, 216
Fibonacci numbers 296
fifteenth above (15ma) play two octaves higher 7
fifteen below (15ma basso) play two octaves lower 6–7
Fifteenth century 205–06, 351
fifth 50, 56, 60, 209, 212

fifth of a triad 126, 134
fifth omitted 212
Fifth Phrase 226
fifth species counterpoint 206
figured bass 142
final 62, 68, 70
final cadence 105
Final Phrase 227
Finale™ 357
fine 40, 310
fingers 59
finite canon 325
first bridge 318–19
first inversion 141–42, 147
first inversion seventh chords 155
First Phrase 222
first species counterpoint 206, 209
first theme 318–19
five beat pattern 46–47
five beats per measure 23
five four time 22
"fixed do" 72
flag 13
flat (symbol) 68–69
flats 3, 8
Flow Gently, Sweet Afton 108
flute 49
folk music 209, 270
folk dances 36
folk songs 316
foreign tonality 159
form 267, 295, 301
formal conventions 303
forte 38
fortepiano 40
fortissimo 38
forzando 40
Foster, Stephen 200
four beats per measure 45
four chord, a 146
four-eight time 20
four-four time 20
four note pitch stack 149
four part example 212
four part style 251
four-three ($^{4}_{3}$) 155
four voice texture 205–06, 210
Fourteenth Century 209
Fourth Phrase 225
fourth species counterpoint 206, 241
fourths 50, 55, 60, 201, 209
free imitation 324

free tone 246
French impressionists 194
French 18th century melody 113
French overture 314–15
French sixth chord 193–94, 262
French violin clef 5
frequency 1, 346, 349
Frère Jacques 269
Fugue 331
Fugue in C Minor from Well-tempered Clavier 245
Fugue in F 272
Fugue in G Minor from Well-tempered Clavier 333
full cadence 105
full close 105
fully diminished seventh 153–54, 178, 384–91
function of a pitch 212
functional analysis 145–46, 229–30
fundamental 346
fuoco 18
Fux, Johan Joseph 206

G

G clef 4
G Minor Fugue 335
Gaburo, Kenneth 293, 296
galliard 35
gallop 35
gavotte 35
general pause (G.P.) 41
genres 283
German folk song 271
German sixth 193–94
gesture 106, 286
gigue 35–36
Glinka, Mikhail 110
God and Man 220
golden mean 295
golden section 295
Goldman, Richard Franco 216
grace notes 15
gradually louder or softer 39
Gradus ad Parnassus 206
grand pause, see general pause 41
grandioso 18, 270
graphing sectional forms 302
grave 18
grazioso 18
greatest density 259
Greek modes 62
Greek system 71
ground 322

ground bass 218, 322
Guido of Arezzo 71
guitar 348
guitar accompaniment 270

H

H (the pitch) 2
Habañera 35
"hairpins" 39
half cadence 105–06, 172, 283
half cadence, melodic 276
half close 105
half diminished seventh 154, 179, 384–91
half note 12–13, 15, 28
half steps 7, 54
Handel, Georg Fredrick 167, 331
Hanson, Howard 122
harmonic 43, 115
harmonic analysis 145–46, 178, 211–12, 225, 228
harmonic cadences 170
harmonic complexity 259
harmonic drive 157
harmonic framework 205
harmonic goal 221, 226
harmonic goal, delayed 182
harmonic intervals 116, 123
harmonic journey 160
harmonic language 260
harmonic minor 81
harmonic minor scale 84, 93–94, 111, 119, 130
harmonic minor scale, construction 85
harmonic motion 149, 158, 205
harmonic progress 159
harmonic progressions 159
harmonic rhythm 166–68, 218, 225, 233–34, 252, 259–69
harmonic sequence 290
harmonic series 121–22, 216, 345, 356
harmonic structure 215
harmonization 250
harmonizing a melody 228
harmony 115, 270
harmony, evolution of 216
harpsichord 252
harsh 116
Hawaiian scale 109
head 317
head of a fugue subject 332
Heart and Soul 160
Helmholtz, Hermann 343, 345
hemidemisemiquaver 13

hemiola 32
Herzliebster Jesu 185, 245
hesitation 173
heterophony 267, 270, 274
hertz (Hz) 1, 350
Hindemith, Paul 122
Hindustan scale 109
historical evolution 346
historical interpretation 15
Home on the Range 276, 312
homophonic 272
homophony 268
homorhythmic 218
horizontal lines 163
Howe, Julia Ward 282
human voice 49
Hungarian dance 36
Hungarian major scale 111
Hungarian minor scale 111
Hungarian scale 111
Hunter's Song 268
hybrid chords 196–97
hymns 210, 220, 316
hypo- 63
Hypodorian mode 62–63
Hypolydian mode 62, 64
Hypomixolydian mode 62, 64
Hypophrygian mode 62–63

I

iamb 37
identifying pitches 343
identifying triads 133
imitation 324
imitative counterpoint 324
imperfect authentic cadence 171
imperfect cadence 173
imperfect consonances 116–17
implied motion 101
implied root 122
impressionistic 110
incomplete 101
incomplete measure 24
increasingly dominant 355
increasingly subdominant 355
independent lines 116, 205
independent lines, preserving 209
inevitable cadence 302
inherent instabilities 158
initial statement 106, 274
initial tonic 182

instrumental music 52, 205, 252
intermediate modulation 182
interpretation 39
interrupted cadence 172
intervals 49, 54
intervals created 116
intervals with accidentals 59
intervals within scales 118
intervallic shape 289
intonation 347
introduction 314, 320
inverted 119
invertible counterpoint 328
inverting intervals 119–20
inverting seventh chords 155
Invention in A Minor 269, 274
Invention in F Major 329–30
inventions 328
inversion 119, 160, 211, 288, 326
inversion symbols 142, 146, 195
Ionian mode 65–66
Irish air 108
irrational meter 23
irregular meter 22–23
Italian 17
Italian sixth 193–94

J

Japanese scale 110–11
Javanese scale 109
jazz 6, 33, 197, 260, 270, 317
jazz conventions 145
jazz notation 40
jazz scale 111
jazz waltz 35
jazz writing 154
Jeanie with the Light Brown Hair 200
Jewish: Adonal Malakh 111
Jewish: Ahaba Rabba 111
Jewish: Magen Abot 111
joules 1
just intervals 346
just intonation 346

K

key 178
key signature 76
key signatures in major keys 75
key signatures in minor keys 89

key signatures using sharps 77
key signatures used to create scales 91
keyboard 50, 150
keyboardist 143
Kodály, Zoltan 36
Kuhlau, Friedrich 257

L

la 71
landler 35
language 34
large (melodic) leaps 222
larger forms 301
large sectional forms 314
larghetto 18, 256
largo 17–18
Latin 2
leap followed by step 259
leading tone 97, 100–01, 147, 152, 170, 202
leading tone seventh 153, 158–59
leading tone to the dominant 178
leading tone triad 159
leading whole-tone scale 109
lead sheet notation 147, 197–98, 395–96
ledger lines 5
legato 39, 40, 44, 47
lento 18
less traditional chords 201
letters of the alphabet 2
levels of detail 303
line 49
line, primary 269
line, subordinate 269
lines 4, 50, 115
listener 48
l'istesso 18
l'istesso tempo 19
Little Morning Hiker 306
location 233
loco 7
Locrian mode 65–66, 70, 189
London Bridge Is Falling Down 106
longer compositions 182
louder 47
loudness 1, 38
loudness, changes in 1
lower neighbor (LN) 235, 246
lowered supertonic 189
lowercase letters 131, 303
Lydian minor scale 109
Lydian mode 62–64, 68–69

M

ma 18
maestoso 18
macroscopic 301, 309
main theme 270
matcato 18, 47
marches 34
major 54
major and minor keys with same key signature 90
major interval 56, 60
major key, key signatures 29
major keys 102
major Locrian scale 109
major-minor seventh 384–91
major-minor system 109–09
major modality 71, 159
major ninth chord 190
major scale 66, 71–71, 76, 101, 145, 362–65
major scale, construction of 72
major scale constructed using flats 73, 76
major scale constructed using sharps 73, 76
major second (M2) 54
major seventh (M3) 56, 150
major sixth (M6) 56, 116
major triad 126, 130, 149, 378–83
major third (M3) 55, 59, 116, 347
mambo 35
Marks, Godfrey 107
mazurka 35
meantone tuning 351–52
meantone system 1/4, 1/5, 1/6 comma 351
measure 19
measure, structure of 21
mediant 96, 100–02, 105, 147
mediant, altered 216
mediant triad 149
medieval plainchant 217
Meistersingers 313
melodies 52, 209
melodic 49, 115
melodic cadences 170
melodic direction 243–44
melodic forms 274
more complex melodic forms 281
melodic intervals 123
melodic manipulation 286
melodic minor 81
melodic minor scale 93
melodic minor scale construction of 82
melodic rhythm 168
melodic/rhythmic movement 256

melodic sequence 290
melodic structure 104
melodic tendencies 101
Melody 49, 185, 215
melody and accompaniment 268
Mendelssohn, Felix 268
meno 38–39
meno *f* 39
meno mosso 19
meno *p* 39
mensuration canon 326
merengue 35
meter signature 20
metronome 17
mezzo 38
mezzo forte 38
mezzo piano 38
mezzo soprano clef 5, 358–60
mi 71
MIDI 343–44
microscopic 301
microtones 8
middle ages 36, 62
The Mill by the Brook 169
minim 12–13
minor 54, 70
minor interval 60
minor keys 102
minor-minor seventh 384–91
minor modality 71, 80, 159, 179
minor modality, determining 89
minor ninth 190
minor scale 71, 80, 145, 366–77
minor second (m2) 54
minor seventh (m7) 57, 150, 384–91
minor sixth (m6) 56, 116
minor third (m3) 55, 59, 116, 347
minor triad 126–27, 139, 149, 378–83
minuet 35–36
Minuet 185
Minuet from *Don Giovanni* 251, 255
minus sign 145
mirror 288
mirror canon 325
mirror inversion 288
Mixolydian 62–63, 68–70
modal scale degrees 100
modal shift 290
modal system 216
modal transposition 290
modality 97, 178
moderato 18
modern keyboard 3, 349

modes 62, 64–65, 108–09
modes become major or minor 70
modulating bridge 318
modulating subject 333
modulation 182–82, 310
modulation formulas 184
molto 18
Monk, William H. 107
monophonic 272
monophony 267
more than two voices 122
morendo 39
motives 283, 329
moveable do 72, 358
movement 34
movement by fourths, fifths and octaves 218
movement by leaps 52
movement by steps 52
moving into inner voice 259
Mozart, Leopold 15
Mozart, W. A. 36, 251–52, 254–55, 257, 273, 296
music 1
music of other cultures 8
musical insights 216
musical rhythms 34
musical symbols 1
muted 43
My Bonnie 103
My Country 'Tis of Thee 25, 268
mystic chord 201

N

naming intervals 60
Nashville numbers 132, 147
nature of music 39
natural 3, 8
natural, evolution of 8
natural minor 66, 81
natural minor scale 87
Neapolitan major scale 109
Neapolitan minor scale 111
Neapolitan sixth 188–89, 193, 261–62
neighboring tone 234–35, 238–39
Nineteenth Century 70, 198, 213, 260, 314
nine-eight time 46
nine notes in a chord 258
ninth 51
ninth chord 190
non-functioning sevenths 197
non-harmonic tones 15, 225, 233, 263
non-harmonic tones, (abbreviations) 246

non-legato 39–40
non troppo 18
Northwestern University 48
nota cambiata 244
note against note 206
number of keys per octave 350
numbers, use for 295
numerology 296

O

O Haupt voll Blut und Wunden 216–17, 221, 223–25, 227–28, 230, 233–34, 247, 249–50
oblique motion 207, 223
observation 211
occuring on strong beat 236
octatonic scale 111
octave 51, 57, 60, 209–10, 345–46, 348
octave higher (8va) play octave higher than written 7
octave lower (8va basso, 8vb) play octave lower than written 6–7
octave equivalence 292
octave point pitch class 344
octo 3
off-beats 21
okta 3
omitting inversion symbols 253
On Top of Old Smokey 167
one chord 146
one fourth of a semitone 350
one hundred twenty-eighth note 13
one-line instrument 49
one pitch change between chords 163
open form 256, 308
open pipe 343, 345
open position 210
open score 211
opera 301
orchestrators 209
orchestral string music 39
ordered 104
organ building 344
organ part 245
organization of time 17
organum 209
original idea 287
ornaments 15
outlining triads and sevenths 218
overtone scale 109

P

pan diatonicism 291
parallel fifths 209
parallel major/minor scales 92, 100
parallel motion 207, 209, 223
parallel octaves 209
part writing 205
Partch, Harry 3
partials 122, 345–46
passacaglia 322
Passacaglia and Fugue in C Minor 322
passing seventh 235, 262
passing tones (PT) 234–38, 246
pause 105
pedagogy 205–06
pedal (point) 245–46, 335, 337–38
pedal tone (Ped) 246
pentatonic scales 110, 348
pentatonic tuning 348
perception 115
perfect 56
perfect authentic cadence 171
perfect cadence 173
perfect consonances 117, 206
perfect octave (P8) 57, 116, 205
perfect unison (P1) 57, 116
perfect fifth (P5) 56, 116, 122, 205, 345–46, 348–49
perfect fourth (P4) 55, 116–17, 122, 205, 345–46, 348–49
period 279, 302
permutations 294
pesante 13
Peter, Christoph 222
percussion music 39
performance space 39
performance style 44
Persichetti, Vincent 198
Persian scale 111
phrases 105, 183, 274, 283, 301–02
Phrygian mode 62–64, 68–70, 109, 217
Phrygian second 189, 202
physical insights 216
piano 38–39, 252
piano building 344
pianissimo 38
Picardy third 159, 226
piccolo descant 270
pickup 21, 24–25
pipe organs 209
Piston, Walter 212–13, 236

pitch 1
pitch augmentation 292
pitch diminution 293
pitch doubling 211–13
pitch goals 170
pitch interval 324
pitch retrograde 287
pitch structures 168
più 18, 38–39
più *f* 39
più mosso 19
più *p* 39
pivot chord 182–83
pizzicato 43
placid 49
plagal cadence 171–72, 224
plagal mode 53, 69
plainchant 272
planing 291
play in all keys, ability to 352
plus (+) sign, use of 196
poco 18
poetic foot 37
poetic meters 36
points of hesitation 170
point of imitation 324
polka 35
polonaise 35
polyphonic 268, 272, 324
polyphonic texture 269
polyphony 267–68
pop music writing 154
popular music 161, 260
position 210
prelude 257
Prelude, No. 6 264
Prelude, No. 7 258, 260
Prelude, No. 9 265
Prelude, No. 20 260–61
preparation 233
preparing dissonances 205
prestissimo 18
presto 18
prevailing harmony 259
primary melody 269
prime 51, 302
progression 160
prolonged phrase 279–80
prolonging 158
Promethean chord 201
Prométhée 201
properties of the octave 3

proportions 295
prototriads 134
psalm tone 63
psychological insights 216
Puccini, Giacomo 291
Purcell, Henry 322
pulse 17, 28, 44–45
Pythagorean comma 349, 351
Pythagorean turning 352

Q

quadruple fugue 338
quadruplets 30
qualities of sevenths 150
qualities of triads 150
quality of minor scales 97
quarter notes 12–13, 15, 28–29
quarter not pick-up 258
quaver 12–13
quick step 35
quintuplet 29

R

Rachmaninoff, Sergei 36
Raga Hanunot 109
Raga: Topdi 110
"railroad tracks" (//) 41
rallentando 19
Rameau, Jean-Philippe 125–26
ranges 64
ranges, vocal and instrumental 160
range (of modes) 62
ratio 29, 31–32, 296, 348–49
Ravel, Maurice 36
re 7
real answer 333
"real" inversion 288
realization 199
realization of a figured bass 142
recapitulation 318–20
recitation tone 62–64, 69
recognizing triads 133
refrain 281, 283
reinforcements 115
Rejoice and Sing 218
relative major 216
relative major/minor 90, 92
relative minor 216, 221

religious processions 34
renaissance modes 68–69
renaissance period (*c.* 1400–1600) 68
repeated pitches 218
repeated statement 274
repeats 41, 302–93
reprised 310
resolution 157, 233–34
resolve 116
resolves (usually) downward 236
resolving dissonances 205
response 275
rests 14
resultant pitch 209
retransition 320
retrograde 287, 325
retrograde-inversion 289, 325
returns 302–03
rhythm 104
rhythmic 47
rhythmic accompaniment 270
rhythmic character 234
rhythmic feel 21
rhythmic figures 19
rhythmic motive 286
rhythmic retrograde 288
rhythmic unison 268
rhythmically 47
ricecare (ricecar) 331
Riemann, Hugo 216
rinforzando 40
risoluto 18
ritard 19
ritenudo 19
ritornello form 316
role of conductor 44
"roll" 258
Roman Catholic Church 62
roman numerals 98, 145–46, 153, 178, 211, 279
rondo form 315
rondo theme 315
root 121, 198, 211–12
root and fifth 252
root and seventh 252
root and third 252
root of harmonic intervals 121
root of triad 126, 134–35, 138
root position 141–42, 164
rough 116
round 269, 324
round, how to write 327
rounded binary form 308–09

Row, Row, Row Your Boat 104, 325
rubato 19
rumba 35
Russlan and Ludmilla 110

S

sacred modes 62, 64–65
Sailing, Sailing 107
salsa 35
Sandole, Dennis 109
saraband 35–36
SATB 206
scale degrees 95–96
scale degree, names 96
scales 64
scales with 9 or more notes 111
Schein, Johann Hermann 219
Scherzo from *Opus 24* 169
Schoenberg, Arnold 292
Schop, Johann 285
Schumann, Robert 185, 285–86, 305–06
Scriabin, Alexander 201
secco 293
secco chords 293–94
second bridge 318–19
second inversion of triad 138, 141, 147, 164, 194, 256
second partial 121, 209
second phrase 223
second species counterpoint 206
second subject 335
second theme 318–19
secondary dominant 174–76, 179, 259
secondary leading tone chord 179
secondary level chords 178
secondary relationships 229
secondary sevenths 178
secondary supertonic 179
seconds 49, 54, 60, 116
section 279
sections 283
sectional forms 301–02
sectional music 321
secular modes 65–66
segno 40
semibreve 12–13
semiquaver 13
semitone 7, 54, 56, 71
senza sordino 43
separate melodies vie for attention 269
septuplet 29–30

Index

sequence 290
sequentially 335
serial systems 198
seven beat patterns 46–47
seven beats per measure 24
seven-eight 22
seven note scales 109
seven (7) root position 155
seven triad pitch-sets 134
seventeenth century 1, 189, 205
seventh chords 149–50, 179, 384–91
seventh chord anatomy 150
seventh chord construction in major scales 152
seventh chord construction in harmonic minor scales 152–53
seventh chords in keys 152, 384–91
seventh chords, root position 155
seventh chords, second inversion 155
seventh chords, types 150
seventh chords, usage 157
sevenths 50, 56, 60, 116
sextuplet 29
sforzando 40
sharps 3, 8
si 71
Sibelius™ 357
silence 14
similar motion 207, 223
simple dances 257
simplified discussion 225
simultaneously 115
sinfonias 328
singable 205, 213
single line 267
six (6) 143, 147
six-eight time 22, 46–48
six-five ($^6_5$) 155
six-four time 22, 46
six four ($^6_4$) 143, 147
six note scales 110
Sixteen-twenty (1620) 331
Sixteenth century 205
sixteenth note 13, 15, 25, 29
sixty-fourth note 13, 15
sixth 50, 56, 60
size 39
skip 234
Slavic dances 36
slow 17
slow tempo 44
slur 39
slurred 40

small homophonic pieces 316
smoother harmonic progression 163
smorzando 39
softer 47
sol 71
solfege 71
solfege syllables 72, 98
solo 274
solo line 267
solo voice 270
sonata 318–19
sonata-allegro 318
sonata form 318
sonata rondo 315
Sonatina in G Major 307–08
song forms 276, 312
sonic elements 294
soprano 205–06, 210, 338
soprano clef 5, 211, 358–60
sostenuto 40
sound 1
Sound Off 274–75
Sousa, John Phillip 270
space 4, 49–50
spacing 210
Spanish scale 111
specified bass note 198
spelling of chords 150
spelling of intervals 150
Spillman, James E. 108
spiral of fifths 354
spiritual 273
split keys 351
spondee 37
stable 102, 116
staccatissimo 40
staccato 40, 44, 47
stack of thirds 134–35, 142, 155, 210
standard blues progression 197
Stars and Stripes Forever, The 270
Star Spangled Banner, The 24–25
statement 275, 335
Steffe, William 282
stem 12–13
stem direction 12
step 234
stepwise descent 105
stepwise descent to tonic 52, 218
stepwise motion to tonic 183
sticks 39
Stollen 313
stopped pipe 343, 345

stressed 37
stretching piano octaves 350
stretto 335–36
strict imitation 324
string music 39
string quartets 301
string vibrations 345
stringendo 19
strophic 283
struck suspension (>Susp.) 236, 246, 250
structure of a beat 28
structures 274
styles 44, 160, 283
style and sound 213
subito 18
subdivisions 44
subdominant 96, 100–01, 119, 147, 172, 215, 256, 311–12
subdominant triad 149
subject 331–32, 334–36, 338
submediant 97, 100–01, 147, 173, 215–16
submediant ninth 191
submediant triad 149
subtonic 97
super dominant 202
super Locrian scale 109
supertonic 97, 100–02, 106, 147, 153, 182, 215–16
supertonic, altered 216
supertonic ninth 191
supertonic seventh 153, 157, 159, 222
supertonic six-five 212
supertonic triad 159
suspension (Susp or Sus.) 234, 236, 242–42, 246
swing 33
Swing Low, Sweet Chariot 272–73
Symphonic Dances 36
symphonies 36, 301
Symphony No. 4 in E Minor 323
syncopation 206
system 261

T

tablature 198
tail of subject 332
tango 35
tarantella 35
taste and tolence (in tuning) 346
Tchaikovsky, Pietr Ilyich 32
techniques 267
temperament 348
tempo 17

tempo marks 18
tempo primo 19
temporary goals 104
temporary tonic 179
temporary tonicization 182, 229
tendencies of harmonic intervals 116
tendency to resolve 117
tenor 4, 205–06, 210–11
tenor clef 358–60, 365, 375–77
tension 101
tenth 1, 51
tenuto 40
ternary form 309–10
tertian triad 125
tetrachords 71
texture 209, 267
theme 302, 312, 329
theme and variations 316
theoretical mode 66
thesis 21
third(s) 49, 52, 55, 60, 212
third inversion seventh chords 155
Third phrase 224
third of triad 125, 134
third species counterpoint 206
"thirding" 195
thirds, major, minor (3M, 3m) 205
Thirteenth century 1
thirteenth chords 195–96
thirty-second note 13, 15
three beats per measure 45
three lines 123
three staves 123
three unique pitches 211
three voice round 328
through composed 313
ti 71
tied notes 40
tied notes with accidentals 94
tierce de Picardie 159
ties 14, 39
timbre 1, 209
time 1
time interval 324
time signature 20, 28, 44
tonal anchors 106
tonal answer 333–38
tonal center 104–05, 289
tonal degrees of scale 100, 213
tonal goal 149, 224, 228
tonal inversion 288–89
tonal quality 1, 38, 43
tonal transposition 290

tone color 1
tone row 292
tongue 39
tonic 96, 100–02, 104–06, 147, 212, 215, 332
tonic chord 146
tonic-dominant 205
tonic, home sonority 159
tonic ninth 191
tonic six-four 170, 172, 213, 256
tonic six-four, cadential 256
tonic triad 158, 256
tonicization 176
tonics, preceded by their dominants 161
traditional chord ordering 159
traditional cowboy song 276
traditional music 209, 270
traditional Scottish song 112
transforming 158
transmutation 290
transposed 119
transposed Dorian 69
transposed Lydian 69
transposed Mixolydian 69
transposed modes 68
transposed Phrygian 69
transposing by clef 358–60
transposing by function 358–60
transposing by interval 357–60
transposing by scale degree 358–60
transposing instruments 357–60
transposing matrix 360–61
transposition 289, 356
transposition within the key 289
treble 4
treble clef 54, 210–11, 358–60, 362, 365, 366–68, 378–80, 384–87, 392–93, 395
treble dominant melody 268
triad tendencies 149
triadic harmony 126, 205
triads 125, 211, 378–83
triads built on the dominant of a pitch 175
triads built on seconds 125
triads built on sevenths 125
triads in first inversion 138
triads, four types of 131
triads, identification of 142
triads, implied 252
triads in keys 145
triads in major scales 126
triads in minor scales 129
triads, inversion of 137–38, 378–83

triads, names of 131, 138
triads, quality of 138
triads, quartal 125
triads, quintal 125
tribrach 37
trill 240
trio 310–12
tripartite form 309
triple forte 38
triple fugue 337–38
triple meter 21, 30, 46, 206, 322
triple pattern 46
triple piano 38
triple subdivision 46
triplet 29, 31, 105
Tristan und Isolde 201
Tristan chord 201
tritone 65, 69
trochee 37
trombone 5
troppo 18
trumpet 79
truncated phrase 279–80
truncated rondo 315
Tschirch, W. 169
tuning 348
tuning systems 150
'tuplet 29–32
twelve bar blues 166
twelve-eight time 23
twelve-four time 23
twelve pitches 349
twelve tone system 198
Twentieth century 292, 314
Twentieth century, beginning of 198
Twentieth Century Harmony 198
Twenty-first century 205
Twenty-four Preludes 258
two (2 or $\frac{4}{2}$ or ($\frac{4}{2}$)) 155
two beat pattern 45
two chord 132
two couplet rondo 315
two-four time 20
two seven chord 153
two staves 210
two-two time 20
Tyrolese Air 305

U

"ump-pah-pah" bass line 259
up beat 21, 45

upper case letters 131
upper neighbor (UN) 235, 246
unaccented 104, 234
unaccented passing tone 235, 263
"under-thirding" 197
unequal durations 33
unifying character 287
unison 51, 57, 60, 267, 274
unprepared modulation 183
unstable B 63
unstable chords 182
unstressed 37
U.S. Navy Hymn, The 272
using clefs to transpose 358–60
ut 71
Ut queant laxis 71

V

variation 287, 317
variation rondo 315
Verdi, Giuseppe 110
verse 283
vertical 115
vertical spacing 210
vibrato 43
violin 5, 348
violoncello 5, 143

visual arts 295–96
vivace 18
vivo 18
vocal motet 331
voice leading 160, 205, 207
voices 115, 332

W

Wagner, Richard 201
waltz 32, 35–36
Ward, Samuel A. 107
wattage 38
watts 1
Welsh Hymn, traditional 284
Westside Story 32
whole note 12–13, 15
whole step 7, 54
whole tone 7, 54, 71
whole tone scale 110, 194
Wie schön leuchtet der Morgenstern 167
Wild Rider 286
wind instruments 39
without accidentals 54
without clef 54
without mute 43
without vibrato 43
wolf fifth 252